MAKING IT WORK

MAKING IT WORK

Women, Change and Challenge in the 1990s

SUE INNES

Chatto & Windus

LONDON

First published in 1995

1 3 5 7 9 10 8 6 4 2

Copyright © Sue Innes 1995

Sue Innes has asserted her right under the Copyright, Designs and
Patents Act, 1988 to be identified as the author of this work.

First published in Great Britain in 1995 by
Chatto & Windus Limited
Random House, 20 Vauxhall Bridge Road,
London SWIV 2SA

Random House Australia (Pty) Limited
20 Alfred Street, Milsons Point, Sydney
New South Wales 2061, Australia

Random House New Zealand Limited
18 Poland Road, Glenfield
Auckland 10, New Zealand

Random House South Africa (Pty) Limited
P O Box 337, Bergvlei, South Africa

Random House UK Limited Reg. No. 954009

Papers used by Random House UK Limited are natural, recyclable products
made from wood grown in sustainable forests. The manufacturing processes
conform to the environmental regulations of the country of origin

A CIP catalogue record for this book is available from the British Library

ISBN 0 7011 6211 2

Typeset by Deltatype Ltd, Ellesmere Port, Wirral

Printed in Great Britain by
Mackays of Chatham, Plc Chatham, Kent.

for Rebecca and Katie

Contents

Acknowledgements

The recurring image for me while writing this book has been of climbing a mountain: well worth doing, with exhilarating views, but the slope was steep and sometimes hazardous with scree – would I make it? Many people have pushed and pulled, encouraged and extended a hand and I am immensely grateful to them.

For the practical support and encouragement without which this book would not have happened I have particularly to thank my editor Jenny Uglow, my colleague Fiona Mackay and my partner John Clifford and daughters Rebecca and Katie Innes, Jessie Lee and my mother, Jean Innes (who may not agree but helped anyway). The women I interviewed deserve special thanks, for their time and thoughtfulness. Not everyone is quoted, but everyone was insightful and helpful. Additionally Fiona Mackay gave me access to interviews which are part of her forthcoming PhD thesis. Kath Davis, Fran Wasoff, Michael Anderson, Carol Craig, Bronwen Cohen, Sally Wainwright, Esther Breitenbach, Alice Brown, Bob Morris, Malcolm Chisholm, Sue Robertson, Marie Cairns, Morag Gillespie, Irene Bloomfield, Eleanor Kelly, Liz Kelly and Susan Hart all gave information and advice. Thanks also to Nadine Harrison, Kathy Sylva, Ellen Kelly and Ellen Galford, and to Cindy Cunningham and Jane and Chris at the Edinburgh Pilates Centre for keeping writer's cramp at bay.

I am also grateful to Shona Munro at the Edinburgh Book Festival for her unhesitating interest, to the invariably helpful staff of the National Library of Scotland, the Scotsman Publications library and the Equal Opportunities Commission press office, and to the Scottish Arts Council for a grant towards research for part of this book.

Introduction

I first began thinking about this book in 1993. The war in Bosnia was a daily reminder that European civilisation cannot be taken for granted; the move to democracy in South Africa showed that much more can be achieved than most of us ever imagine. At home, the anniversary of seventy-five years since the first tranche of women's suffrage in Britain encouraged reflection on what had changed, and what had not.

That question is at the centre of this book. The past twenty-five years have, without doubt, been a time of change for women in Britain. Yet with equal certainty you can argue that a great many things in women's lives haven't shifted at all. In my work as a journalist, as I talked to women about their lives I began to question what had really changed for women since 1970? A young woman I met in a workshop said: 'Things are changing. But they're bloody well not'. She had spiky maroon hair and a tough, independent style. But some things, she reckoned, were still the same: 'Are you courtin' yet, hen?', she mimicked the irritating question. 'People treat you differently if you're with a man.'

What hasn't changed is all around us. Go shopping at lunchtime and the supermarket is crowded with women buying groceries and a sandwich to take back to their desk, and the very occasional man (probably older); round the corner in the pub the men are sitting down to a proper lunch, plus the occasional woman (probably younger). I don't have to explain the idea of sex roles or job segregation by gender as if they were curiously out-dated phenomena. 'Girls don't do that sort of thing,' says my daughter Katie – and mainly we don't.

What *has* changed is part of everyday life too. Ask any woman and she'll talk about women bus drivers and bank managers, or about divorce and more women bringing up children on their own. There are professors of feminist theory in universities and equal opportunities officers in the local council. Confident and female are no longer contradictory: assertive, intelligent women don't have to hide it any more. Women have pioneered new roles in management and politics, in medicine, law, the police, the arts and media, and science and technology (though rather less so) and that is beginning not to seem worthy of special comment.

I went to buy shoes. Another customer beamed at me: 'I never knew you could buy such smart, *comfortable* shoes for women,' she said. You have to have limped through the past twenty-five years of women's shoe styles to realise how much that symbolises progress. That same day, though, problems at work reminded me how marginalised women 'fitting in', working in less orthodox and therefore less secure ways, can be.

Star Trek has divested itself of gendered language and boldly goes where no one has gone before. A woman shepherd and her dog won on *One Man and his Dog*. A Church of Scotland prayerbook includes a prayer addressing God as Mother, something a friend of mine caused an extraordinary storm among theologians by doing only ten years ago. The ban against advertising sanitary protection on TV has been partially lifted; that something as natural and healthy was unmentionable did nobody any good. We paid for it with new designer san pads costing five times as much. Protests were mounted when Beth and Mandy Jordache in *Brookside* were found guilty; fiction reflected reality: Women's Aid have only a third (in England) and a half (in Scotland) of the recommended number of refuge spaces but fewer people know or care.

Look at who looks after the children and worries about granny, at access to resources and vulnerability to violence and harassment, and not so much has changed. Family sizes are smaller yet more elderly people are in need of care. Three carers in every five are women; the work carers do has an estimated value of £34 billion a year but is invisible to public accounting. Only one in six women retire on a full state pension compared with two in three men.[1] Restrictions on public spending affect women most as more of us live on means-tested benefits and in council houses. One of the most positive changes has been in the visibility of lesbians – women in their forties now say they didn't even know the word when they were young, let alone think it chic. But discrimination on grounds of sexuality is still legal.

Change in attitudes and awareness has not been accompanied by as great a change in the infrastructure of unequal opportunities. British women are in paid work in record numbers under an umbrella of law and policy yet the gender gap in pay persists as do pay differentials among women related to family status. Black and ethnic minority women face high levels of unemployment: more than three times the recorded rate for white women. Low pay remains a widespread problem with at least four million women workers low paid: more than half of women checkout operators earn less than £3.60 per hour.[2]

'Paradox' was a word I kept coming back to. 'Women are still assumed to have the primary, if not exclusive, responsibility for children and the public world of institutional power remains dominated by men,' Mary Evans wrote in 1994.[3] She could have written it in 1974, yet she is doing so now as a professor at the University of Kent, not in a women's group meeting round someone's kitchen table. Young people are taught the facts of inequality at school, learning that few women are in decision-making roles – and then see that replicated when most teachers are women but most schools are run by men. The tribal groupings of the environmental movement challenge power politics in radically new ways but men in them behave towards women in the old familiar ways. The Labour Party begins to use quotas to increase the number of women in Parliament and its opponents mount a challenge on the grounds of sex equality.

Back in the early 1970s, it is salutary to remember, women couldn't be newsreaders because we 'lacked authority'. We couldn't fly commercial planes because we had periods, couldn't be allowed into medical school on merit alone or we'd keep deserving chaps out. Now a headline like *Sexism in social work attacked* is mainstream not *Spare Rib*; on International Women's Day in 1995 the *Scotsman* became the *Scotswoman*, 'to give voice to a women's perspective'. But very few older women stay in visible roles in television and no women edit broadsheet newspapers in Britain. Some of the arguments used about 'a woman's place' only twenty or so years ago seem simply silly now, while ideas which were radical in the 1970s have become incorporated into common sense: supporting equal pay defined you as feminist then, now it is argued for by people who find the F word troublesome. And a lot of people do, especially younger women – yet their view of the world has been shaped by it. The comments about women's inequality John Major made when he launched Opportunity 2000 in 1991 would, twenty years before, have led to the accusations of zealotry that are levelled at Clare Short today. Discontents and demands voiced by a minority of women have entered the mainstream, albeit often prefaced with the useful disclaimer, 'I'm not a feminist, but...'

Then again, people who used to say 'I may be an old-fashioned chauvinist but...' now say 'At the risk of seeming politically incorrect...' And there still aren't many women surgeons or pilots.

The dilemmas of managing change face most women in Britain today; and dilemmas created by partial change and by apparent change which becomes elusive when you reach out your hand for it. Most of us confront the task of trying to create a workable, liveable equality in relationships and households and workplaces. An awful lot of women seem to feel, to paraphrase the woman in the workshop, 'we are equal – but we're bloody well not'. How do we handle that, every day?

Recent accounts of women's lives today are highly polarised: between a 'power feminism' which asserts that all we have to do is reach out and take it; or a gloom and doom feminism which sees no meaningful change for women anywhere. Neither seems to me true. Nor does the bland account of everything for the best (almost) given by the government.

The account which comes closest to a feminist orthodoxy, I think (though there isn't really such a thing) is by Vicky Randall and Joni Lovenduski in their useful book *Contemporary Feminist Politics*. 'The legitimacy of claims to equality in employment, of a mother's right to go out to work, of a pregnant woman's right to say how she wants to give birth, and so on are now well established. But the effects of continuing economic liberalism combined with the recession will ensure that it is, for the most part, only a privileged minority of women who benefit from the new opportunities that result.' The central thesis of Kate Figes' book *Because of her Sex* is that 'discrimination... not only survives but is worse than ever.' And that 'In the arts and advertising, as in pornography, representation of women as weak and subjugated reflects a culture which still places a lower value on a woman.' The view from America is even bleaker: 'The last decade has seen a powerful counter-assault on women's rights, a backlash, an attempt to retract the handful of the small and hard-won victories that the feminist movement did manage to win for women,' Susan Faludi wrote in *Backlash* in 1992. Young women are bombarded with 'you've-never-had-it-so-good Backlash-think' the magazine *Everywoman* said in a 1994 editorial, 'But the gulf between these raised expectations and the real opportunities on offer is wide and may be getting wider'.[4]

It is because we've been told once too often that 'we've won' that women in Britain find it necessary to gainsay it. It's as if once we acknowledge any achievements we'll become culpably complacent. So, ironically, we are in danger of denigrating women's real gains and ignoring the greater sense of freedom so many women express, even those whose room to manoeuvre may seem limited. It is hard too, when the demands raised in the 1970s haven't been met, to see that the world has changed and the arguments have shifted.

The more positive accounts of change have come mostly from outside the women's movement, apart from Naomi Wolf's confident naming, in *Fire with Fire*, of 'the era of the "genderquake" ', in which 'the meaning of being a woman is changed for ever'. For example the Social Justice Commission's declaration that 'The social revolution is a revolution of women's life chances, of family structures and of demography'. And Helen Wilkinson's report for the 'new middle' think tank Demos, *No Turning Back*, claims that we are living through 'an historic change in the relations between men and women: a shift in power and values that is unravelling many of the assumptions not only of 200 years of industrial society, but also of millennia of traditions and beliefs.'[5]

Similarly polarised accounts of women's lives today were a feature of the Parliamentary debates on the progress of women towards equality in March 1994 and 1995. On the one hand women were seen as trapped by low pay, limited opportunity and the lowest level of publicly funded childcare in the European Union (EU) (as Clare Short and Harry Cohen saw it), on the other, the Minister with responsibility for women's issues, David Hunt, praised women's advance in science, information technology and the civil service and the new flexible job opportunities 'that women find most attractive', and Elizabeth Peacock hymned the advantages of an 'old girls' network'.

The last time sex discrimination was debated in the House of Commons, in 1975, at the second reading of the Sex Descrimination Bill, very similar things were said, if rather more hopefully. Left and Right competed to insist how unjust and economically damaging inequality between the sexes is and how determined they were to end it. The arguments for parental leave, more and better childcare, more realistic working hours for Parliament and more women there sound strangely familiar.

Perhaps the most telling comment came from Helen Jackson, MP for Sheffield, Hillsborough. Everyone, on both sides of the House, she said 'agrees that gender inequality is something that they do not like and that it should not exist in society. Everyone says they have never practised discrimination and that they are working very hard to achieve gender equality'. And they say so 'in this place with its 91 per cent masculinity'.[6]

The report on equality for women in the UK published by the government in the run-up to the UN world conference on women in September 1995 puts an unembarrassed face on minimal change. Introducing the assessment of progress made over the decade Employment Secretary Michael Portillo could only say: 'Much has been done... but there is no room for complacency'. Indeed there isn't: so little is there to boast about that the press release accompanying the report could only be headlined UK ON TRACK TOWARDS EQUALITY FOR WOMEN. Which is true – the question is how far into the future the track stretches.[7]

The list of achievements includes several things that count: the fact that women now take up around half of all further and higher education places and an increase in flexible access courses which has benefited 'women returners'; the independent taxation of married women; the amendment of equal pay legislation to include equal work of equal value (a consequence of European law); enhanced maternity rights (again won through Europe). But it is a shamefully short list and several other 'achievements' it includes are at best ambiguous. The new Cabinet Sub-Committee on Women's Issues is, I dare say, a thoroughly good thing, it's just that no one knows what it does and few know that it's there at all. The same goes for the new ministerial group on domestic violence. Equal retirement ages for women and men at 65 is an 'achievement' which the Equal Opportunities Commission (EOC) and most trade unions argued against.

Other achievements listed are dubious. There have been steady increases in women's average earnings relative to men's, but if the law worked well, if it was easier of access, and if there was not persistent job segregation with little to challenge it, equal pay would be a reality not a distant hope. 'Government support for childcare' (don't laugh) means plans for after-school and holiday childcare – welcome of course, but rather more needs to be done to meet a widening 'childcare gap'.

And some 'achievements' are very dubious. Although there was support for the principle, very few people would now claim the Child Support Agency as an advance for equal opportunities. That the new national targets for health include cervical and breast cancer is scarcely an achievement. It is necessary because women's deaths from cervical cancer in Britain are the second-highest in Europe and from breast cancer the highest in Europe: and far higher than they would be if better diagnosis and standardised treatment was available throughout the country. And the target is *limited*.

Independent reports to the UN Conference were prepared in Scotland and Wales. The extent and seriousness of women's poverty was the main omission in the government's account highlighted in the Scottish report, a criticism also made by the Women's National Commission. Cynulliad Merched Cymru, the Wales Assembly of Women, comments on the lack of women in senior posts in the University of Wales and says that 'Wales remains the area of the UK with the worst record of neglecting the provisions of the Equal Pay Act.' Also rather different from the government's account is the United Nations report for Europe which was presented to a conference in Vienna in September 1994. It said 'women's jobs are still segregated at the lower end of the labour market; upward mobility and career prospects are limited; and many women are left outside the full-time labour market. Nor is the existing social infrastructure adequate for balancing women's work and family obligations.' Though, in the longer term, women's integration into the labour force was one of the most important European trends for the 1990s, as a consequence of recession 'the economic situation of European women is deteriorating'. It also cited the poverty of female-headed households.[8]

What had *really* changed remained a question for me, even (or perhaps because of) writing about 'women's issues' for ten years. In the 1970s I had been very involved in the women's movement. The ideas which ran through the land like wildfire, or at least through its institutions of higher education, seemed to fit like a glove. But after I had my first child in 1980, the difficulties of trying to look after her and find a way to earn a living at the same time, and of living in the country with no car, a large garden and impractically green aspirations, meant political commitments were hard to sustain. Disillusion would be too strong a word: lack of relevance certainly. Yet my personal struggles lay along the axis of inequality: work and family.

Making it Work reflects my own concerns and priorities as well as the ideas and insight of the many women who took time to explore them with me. I have talked to women both formally and informally, in long, illuminating interviews and in brief snatches of conversation which sometimes threw new light on whole areas. Whenever I met any woman and mentioned what I was doing she had something, usually plenty, to say on the subject. I've talked to women on trains and buses, at the school gate, in university corridors, at conferences, late at night over bottles of wine, and in discussion groups where I presented an early draft of my ideas. In so far as I sought out women to talk to, I wanted to talk to women who were likely to be reflective about change in women's lives, and who would bring diverse perspectives to that discussion, which would include differences of ethnic background, age and sexuality. Mainly I avoided anyone who had to speak on behalf of a particular organisation.

This is a book about Britain written from the perspective of a Scot; the women's movement in Scotland and the campaign for equal representation of women in a Scottish parliament have been important influences. It is about Britain, not the UK, and does not include Northern Ireland because the social and political situation is sufficiently different to demand rather more attention than I could give it. And my perspective is that of a mother of two daughters, living with their father in a small, city-centre family. Most of all this book is informed by my years as a journalist and the thousands of women I have talked to or who have written to me through that work. A journalist is, I think, a kind of a magpie. You ask questions and seek out information but you also use what comes your way. In the way that a more disciplined inquiry cannot, journalism has the freedom to explore ideas with a broad brush, to make space for raising impossible questions.

My central focus is work and the family, but neither can be explored apart from the other or without raising questions about politics and the economy, popular culture, feminism and femininity, masculinity, the future of welfare. I began with neat categories but they soon leaked into one another. Most women's lives are lived across boundaries; to try to think about work and the family separately is to follow a false conceptual division which is at the root of many problems. If this has created a structure where ideas and arguments seem to circle round on each other it is because that's what happens in life. If there has been one comment which has provided a recurrent motif during this time of research and writing it is something the sociologist Liz Stanley said: that always 'it's more complicated than that'.

So the question which is at the centre of this inquiry has no single, or simple, answer. Change and continuity are contradictory, elusive when you get up close. 'History as lived is confused and illogical,' the French feminist Christine Delphy comments.[9] Can we begin to make sense of it? Yet we make sense of it in our everyday lives, and we need to.

Part I

Life, Love and Earning a Living

Chapter 1

Paradox and Pandora's Box

We see change differently according to our own experience and what we see of the world around us. I have talked to women who've said, as novelist Zoe Fairbairns did, 'People who say things haven't changed must have very short memories.' And talked to others who have argued that real change cannot be demonstrated. Valerie Amos, former chief executive of the Equal Opportunities Commission (EOC), for example: 'When we talk about change it seems to me that we always assume that things have got better and I'm not actually sure that that's true. Fundamentally I think that things haven't changed that much for the majority of women.'

'Things have definitely changed,' Edinburgh councillor Susan Dalgety says. 'There's mair expected of us. You want to have babies, you want to have a career, you want to have a nice house, a good social life, you want to be politically involved. I mean the burden that women carry – while the opportunities have increased, the burden has.'

'There's no very many men will be sitting in a meeting and think "hell – there's nae bog roll", or "what are they going to have for their tea the night?" I'm no talking from a single parent perspective, I'm just talking from a woman's perspective. We carry the house and the kids in our heads all the time. While it can be exciting and challenging it can also be bloody difficult.'

'It's now you see it, now you don't,' author and researcher Cynthia Cockburn said. 'There are moments and places when you would say – oh, yes, look, she's taken seriously, they can't ignore women, that could *never* have happened before. When it's quite clear that women can operate adequately and effectively and are part of mainstream culture. And at another moment you can think that nothing has changed at all or that it's gone backwards – and even the same kind of phenomenon can be read both ways.'

For Marian Bell, an economist, the biggest change has been in men's behaviour, and others have agreed. Council women's officer Ellen Kelly – again not alone in saying so – thinks men's behaviour is exactly what hasn't changed. 'Well we can go back a stage and ask what caused that,' says Marian Bell, 'but there's been such a change in men – a greater willingness to do the housework and so on, you just need to look at men of my generation and how much they contribute to a household compared with men of my father's generation ...'

What hasn't shifted? Ellen Kelly had no hesitation. 'How men see themselves. I think that's where an enormous amount of conflict is coming from. Particularly in the workplace, so many men don't listen and aren't showing any signs of wanting to listen. So many men still like to pretend to themselves that they're the major breadwinner and their wife's only working for the holidays and the sweetie money. The patronising attitudes some men have towards women! I look at men at work and think: if you go home and treat your wife like that I don't know why she disna' take a frying pan to you!'

'Fitba' and Fixations

How can I possibly even consider that things haven't *really* changed, I think to myself, walking home from work the day after the Scottish Episcopal Church voted to ordain women as priests, in June 1994, meaning that the Church of Wales was the only remaining Protestant Church in Britain not to have done so. The placards outside our local newsagent's advertise the *Evening News* 'Free us from Fear' campaign against domestic violence. Twenty-five years ago a newspaper editor would have laughed in your face for even suggesting such a thing, let alone see it as a selling point. The bus goes past, carrying the black and white Zero Tolerance message: NO MAN HAS THE RIGHT. Twenty-five years ago some local councillors would not have been ashamed to argue that they did.

I think the first time I noticed how perplexing change is was when

4

my suggestion of a radio feature on rape crisis centres was turned down because it was an 'old story'. When I had previously worked in radio, in 1975, my boss wouldn't let me cover the campaign to set up a rape crisis centre locally. It was seen as too radical an issue then, probably embarrassing. The 'story' has moved from being inadmissible to nothing new but there has been no diminution in the number of women being raped, only a small change in women feeling able to report it. (A breakthrough was the documentary about Thames Valley police, which had significant consequences for police practice, broadcast in 1984.)

But every sunny morning of the summer term as I walk my younger daughter to school, seeing girls playing in the football game which goes on semi-continually in the playground – in a country in which nothing is more highly valued than fitba', how can I think nothing much has changed? This is not a result of positive action, since there was none, but a change in attitudes. Women even play rugby. Even in 'the male, macho heartland of the Scottish Borders,' as a BBC sports reporter wonderingly put it. Lord help them if the sniggering attitudes of the players who discussed it in that programme are typical. Then again, women's professional football is massively under-resourced and unregarded in comparison to the male game. By secondary school few girls are still playing. As girls have not had much experience of playing they are caught in the trap where their lack of experience makes it difficult for them to get more. The game remains segregated and to play you still need to be unusually confident and quite good. I'm longing for my daughters to play, but I don't say anything. Then the little one came home one day with, mixed into all the other tales of her day, how when she and two friends started playing football in the playground 'Joseph ran in and kept tripping us up'.

They trip us up even on the Internet, than which nothing, apparently, could be more gender neutral. Yet sexual harassment rapidly became a problem. In the mid-1990s it was a new medium with an old message: keep out. Net users are mainly men. Since some men use female personae and women have been advised to adopt male pseudonyms to avoid hassle it is hard to tell how much they dominate, but it was variously estimated at between 80 per cent and 90 per cent in 1994. Women complain of anonymous abusive and sexually explicit messages. Advice on how to avoid 'net harassers' has a strangely familiar ring: we must be careful about what messages we post and where, and write in ways that cannot be open to misinterpretation. (Don't walk home late, and if you wear a skirt that short what do you expect ...) Scarcely had the possibility of downloading and manipulating visual images on computer screens become possible than computer porn was every second nerd's latest wheeze, and many schoolgirls' embarrassment and intimidation.

An absolutely central paradox is that the increase in sexual freedom for women has occurred alongside a steep increase in the commodification of sex, in sexual exploitation and in pornography. Women are equal now – and the richest man in Britain is a pornographer, Paul Raymond. The Page Three girl has become a national institution. (You can't say Page Three *woman*, somehow.) Bare breasts of the sort not normally classed as pornography ('just a bit of fun' is, I believe, the official category) are now everywhere, though the star status of Samantha Fox and Linda Lusardi, who once said on television that pin-up pics had 'nothing to do with sex', has waned in favour of the supermodels who show ever more of their elegant selves in the newer men's mags, on catwalks and occasionally in the pages of the broadsheet press.[1]

It's not so much the bosoms that are troubling as expressions that are also required to be pert and fully formed and say 'I'm only here to please.' At least supermodels sulk. (The *Sun's* own brand of prurience-cum-puritanism reached a high point when, in the spring of 1995, Princess Diana was seen on holiday in a T-shirt and no bra: they ran a feature solemnly condemning her for doing so alongside a full spread of photographs so we wouldn't miss the point, or rather, nipple.)

The breast fixation of Western men grew apace with women's autonomy, Brigid McConville observes in her interesting book, *Mixed Messages*: 'Bare breasts, vulnerable breasts – on display everywhere ... the decorative sex, to-be-looked-at-sex, the bearers of "boobs", "jubblies", "titties", the to-be-ridiculed sex.'[2] Few women miss the put-down that lies behind the pin-up. And it is a most curious contradiction that while it is sexy to show a bit of breast – wholly advantageous if we are to believe Wonderbra and Gossard – it may be considered offensive to feed a baby in a public place. Women still report being asked to leave restaurants for feeding a baby or told to go and do it in the loo, and in a survey in London in 1994 a high proportion of men asked said they objected. Male discomfort with breastfeeding is, midwives say, a common reason for women giving it up.

Brigid McConville's central argument is an important one: until we disentangle cultural attitudes around breasts, the mix of sex, comfort, embarrassment and fear, then breast health care will continue to be affected. The lack of it means breast cancer is the biggest killer of women in mid-life in Britain today.

In the 1990s we are, apparently, in the throes of the second sexual revolution. 'Free love' meant quick sex and lots of it, but the postmodern (naturally) post-AIDS sexual revolution was about quality rather than quantity, 'perverse lingering' rather than instant gratification. 'Vanilla sex' was passé and clubs on 'The Scene' were celebrated for their 'penetration-free orgiastic atmosphere'. And if the floor show calls for volunteer submissives, it's all right because power is *really* with the submissives ...[3]

How many women are still waiting for the first sexual revolution, called paying attention to their feelings and needs?

Change in relation to violence and sexual violence is particularly difficult to assess. We don't know: it may only be more visible. That there is more sexual harassment and more, and more violent, pornography is demonstrable. And more pressure on young women to be sexually active, but some of the same penalties if they're *too* active. If women won sexual freedom at the expense of the right to say no, as critics of sexual liberation claim, that right is being reasserted. The illegality of rape in marriage was one of the suffragettes' demands, which gives some perspective on how long change can take. The law was changed in Scotland in 1982 and 1989, and in England and Wales in 1991, though it remains difficult to get a conviction. The 'date rape' debate which has been writ large through several court cases and in college campuses the length and breadth of the land has been about redefining permissible sexual behaviour: that no means no, no matter where, or when, or whatever she was wearing. But we still think we know where the line is between *nice girls* and slags.

There are resources for women victims of violence now that did not exist in 1970: Women's Aid refuges and rape crisis centres, and changed social service, medical and police practice. Such provision as exists is, however, seriously under-resourced. There are new laws and policies, new concepts like 'acquaintance rape' and 'sexual harassment', yet old ideas are usually not far under the surface: 'she was asking for it' still affects trial outcomes to a demonstrable extent and prejudice is still rife in the criminal justice system.

Protest is more visible and more mainstream: last year you could walk down Princes Street in Edinburgh, where I live, and read a full set of statistics on the reality of sexual violence against women and children. The Zero Tolerance campaign begun by Edinburgh District Council in 1992 has been a remarkable success, taken up by eleven other Scottish councils, in London (where it was modified and had a less positive impact), seven other English cities and in Europe and Australia. Most of the football clubs in the Scottish premier league now advertise the Zero Tolerance message. Birmingham City Council has begun a ten-year commitment to campaigning against domestic violence. Publicity carries the clear message: 'Women have the right to live – free of fear, intimidation, harassment, abuse and attack'. Following a remarkable speech at the Scottish Conservative Conference in 1992 by a Conservative woman activist who had been sexually attacked, a Scottish Office crime prevention campaign of posters and television advertising stressed that domestic violence is 'socially unacceptable and a criminal act'; it sought to achieve 'an atmosphere of public disapproval and a greater openness to address the problem'. Leaflets published by the Home Office carry the message that 'domestic violence is a serious crime' and that 'you have the right to be free from fear and abuse. It is your partner whose behaviour needs to change.'[4]

Twenty-five years ago even, most police officers did not take 'just a domestic' seriously. Even sympathetic community workers thought there was nothing that could be done. Twenty years ago Women's Aid was seen as 'a lunatic group'; now it is a professional organisation with an input into legislation. In the 1970s 'Stand by Your Man' was sung without irony and with full throttle in clubs up and down the land. In 1993 it was the soundtrack for the uncompromising Women's Aid film *Don't Stand For It* for which the Home Office and the Midland Bank paid the distribution costs.

But violence against women by the men they live with, or used to, is still a quarter of all reported violent crime and almost certainly the most common violent crime of all. We know that the true incidence remains hidden: one estimate is that almost a third of women experience domestic violence in their lifetime.[5]

Politics, Priests, Money ...

And the big questions about male power: in decision-making, running organisations, running the country, running the world?

There has been much talk and some progress on positive action to get more women into both the House of Commons and the European Parliament. All the British political parties, one way or another, are exercised by the need for more women MPs. In 1993 the Labour Party, albeit with some grumbling, introduced women-only shortlists for half of winnable seats, and reaffirmed that intention in 1994 without the scrap the press had been looking forward to. By March 1995 a start had been made in selecting women candidates and one would-be (male) MP challenged the policy as against the Sex Discrimination Act. Described as 'a jobs-for-the-girls political racket', this 'plan to pack Westminster with women' would, at best, mean an increase to around a sixth of all MPs women. A new organisation on American lines, Emily's List was founded to support women candidates to a chorus of media disdain. Scottish Labour women tried to go one further: why not have all-women shortlists in *all* the available winnable seats in Scotland? It would ruin the careers of 'a whole generation of able young men', Labour MP George Foulkes rumbled in horror, echoed by most of the Scottish press.[6] There were few tears for the generations of able young women. In Scotland only seven MPs are women, only four of them Labour (but 45 Labour men).

The Scottish Constitutional Convention finalised in 1994 plans to ensure equal female/male representation in a Scottish parliament, meaning that *if and when* it happens it will have the highest proportion of women parliamentarians in the world. An agreement between the Scottish Liberal Democrats and Labour (the two electorally dominant parties in Scotland) in March 1995 introduced an innovative electoral contract by which they would agree to select and field an equal number of female and male candidates, with an additional member list as a back-up mechanism. On 1992 voting patterns it would deliver 40–45 per cent women MSPs. There were rumblings of dissent in private, within the Labour and Liberal Parties, and the SNP was ambivalent but public support in Scotland for getting more women into politics was very high.[7]

The government's own analysis of the forward march of women in public appointments, despite multiplying opportunities in quangoes, show it to be painfully slow: 19 per cent in 1986 (the earliest year for which figures are available) and 28 per cent in 1993 of people on public bodies in all government departments and their agencies were women. Of the 2.3 per cent of public appointments held by people from ethnic minorities, only a quarter are held by women. 'Representation of women, and hence their scope for influence in key decision-making areas, in national parliamentary posts, in the judiciary and in international affairs, remains limited,' the government says in its report to the United Nations world conference. 'It's like watching paint dry,' as one woman said.[8]

In March 1995 there were two women members of the Cabinet and seven women junior ministers, and at July 1994 women formed 10 per cent of the membership of House of Commons Select Committees. And there is Betty Boothroyd, the first woman Speaker of the House of Commons, who is such a popular figure with the public that a lot of us want her for president, come the Republic.

Double messages about success, feminism and femininity continued to be spread. If Conservative women were seen as part of a tradition of hang-em-high Tory Ladies, with a new sexual allure courtesy of Edwina Currie's *A Parliamentary Affair* ('where politics equals sex, power and ambition'), Labour women, *especially* if they tried to organise as women, were seen as humourless do-gooders. The killer adjective 'earnest' was wielded, as it has been against feminism for most of this century.

When John Major formed his first Cabinet in November 1990 there was protest that it included no women: the fact that the mainstream press noticed and that he could be embarrassed on the subject was evidence that something had changed. But for women in the House of Commons it still feels like the 'self-contained male club' Barbara Castle described it as in the 1960s. Angela Eagle, MP for Wallasey, described it to me in very similar terms, though she believes it won't be that way much longer: 'a critical mass of around 20 per cent women and the House of Commons would become unrecognisable – and if 40 per cent of parliament were women ... no national strategy for childcare, the high rate of women's deaths from cancer, these things would not be tolerated. And the ridiculous hours we work! Women have not been fully involved in the political process since the fight for the vote.' But she believes we could be on the brink of much greater women's involvement. 'The political process has ossified – it needs women and it needs far-reaching constitutional change. Getting in more women would change it more rapidly than anything – easily, cheaply!'

A lot of politically active women don't just want a bigger slice of the cake, they want to change the recipe. If you include participative politics, community action and pressure groups as well as representative government there are almost certainly more women who are politically active than there are men: in decision-making the reverse is true.

Between 1970 and the most recent election the proportion of women MPs more than doubled: but from 4.1 per cent in 1970 to 9.2 per cent in 1992 it is still very low in comparison to most European countries. In Europe only France, Portugal and Greece have lower figures for women's representation, and half of EU countries have over 20 per cent women representatives: hardly good, but better. Sweden, which has the highest proportion of any democratic country, has 40.4 per cent women in parliament. Nor has it even been straightforward progress in Britain: the proportion fell in 1979 (to 2.9 per cent). Such fluctuations are all the more likely when numbers overall are low. An increase of 2 per cent between the 1987 and 1992 elections at a time when there was a great deal of lobbying to improve the situation can scarcely be identified as an onward march of reverse discrimination (though it is).[9]

There is no comprehensive audit of local authorities in England and Wales but research indicates that the number of women councillors has increased: from an estimated 19 per cent in the mid-1970s to an average of just under a quarter now. The proportion varies considerably, with urban councils more likely to have more

women than rural areas. The possible impact on women's representation of change to councils in England and Wales is an issue now
beginning to be examined. In Scotland the proportion of women
councillors is 22.4 per cent in the new 'shadow' unitary authorities
elected in April 1995, an increase of 0.5 per cent on the 1992 district
results.[10]

Women now form 25 per cent of members of the European
Parliament, an increase from 18.5 per cent at the previous elections.
Britain, with 13 per cent of our MEPs women, is one of the three with
fewest countries; most European countries now send a third of
women MEPs. The European Commission wields most of the
power, and here there are four women out of twenty-one members,
from Germany, Sweden, France and Denmark.[11]

But the major change, though nowadays a lot of people are trying
to forget it, was our first woman Prime Minister. Living through the
thirteen years of her reign was a contradictory experience. Though
the cliché quickly spread that as a woman she had done less for
women than any man had, or might have dared, the jury is still very
much out on her significance for women. Equally, we used to say
that *at least* no girl could grow up now thinking of the top job as a
male preserve. I tested that one out on my daughter, aged four at the
time. 'Who is Mrs Thatcher?' I asked her. 'Ummm – isn't she
President Reagan's wife?' For me a defining image of the 1980s was
Margaret Thatcher heading a war cabinet while women at Greenham
Common asserted women's essential peacefulness.

Notoriously, there was 'not a man to match her'. But in Defence
Secretary George Younger's memories she was 'very much a lady'.[12]
Tougher than the boys – but she was *Mrs* Thatcher, as if to emphasise
her respectable femininity, less often Margaret Thatcher (though we
say *John* Major, *Tony* Blair) and never, *ever* Ms Thatcher.

Underlying constructions of gender were crucial to the way in
which she was promoted and seen, from the very first good
housewife images on. She was described and reviled in ways
permeated with sexual imagery: Alan Clark's flirtatious talk of her
slim ankles, sexist slogans like 'Ditch the Bitch' on demonstrations,
images of her as cruel mistress, as dominatrix, as nanny. And now as
the madwoman in the attic. Her occasional breaks for freedom
embarrass the men who are back in charge, creating havoc until 'she is

again locked safely away'. In her memoirs *The Downing Street Years* she sorts her cabinet ministers into several categories of inept masculinity: the waverers, the ditherers, the fainthearts and moaning minnies. They lined up to reply in kind: she was a sour and peevish old woman, embittered, a woman scorned, vengeful, petulant and *not statesmanlike*.[13]

Margaret Thatcher was Prime Minister and First Lord of the Treasury but not entitled to full membership of the locus of behind-the-scenes Conservative power, the Carlton Club. As an outsider she didn't play by the rules; it was her strength and her downfall. It is salutary to remember that before she ousted Ted Heath as leader of the Conservative Party there was a strong body of opinion that as a woman she couldn't do it or take it, would not be strong or well-connected enough. The verb 'to handbag' entered the political lexicon soon enough. When it was first suggested that she go she reflected, she says, 'that if the great and the good of the Tory party had had their way, I would never have become party leader, let alone PM'. Her personal creed became a political philosophy: taking tough decisions, showing boldness, admitting no weakness or failure. 'I'm sure I was wrong on a number of occasions,' she told David Frost, 'but I cannot think of anything immediately.' Her condemnation of one-nation Tories as 'wet' echoes girls' playground cries of 'wimp' and 'sissy'.[14]

Her cool account of the Brighton bombing makes particularly fascinating reading: the detail, the determination on control and the appearance of control. She was still awake at just before three in the morning, working as ever. Her personal assistant 'Crawfie' (intriguingly, the same affectionate name as the Queen's nanny) gathered together her vanity case, blouses and two suits; her private secretary collected government papers and her speech. Someone has just tried to kill her and come close to succeeding. 'I knew I could not afford to let my emotions get control of me. I had to be mentally and physically fit for the day ahead.' What mattered most was to open the conference on time, and at 9.30 precisely she did so: 'to show the terrorists that they could not break our spirit'.[15]

Notoriously, she only ever included one woman in her cabinet, Baroness Young, who was briefly present as Leader of the House of Lords. Endlessly Thatcher was photographed in bright blue suit against the grey ranks of male anonymity and loved it. She adored her father and left her mother out of her entry in *Who's Who*. 'Mrs Thatcher offers her own life and career as proof of the folly of feminism,' wrote Wendy Webster in 1990, in her book on the Thatcher phenomenon. 'Since she has achieved power and success, she sees no reason why other women could not do so if they wanted. But curiously, she usually does not think they ought to want to.' And: 'Mrs Thatcher's profound division from other women is a central theme of her life, thought and publicity. In Thatcherism which bears a woman's name there is no room for other women to be like her.'[16] In that she acted much as a right-wing woman of her generation might have been expected to. She cut the budget and staff of the EOC, but encouraged the promotion of women in the Civil Service, introduced separate taxation for husbands and wives (in 1989). In 1987 I went as one of a party of women on a trip to China. We met representatives of the Chinese Women's Federation. In a country run by two women, they said, women must be very powerful. (The other was the Queen.) No one knew the Chinese for 'Queen Bee'.

Margaret Thatcher dominated government and arrogated collective responsibility; in the unwritten British constitution the PM is first among equals, a uniquely difficult status for the first woman PM – easier to be a bossy headmistress (see George Younger's account) than to be equal. Her memoirs talk of betrayal, desertion, treachery. From Kenneth Baker's account of her downfall you get a powerful sense of men as scheming and superstitious, tiptoeing in, one by one, each with a knife in hand – destroying a woman who had become too powerful. (Kill the witch.) He suggests that if she had seen them together rather than separately she would have successfully faced them down.[17] Her shadow hangs long and dark over ambitious women in politics.

But what about *spiritual* power? Admitting women as priests is a decision which was important because of its symbolic meaning even to people who don't go to church. The Christian Church is a carrier of patriarchal values in unusually pure expression: the reason women couldn't be priests was because we could not stand for God, could not consecrate the sacrament, give blessings or absolution. Which says a great deal about how women are seen and how God is seen.

I remember watching the televised Church of England debate on women priests: a particular group of women deacons, shining blonde bobs, swinging earrings and dog-collars all in a row, suggested the acceptable face of the Church. Almost since its inception (with a couple of interesting heresies as exceptions) Christianity has insisted on the lower status of women and has ensured their role as men's servants. It has used guilt and prescription as a way to control women. Biblical diktat has been responsible for 'a few millennia of women's work being defined as stitching altar-cloths, and having lunch ready when the men come back from the Synod,' as theologian Elizabeth Templeton puts it.[18] Christian churches and organisations, which might have taken a lead in condemning violence in the family, have, with some few exceptions, done little actively to oppose it and the refusal of many clergy to countenance divorce means that some women stay in violent marriages.

The arguments against ordination were revealing in an age when institutional sexism is more usually disguised. When new priests danced in the aisle at York accusations of witchcraft made clear how deep the roots of opposition went. One (Scottish Episcopal) opponent, saw floodgates opening to 'militant feminism, greater acceptance of deviant sexual practices, trendy liturgies and all manner of strange and erroneous doctrines'. The ordination of the Church of England's first thirty-two women priests in Bristol Cathedral (in March 1994) was greeted variously with jubilation and gnashing of teeth. A team of vergers with walkie-talkies discreetly patrolled the aisles 'to look out for known traditionalists who might make trouble'. Surely this was real change – ending, as one report put it, 'more than 1,000 years of male domination of established religion'. And Roman Catholic women have renewed their campaign for ordination in consequence. But a report a year later showed that a third of women priests in the Church of England were still without paid jobs although 1,387 had been ordained. A spokeswoman for the women priests' organisation Watch said some traditionalist bishops had been 'obstructive' and that several parishes which had asked for a woman had been sent a militant opponent of women priests instead. However, relatively fewer opposing priests than expected have resigned on the issue.[19]

The Church of Scotland took the decision that women could

become ministers over twenty-five years ago. The message from Scotland to the new English priests must be that they have been freed to face merely mortal discrimination: although their presence in the parishes has had an impact, since only 10 per cent of ministers are women their voice in the Church remains marginal and the major decision-making committees remain male dominated. Women's role is still seen by many as that of tea-makers and Sunday School teachers, wives and helpmeets – and the majority of the congregation. Interesting light on this comes from Mary Levison, the woman minister who led the struggle for the ordination of women in the Church of Scotland. She says she still feels an outsider.[20] (The Congregationalists have had women ministers since 1917, the Baptists since 1925.)

As the main Christian Churches respond to more egalitarian times (though the Catholic Church has set its face firmly against women's demands) there are reports of record numbers of women converting to Islam, with its rigorous and defined – though that definition is contentious – gender roles. The rate of conversions is, according to the Association of British Muslims, increasing, and Islam is attracting more women than men, and mainly single, educated women. Within Islam there is also change: a vigorous debate about women's position in which women theologians argue that true Islam demands respect for women and offers them a powerful role and that 'unlike capitalism and much of feminist discourse, Islam recognises the importance of women's life cycles'.[21] 'There is an awareness of women's position which is very different from the perceived position from the outside,' says Farkhandra Chaudhry from the Muslim Women's Group in Glasgow.

Bond Girls, Trading Women

With reference perhaps to the real Stella Rimington, head of MI5, the new 'M' in the seventeenth James Bond film is played by Judi Dench, and the Bond girls are apparently now to be known as Bond women. (Does this mean they don't have to take their clothes off?) Corporate woman is chic. But very few sit at the head of the table in real life. A woman makes the decisions, tilting her head charmingly, in the Vauxhall Astra ads: the firm's real chief executive is Charles Golden.

PARADOX AND PANDORA'S BOX

Kenco, where the silly, sexist foreigner wants to talk to the real boss, is a trade name used by General Foods, a subsidiary of tobacco giant Philip Morris Inc. (USA) and the real boss, in the UK anyway, is Ronnie Bell (Ronnie as in Ronald, not Ronalda). No woman that I could find out about heads a coffee company. In advertising the woman is a marker of modernity, judge of quality and good value, contrasted, often as not, with a bumbling older man. In real life her judgements still run against the grain and older men are firmly in charge: Anita Roddick of the Body Shop, Penny Hughes who until recently ran Coca-Cola UK, and Margaret Seymour, MD of a successful swimming-pool business in Scotland (which in itself shows entrepreneurial spirit above the average) are conspicuous because they are still unusual. Although the female membership of the Institute of Directors (IoD) has increased, from less than 2% in 1975 to 6% in September 1994, most are the directors of fairly small companies, 60 per cent running companies with a turnover of £2 million or less. In the flurry of controversy about how much top executives get paid which ran from late autumn 1994 onwards, no women's names featured. Financial journalist William Kay's account of *The Bosses* – interviews with 'the major players... the movers and shakers', the 'fresh generation of managers' – was an account of the growth industries of the future and, rather less freshly, 'the men who lead them'. No women were apparently playing big enough to matter.[22]

The proportion of women who are starting their own businesses, on the other hand, is rising rapidly – reckoned a positive outcome of 'the glass ceiling'. It's a trend in which 'Women who think laterally move sideways,' as one woman said. A large proportion of the IoD's women members (65 per cent – and it has not been known as a hotbed of radical feminists), do not believe that equal opportunities for women exist, and 88 per cent felt that women face obstacles at work not encountered by men. What obstacles? 'Men's attitudes.'

If high-flying City woman was the 1980s icon of progress, the sex discrimination case fought by stockbroker Samantha Phillips in August 1994 tarnished the dream. Women trading in telephone-number figures was change indeed. Suffering sexual advances from senior management and being called a bimbo – no change there.

What's newer is women fighting back. With the support of the EOC and a London law centre Phillips won £18,000 compensation for unfair dismissal and discrimination. A different kind of change: thirteen women who work at the company in question, underwriters Willis Coroon, wrote to the *Guardian* to say the company has 'a non-sexist atmosphere' and that 'everyone should be able to survive the normal rough and tumble, cut and thrust of office life'.[23] Less of a change: since she was blonde and youthful the papers devoted extraordinary acres of newsprint to photos of her and still further acres to the story. In the 1970s it was observed that women were much less likely to be the subject of newspaper articles but much more likely to be represented visually. That rule still seems to hold.

'A head-hunter had warned me before the industrial tribunal that I would not get work again in the City if I went ahead with it,' Samantha Phillips said later. 'Whether or not you win, if you stand up for your rights you are marked as a troublemaker.' After the original advances from the manager she had not complained – 'I took the view we were grown-up people and it would blow over' – but he persistently made unpleasant and personal comments to her, she said, and encouraged others in the office to join in. After she complained she was dismissed.[24]

When the stock market was opened to women in 1973 it was acclaimed as a step forward. Now 'sexual harassment in the City is an everyday thing,' a woman broker told me, although another woman working in the City commented that it seems to vary according to status – the higher you are promoted, the less the groping at the photocopier. Samantha Phillips described a 'swaggering atmosphere' and a habit of sexual innuendo in the office where she was the only woman. Men outnumber women by around twenty to one in the City's financial institutions; few City firms have official complaints procedures and there is anger at women seen as destroying office culture. As a male futures dealer told the *Observer*: 'it's all good fun really. If the girls can't take it they should get out.' In City argot a successful trader is a 'big swinging dick', and a successful woman trader an 'honorary big swinging dick'.[25]

The picture of the working culture in high finance which emerged from Samantha Phillips's tribunal was much the same as life on a manual work team described to me around the same time by a woman working alongside eleven men on a conservation team in northern Scotland. It was aggressively, endlessly, crudely sexual and if she didn't like it, well she could leave, couldn't she? She felt she had to take it because if she complained it would only make things harder for her. The messages to women seen as trespassing on male preserves are remarkably similar, from Armani-suited offices to wellie-booted hillsides and, indeed the armed services.

Sexual harassment has been a serious problem for women police officers. A strongly masculine working culture in the ranks contrasts with statements about equal opportunity at the top. The hassle and intimidation women face, and are supposed by that ethic to be tough enough to take, is not only a problem for women officers but a major barrier to creating policing that is equally responsive to both halves of the population and that women can trust. One survey found that one in ten women officers had given serious consideration to leaving because of harassment and another study, of 1,300 policewomen, found that 60 per cent had suffered unwanted touching by fellow officers in the previous month and 6 per cent serious sexual assault. In this culture, Frances Heidensohn, a sociologist who has studied life in the police writes, 'categories ... are few and polar: police-women are either dykes or sluts'. That it's not easy to seek redress is shown by what happened to Sarah Locker, a woman police officer with the Metropolitan Police who won a record settlement for sexual and racial discrimination in December 1993. She met with hostility on her return to work: fellow officers refused to talk to her, she received anonymous phone calls, and made a suicide attempt in consequence. Women form less than 15 per cent of police officers in Britain and they are more likely to leave than men.[26]

A large-scale study of junior barristers' training and work, published in early 1995, shows that three out of four young women barristers see sexual harassment as a problem at the Bar and 40 per cent have experienced it personally during their studies or first years at the Bar. Four out of five young barristers said sex discrimination was a continuing problem. As the controversy grew, Barbara Hewson, Chair of the Association of Women Barristers, said she knew of a number of students who had been offered pupillages in return for sex.[27]

Sandra Valentine, the only woman among 178 pilots working for

Airtours, was subjected to 'a relentless onslaught of sexual harassment and discrimination,' her lawyer told a tribunal in Birmingham in January 1995. This included being propositioned in front of passengers and other colleagues and sent pornographic material at work. When she complained of a trainer using coarse language he replied: 'If you want to play in a man's world you had better get used to a man's language'. (No decision was expected until later in 1995.)[28]

In 1970 no such case could have been taken. Sexual harassment only became actionable as sex discrimination after the Porcelli case in 1986 against Strathclyde Regional Council, and no sex discrimination, of course, was illegal before 1975. A number of organisations and companies have now introduced policy procedures on sexual harassment. The EOC reports a steady increase in sexual harassment enquiries, which they think demonstrates an increased confidence that something can be done. The sort of salacious publicity that harassment cases attract is, however, a significant disincentive for many women. Taking a case can be distressing and unpleasant and a 'can't she take a joke' response is still common.

Complainants of sex discrimination at work are now winning an average of almost £22,000 in compensation, seven times the awards being made before European law raised the ceiling on awards in 1993. The EOC notes that this has led to a rapid rise in awareness of equality law among employers. Until early 1993 industrial tribunals were limited to a maximum payment of £11,000 for sex discrimination and the average tribunal award, before the test case in the European Courts, was a little over £3,000.[29]

The cost of discrimination was brought home when the Ministry of Defence (MoD) found itself paying 'jackpot awards' to ex-servicewomen it had dismissed for pregnancy after a 1990 European Court ruling that the policy operated by the MoD of dismissing servicewomen in their sixteenth week of pregnancy had been illegal since 1978. The cost to the MoD at September 1994 was £30 million, with more cases in the pipeline. However, an appeal tribunal in July 1994 ruled that the 1,700 cases still to be heard would be assessed on the percentage chance of the woman returning to work rather than the 'all or nothing' measure that had previously applied, and called for future tribunals to 'keep a due sense of proportion'. Awards had been 'manifestly excessive,' Mr Justice Morison ruled. After this the average settlement was £10,000 and Helen Homewood, an ex-army major who won a record compensation award of £300,000 came to a private agreement with the MoD after it appealed. In February 1995 the EOC backed the case of a woman who had been sacked because she was pregnant after the MoD changed its policy of automatically dismissing servicewomen when they became pregnant; the woman, who had been in the RAF, won £15,000 in an out-of-court settlement.[30]

On 1 February 1995 equal treatment for women and men in the armed services became law in Britain, following a campaign by the EOC: this means that women and men in the armed forces will have the same rights as any other employee to protection from sex discrimination. The equal pay laws do not, however, apply in the armed forces.

The equal opportunities provided by service life had already been praised by ministers when, after seventy-six years, the Women's Royal Air Force was, in April 1994, integrated with the RAF. Only two jobs – fireman and the symbolically appropriate aerial erector – are still barred to women in the RAF. 'Women ... compete on equal terms with men for appointments, training places and trades,' armed forces minister Jeremy Hanley said.[31]

That it is not, sadly, quite as simple as that is suggested by the experience of the Wrens. The Women's Royal Naval Service was integrated with the Royal Navy in November 1993. However, an internal Royal Navy report seen by the BBC television programme *Public Eye* revealed that women in the Royal Navy suffer from verbal and physical harassment and some are extremely unhappy with life at sea. The report said that men of all ranks are hostile to women serving at sea and are overtly sexist. Women on HMS *Ark Royal*, who are outnumbered ten to one, told of endless abuse and different standards: 'If a fella drops something he's just dropping something, if a woman drops something it's because you're a stupid woman'. Men interviewed by *Public Eye* (April, 1994) said they should 'stop dripping about it' and that women should learn to 'take it like a man – they want equal rights and equal jobs, they should take an equal amount of mickey. We take it!'

The Politics of Glitz

For my sins, I spent about a year of my journalistic life as a fashion editor. It was long enough to realise that it was true that fashion is often an uncannily accurate social barometer. But if so, then some of the mid-1990s messages are bizarre. If the women's liberation movement looked forward to a time of Mao jackets and rational dressing, the Baby Doll look and return of pastels might seem the apotheosis of reaction.

Yet, approaching a pink 'n' glitz femininity not otherwise attempted since Doris Day by anyone actually female, this was a kind of quoting: girls dressing up as girls. In sequinned slips, ostrich-feather bras and outrageous silver platforms a woman was 'dragged up'. Wearing denims, Docs and a lumberjack shirt (technically cross-dressing, after all) she wouldn't be seen to be. It is a style which fits rather perfectly with both theories of postmodernism and womanliness as masquerade: the idea expressed by Simone de Beauvoir of femininity as a game with clothes and make-up its props. The question, then and now, is how far women manipulate this game, how far they are trapped by it.

Fashion semiotics is never more needed. Because what is also intriguing are the mixed messages: the first femininity as costume, the second as uncertainty. Dress code is as complex off the catwalk on the street – angora bikinis for clubbing to a shorn and sleek baby-dyke look from which presumptions about sexuality can no longer safely be drawn. Briefly there was a post-St Trinian's look which seemed designed to bring out the dirty old man. (One day, walking towards an Edinburgh secondary school I met a woman of reasonably mature years in mini-gymslip, white blouse and striped tie – probably Laura Ashley – closely followed by several hundred schoolgirls most of whom were in jeans and anorak.) But by 1995 there is still no look that sums up the decade as we can do so easily for the 1920s, or 1960s, 1970s or 1980s.

The saddest version of pink and pretty I saw was in Evans outsize window: a large and smock-like garment in cheesecloth called, unblushingly, a Baby Doll blouse. According to the *Independent* though, in 1994 'The message for spring is this: you can dress like a sex kitten and still be firmly in control.' The article is worth quoting further, such contradictions being the essence of the times. 'You may wonder what these pictures are doing here in these politically correct, gently feminist times. You may wonder if these teeny-weeny skirts and this fluffy-bunny cutesiness is yet another plot by misogynist male designers to make women look silly. You would be wrong.' (Phew!)[32]

'This is not about being sexy and fluffy. It is about being sexy and fluffy and strong all at the same time.' The article concluded with a quote from the accessory and shoe editor of American *Vogue*: 'women have arrived. They have done their struggle to the top. The power suit is out! You can be sexy and still command the boardroom.' So much for all those women who thought they did look sexy in their suits (but still weren't even in the boardroom). And the stiletto was back. And constricted, tight, pencil-line skirts. (Control?) What actually walked out of the shoe shops were to all intents and purposes androgynous boots. Mothers who were teenagers in the 1960s and 1970s looked on with some amazement as their daughters went to school in Doc Martens – not so *very* different from the lace-ups the lady supervisor had advised which they wouldn't have been seen dead in.

The Paris collections for spring/summer 1995 showed dirndls and dresses Kay Kendall would have felt happy in: the Baby Doll look was growing up and heading for the kitchen. *Scotsman* fashion writer John Davidson described it as 'hausfrau style', harking back to 'perhaps the last time when women were really womanly'. (Gee thanks, John.) 'Do women have nothing more to prove?' he wondered. The *Guardian* headlined it THE NEW FEMININITY although it looked rather like the old one to me, and wrote of 'a return to glamour and femininity after the sombre, sexless years of deconstruction'. However – and it appeared to be true – 'nobody seems to get a handle on what constitutes femininity for the contemporary woman: too many designers are retreating into tired old clichés' and a 'spew of sexual stereotypes'.[33]

Both papers pictured a remarkable garment by Comme des Garçons in which a complex organza ball skirt was somehow sandwiched between a tailored tail coat and striped trousers. Its designer, Rei Kawacubo, said something incomprehensible about 'transcending Gender: The Presentiment of Femininity in the Play of its Disappearance'. Aaah – so that's what's going on ...

But you still mainly can't wear trousers to work. Even where dress codes are not formalised most British working women find skirts more appropriate; there are quite strong unwritten rules about looking smart but feminine, especially in the more conventional sectors. Men may wear ponytails to work (Safeways was found guilty of sex discrimination for sacking a long-haired man in December 1994), and in January 1993 schoolboys in Dorset won the right to keep their earrings in, but the legal situation, based rather tenuously on the unsuccessful appeal against unfair dismissal of a woman bookshop worker in 1978, suggests that employers can require women to wear skirts with impunity, providing there is some sort of vaguely equivalent dress rule for male staff. (Kilts would seem to complicate the law, but there hasn't been an appropriate test case.) New customer relations staff in our pre-privatisation railway companies might want to test it, I'd have thought – the young women standing around in smart red coats and navy skirts on Waverley Station, Edinburgh, where howling gales hit at knee height, would be much better off in trousers, and it's difficult to see that it would impede their capacity to answer questions and direct travellers to the right platform. At Manchester Piccadilly there was a rumbling of protest when Regional Railways went so far as to insist on 15-denier black or barely black stockings, again hardly relevant to the job. But then, research done by the managing director of Colour Me Beautiful image consultants – not perhaps the most objective of observers – shows that women who wear make-up earn more and get promoted faster.[34]

I was surprised when I read in January 1995 about a schoolgirl protest over trousers, since most schools I knew about were relaxed on the issue, and some local authorities have 'no uniform' policies. But almost every winter, the EOC said when I asked, the issue of skirts as school uniform comes up, mainly because of the cold, though sexual harassment is also a concern. In the absence of a test case what schools can insist on is unclear, though the EOC believes that requiring girls to wear skirts to school may be inconsistent with the Sex Discrimination Act. The EOC observes, however, that any challenge to an individual school ruling would have to be mounted in the County or Sherrif's Courts, where female advocates are required to wear skirts, as are female judges, and that 'this would not be a propitious venue in which to press for a new order'. When, in early 1995 the head of a mixed comprehensive in Gloucestershire threatened fifteen female pupils with suspension after they wore trousers to school, he said 'Boys wear trousers and girls do not, that is the convention of society.' 'Cross-dressing is not just acceptable for a Nineties Person, it's essential,' a *Guardian* fashion page had declared a few months earlier. Should someone tell him?[35]

Thinking about Women

I like train journeys: the passing theatre of rain-sodden back gardens, grubby bathroom windows, smart new patio doors and other people's washing. Unfamiliar ochre and softened red brick, Victorian back-to-backs, converted warehouses with postmodern balconies: Preston, Salford, Manchester, industrial towns I knew only as names from history at school. Travelling to meet Liz Stanley, reader in sociology at the University of Manchester, early in this journey of inquiry I thought about how little I knew of the north-west of England. And the wider question: how can I begin to know anything of women's lives other than my own and those of women I knew or have interviewed? I was trying to write about women, the real texture of whose lives is only a little more visible to me than the snapshots of lives endlessly presented through the train windows.

The category 'woman' can silence women; it puts our lives and experiences and thoughts and perceptions into the blender and ends up with something far too homogeneous. It presents us with really basic muddles: so that arguments are routinely put forward in terms of a women's position or interest – I'm thinking of articles in the broadsheet press, for example, and of local authority politics; so that, as campaigners, as feminists, we want to say, we *do* say, women this ... and women that ... But to do so is to make invisible the experience of women to whom those particular arguments may not apply. We cannot talk accurately of women as a group or class; we also need to.

Are these paradoxes a consequence of how we look at change, and at women? In part because of the way in which questions are posed, an answer, it seems, must be one thing or the other. This comes from the sense of a grand narrative: that there are broad and sweeping explanations. Tangled in with our sense of change, too, is a model of culture as continuous progress.

We are learning to be suspicious of sweeping statements and grand theories, of 'general diagnoses and general remedies for the ills of society'.[36] We are learning that there are few straightforward answers and that progress is rarely guaranteed. We are learning that either/or thinking stops us recognising a more complex position, that an answer can be 2 per cent of this and 8 per cent of that. To think otherwise has been a feature of the Enlightenment thinking that feminism has contested. If 'man' cannot stand for all of humanity, can 'woman' stand unproblematically for all women?

As I began the research for this book I came hard up against the question of 'difference' which has been of major theoretical concern for feminists for the past ten or fifteen years or so, and a practical concern in women's groups and organisations. Simone de Beauvoir first articulated the positioning of woman as 'other'. The influential American black lesbian feminist Audre Lorde later showed that as 'white women ignore their built-in privileges of whiteness and define *woman* in terms of their own experience alone, then women of Color become "other"'.[37]

If the question of difference was first and most clearly articulated by black and ethnic minority women, in a critique of feminism as expressing Western, white, mainly middle-class values, it has also chimed with other women's experience. As a Scottish woman from a working-class background I have found this a resonant argument since much feminism is positioned in a (not always conscious) metropolitan viewpoint and partially exclusive. The women's liberation tenets of sisterhood and solidarity made unwarranted assumptions, defined women without their consent. We cannot assume shared priorities. If I do so in my role as columnist for *Scotland on Sunday* the occasional reader is inclined to write and ask me why I presume to speak for her. Quite rightly, even if it is a useful short-cut in argument or rhetorical flourish.

But if we cannot easily talk about woman without constructing some sort of monolithic category are we in danger of losing the capacity to talk generally, and hence politically, at all? As Mary Evans has written, from an acknowledgement of diverse inequalities has followed the difficulty in developing a single feminist politics.[38] (Although you can also reverse it: the difficulty in developing a single feminist politics has led to more attention being paid to differences between women.) It is an argument that has seemed to lead to stalemate, to a point at which there is little that can usefully and generally be said about women. Yet 'women' are still vulnerable on dark streets at night, and paid less than men. Life is about the particular and the specific. But to write at all you begin to move away from that.

Which was why I was travelling to Manchester to talk to Liz Stanley. Her thinking had been crucial for me in getting beyond that impasse. She had written: 'A concern with the details of particular lives … stops in their dubious tracks "women this" and "women that" categorical statements by showing the importance of time, place, gender, community, education, religious and political conviction, sexual preference, race and ethnicity, class, *and* of the indomitable uniqueness of people who share social and structural similarities.'[39]

Liz Stanley is feisty, straightforward and warm. A senior academic, her route into academic life was as independent as her thinking often is: from a working-class family in Southampton, she left school at 16 to work in a corset factory and only later began a degree part-time at a further education college. She lives in Manchester with Sue Wise, with whom she wrote the books *Breaking Out* and *Breaking Out Again*, titles which seem to sum up her refusal to settle for any easy orthodoxy.

We met in her office and talked for about four hours, intensely, connectedly, about operations, frocks and epistemology. Feminism had been guilty, she argued, 'and I know I'm as culpable', of thinking about the world in terms of over-simple dichotomies. 'Feminism was saying very powerful things, which were as powerful as they were because they offered a very stark vision of the world – good and evil, male and female. And if one lot of them, the baddies with the dangly bits, had the power then the other lot didn't – didn't have anything, there were just oppressors and victims. I think that we're now reaping the whirlwind of that – in deconstruction, which is saying all there is is complexity and there's nothing like gender, or racism, or sexism. And you lose any notion that there are structural inequalities.'

Later, the same issue of the elision of structural inequality in the way we now talk about women was raised in a differently focused conversation with Valerie Amos. She recognised the same difficulty in the language of equal opportunities and the world of 'the policy community'. Valerie has spent her working life in equal opportunity, mainly in local and central government. Now working as a management consultant, until December 1993 she was chief executive of the EOC but left soon after the new director Kamlesh Bahl arrived. Smart and helpful, self-contained, carefully and deeply thoughtful, she came to Britain in the 1960s from Guyana with her parents, who are teachers. She now lives in London with her sister and her sister's children.

'I think that part of what's happened is that we no longer have a language with which to talk about what's happening to women. To talk about being a feminist is perceived as being outmoded. All the language of managerialism and bureaucracy and economics has kind of crept into the way that we talk about equal opportunities. It's helpful in one respect, in terms of creating change in organisations, but it's not helpful in a broader, societal sense because then you're not talking about social justice, you're not talking about structural discrimination.

'We seem always to be talking about things on the periphery and it no longer seems to be acceptable to say *fundamentally* in the way that our society is structured women are oppressed.' Which has meant a return to a sense of any problems as women's problems, not society's. 'Women are seen as unable to sort themselves out. And women have internalised that a bit, because it's very hard otherwise, you end up appearing as if you're moaning the whole time.'

'Part of the problem is that arguments and debates have not kept pace with the rapid change that's going on, not just in the UK but more broadly ...' All the talk of individual choice 'denies the reality that we don't all actually start from the same place'. It has also become increasingly more difficult to talk about class and poverty, and this ethos hides the fact that 'access to decision-making and influence still remain closed to the majority of women and the majority of black people ... The way society operates is through pressure to say "I'm different", "I'm an individual, if I work hard enough ... There are all these role models of people who have made it. You can too.'

So do the same arguments have to be made? 'We may not have to use the same language but we do have to find a way of getting beyond talking about discrimination in the way we are currently talking about it. I feel that very strongly. Because the context has changed, socially, economically and politically. Because if we don't do that then we haven't got a collective means of acknowledging what the issues are and thinking about how to move beyond that.'

Chapter 2

Facts of Life and Labour

My research had begun before those conversations, and rather unexpectedly, in a hospital bed. A week after I started work on this book I was in hospital having an operation to remove a growth on one of my ovaries. I was *furious*. I didn't have *time* to be ill. It seemed a bitter comment on my ambitions that I should be held up by a quintessentially feminine part of me malfunctioning.

I think it was on the third day, still dozy with dope and disorientation, that I realised all female life was here. I exaggerate: I would not wish to define women in terms only of our reproductive parts. But that week in hospital threw into conspicuous relief so many of the themes which underpin women's lives in the 1990s. In a gynae ward issues of reproductive health and sexuality are of course paramount, but as the week went on and we crawled, wincing, from our beds and began to talk to each other, so the economics of our lives and those of the women, nurses and auxiliaries, who cared for us, became equally visible.

I made some notes on those themes:

- the warmth and pleasures but exhaustion and dependence of women's traditional role; women at the centre of the family – taken for granted there;
- the erosion of women's traditional role – less valued, less sure – the fragility of new roles and identities;
- money worries, work worries, overwork;
- health, energy, ageing;

- femaleness as a source of pleasure, anxiety, humour, sometimes danger and ridicule;
- resources/resourcefulness;
- caring skills – formal and informal – kindness, humour, intelligence, empathy, handling emotion and understanding relationships – all undervalued qualities which are so important. Abilities and power that women seem unable to free and utilise for so much of the time – for ourselves anyway.

Women's economic position is central to any understanding of change but it is embedded in issues around femininity, power and vulnerability, the family and how we see ourselves. The two main arenas of change are how work itself is changing, and the family and how caring tasks are managed. Change in women's participation in paid employment is played out against that broad backcloth. Changes in when we have children, the nature of our relationships, and whether those relationships last, intersect as both cause and consequence. The image that comes to my mind is that of the waltzers at the shows or fairground. Are they called waltzers everywhere? It's the ride where the base goes round in a circle one way, but also undulates, and your car turns on its own axis against it. What people do at work is changing: that goes one way. How we see ourselves and what we expect from life: sometimes that's in rhythm, sometimes it isn't. So is how other people see us and treat us. Most women work, inside and outside the home, and that turns us in one direction. Most women have children: that turns us in another, and speeds things up. The metaphor gets stronger – in Scottish shows anyway the contrary motion is increased by the car being caught and pushed in the opposite direction, usually by young men! The broad patterns of change and continuity are not confined to Britain. Women's formal labour-force participation has been rising in most industrialised countries since the 1950s (though the East European countries now show a complex picture, with women in some countries leaving the paid workforce). Woman-headed households and single-parent families are rapidly increasing in number throughout the world, including the Islamic countries.

The facts of most women's economic life are straightforward enough: at the centre is an interlocking triangle of low pay, limited

opportunity and caring responsibilities. Have those interrelation-
ships changed significantly? The dominant female image of the 'post-
feminist' 1980s, the besuited, sleekly sexy high-flyer, never came
near most women's lives. The rate of progress towards equal pay is
slow: full-time women earn 79.5 per cent of men's average hourly
earnings (at December 1994: 85 per cent in Wales, 81 per cent in
Scotland and 79 per cent in England). In 1970 it was 63 per cent and in
1975 when the Equal Pay Act became law it was 71 per cent. If the
rate of average increase stays the same – though we cannot assume it
will be neither faster nor slower – it will take between 33 and 60 years
to achieve parity (depending on different estimates). There is a wider
pay gap now between non-manual women and men workers than
there was in 1982.[1]

The pay gap for part-time women workers is much wider: 59 per
cent of the male hourly average and 74 per cent of the average hourly
earnings of female full-timers. The gap between the average *weekly*
earnings of women full-timers and part-timers widened considerably
between 1982 and 1992 at a time when the proportion of the
workforce working part time was growing rapidly.[2] The equal pay
legislation is complex and not as effective as the EOC argues it could
be, although the equal value amendment introduced in 1984 has led
to an improvement.

Low pay for women remains endemic despite improvements over
the past twenty-five years. A smaller proportion of full-time women
workers are low paid now than in 1970: a comparison by the Scottish
Low Pay Unit shows that three quarters of women working full time
aged 18 and over were low paid in 1970 against 41 per cent in 1994 (in
Britain; the figures for Scotland are slightly higher in both cases). The
improvement is a consequence of the Equal Pay Act. However,
many more women than men work for low pay: three-quarters of
part-time women workers are low paid.[3]

The poorest women don't even appear in the statistics so the true
picture is worse still. An estimated 2.3 million women are earning
below the National Insurance threshold, over two-thirds of employees who are paid below that limit (£57 a week in March 1995). Their
number increased three-fold between 1980 and 1992. They are not
counted in the unequal pay statistics and are not eligible for
retirement pensions and maternity, redundancy and sick pay.[4]

It means that, working or not, financial dependence within the family is still a reality for most women who live with men, and that is backed up by how public policy works – the social security system and pensions policies in particular. In 1991 the independent income of women (from investments, earnings, social security and pensions), on average, was half that of men on average. Women's incomes also vary much more than men's do by age, marital status and whether we have children; women are much more likely than men to have no independent income. Women's lower earnings and greater dependence on Income Support cashes out as poorer housing, social exclusion, poor health. All of which has a further, cruel twist in old age: the poverty suffered by almost half of women pensioners is a direct consequence of low pay and employment interrupted by bringing up children.[5]

I could have written most of the previous page and a half in 1970. Fewer of the details which flesh out a bleak picture were known then. The research has been done now and detailed arguments, such as the relationship between women's caring roles and poverty in age, have been pursued. The connection between low pay, motherhood and lack of childcare was always argued. Now it is demonstrable with reference to – well, I can think of five studies without looking too hard. Rhetoric has been shown to match reality.

Five interlocking changes have cut jagged swathes across that continuity nevertheless: changes in the family; demographic change; changes to the welfare state and the private/public balance in caring responsibilities; more women out at work and more women who are breadwinners, and in different sorts of work – the larger number of women in professional work, women's changing aspirations, and educational achievements; and the changing pattern of work itself and how it fits into our lives. We routinely discuss work and the family separately but you cannot so easily separate them in reality.

Almost half of the (paid and recorded) workforce is made up of women now. Almost half are working part time and almost half have children at home. In 1971 women were 38 per cent of employees; in winter 1994 we were 48 per cent. Both full-time and part-time women's work is increasing (by 14 per cent and 19 per cent respectively over the past 10 years) and that is predicted to continue with eight out of ten new jobs going to women, although there has been a recent slow-down. Women are already half of all employees in some regions; if we could accurately add in undeclared workers in the 'grey economy' probably women are a majority of employees. If you add in the self-employed, however, three-quarters of whom are men, women are 45 per cent of those in work. Women's earnings have been a steadily increasing share of family income: contributing a quarter on average in 1971 and 35 per cent by 1991, with full-time workers bringing in almost half.[6]

Much alarmed attention has been paid to the fact that most new jobs are now going to women. A majority of those 'new women' are mothers of dependent children. Although it is seen and presented as a relatively new phenomenon, this continues a trend evident over the whole post-war period of sustained growth in both women's employment and part-time working. There was a steady increase throughout the 1960s, a dramatic increase in the 1970s which slowed towards the end of that decade, and a further steep increase at the end of the 1980s. This continued in the first half of the 1990s, although the rise has not been as steep since 1992. The proportion of women with a youngest child under 5 out of work has doubled since 1973, from a quarter to a half.

Employment Department figures continue to give married women as a separate category, which seems anachronistic. Married women's working behaviour (as opposed to that of women with children) is no different from that of all women, nor would we now expect it to be. But in 1970 it was different. In what's sometimes called 'the phenomenon of the disappearing housewife', half as many married women are classed as 'economically inactive' now as were in 1971, though economically inactive is scarcely an accurate way to describe the contribution they make – and for most the housework hasn't exactly disappeared with the label. Interestingly, since 1990 there has been a slight rise again in the numbers of women who say they are not working for family reasons. The most significant recent change is that many more women work when their children are young, and although most mothers of young children stop paid work for some time, many more go back to work after maternity leave or after a shorter time away. Less than a third of women with dependent children who have an employed husband or partner are now not in work or looking for work. The steepest increase over the last decade has been in women with children under five working: up from 37 per cent in 1984 to 52 per cent in 1994.

This can't be read as unequivocal progress, though it appears that way in much rhetoric, both government and some feminist. I heard one woman journalist accuse another of the current front-running sin of 'seventies thinking'. Things are different now, she said; all the new jobs are going to women: 'women have economic power'. Do we? Most have more – how *much* more is the difficult question, and at what cost. A pay packet of one's own is a thing to be treasured, less so the double burden of work plus housework and childcare, and what's come to be called the triple burden: work, housework and public life/changing the world. Which we still need to do (only after cooking the tea). As the journalist Yvonne Roberts rightly observes, the triple burden means all that men who oppose change need to do is nothing: 'Exhaustion then steals away a woman's anger and her conviction that she has a right to something more, if she so chooses, than the role of mother and wife.'[7]

Most women still take on most of the work of family life. You can sing along with the major change for families to a country tune: 'D.I.V.O.R.C.E.' Which is not unconnected, of course, to women's greater role in the workplace. The rising rate of divorce, the rise in cohabitation and in babies born to mothers who are not married, and the rise in the number of single-parent families are the most conspicuous changes to the family, though not the only ones.

Marriage was probably never a meal ticket for life; nowadays we know it, or don't hide the fact that we know it. More families with children depend on women's wages, wholly or partly. Put this together with the major demographic changes of an ageing population and falling birth rates – which affect and are affected by the changing roles of women – and change is considerable, though the continuities are considerable too and rather less remarked. More women are creating a different pattern of work and family, possibly with different priorities: women are marrying later, if at all, and waiting longer before they have children. Fewer women are having children – though most still do.

Of immense importance to women's working and family lives is the erosion of the welfare state – with demonstrable effects on women's employment and exhaustion levels. It affects women more, although of course it also affects men, because we are the 'default' carers when public spending cuts mean kids sent home from school or fewer home helps for the elderly, and because so many women work in the public sector.

Both Margaret Thatcher's and John Major's governments have ostensibly given high priority to rolling back the welfare state, and indeed their success would not be doubted by many people at the receiving end of diminished services. But both have also ended up spending more on it. It is a project more constrained by circumstance than their speeches and stated intentions have suggested; spending on welfare has not fallen, though it has failed to keep pace with need. Alongside (continuing) public spending cuts is increased social security spending primarily because of continuing high levels of unemployment.

Changes in the care of the elderly affect women most because women *are* most of the elderly as well as most of those who care for older people, in families and professionally. Nursing homes are one of the main growth areas in the flexible workforce of women, often paying very low wages. One of the first of the deregulatory measures allowed the expansion of private and voluntary sector nursing homes: their numbers have tripled over the past five years. While some are good, profit margins connect directly to the standard of care, to staffing levels (often poor: there are no nationally agreed minimum levels), staff training (often inadequate), and practical things like carpets and even the number of incontinence pads per patient. The mechanisms by which health boards and the social services can ensure standards are weak. When we hear of elderly people living in inhumane conditions, kept 'like livestock', it is mainly women we are talking about and it is the fullest expression of our society's failure to value older women.

Those words were used by Scottish sheriff Daniel Convery, charging a couple who kept an old peoples' home in Glasgow in September 1994. It was, he said, 'a squalid enterprise, keeping frail and confused residents as human livestock for the income they generated from public sources'. The fatal accident inquiry into the death of one 79-year-old woman revealed that the weekly food bill for nine residents was £50; the heating was often turned off even in winter and baths and showers were rarely allowed. Some other conditions which have been uncovered in small private homes have been 'scandalous and shocking', says Mary Marshall, director of the Dementia Services Development Centre at the University of Stirling. The largest nursing home company, Takare, was accused of inadequate staffing, poor design and serious failures in care in a Channel 4 programme in early 1995.[8] Share prices did not, however, fall.

The moves to end NHS responsibility for care of the elderly have only begun to have impact. The closure of long-stay beds for the elderly and mentally ill since the NHS and Community Care Act 1990 began a process which was continued in the August 1994 Department of Health guidelines on how long-term care of the elderly should be paid for, drawing a distinction between medical care and social care which can be means tested. This in effect privatises the NHS for the most vulnerable, costly and ever-growing group, but a group with no voice. It met with remarkably little protest. (Do we all cross our fingers and think it'll never happen to us?)

The Changing Workplace

Work itself is changing – what we do and where and how and when most people work. Coalminers have become less common than university graduates; car workers than childminders. But women doing 'women's work' and men doing 'men's' has changed very little. The decline in manufacturing and the growth of the service sector, where women have always been more likely to work, has had the greatest impact on women's working lives. There is accelerating change in the ways in which working time is organised: deregulation, meaning casualisation, 'contracting out' and more part-time and other forms of flexible working continues to cut a swathe through how we work, with good and ill consequences which we are only beginning to engage with seriously. Britain has the largest part-time workforce of any EU country, and one of the highest rates of women's participation in the formal labour market: almost half of women employees work part time whereas in 1971 the figure was 34 per cent. The equation between female and part-time work perpetuates patterns of job segregation.

Unemployment – women's and men's – and its impact on whole

communities has been a considerable change. In recent years a high level of unemployment has been treated as tolerable ('a price worth paying', in Norman Lamont's notorious phrase), although recently more political attention has been paid to the ill-effects of male unemployment. It's worth remembering that Edward Heath's U-turn in economic policy in 1972 was occasioned largely by the desire to avoid one million out of work: now no one has any very convincing ideas about how that sort of low level could be achieved again. Black women are almost three times more likely to be unemployed than white women, and have lost jobs in manufacturing at a greater rate than other workers.

Research published in February 1995 shows that after twenty years of equality legislation job segregation is still pervasive: women work where they've always worked and men where they've always worked. The only surprise is the lack of change. Women work in the service industries of retailing, education and medical services and as clerical and admin workers; in manufacturing only the clothing industry employs a majority of women. So women mainly work with other women, and men with other men, and where that is the case, the report shows, women workers are much more likely to be low paid: 'Establishments that had a female workforce of 70 per cent or more were nearly three times more likely to employ low paid workers than establishments with a predominantly male workforce.' Nor did many firms have any method for guarding against gender bias in the setting of pay, and there was evidence that promotion and regrading opportunities were slanted towards men. Other recent research shows that women and men with qualifications at degree level are also most likely to work in jobs where the majority of workers were of the same gender, although academically qualified women were more likely than other women to be working in a gender-mixed or male-dominated area.[9]

It is more evidence, if that were needed, of why equal pay may be the law but doesn't happen. It shows widespread continuing positive discrimination in favour of men.

The Equal Pay and Sex Discrimination Acts and European equality legislation, beginning with the Treaty of Rome in 1957 and developed in key directives and European Court judgments, have had a positive impact on women's working lives, as has the introduction, if patchy, of equal opportunities policies. Both the new breed of 'femocrats' and trade unionists have played an often unacknowledged role in consistently developing and building strategies. But a number of women active in equal opportunities in employment have expressed disappointment about the limited achievement of brave new policies and say we need to 'go back to the drawing board'. There is concern about the low level of take-up of opportunities but this is hard to assess because it is something that few companies monitor. The most demonstrable positive impact of equal opportunities policies has been in the public sector. Some local authorities and area health boards have well-developed policies and can show that women are moving up the hierarchies as a consequence. The BBC has a model policy and can demonstrate a rapid move by women into some senior areas of work – though the initial success may have been because so many under-promoted women were pushing at those doors already.

New management styles like HRM (Human Resource Management) and TQM (Total Quality Management), slippery terms which mean different things to different people, are double-edged for women. Discretion creates room for management bias which may be harder to track, but, with appropriate training for those making assessments, a less rigid workplace can also mean more opportunities for 'non-typical' employees. Newer recruitment practices explicitly assess employees not just on their competence but on their ability to fit in to corporate culture so have implications for 'outsider' groups, given the evidence that managers recruit in their own image.

Equal opportunity models have changed from the 1970s concern with formal procedures against positive discrimination, through arguments for parity of treatment of 'different but equal' groups to the 'diversity' concept which is now fashionable, and that 'equality can be a way of achieving quality'. Newer thinking emphasises the need for the best talent from a broad section of the population and for the different ideas and initiatives which may come from 'atypical' employees. The 'business case' for using and not losing talent is the central argument of Opportunity 2000, which was launched by Business in the Community in 1991 and has had considerable success in getting large private sector companies to make a commitment to improving women's employment opportunities, particularly at senior levels, with 282 members by Spring 1995 (there were 61 when they launched) employing a quarter of the workforce. 'Mainstreaming' is a current catchword – ensuring that equality issues are understood as affecting all or most of company policy rather than confined to a special category for special effort labelled 'women'. Awareness of the business case for equal opportunities has increased dramatically over the early 1990s, Opportunity 2000 says; 'top managers' have a much better understanding of it now, and 'see women's potential in helping them to better serve customer needs, and bring a different perspective to creative or organisational thinking'.[10]

Janette Webb at Edinburgh University has analysed changing thinking around equal opportunities, and says 'there is no convincing evidence that historically established, deep-seated beliefs in the significance of gender as a means of allocating people differentially to jobs and opportunities is declining.' Despite greater awareness of the unacceptability of overt sex discrimination 'the private sector, including the female-dominated financial services, continues to route women into lower paid, less responsible jobs and to find rationales for barring women from jobs which constitute steps on a promotion ladder.' More optimistically, however, she also thinks that 'twenty years on there is better understanding of the likely process of change surrounding Equal Opportunities initiatives, including the need for commitment at senior level, resources, and regular monitoring.' There is also a greater willingness to recognise and 'respond to the defensive reactions of many men'.[11]

Valerie Amos sees the changing pattern of women's work as both the main negative *and* the main positive change. She is worried by changing conditions of work for the least protected workers. 'There is a wholesale shift towards greater flexibility in the labour market. Whilst there's a sense in which we can say some of that is positive for women, I don't think we sufficiently explore the negative effects of that on women. Contracting out, short-term contracts, annual hours, that whole shift is potentially dangerous for women, in terms of their protection, pay, training – all the things we talk about but don't seem able to *do* anything about.'

'I think the majority of women in employment aren't necessarily better off. Although you talk about net employment growth for women to the year 2000 you have to talk about what *kinds* of jobs. And for black women all those problems are magnified.' But the attention paid to women at work has been valuable in itself. 'Despite what I've been saying, there is an acknowledgement and acceptance that women are there and they have an important role to play – which was not the case twenty-five years ago.'

'There is now a total acceptance that women work because they need the money. That's very, very basic,' Ellen Kelly says. 'What that carries with it is a whole value system – women's right to self-determination. Of course that's hard to back up – you can't stroll into the street and say, oh, there's a self-determined woman. But I graduated from college in 1970 and the expectation very, very clearly was that I would teach for a couple of years and then get married to some nice chap and I would stay married to him no matter what.'

Ellen is policy officer in the women's unit of Edinburgh District Council, a job which brings her into contact with women across the city. She grew up in Drumchapel in Glasgow, trained as a PE teacher and married at 22; after six years she left both her husband and teaching and came out as a lesbian. Both her work and her experience of life gives her a strong sense of how women's choices depend on work and education. 'I was unusual in having gone into higher education. I was the first person in my whole family to do so and out of my class of twenty-eight girls who left school at the end of fifth year, four of us went into higher education. That proportion would be very much higher now.' Education meant escape, meant getting out. But only so far. 'There was this expectation in college, you'd get a boyfriend, the whole of your social life as a single woman was just geared to that. There was a part of me that thought, "This isn't right" but there didn't seem to be any other choice. Everything was geared towards getting and keeping your man. So I shared in it – I did it!' The young women she meets now have rather wider horizons: 'they want the boyfriends, but those who go into higher education especially are very clear they are not tying themselves down, they expect to get married at some point, but they're gonna have a career.

'And I think, more recently, women realising that demanding decent childcare is OK, that's a big change – that there should be a recognition of the enormous burden that most women carry and that decent-quality, affordable childcare would go some way towards lessening. For so many years women just accepted the fact that because they weren't high-flyers and didn't earn enough to pay for nannies or nurseries they would have to stop work, would have to wait until their kids were in secondary school before they went back ...' But many still do. 'But they resent it. They resent losing their skills and their place in the job market, they resent the restriction on family income. Not every woman does, of course, but an awful lot do ...

'There's this growing sense in women – that they have the right to a life on their terms – they are not going to have lives dictated for them by their fathers or brothers or husbands any more. Young women have an expectation that they will live a life on their own terms, and not just young women – older women are less prepared to just accept things. This acceptance of women's self-determination, in work, in education, in marriage ... Those are *it*. On that all else is founded.'

A Life on Their Terms?

The first time I went to interview Harriet Harman, MP it didn't happen. There I was, notebook poised, when a call came from the Shadow Minister's son's school to say he was ill, and in a flurry of anxiety and colour-matched tweeds she apologised and left, re-arranging matters in hand as she went. I mention it not because it is a particular problem for her as one of Britain's most senior working mothers, because it isn't, she said, the sort of thing that usually happens. Which I'm sure is true. She has three children, Harry, Joe and Amy, and you do not rise to high office without almost cast-iron childcare. A childless friend sternly described a similar situation as unprofessional behaviour but I could only sympathise, because it had happened to me. For the first time in the history of government in Britain someone who has personally experienced the conflicts that more than a quarter of the workforce also faces is in a position to influence, and likely to be in a position to make, employment policy. At a time when more mothers with young children are employed than (probably) at any time this century it is extremely apposite – and itself a marker of change.

There are a lot of women whose working lives, without support either at home or at work, have become harder now, Harriet emphasises. But 'the general entry of women into the world of work has in itself made things better for women there. Every woman who does it makes it more possible for another woman. By the time I was thinking about what I wanted to do already a whole load of women were working and had children and both made it seem possible and made it easier. That certainly wouldn't have been the case fifty years ago.

The crucial changes for women since the early 1970s, she reckons, are the larger number of single parents and more woman-headed families; in education – the continued increase in women's qualifications; and more and more women going out to work. It has amounted to 'an immense social and economic revolution' which employment and social policy is way behind on: 'women have changed, structures haven't'.

Ironically, of those with whom I discussed it, the Shadow Employment Minister had probably least to say on women in employment – because she's said all of it so many times before and is very clear about what she wants to see. All she wants is the chance to make it work. She summarises her priorities in three terse headings: childcare; equal rights for part-time workers; and a minimum wage. The key problems are the absence of those. Have these needs changed at all? 'Only in that the more that women are at work the more important they become. As does men's participation in the home.'

'But the arguments are getting through. It's not a huge breakthrough but it's not deadlock either – it's the catching-up process. At the moment there is a lot of insecurity and increased difficulties. What makes me optimistic is that we do know what to do, there is much greater understanding. For example Gordon Brown as Shadow Chancellor always includes childcare in his speeches. Since *Moses* I've been talking about childcare as part of the economic infrastructure, as important to workers as the roads and railways which get them there – and now the CBI say it, it is part of generalised commonsense.'

When you talk to girls and young women now they take it for granted that their work will form as integral a part of their future as relationships and home life. And why wouldn't they – they will be very unusual if it does not. Some exceptional women have assumed this for most of this century. Now it is exceptional not to take work reasonably seriously. Girls who leave school at 16 and haven't got much out of education are still channelled into sex-segregated work with low pay and limited options. But even if their teachers and general perception do not validate those directions as clearly as the ambition to become a doctor or a lawyer, for example, young women of 16 themselves will talk in terms of a career and describe their plans in the same words and ways as do more academically able young women with what the world sees as a career ahead of them.

Hairdressing does not look low paid from the perspective of someone on pocket money; it looks glamorous. And when you're still at school, given armfuls of careers advice leaflets and encouragement to choose a direction, unemployment is something that happens to other people. When Edinburgh schoolgirl Susie Bell, now 16, was young she wanted to be a doctor, by the end of primary school she wanted to be a nurse, and by first year of secondary had fixed on being a nursery nurse. If she gets the standard grades she needs she will go to a local college to do a childcare course. Hers sounds a typical route of diminishing ambition. Nor has anything in her school life made her question that. But we at least need to question the ascription of value: Susie's future is likely to be low paid because of the low value we place on caring for children; it doesn't mean it's any less important to her.

For Susie and other less ambitious girls of her age, just as for the very able girls who are getting top marks at A level and Higher (the Scottish university entrance exam), work is no longer 'something to fall back on'. Perhaps it never was for most – but there was encouragement to see it that way. Zoe Fairbairns was one of the bright girls and she remembers that when she was 16 in 1967, girls were not given proper career guidance 'because it was assumed that girls didn't need it. There was this wonderful phrase about taking a shorthand-typing course because then you would have "something to fall back on", meaning if you did not succeed in getting a man to support you, you would be able to do something else.' Writer and researcher Sue Sharpe talked to girls in four schools in Ealing in London nineteen years apart, in 1972 and 1991.[12] She describes a major change in how working-class girls in particular see their future.

The almost unquestioned priority given to marriage and family by the girls she spoke to in 1971 has gone. 'In spite of, or because of, the knowledge that jobs are scarce, the importance of having a "career" is automatically endorsed.' There was no clear-cut separation for either working-class or middle-class girls, as there had been in 1971 'between themselves and someone who was "going for" a career'. Not everyone will get one, 'but it no longer applies only to a special sort of girl'.

Ambition is allowed, if hedged by a need not to seem too self-seeking. What was once considered exceptional is normal and desirable. Anna Sommerville is a self-assured and thoughtful 17-year-old with long silver nails and swinging earrings. When I spoke to her she was undecided between university and art college. Some careers advice is irritating, she said. 'You have videos with women saying *I'm* a pilot, *I'm* an architect – as if you didn't think they could be. And special days for girls for computing, things like that – it's a bit insulting in a way.' It is telling that young women who have been encouraged to see themselves as able to do and be whatever they want, now, because of the very success of that message, may see it as patronising. Anna is well aware that although women can, few women do have the top jobs. The main reason why, she thinks, is because men who have the top jobs control the appointment of their successors. 'I don't think men want to change it.'

The things Zoe Fairbairns remembers as irritating and patronising are 'jobs vacant columns in newspapers divided into male and female jobs, and for it to be absolutely *normal* when a job was being offered to male and female candidates to have two rates of pay and to have that advertised. Now, I'm not saying this does not still go on but at least you are not allowed to say it in public. But that was normal practice. It was defended by people like trade union leaders on the grounds that men have families to support.'

The partial contradiction between changes in perception of what women can do and what most women still *actually* do that Anna expressed in her comment on women pilots is widespread. That women have as much likelihood of working as men is taken for granted – the idea of a 'right' to work would be meaningless to young women now. But even for girls with little prospect of high-flying careers and women in jobs that aren't bringing in much money, or who are at home or unemployed, the relationship of work to home and family is perceived differently. The cultural/perceptual change is ahead of opportunity and economic change. Personal change and cultural images allied to an extension of opportunities, however hedged-about with complications, have cumulative and far-reaching consequences on how women see themselves and their lives.

The changes in women's employment have been more marked for some than for others. Most of the new jobs have gone to women in two-parent families with an employed partner. Women with a partner working are almost three times as likely to be working themselves as those with an unemployed partner. In Britain mothers in two-parent families are more likely to be working than single mothers are; the opposite is true in all other European countries. As the participation of married women in paid work has increased, the proportion of single mothers at work has decreased. The forecast continuing growth in women's employment also excludes black and ethnic minority women, who are more likely to be working in declining or slow-growth areas.[13]

For a substantial group of women recent changes may have involved a deterioration in their position. The abolition of the wages councils has had most impact on women: three-quarters of the jobs that used to be covered by them were done by women, some of whose wages have fallen since.[14] Many women are doing very poorly paid work; public sector cutbacks and the erosion of job security and conditions of work disproportionately affect women workers.

Lorraine Mann lives and works in Highland Region, and is an independent-minded, energetic woman of wide interests. The Highlands are cohesive and small enough – in population, not geographically – to allow an overview of women's lives and how they intersect with the local economy. 'Issues for women working with kids are not so different in rural areas but they are magnified,' she says. The survey she conducted in 1991 for Ross and Cromarty District Council identified two main constraints on women working: lack of childcare, and a lack of suitable, available jobs, particularly to fit in with school hours – the same constraints as almost everywhere else, 'only maybe a bit more so'.

She talked of one woman she had met who had an honours degree in zoology and botany and was working as the cleaner of the village hall because she could take the kids with her. 'In some ways it doesn't matter what your skill or income level is; if there is no childcare available and you have no relatives nearby, then the only jobs you can take are ones where you can take the kids, and that's in the low-paid, service sector. That's not just a waste for the individual woman, it's drastic for her and it's a disaster for the local economy. It's not just a problem for the Highland economy but for the UK as a whole, but it shows up to a greater extent here.

'Certainly for some women, for middle-class, articulate women things have changed, particularly in terms of opening up of some of the sorts of jobs we do.' Lorraine herself now works on reports and research for organisations throughout Britain, using information technology, and is an enthusiast for the benefits it can bring to people in 'remote' areas. But she argues strongly that although for people in lower income groups, both men and women, life has changed radically, that has not delivered any more choice. 'Who has a burning desire to go and clean old folks' homes at £2.10 an hour? It is just not on to describe as choice most of the low-skilled jobs people do. In our area, people working in fish-processing plants, it is smelly, cold, hard work – nobody actively wants to be doing that, they're there because they have to be, because there's no other way of making ends meet.'

That much women's employment still offers poor prospects and low wages (and some wages have recently fallen even lower) creates a gloomy picture. It is true, but is only part of the truth, which includes a greater polarisation between wages and work opportunities for different groups of women. A focus on low pay and limited opportunities, real though they are, can serve to obscure more positive developments. Indeed, it obscures them so successfully that even the Employment Department, whom I expected to be bullish about improved prospects for women and whose publications put a very glossy face on it, said they didn't think real, positive change for women in general in employment could be demonstrated (in an unattributable briefing, of course).

But the broad picture both conceals considerable regional varia-tions and obscures developments that present opportunities for women workers. Although women's work has continued to be segregated in the service sector of the economy and over half of female employment is in catering, clerical and related, this sector is itself becoming more economically important. The familiar argument that women work in low-paid, part-time, service-sector work needs to be picked apart: some work is low paid and with poor prospects certainly, but in a sector which includes financial and local authority work, education, health/medicine, some also isn't and those better jobs are increasing in number. A specific focus on those regions where women are half of the labour force already and where average pay is high would repay attention.[15]

Two caveats need to be made before going much further. Any account of women's work will underestimate its extent firstly because so many women work in the 'informal sector' – cleaning, some childminding, the growing 'grey economy' around care for the elderly, bar work, the sex industry ... But a valid definition of work or economic activity would also include domestic work, the work of bringing up children and caring for elderly and disabled people. It is wrong that work which remains invisible when done by a family member, for example childcare, once you actually pay someone else to do it, for example a childminder, then adds to the country's GDP.

Secondly, it is hard to talk accurately about changing patterns of women's paid work not only because in the past it has often been invisible to official statistics – as it still is to some extent – or not recognised as economic activity but because women, as I am well aware from my own family, have always worked outside as well as in the home, but where that has conflicted with the dominant ideology for married women it has been partly hidden. Liz Stanley, describing her family, said: 'My mother was one of those women who never worked – which meant she was a cleaner in a local pub and a local shop.' My own grandmother 'went to the herring', which meant following the fishing fleet on a yearly cycle to ports as far apart as Lerwick and Great Yarmouth where women gutted and packed the fish in great barrels of salt. Their children came along, plus pots and pans and belongings in strong wooden kists, sent ahead on a lorry. The women worked in teams of three, and with her cousins my grandmother seemed always to manage it that one would be pregnant or nursing and care for the children while the others earned the money.

Social historian Professor Rosalind Mitchison is retired from teaching at Edinburgh University but retirement is not otherwise a meaningful description of her life, which currently includes research and writing a book on the history of the Poor Law 'My mother was of the generation which established that women *could have* education and the qualifications for an outside job. I regarded my generation as showing that *married* women could do this – and I think this has been a big change, the idea of married women doing things in their own right. You really do hear rather less of the "helping my husband in his school" sort of thing, fewer devoted slaves of the Bishop of such-and-such, and more women who have done what they want to do.' Her mother was one of the first women at Cambridge, and was widowed in 1927 with six children, the youngest only six months old. 'My mother worked to get a home together and taught history all her life – she retired at the age of 86.' Professor Mitchison's mother-in-law, the writer Naomi Mitchison, is another example of indefatigability: she is still writing at 97.

For most of her working life she was concious of being discriminated against for jobs because she was married. 'One letter made it clear it was a *permanent* post so the assumption was it wouldn't be appropriate for me.' Most of her writing (on ecclesiastical, political, economic and social history) has been done since her children have grown up: 'my youngest child was born during my first book – in the middle of Chapter 11'. She studied for a degree at Oxford from 1938 to 1942 and describes as 'luck' the way she got jobs 'when there was nobody else to take them'.

'The attitude was that married women were liable to "abnormal circumstances" which made them unreliable – and that concept of married women's status was impossible to argue about. Women were seen as extra-liable to mental stress.' And, she adds, 'there are people still in this university who feel women are intellectually inferior – or a menace!' What made her work possible was 'adequate income and a lot of stamina, and not all women can be expected to have these.

'My mother was insistent that the girls should have as good as a chance as the boys and one simply took equality for granted. We did have the notion that boys were not very good at domestic work but they were expected to do a certain amount of it. My husband was brought up with the idea of intellectual and career equality so there's never been any query as to why one should do this, but his family being better off he wasn't used to doing housework.' They had four children and she remembers being 'fairly heavily submerged domestically, and just running on behind Hugh'. Even getting out occasionally to a library was difficult. 'I've always … I've never given up totally, put it that way. I did coaching at home and so on – though I took for granted that one didn't have a career if one was married. You can see the ambivalent attitude. I always took it for granted that I was a housewife – but a housewife doing university teaching! Then later I got further back into it.'

It is widely described as new, and as a characteristic of 'the crisis in the family', that the majority of British families now have both parents out at work but this has always been common in working-class households, although married working-class women working outside as well as within the home also became more common as families became smaller and children were not permitted to work. Seeing women in the workforce as such a change is a reflection of the dominance of middle-class ideals of family life in how the world is described, and in part the dominance of norms formed or at least solidified in the 1950s. Increasing prosperity (it was true that they never had it so good), the post-war focus on home, family and traditional gender roles, and full male employment meant that a higher proportion of families followed the breadwinner/homemaker model then than probably at any other time.

Indeed it was something that many working-class families saw as an achievement. Although that period is still taken as a starting point from which subsequent change departs, in terms of most women's working lives the 1950s is the exceptional decade of the twentieth century. Even at the height of Victorian 'angel in the house' ideology there were far more women working and responsible for dependants than history has allowed. And in the 1950s, when men were men and women wore gingham, there was both more hidden paid work for women – much of it home based – and a steady increase throughout the decade in married women working. It was never as Janet and John a family as we now think.

Professional and Related

One morning my nine-year-old daughter, Katie, came in puzzled, with a riddle she couldn't work out. 'A father was driving his daughter to school when their car was hit by an oncoming lorry. The father wasn't hurt, but the daughter was injured and was raced to hospital by ambulance. She was wheeled into the operating theatre. The surgeon took one look at her and said: "I can't operate on this child. That's my daughter!" Why not?'

What puzzled Katie was why was this a riddle? Why shouldn't the surgeon be her mother? The riddle doesn't work any more because it depends on the incompatibility between our image of a surgeon and a woman which has faded almost completely. Katie wasn't to know that women are still less than 3 per cent of general surgeons, and women with children a minority in that minority. Our expectation now is that women can and will do almost all jobs. Maybe Katie will see it as a riddle – though I hope not – only when she's 30 or so and has tried to combine work and having children. The credibility gap has gone: the reality gap hasn't.

Nevertheless, there has been fairly steady growth in women entering the professions and 'careered occupations' since the 1960s, and more recent growth in women with children doing so, and in most areas that growth curve has become steeper. The growth rate in the late 1980s in the numbers of women in professional and related occupations was doubled that of men, though from a lower base. However, 'professional and related' is still one of the three categories with the lowest proportion of women (the others are 'craft and related' and 'machine operatives'), and professional women are most likely to work in government, education, health and welfare: 84 per cent do, almost twice the proportion of men who do and a slightly higher proportion than in 1975. Even so it means women moving in growing numbers into better-paid and influential sectors of work, in new jobs and old.

Research on 'Highly Qualified Women', using data from 1991 and 1992, concludes that efforts to attract more women into professional work and management 'appear to have been partly successful. Although women still make up a very small proportion of science and engineering professionals, there has also been an unprecedented rise in the number of women entering into higher-level professional occupations such as medicine, accountancy, law and pharmacy.' It also shows that policies designed to attract women into the most traditionally male-dominated sectors of the labour market have had less success; most women with degree-level qualifications still work in teaching or for the NHS. Career opportunities and pay for women and men with high-level qualifications remain unequal and 'women with higher qualifications did better in the labour market than less qualified women but they fared less well than men qualified to a similar level.'[16]

There may be far fewer 'women at the top' than cultural images suggest, but even if the career woman's progress has made little impact on the overall statistics on women's employment that does not mean it has been insignificant. We might have expected women's presence to have made more impact on the professions over twenty-five years, certainly, and to have seen even greater change – but are we now seeing it? Women consultants, senior policewomen, QCs and engineers are becoming a more vocal minority, less afraid than they were even ten years ago of rocking the boat and criticising the male hand on the tiller, or of using equality law to right wrongs that at one time they might have just put up with. All sorts of discrete barriers may still be in place and promotion policies and processes within many organisations remain rife with indirect discrimination,[17] but women are becoming cleverer and more determined in negotiating them.

Marian Bell, a treasury economist with the Royal Bank of Scotland in their City HQ, is one of the *Guardian*'s team of 'Seven Wise Women' commentators. She has two young children and was the first woman at her level of seniority to take maternity leave. Banking and finance have seen a significant growth in the numbers of senior women, albeit from a low base. 'I don't think it's tokenism, I think the women that have got there are there because they are good,' Marian said. 'But there is much more awareness on the part of organisations, and of course explicit policies. I can remember in my working lifetime, which isn't all that long, ten years or so, women being told there's no point training you because you'll go off and have a baby and that sort of thing. As equal opportunities are espoused it becomes less likely that managers, even if they actually believe that, are going to say it.'

Remaining barriers tend to be more subtle, less explicit. 'Sometimes the skills that are needed for a job, or the skills that are perceived to be needed, tend to be skills that men more readily have, or are seen to have.' Going to the pub after work still matters. 'There's a male way of friendship that is different from a female way of friendship – a lot of the corporate culture has been built around those things.' But the role of male networks, she suspects, may be diminishing. 'And I do think there are some people that like to be seen to have a senior woman in their camp, because it looks as if they're modern or good in some way ...'

I am conscious as I write this of a hundred and one arguments about the barriers and problems women face on the career ladder. We are more familiar with those arguments than with counting the achievement. It is important, of course, to recognise that although at most a third of managers and administrators are women (estimates vary from under 10 per cent to 33 per cent, depending on how you define 'management'), what a woman manager actually does and where she does it, as well as what she's paid for it, will typically be different from what a male manager does. Women managers are much more likely to work in the service sector and public administration and health; the earnings gap between female and male managers widens higher up the management ladder. We need to know that male GPs are much more likely to be high earners. And that although women in law are relatively numerous, they are less likely to hold partnerships, tend to earn less, and are unlikely to be judges. We need to recognise that the barriers to power and influence are both subtle and considerable.

But we also need to recognise that this change marks real achievement – by individual women and in changing the climate of expectation, among younger women especially, and some employers. It means, among other things, that far fewer able women are being channelled into 'more suitable', less ambitious work. But an enduring stereotype of the feminist is the woman with big hair and power shoulders fighting her way up the career ladder and treading on other women to get there. Perhaps for fear of seeming like that, success at work is a subject treated by many feminists with ambivalence and by some as anathema. I've noticed how reluctant many women are to say very much that is positive. Instead, the argument is that as long as the majority of women are in low-paid, marginalised work then the achievements of the minority who have fought their way on to the board or the Bar have little meaning. Successful women are seen as playing male games; 'power dressers in sexy underwear,' as one woman sniffed. The more worthy successes, as someone observed of women in politics, are criticised when they dress smartly and criticised when they don't. And the socialist feminist priorities of probably the majority strand of British feminism to date have been elsewhere. Successful women are in theory well paid and can afford their own transport and help with housework and childcare, so campaigns on those issues do not seem to apply to them. Then too, most women with access to public means of expression have themselves been among 'the relatively privileged' and many have not wanted to seem to be saying 'I'm all right, Jill'. But it is not a question of either/or: the position of women who are so busy hoovering the office floor they haven't even looked to see what the ceiling's made of is *not bettered* by other women bumping their heads on the glass.

Nor is it always all right. As Gillian Pascall argued in 1994: 'Women in careers may be more able to accrue the advantages attaching to a more 'male' working life: in particular, resources to pay for childcare with the ability to sustain continuity. But their career pattern shares features with that of less advantaged women. In some ways they meet special hurdles. If careered occupations are organised as a continuous, upwardly mobile, single-minded pathway their structures put women at a peculiar disadvantage.'[18]

Again it is one of those on the one hand/but on the other sorts of changes. The Hansard Commission's 1990 report *Women at the Top* was concerned about lack of women in top positions in public service, corporate management and key areas of influence – media, universities, trade unions: 'In any given occupation, and in any given public office, the higher the rank, prestige or influence, the smaller the proportion of women.'

Nine out of ten senior positions in Whitehall are held by men although half of all employees are women. The civil service has a classical triangular work profile: lots of women at the bottom and in the lower grades and fewer as you get to the top. That was the case in 1971, and still is the case although there has been an increase in women at all grades. A Cabinet Office report in March 1995 on ten years of progress since the first programme of action for women in 1984 reports that the proportion of women staff has grown to just over half (although staff numbers overall have fallen). In the senior grades the proportion of women has doubled but their numbers are still very low: less than 10 per cent of staff in Grade 3 and above are women (4 per cent in 1984) but almost 80 per cent of the lowest grade are women. Six departments, including the Department for Education and the Inland Revenue, have only men in the top staff jobs. Only 2 per cent of science, technology and engineering posts are held by women. The report does not give the proportions of ethnic minority women.[19]

In local authorities again the number of women in charge remains low, and the number of women in low grades high, although there has been an increase in recent years in women in middle management. Women are 66 per cent of the local government workforce but there are only sixteen women chief executives in the 449 local authorities in England and Wales. At the next most senior grade women are 5.4 per cent. The position in Scotland is similar.[20]

Architecture remains strikingly male dominated, as does planning, which matters a great deal since it results in a continuing 'man-made environment'. Only 9 per cent of Britain's 30,000 architects are women, according to a new survey. And at the top of the profession there are even fewer: of twenty-four leading architectural practices questioned only one had appointed a woman as a senior associate and only three had women partners or directors. The drop-out rate for women architecture students has been higher than average for a number of years. Lengthy training, long hours of work when you do qualify, and sexism in the construction industry have all been identified as putting women off. Women are 20 per cent of qualified town planners and 42 per cent of student planners; but less than 5 per cent are in policy-making positions.[21]

Medicine and law have been key areas of change: there are equal numbers of female and male students in both. Even if women are not getting the most senior jobs within those professions, there is now a substantial and continuing increase in women. In 1975 women were less than 7 per cent of all doctors and 35 per cent of medical students; quotas restricted their number to below 20 per cent until that year when it became illegal to do so. Women are now a quarter of GPs, 16 per cent of consultants though less than 3 per cent of general surgeons. Just over half of newly qualified solicitors are women, as are a third of solicitors overall; the figure was 10 per cent in 1974. Women are still less likely to be barristers (22 per cent) and advocates (18 per cent), less likely to be QCs (6 per cent in England and Wales and 7.5 per cent in Scotland) and although the number taking silk is increasing, in the judiciary women are now just under 8 per cent.[22]

Of course it matters. We all need a doctor one and it matters a lot to most women that they have the choice of having a woman GP. Most women won't become lawyers but many women are happier talking to another woman about the difficult personal issues that family law deals with. Not all women are necessarily more sympathetic than are men, of course – but you're in there with a head start and are much less likely to be patronised and talked down to. After rape or domestic violence it is particularly important that women have the choice of a woman doctor to examine them, though it doesn't always happen. In parallel, specialist teams of policewomen dealing with sexual violence have been an extremely important introduction.

Women academics remain a minority even though their numbers have doubled since 1970 (from 3,000 to 6,000 in the 'old' universities; 5 per cent of professors, 12 per cent of senior lecturers, 27 per cent of lecturers, almost half of contract researchers).[23] Women are beginning to change the priorities of what is researched and taught: courses like 'Women in Politics' are very popular, women's studies is a thriving area of academic life which did not even exist twenty-five years ago and in that short time several centuries of women's history has been reclaimed. Women head several publishing companies and roughly equal numbers of men and women enter publishing, though a 1995 study claims that although in sixty interviews 'there was no evidence to suggest that women had lower aspirations than male employees' there are 'covert barriers' to women reaching board level. Before Carmen Callil proved with Virago there was a market, it's worth remembering, the notion of a woman's book was confined to Mills and Boon. (Virago was set up in 1973.)

Management is an important area which shows a contrary trend:

an Institute of Management survey in 1994 showed a drop in the number of women managers for the first time in twenty-one years (although the 1995 survey showed an increase again, to an all-time high of 10.7 per cent. The predictions in 1994 by the Institute for Employment Research at the University of Warwick show growth in almost all areas of work for women except management. The 1995 survey showed almost half of women managers are employed in the two last senior categories. Only 1 per cent of the women interviewed in the 1992 Women in Management survey had flexible working hours, and nearly six in ten had never taken a career break.[24]

'I'm not at all surprised,' said Anne Rennie, executive director with Reed Employment. 'It's not just the long hours but a hierarchy and working culture which I think many women find antithetical.' In her previous work as equal opportunities director with National Westminster Bank she had found, she says, that most women put quality of life ahead of status. Angela Giveon, editor and publisher of the magazine *Executive Woman*, puts it succinctly: 'A good woman will succeed, whatever. Though there comes a time when she says, oh sod them, I'm going to start a small consultancy from home.' Research in 1993 by Professor Janice Morphet on high-achieving women in local government would seem to have implications for a range of management and professional jobs. Strategies for successful career development, she found, were: pre-planning; specific support when growing up; finding a sponsor or patron; a supportive partner; minimising any career break for having children; hard work and unsocial hours. A list like that makes you wonder how any women at all make it through.[25]

The Women in the Middle

Oddly enough, the areas 'in the middle' in which most women work usually feature least in discussion. From most accounts of women's employment and its ills you could be forgiven for thinking that working women are all either high-flying lawyers or exploited cleaners. But there has been a continuing movement of women into jobs at intermediate levels: good, interesting jobs in all the traditional areas of the caring professions and the public sector and also in accountancy, pharmacy, tourism and recreation, and information technology. Job segregation, I would argue, is less a problem than its consequences: a continuing narrowing of choice, and the way 'women's' work is valued, or rather isn't. Which in turn connects to how it is seen to relate to what is done domestically for free anyway – including and especially interpersonal skills. But these value judgements are not fixed; there are interesting questions about whether they are changing, and why.

Nursing has been, since its inception, an important area of women's work and the changes it has seen over the past 25 years are illuminating. As a profession it has been undervalued because it is female dominated – over 90 per cent – and because, though the technical skills are high they are allied to personal, psychological skills which are no less important in health care but look like women's 'natural' skills. Nevertheless there has been a professionalisation of nursing, including the rapid growth of degrees in nursing and the move to nurse education as primarily college-based, and wage levels and training have increased if not commensurately then to some extent. (The 1 per cent pay offer made to health workers in February 1995 suggests that revaluation still has some way to go.) As the nurse has become more of a specialist (with nurse prescribing and nurse practitioners, for example, and ward sisters becoming ward managers) a range of nursing tasks have been passed on to less highly-trained and well-paid auxiliaries, although there is now a growth in vocational training for this group also. Change also varies in varying settings – the nurse's position and skills in, for example, a poorly-managed and funded geriatric ward may not have changed for years and be characterised by a low level of education and training, and contrast strongly with the clinical nurse specialist in, for example, a cardiac ward.

It has also seen more men entering general nursing, and a sorry irony in the speed with which men have climbed hierarchies: although women outnumber men in nursing, men in the mid-1980s had half of all senior posts and 80 per cent of chief nursing officer posts, and although women are now better represented in senior nursing positions (71 per cent according to 1995 research) men are still disproportionately likely to be in senior posts. In 1993–4 there was a marked increase in the numbers of men coming into nursing (15 per cent against the 10 per cent which has been fairly constant since the 1960s). Male nurses are still more likely to work in mental illness or mental handicap however (where they are between a third and a half of nurses) and much less likely to be in community nursing or health visitors (where men are 1 per cent).[26]

It is ironic that although nursing is seen as feminine those nurses who least match the traditional female role are most likely to get ahead in it, with promoted and senior women more likely to be single and married women much more likely to be staff nurses, rather than in higher grades – almost twice as many were as were sisters or in teaching posts, according to research in 1983, and 1985 research found that while almost all male chief nursing officers were married, mostly with children, only 18 per cent of the (minority of) women chief officers were married, and only 14 per cent had children. Women were discouraged from remaining in nursing after marriage even as late as the 1960s and, although the career problems faced by women with families have lessened, 1995 analysis shows senior women in nursing were still less likely to be married or have children than senior men were. A high proportion of women in top management in the NHS were also single and without children and they had usually taken longer than the men to reach top management. For both senior nursing and management posts the women were better qualified academically. Although job-sharing has become more available recently, as have other more flexible ways of working, most nurses who work part-time do so in the lower grades and with less access to further training, and job-sharing is an option taken wholly by women. Discrimination against black nurses is also of concern: evidence from the Royal College of Nursing, the Campaign for Racial Equality and NUPE all show stereotyping and discrimination in pay and promotion for black nurses.[27]

Although the situation is multi-faceted, and changing again because of the move to hospital trusts, (local and performance-related wage negotiation may undercut some of the progress on pay of the 1970s and 1980s and there are no longer nationally comparable career paths), nursing also serves to illustrate that once determinist connections between 'women's' skills and female-dominated work can be broken and subject to revaluing. The way in which nursing is affected by being a female-dominated profession is hard to unpick precisely because it is quintessentially *the* female profession. We say, because it is necessary still, *woman* doctor and (sometimes) lady policeman, but *male* nurse. The identification is very close: to nurse also means to breast-feed a baby. Public perception of nurses suffers from sexist and sexual stereotyping: angel, battleaxe, tart. Trousers, which would be more practical the RCN think, and may have a role in preventing common back injury, are not normally worn because nurses must be feminine. Nursing skills are seen as subservient to the male-defined skills of the doctor, though they are complementary. Like mothers, nurses represent a feminine paradox: they are expected to be sweet and kind and understanding, yet deal everyday with piss and blood and unruly behaviour.

We seem to believe, as we do of good mothers, that nurses are born, not made. A DHSS recruitment poster in the mid-1980s showed a little girl dressed in nurse's uniform with the words 'The best nurses have the most essential qualifications before they go to school'. Nursing, it implied, was mostly about inborn compassion and girlishness.

Nursing's status has risen with the extent to which it has presented itself as professional and technical, rather than doing what comes naturally to women anyway. June Andrews at the RCN summarises the differences as towards autonomy and individual responsibility, away from regimentation, mixing continued team work with a high degree of individual judgement: '25 years ago you had a guaranteed job, a fairly automatic consolidation of experience, stability, steady progress. Now there are greater risks but also greater rewards.' It is possible that the growing emphasis on holistic care rather than medical intervention also has a role in nursing's changing status, revaluing a more 'female' and emotionally-sophisticated approach. It may also be that just as the 'male bastions' of law and medicine and (to a much lesser extent) architecture and engineering are becoming more open to women, so one of the few female-identified areas of professional work is also becoming less gendered in how we see it.

Most married women now stay in nursing. However changes forced by the more competitive attitude to employment within the Trust hospitals may make it harder for some. The overall number of nurses has been reduced slightly (and in some areas steeply) while the volume and intensity of the work has grown, meaning fewer nurses doing more. There has also been loss of job security – a UNISON survey in September 1994 reported two in three nurses were worried about keeping their job and there has been an increase in short-term contracts with loss of maternity pay and other benefits.[28]

There are parallel questions about the cross-relationship between women's work, pay and perceived value which might be usefully posed about teaching, again a profession in which women are a majority but which in management, and some would argue hierarchical style, is male dominated. In England while men are only 17 per cent of primary teachers they are just under half of primary headteachers and in Scotland men are 8 per cent of primary teachers but almost a third of headteachers. At secondary level the discrepancy is different but also acute: women are just under half of secondary teachers but only a fifth of secondary headteachers in England and less than 3 per cent in Scotland. Those proportions have changed only marginally since 1990. Education, says ex-headteacher Margaret Macintosh, 'is lop-sided … it is designed, planned and managed almost entirely by men'. The concentration of decision-making in the hands of mainly white, middle-class men has meant, she says, 'a fairly narrow set of experiences' has been allowed to dominate educational agendas. Among the consequences for schools, she thinks, is that passing exams is given much higher priority than children's safety, happiness and creativity.[29]

Throughout the century differential valuing of teaching has a demonstrable relationship to gender. Steps towards equal pay in teaching in 1919 were reversed because of concern about 'the dearth of male teachers', a concern that has recently been echoed as women outnumbered men as entrants to secondary school teaching in 1993, with calls for positive discrimination to restore a balance.[30]

Rather than a growth in status and position, however, although the training discrepancies between nursery, primary and secondary teaching have lessened with the incorporation of teacher training colleges into the universities, there has been an erosion of pay and status for teachers – more markedly so in England than Scotland. Teachers' salaries have fallen from 137 per cent of average non-manual workers' salaries in 1974 to 99 per cent in 1992.[31]

Values and Value

In a market economy what you are paid in the marketplace has become almost the only functioning measure of value. It is only in radical attempts to depart from standard economic models that different valuing can emerge. A good example of this is in the LETS (Local Economic Trading Systems) schemes that have been growing rapidly throughout Britain in the early 1990s: an idea first introduced in 1982, there were 25 in 1993 and by 1995 around 350 – some of them sizeable. These trading schemes substitute a local currency for cash – in Manchester 'bobbins', in Stoke 'stokers', and so on – to allow what is essentially a sophisticated system of barter. Aimed particularly at areas of deprivation and high unemployment where people have no cash but often time and skills, the initial schemes seem to be rapidly moving beyond baby-sitting-for-plumbing swaps into deals with local shops and councils; a school and nursery in Wiltshire now operates on a part-LETS system and there are plans for other nurseries. Rather than banks and multi-national companies taking profits from a community and putting back only a fraction of that in wages, the LETS system encourages the parallel local production of goods and services. Importantly, the currency has no value outside the local area: as a symbolic currency it can ring fence the direct exchange of goods and services by people in economically disadvantaged areas. It has been an important way for some local communities to assert control in the face of desertion and ravages of the formal economy.[32]

Women's participation is – as it is in most community activism – considerable; it's estimated that two-thirds of transactions are done by women. And the relative weight given to traditionally male and female skills has a different balance in these local economies, Ed Mayo at the New Economics Foundation says. 'You don't set prices in the formal economy, the supermarket does it for you. In LETS you can see what people really value coming through.' Childcare and babysitting is relatively better paid in local currencies than it is in real money, reflecting the level of responsibility entailed. He also gives an example of women workers in Leicester who found they could sew curtains for a better price in the local currency than they were getting from the international market.

Central to the continuing disadvantages most women face in paid work is the different value we still give, as a society, to skills which are seen as 'women's' and 'men's', and now to skills which are seen as gender neutral (even if in practice they are male dominated). Arguably now the 'gender-neutral' areas of skill are most valued, which in itself opens opportunities for women. There is higher value placed on the 'female skills' of communication and building teamwork, and the caring skills involved in nursing or physiotherapy are 'female' skills defined as such and so have been partially revalued in consequence. But most women's skills are still systematically undervalued. Three of the main areas where women work are cleaning, catering and childcare – all are essential to life, replicate the domestic division of labour, are poorly paid and seen as low-skilled. Barbara Castle writes in her memoirs, about the run-up to the Equal Pay legislation, that the Engineering Union had for years 'tolerated a pay structure hierarchy which descended in the following order: skilled workers, semi-skilled, labourers and women'.[33] It is a useful benchmark: no longer *wholly* true, but where women have achieved parity it has been mainly by moving into male-dominated areas (often with attendant stress and harassment), working full-time and not taking career breaks. The different worth put on brick-laying, for example, against caring for the elderly demented (check the Job Centre), or gardeners and dustmen against cleaners and school dinner ladies (as the process of CCT demonstrated), or nurses against senior civil servants (the 1995 public sector pay limits), still has different consequences for most women and men.

Claims for 'equal value' under the amended equal pay legislation only scratch the surface of this. In theory they create an opportunity for scrutinising stereotyped ascriptions of value, but in practice legislation which is both narrow and infamously complex scarcely allows this, though it may have thrown renewed light on how value in work is gendered, as have new forms of internal job evaluation. The legislation gives little direction as to what equal value might be, but with circular logic says a case must examine whether the employee's 'effort, skill and decision-making' is of equal value to that of a man in the job being compared. One case has been trying to disentangle that for almost ten years.[34]

The hospital ward where my inquiry began seemed in several ways a metaphor for the world outside. The nurse who admitted me left at the end of the shift to sign on as unemployed. The hierarchies of class, gender and race were explicit: with the exception of one female consultant the hierarchy ran from middle-class white men (professor, consultants), through non-white men (the doctors), then middle-class white women (junior doctors, senior nurses) with older working class and black women as auxiliaries, tea ladies and ward cleaners. At the end of the corridor was the theatre; that was where the men were, the surgeons, the anaesthetist, the porters, all in green overalls. Their world was secretive, arcane; we were delivered to it as malfunctioning reproductive systems. Afterwards we rejoined the world of the ward: a calm, womanly place, its rituals of caring transparent, intelligent, comforting.

Good nursing, according to June Andrews at the RCN, is like invisible mending: 'you don't see it most of the time. Think of an old woman, dressed, comfortable. You'll only notice if she's wet and in a mess.' It shares the characteristic of women's domestic and maternal work that we only notice it when it isn't done. Empathy, handling emotion and understanding interpersonal dynamics, kindness, perception and humour are part of professionalism for health care workers – but vital in almost all areas. In a curious reversal typical of our culture they are undervalued because they are seen as coming naturally to women, and perhaps too because acknowledging their importance is to acknowledge vulnerability.

The strongest strand of change and the most far-reaching in women's lives since the 1970s has been in paid work and this is true in all the OECD countries – women's paid work has increased whether social policies and hostile trades unions have determined to keep women at home and where social and labour market policies have supported working women alike. Equal and unequal, paid work has meant greater independence for many women and has begun to change the balance of power in families, albeit neither consistently nor completely. It has led to much more work for many women and though more women are making and benefiting from new possibilities there are also growing pressures in the insecure climate of the 1990s.

More opportunity for more women in paid work was and is important: the next step is to think much harder about how work and caring fit into all our lives, why value accrues as it does and how we measure and reward it.

Chapter 3

'Fatally Torn'? Love and Work

In a new introduction to her first novel, *The Shadow of the Sun*, published in 1964 and reissued in 1993, Antonia Byatt writes about the central conflict for young, educated women of her generation. They were, she writes, 'fatally torn' between hopes of marriage and hopes, barely articulated, of work. 'Men could have both, work and love, but it seemed that women couldn't.' Her words echo those of a novelist of the next generation. Growing up, Zoe Fairbairns said to me, she saw that women had to choose. 'You could have work but that meant being single and pitied; you could have love, but you paid for it by doing housework.'

Work and love are central and defining human needs. For much of this century and the last they have been separated according to gender, with men doing 'serious work', women keeping the flame of love and the home fires burning. The destructive consequences of that separation are part of what led to the demand for a more equable division – and to all the complicated, exhausting, creative ways women are finding to have and do both.

Are women still 'fatally torn'? Or torn perhaps, but less often fatally? Byatt writes of the need to be 'normal': 'a word dated now, full of ancient pressures to conformity, backed by a crude psycho-analytic chatter'. I'm not so sure the pressures *are* a thing of the past, though talking to women now suggests there are more ways to evade or refuse them, and more role models. Cynthia Cockburn said firmly: 'the sort of education and upbringing I had as a middle-class girl in the 1950s – that wouldn't happen now'. She is an intellectual and a writer, but 'I didn't go to university because nobody thought it was really worthwhile my going, despite the fact that I got good exam results. And it didn't cross my mind not to get married, or to have children – it didn't cross my mind to ask why, even. It was a very tightly controlled world for women.'

She grew up in Leicester, in 'a very uptight, covertly patriarchal family and they sent me to a boarding-school which exactly matched their ideology. It was a lethal combination of subservience and authority.' Her two daughters were born in 1965 and 1969. 'It took me until 1972 or so to stop thinking of myself as the little woman with children, hanging on to her husband ...' The end of her marriage was painful but brought real freedom.

Bridget McGeechan is also in her fifties, divorced, and with eight children. She came from an Irish Catholic family who were not well off but passed her 11-plus, went to grammar school, then trained as a primary teacher. 'I remember the local doctor coming to our house and asking my mother if she would let me go and work in his house. I remember my mother saying, 'No, Bridget is going to finish school'. She was traditional but she always believed her lack of education was a great barrier to her ... just felt she'd had to work all her life, cleaning and farm jobs, very hard work. She didn't want us to have that kind of work, she wanted us to have something better – like teaching or nursing or secretarial work.' Bridget is a fundraiser and organiser for Childline in Scotland, and until May 1994 was a Labour councillor in Strathclyde Region. When she first married, 'it seems terrible to say it now, but I really felt it was the woman's job to do everything in the house and make everything easy for the man to do his job. Because my husband was good with the children I actually thought I had equality – it was only later on that I realised it wasn't equality at all, I was only being allowed to do certain things. If I had stepped outside of that ...'

She too talked of difficulty at the end of her marriage, but also of the freedom to be herself in ways that hadn't seemed possible. When she thinks about change: 'in lots of ways my daughters have got it harder – my eldest daughter, who works, has two children, has a husband who's working, really has a very hectic life. I don't think they have as many choices as I had. My mother didn't have choices at all – she was out working at 12 and so were all her sisters. I had the choice to go to college because I got a grant, and that's changing now. I'm afraid women are losing a lot of the choices they had.'

'Normal' now includes more. In part in reaction to the increased demands that have come with increased possibilities, there's a renewed sense that maybe it's less possible to do it all – but greater pressure to keep trying: financial pressure and competition for jobs. Rather than having been wholly vanquished, some of those pressures have been recast. Success is still defined differently for women and men. Rebecca Abrams interviewed ten prominent British women from what she calls 'the lost years between the suffragettes and the feminists'. They include Betty Boothroyd and Helen Brook. 'Success,' she says, 'is a particularly ambiguous term when applied to women's lives, since fulfilment is rarely linked purely to professional achievement ... For these women ... success was often bought at a high price.'[1]

Has that changed? Or is the price still high? Abrams thinks it is and comments that, like the women she interviewed, 'young women today are juggling the conflicting demands of family and career without adequate support systems for doing so'. Many women would agree with that double definition of success – a man will be called successful if he has high office but miserable relationships or is slovenly and overweight. If women once were supposed to be bright *or* beautiful, mothers and wives *or* serious about work, now we must try to be both. We assess women's achievements on a tougher measure. It has an impact on how we see ourselves, inevitably.

More women are finding ways to do it differently, many women pay those costs cheerfully, but there is a trade-off which is still real for women in a way that it is not for most men. Most women who are in senior decision-making roles don't have children. Partly that is now an 'age effect' – more younger women are saying they're determined to have and do both. But I think of the consultant gynaecologist in her thirties who told me she felt she had to choose between her work, to which she is passionately committed and through which she makes a unique contribution, and having children. I think of the colleague who put her children's need to stay where their friends are before the new job she wanted in another city. I think of women who put their own priorities, big and little, to one side all the time, as everyday habit. Penny Mansfield, at One plus

One, the relationship research charity, comments that 'it is telling that so many working women see marriage as an obstacle to self-fulfilment'. The evidence from their research, she says, 'is quite clear that while the ideal of sexual equality and task-sharing is strongly upheld in principle, in practice becoming a wife – and especially becoming a mother – will mean the diminution of women's career opportunities'.

A close look at women's increasing participation in professional and management jobs shows that women without children have been twice as likely to take up those opportunities. Evidence to parliamentary hearings held by the International Year of the Family on 'Families and Work' in June 1994, and by the Employment Committee throughout 1994 on 'Mothers in Employment' makes clear that it is still very difficult to do both, and that a great deal of stress is involved in trying.[2] Although there is now much greater social acceptance of 'working mothers', practical social support has not kept pace with demand. Where a satisfactory balance is achieved it has been either through the remarkable abilities of the woman concerned or through taking a 'non-standard' option (or both) – and the ability to pay for help. Those who have an arrangement that works – and there *are* more who do – are conscious of being lucky or (though they wouldn't usually say it) exceptional.

No more Superwoman

At least four times broadcaster Kirsty Wark emphasised how privileged she is. She was saying so not out of an excess of liberal guilt but because on the days when she's practically the only woman on the London shuttle, or the days when she is able to pick up her daughter Caitlin from nursery, as she looks around her at women whose work is neither as well paid nor as interesting, or women who work alongside her but whose jobs demand much longer hours, she simply knows it's true.

Money is the secret, she says immediately. 'It is critical. It is such a struggle anyway to combine everything, that if you're having to make ends meet the whole time, can't afford childcare or very much of it, I can't imagine the pressure that women are working under. I have a nanny four days a week and I can afford that.' Caitlin is four and James three. 'One of the key things that's enabled me to work is the feeling that my kids are secure and happy when I'm not there.'

Living in Glasgow and working some of the time in London means a high-pressure schedule. She presents the BBC flagship current affairs programme *Newsnight*, and she and her husband run an independent production company. But compared to some, Kirsty thinks she has it easier. 'It's possible because I am a presenter. Producers have incredibly long hours and have to go away from home at short notice.' She finds it depressing that 'so little has moved on'. It hasn't moved on for men either, 'but this is still seen as a women's issue. What makes my hackles rise is when everyone comments on how Cherie Blair is able to combine a highly successful career as a barrister with bringing up three kids – it isn't that Tony Blair is able to combine a highly successful career as a politician with bringing up three kids. As long as that reinforcement keeps being made then this is only a one-sided story – it isn't and shouldn't be …'

Fiona Mackay is a postgraduate student finishing a PhD on women in politics, but her background is in journalism in the North of England. She has an eight-year-old daughter, Georgina, whose birth occasioned a major career swerve. She worked in television in the height of the yuppie eighties, from '83 to '87, when she was in her twenties. Looking at the generation of women before her who had been very successful – 'not that there were that many' – made her wonder whether it was what she really wanted. These were women who had got there, it seemed, by being tougher than the men. 'You found out by accident that they had children, they never talked about them. They were just incredibly macho – confrontational, unsympathetic, deliberately different from how you expect women to be.' It was an approach to pregnancy and children 'based on not letting it stop you. When I was pregnant I got very angry about that. These women made things incredibly difficult for other women.'

Kirsty Wark feels her ambition to have both work and a life is now seen as legitimate – 'and that's a change. Having said that, it's a lot to do with where I am now in my profession, because I've had a measure of success, lots of women feel they have to prove themselves.' She doesn't feel that she must hide her maternal side. 'If anything I don't do that because I want people to realise – I want people to know it *isn't* Superwoman, and it *is* guilty, and it is not having it all.'

Ginny Dougary, attending a television conference, described in her 1994 book on women in the media, found the same arguments being rehearsed. The two main themes which emerged from her inquiries, she says, were 'power, or the lack of it, and the desire of many women to extend the definition of "success" beyond the purely professional.'[3]

'A major preoccupation of the younger women was how they were going to combine career with motherhood ... Most of the women I spoke to in their forties and older felt that such an option was neither possible nor advisable ... It is not always spelt out, but when I speak to the younger women the sub-text is clear: women of this generation are not prepared to sacrifice their personal goals for professional success. They believe, or want to believe, they can have it all.' What she reports echoes what younger women without children, from several backgrounds, have told me. It is a marker of change that many well-educated and ambitious women see this as a false choice. Clearly they can say little about conflicts they can still postpone for a better day. Their determination bodes well.

But preliminary results in 1994 from a British Film Institute study of 500 creative staff in television show how hard it will be: that women in television find it almost impossible to have children because of the hours they are expected to work and the insecure nature of their jobs. While two-thirds of the men in the study have children, less than a third of the women do. This is not just because it is a young workforce: in the over-40 age group just over half the women had no children compared with 15 per cent of men.[4]

'It's not just if you have children,' Fiona Mackay said, 'you want a home life, time to see your friends, go to art galleries, have a life.' She went into journalism straight from school and, looking for a more flexible, less pressured way to live, applied to do a degree in politics and history at Manchester University. 'People say, well done, you managed a degree with a young baby. But in comparison it was easier.' After university, with Georgina in nursery school she went back into television for four months. 'But it was impossible. If I was going to have a child I wanted to spend some time with her. But I didn't feel I could say that – it felt like a conservative and retrograde thing to be saying, you were seen as letting the side down.' She remembers one of her producers saying that when she left she'd sold out. 'I'd quit – I'd let myself down.'

A big change, Kirsty says, is 'the way women are treated at work as professionals – it's taken a whole generation of men to retire before that happened. At least *intellectually* men now know that they have to have a different attitude, whereas the dinosaur breed that's hirpling off to retirement now didn't really believe it.' What hasn't changed are the structures that would allow most women to take advantage of the opportunities: 'and why have kids if you never see them? There's been a sea change in attitudes. But unless you can buy the support you need there's been no real change – and that is very disappointing.'

High-flying women of Fiona's generation are having their children now, in their late thirties. It will be interesting to see if they insist on a better deal, using their experience and confidence to ensure their needs are met, adding yet another layer to the multiple patterns of women's working lives. Then again the threat of ageism – alive and well in the media – is only round the corner. There was some useful growth in job-shares and high-level part-time work in the late 1980s – but only if you'd proved you were too good to lose. Against that the growth of short-term contracts and tighter budgets has narrowed opportunities. A sense of realism makes Fiona doubtful. 'When there's a job in hand, a deadline, tight budgets – what are you going to do, are you going to say, well I'm going home now it's six o'clock?'

The media is hardly a typical working world but it is highly relevant to this study – first, because it is an area in which women were making rapid progress in the 1980s. Ginny Dougary argues that this has now slowed. In 1995 80 per cent of decision-making jobs in national newspapers were held by men, though more women are deputy and assistant editors and more women are news reporters. It's also relevant because the long hours and work-centred lives demanded in the media are becoming more common almost everywhere, even in once-civilised working environments. And, because the composition and values of a media workforce have an impact on how the world is presented to us, who they are has a significance well beyond the individual. The BBC has recognised this in acknowledging the importance of portrayal in its equal opportunity policy: 'as long as managers and production staff are overwhelmingly white, able-bodied males then this will be reflected in the output ... a national broadcasting organisation cannot afford to ignore or misrepresent large sections of its audience'.[5]

Looking Outward

Liz Lamb faces many of the same issues in a rather different working world. She is a health visitor with two part-time jobs: one in a more conventional role in a well-heeled part of Glasgow, the other working in the pioneering Community Health Project in Drumchapel, a housing scheme on the outskirts of the city, with some of the worst health and social problems in Europe. She is deeply involved with the problems disadvantaged women and their children face and faces some similar conflicts herself.

As for change, she sees women doing more and coping with more difficult problems: 'There's not been a big move, has there? Some issues relevant to women have been taken up but there's been no big shift to equal responsibilities.' She has two children, Ruaridh, who is four and a half, and Kara who is two and a half. When Ruaridh was born she went back to work full time. 'I seemed to take it in my stride and he settled very quickly with the childminder – I even did some evening work.' She wonders now that she had the energy.

After Kara was born she worked part time, but her husband Michael, who had been a lorry driver and then a mature student finished his degree and became unemployed. He now looks after the children three days a week, and the children go to a nursery two days a week. 'It works quite well. The main pressure is that he is unemployed. He's better at home than I'd have thought – he didn't take much responsibility at the beginning of the relationship, that was something we had to sort out.

'I take total responsibility for the kids in the evening – it's very tiring but I feel I have to, I'd not see them through the week if I didn't. My tea's on the table when I get in' – she grimaces guiltily. 'Financial need is the main reason I work. I wouldn't want not to work but I'd rather work part time. I do enjoy my work, but it's having only the weekends with the kids. It's not even so much guilt, it's wanting to be able to do everything with them, go swimming and everything.' Time for herself is non-existent and she's conscious she has very little for her partner. 'I tell people, "You've got to have time for yourself, for your partner – give it priority." I know it's good to do that – but when I get the children settled at 9, 9.30 I usually go to bed myself. And I know Michael's probably never had an adult conversation all day …'

Energy comes from working with local women activists. 'Seeing them come out of drastic situations and taking action. To be there to support them is great.' There are several women's groups in Drumchapel now plus the women's health network and post-natal depression and breastfeeding support groups, which Liz runs. 'I don't think things are a lot better for women with children generally. For some individual women, though, life is better, for some of the women who've got involved here.' At work there is no formal help with childcare costs or recognition of her multiple roles. She looks slightly surprised that I even ask. 'No – it's seen as an individual problem for you to solve. But at this project it's a big advantage that all the workers have young children, there's a lot of empathy.'

Lorraine Mann was a teacher before she had her three children: Liam who is 15, Caitlin 12 and Bryony 9, and then at home looking after them for ten years. During that time she became actively involved in anti-nuclear campaigning, in particular against the Dounreay nuclear reactor in Caithness.

'There is as much pressure now on women to go back to work when they have kids – women with careers especially, and in families with very low incomes – as there was on women not to. I think we need to question how exploitative the whole thing is or may become. Women now have to go back to maintain their place on the career ladder, all the more so because of possibilities fought for and won – it's ironic, really … How do you compare the pressure on a woman who wants to be at home for the early years and is having to go back with a woman who desperately wants to go back and can't because there's no childcare or no suitable jobs? I'd like to see recognition of the skills developed during childcare. We are in danger of changing the burden of non-choice rather than widening the range of choice.'

Rosalind Mitchison, for all the prejudice she faced in her early career because she was married with children, emphasises the positive side of doing both. 'There are enormous advantages in the whole female experience – and I do find small children enormously interesting. Having children has given me enormous satisfaction. Concentration *is* an issue. I've always done my serious work out of the home ... You're not going to do the quantity of work that a man with a wife looking after him will – with that set-up totally designed to protect him. Nobody is ever going to protect *her* to that degree. But don't they miss out as people more than if they had to muck in a bit? Do you measure life entirely by a stack of enormous books?'

'We need a different way of viewing the broadening of experience and other advantages gained from a career break,' Lorraine Mann argues, 'so that it is seen as an advantage, not a disadvantage – that you wouldn't be knocked down the ladder for that – against somebody in the same establishment for twenty-three years and they've never done anything different. Well it's a big, wide world out there ...'

Expectations and Relationships

'Increasingly, many women are not in a position to make a choice between going to work and staying at home,' Harriet Harman emphasised. 'It is only a choice if you have support at home and flexibility at work – a lot of women don't have either.' It's estimated that around a quarter of women out at work would rather be at home and about the same number are at home and would rather be working.[6] Women with young children are still particularly likely to be doing work which under-uses their abilities and training, although that can be a problem for all women.

But, while not ignoring the constraints that hinder many women, at work and at home, I want to focus on the way possibilities *have* widened. And on how women – arguably the majority – have, one way or another, made new combinations of work and family life work for them.

In asking whether women – ordinary women, not just exceptional women – can have both love and work, I'm asking really two questions. About women and children yes, but also about sexual relationships with men and whether it is possible to achieve equality in female/male relationships, to manage a relationship which allows both partners to grow and change and achieve some of the things they set out to. This is inevitably to focus on what a gay friend of mine calls 'the heterosexual crisis'. Although lesbian relationships have tensions of their own, socially sanctioned male dominance is not one of them, nor the complications of the tender male ego.

For the women Rebecca Abrams talked to, the further up the scale they climbed and the more traditional the profession they sought to progress in, 'the less compatible it appears to have been with the more conventional expressions of female fulfilment, marriage and mother-hood. These women were ahead of their time: they were challenging notions of how a woman could live her life. But what they could not always do was find the men who would also accept their revised versions of female identity: men remained largely unchallenged and unchallengeable in both the domestic and the professional sphere.'[7]

How much has that changed? I think of the women (in their thirties and forties mainly) who have told me clearly and often that men can't relate to independent women. They're single or divorced, heterosexual, and they've pretty much given up looking for a sexual relationship: the men they meet need them to give up too much. As the saying goes: when a man's under pressure he's got his wife to support him, when a woman's under pressure she gets a divorce. These are differences which are hard to give chapter and verse to, compared to issues for working women with children which are endlessly investigated. But they play a role, certainly, in the high divorce rate and the reluctance of a growing group of younger women to marry or even to live with men.

Women's right to work when our children are young is not an issue now in the way it was in the 1970s and earlier – it's interesting to track how the arguments have shifted: from married women working at all, to maternal deprivation and latch-key kids, from grudging acceptance to actual pressure on many women, especially single mothers, to earn. Labels common in the 1980s – 'career woman' and 'working mother' – seem outdated. There has been a shift in attitudes and some (small) concessions: 'If you've got kids and you want to go back to work – can you afford not to?' The voice is reassuring, encouraging: it is an advertisement for the childcare provision now available on Family Credit. But many of the practical problems are exactly the same.

Putting Things Off

Although more women are finding new ways of having if not it all, then more of it, other women are resolving these dilemmas by not having children, or by having children later, and by remaining (or becoming again) single. We cannot always assume this is a matter of choice, but these are changes which are now sufficiently widespread to show as significant in population statistics, and across social class. Alongside steeply falling marriage rates and an increase in the number of younger women living alone, this shows a turning away from what marriage and childbearing entails. Our culture places a low value, in practice if not in sentiment, on mothering and caring roles. And while most women expect equality within marriage, many men don't – or don't really know what it means.

Smaller families are part of the same pattern. Family size has been falling in Britain throughout this century, with the exception of the years following the Second World War when it rose (to 2.6 for women marrying in the late 1950s) before falling again from the 1960s. The average number of children among married and cohabiting families is now 1.9, and in lone mother families, 1.7. That average has remained stable since the early 1980s; in 1971 it was 2.0. There are many more only children, and families with four children are now described as 'large'. (Scotland has an average family size larger than for England and Wales but that difference has been narrowing; Asian families are also, on average, larger than white or black families.)[8]

Far fewer women are having children. Most women still have children at some point in their lives, but the proportion of women childless by the age of 30 has doubled in twenty-five years: over a third of women born in 1960 reached 30 without having any children; half that proportion of women born in 1945 did so. Because having children later is first becoming quite usual, predictions are risky. Nevertheless it seems unlikely that delayed childbearing will be widespread enough to completely reverse this trend. Current projections by OPCS are that 2 in 10 women born in 1980 will not have children, against 1.5 in 10 for women who have now passed the childbearing years. Part of this could be due to increasing infertility, for which there is some evidence. However, research by Jane Bartlett and from the Family Policy Studies Centre suggests that many more women are choosing not to have children, some of them because they see work and childbearing as an almost impossible combination.[9]

The trend towards having children later, has been most marked among better-educated and better-off women but is no longer confined to them. Mothers' average age at first birth has risen steadily as has the average age of giving birth: in 1993 in England and Wales it was the highest ever recorded for married women, at 28, and in Scotland in 1994 again the highest, at 27. (Single mothers are usually younger at first childbirth; Asian women are more likely to have children at a younger age.) Since the early 1980s there has been a noticeable rise in women having first babies in their thirties and early forties as well as in overall fertility rates for that age group. Between 1981 and 1991 there was a 27 per cent increase in first babies at 30–34 and the proportion of women having first babies between 35 and 39 almost doubled. But in the early 1990s the fertility rate for woman in their early thirties declined again (consistently with overall fertility rates) but births for women over 35 continued to increase; for women of 40 and over by 6 per cent.[10]

In the context of the whole post-war period the numbers of women aged 30 and over having children is not unusual, but what is new about trends since 1980 is the change in the timing of childbearing. The degree of change shows if you compare the fertility rate of women in their early twenties to women in their early thirties: in 1990 it was only slightly more for the younger women whereas only ten years before it was a third more.[11]

These are striking and significant changes. But as ever, change is more conspicuous than continuity. Fertility rates for women in their twenties have fallen steeply since 1980, especially in the 20–24 age group. But 20 to 29 are still the ages at which most women have children: almost three times as many births in 1993 were to women in their twenties as to women aged 30 and over.[12]

Social attitudes to 'older' mothers have changed quite markedly over the same period, as has medical opinion, if to a lesser extent. First-time mothers over 27 are now much less likely to be labelled 'elderly primigravida' – as I was in 1980 – which is possibly just as well since what was 'elderly' then is the average age at childbirth now. Advertising soon reflected the shift, with older and perhaps wiser mothers cooing over their babies: someone had figured that older mothers have more money for cough medicine. Quite quickly a 35-year-old and 40-, then 45-year-old first-time mother came to seem not so unusual – though the number of women having babies in their forties is still low – and quite youthful really once we were presented with the medically managed post-menopause baby. According to the chair of the British Medical Association's ethics committee in 1993, in ten years pregnant women in their fifties will be 'commonplace'.[13] The 'Christmas miracle' that year of twins born to a 59-year-old woman occasioned outrage, though if the situation had been reversed and the woman 45 and her partner 59 nothing would have been said. A rich woman had done something that rich and successful men do all the time. (It was ironic that most of the arguments were couched in terms of the children's interests, in a society which week after week after week demonstrates its neglect of children.)

This woman's extraordinarily late start was only taking to extremes the advice that is now routine for career women: establish a career before having children. The consequences of delaying child-bearing can be considerable. 'A later start to marriage and particularly motherhood gives women the increased opportunity to obtain educational qualifications, occupational training and job experience,' says Kathleen Kiernan in an analysis of changes in marriage and childbearing across Europe. It can mean 'more self-assurance and greater resources to express and negotiate their needs'.[14] But a later start to childbearing is also becoming a commoner intention among women who don't fit the 'career girl' mould as well as those who do.

Although postponing childbearing has some clear advantages in work and career terms it is not always a strategy women can rely on. Contraception is not infallible and for some women waiting until their late thirties can mean fertility problems. Then too there are the practical problems: of not having found a partner; of having got used to a certain lifestyle and income – as one woman said, 'I'll have to give up so much.' This approach is derided as selfish, but no one expects a man to give up much more than a few nights out with the lads for a bundle of joy. Nor does it necessarily make the dilemmas facing working mothers any easier. Some women say it intensifies them. They're used to full-time work and the public world but having waited so long to have children they want to be 'hands-on' mothers too.

As more women delay childbearing, the difference in women's and men's reproductive lifetimes seems increasingly unjust. As more women see their need for economic independence as legitimate and find ways to ensure it, it is at the cost, in a working culture still dominated by male norms, of a hard choice between financial security and satisfaction in work, and having children in the years which are optimum for childbearing. The 'biological clock' is cruel. But the problem is a social, not a biological, one.

Identities

The major change that Zoe Fairbairns talked about is the greater chance now of having both love and work. 'I think the thing that oppressed me most as a girl growing up was the knowledge that only one of two things was going to happen to me as an adult woman, either I was going to get married, which would be awful, or I was going to fail to get married, which would be awful. The whole of life seemed to be between those two decisions. There were no other identities to seek for yourself. I don't think that's true any more.'

Zoe grew up in London and still lives there. She has been writing fiction since her teens: her novels include *Benefits* and *Daddy's Girls*. She also works for ITN as a subtitler. It is a way of life which once she never would have dreamt was possible. 'I was very much a beneficiary of the post-war boom. I passed my 11-plus and had a grammar school education and free school milk and everything coming off ration – I really had quite a privileged childhood with lots to hope for and lots to enjoy … Things like being validated and praised for your achievements, and having your own room, being able to go off on holiday by yourself or develop your own interests. As far as I could see married women weren't allowed those things and if single women had them it was only to make up for the fact that they hadn't married.' Yes, there were some adult women who didn't fit those categories but the low social status of women who didn't marry was clear to her. 'The overwhelming impression was that that was what waited for me, that choice; and marriage seemed to me the end of all the things which as a girl and a teenager I was encouraged to strive for and enjoy.'

The starkness of that choice may have gone, I said, but I see women still making compromises that men do not have to make. 'But there was no real choice before at all. I think now it is much easier as a woman to make the decision not to have children and not be considered a freak. I'm not saying that that's an easy choice or even the right choice always – I'm saying the choice is there. And similarly the decision about what proportion of your energy you give to your work and what you do about your relationships: those are ongoing problems, but the parameters within which those decisions are made are much broader.'

What made it possible for her to evade those dreadful fates? 'Feminism. Before that I'd just thought it was my problem, I hadn't realised that anyone else felt as I felt. Suddenly to discover that there was a national, a world movement of women thinking and saying those sorts of things … It was enormously liberating – there was a strength in making your own choices which came from that sense of being part of something bigger. Of course a very important legislative change was that divorce became easier, and so marriage was no longer a life sentence. Or you could be single but live with a man, which is what my choice has been, and people, the people you cared about anyway, were no longer going to click their tongues and call you a fallen woman.'

She lives with John Petherbridge, her partner of the past eighteen years, 'within our terms on a basis of equality. I have not had to deal with the very stark choices between career or love which some women I know have had to.' They haven't had children. 'There are always the roads not taken. If I had my life over again, I still don't think I would have had children – I don't think I will now have children. But I feel it is the right decision perhaps for the wrong reasons. 'Because it seemed that the whole business of domesticity and wifehood and motherhood was just one long ordeal, it just never really entered my head that I would have children any more than I would voluntarily chop my foot off. Now that I have friends who have had children and I've seen those children grow up and the friends come out the other end – and they're still OK and their other lives have not ended – that makes me think maybe that decision was based on a misunderstanding. Then, that was not a life pattern that seemed believable to me. Now it seems to be, for some people.'

My colleague Joyce Macmillan has written about her regret about not having children (she is divorced) and when I spoke to her we talked first about the pressures on upwardly mobile women of her generation, in their twenties in the early 1970s. Joyce is a theatre critic and political columnist on *Scotland on Sunday* and also writes for the *Guardian*. She is unusual as a commentator today in that she addresses family issues in the same context as she will address, for example, constitutional change, or the latest failings of the government.

Does she think women can now have both work and love? 'I think there are lots of women who do – but I think there are still quite strong built-in difficulties. It is still extremely difficult for men in our culture to really not resent women's work. Whether it's the way we bring up boys, whether it's a profound psychological thing, it seems to me that most men somewhere in their psyche feel that looking after them should be the key function of women's lives, or at least of "their" woman.' She reminded me of a scene in Ena Lamont Stewart's play, *Men Should Weep*. 'The women are gossiping and suddenly this voice roars down the stairs: "Hey! You – I'm wantin' some attention!"' There might be more sophisticated ways of expressing that need, we agreed, but none the less 'it seems quite characteristic at a deep level of how men think it should be between men and women.

'I suppose at least it's a kind of bond. But it is very difficult for women whose work is demanding. That causes untold break-ups of relationships. Because men *do* go off with women who pretend to believe – or actually believe – that men's concerns are more important, or with women who are prepared to put their own professional lives second.'

Then there are children, who make the same sorts of demands and make them much more intensely. 'We need a society which actually recognises that dilemma, actually encourages people not to give in to it. I think one of the worst things about our society is the assumption that if you've got something you really want to do then you probably shouldn't have children – it's this feeling that not having children is a jolly nice viable option for people with something else in mind. I feel very strongly that that is not the point – you can have an awful lot of things in mind and still have a life that is impoverished by not having children.

'Of course it's a viable choice not to – it's good to live in a society that doesn't pressurise people into having children. But society should be built on the assumption that having children is a normal part of almost everyone's life.' Like many of the women I spoke to she thinks longingly of 'the kind of social statement of intent that is fundamental in countries like Denmark and Sweden. It makes an immense difference to the way people feel about their right to be both parents and to make a contribution to society.' In Britain, 'I think we still feel that people should have to make these harsh choices and trade-offs, and that's life ... I think that kind of harsh choice is completely unacceptable and damaging.'

Maternity Rights

The time most women spend out of formal work when they have children has shortened very significantly over the past twenty-five years. The 1991 study *Maternity Rights in Britain*, a national survey based on Child Benefit recipients, showed that in 1988 nearly half of women were back at work within nine months of childbirth, double the figure for the beginning of the decade. A further fifth were looking for work. A study by IDS in March 1994 of 39 large companies and 12 public sector organisations found that the proportion of eligible employees returning to work after maternity leave had risen from around half in the early 1990s to 70 per cent.[15]

Twenty-five years ago it was unusual for all but the poorest women to return to work soon after having a baby: less than 10 per cent did. By the end of the 1970s the number returning to work had risen to a quarter of women returning to work within eight months, plus 14 per cent looking for a job, which was seen as 'a major change in the labour market' at the time. It is now very unusual for women who have children never to return to paid work, though common to take some time out of paid work beyond maternity leave. Very, very few fathers do so, and paternity leave is not generally available.[16]

Statutory maternity rights (the right to reinstatement, maternity pay and protection against unfair dismissal) were introduced in 1975 but there was no widespread take-up at first. The first study of the effects of the legislation suggested that changing attitudes towards women with young children working was at least as much the reason why more were going back to work as increased rights.[17] One woman teacher I spoke to had a first pregnancy in early 1975, which miscarried. She had her first baby a year later, by which time the new rights had come into force; that made a very practical difference and she decided to return to work, which during the first pregnancy she had felt she wouldn't be able to.

Fewer than half of working pregnant women were eligible for maternity rights, however. In October 1994 extended rights were introduced as a consequence of a European directive adopted in 1992. Women now qualify irrespective of their length of service and the hours they work, though women earning below the NI threshold do not. (There are additional financial benefits for longer serving, better-paid employees.) It is an important advance and will extend maternity protection to a further one in five pregnant employees, the EOC said, though they were concerned that the complexity of the scheme would make it difficult and expensive to operate. The EOC still commonly receives complaints about women who are illegally sacked when they become pregnant and has estimated that around 4,000 pregnant women a year are losing their jobs.[18]

Some business leaders have said that increased rights could lead to employers refusing to take on women of childbearing age. Two-thirds of women members asked by the Institute of Directors in September 1994 said they thought job prospects for women of childbearing age were being damaged by the extended rights, and employers would be chary of employing such expensive workers. Exactly the same argument was put in 1975.[19] As the number of women in the workforce has risen steeply since then it was not, apparently, an insurmountable problem. (The EOC also points out that the issue needs to be kept in perspective: each year only 3.5 per cent of women in work are pregnant.)

More women are also returning to work full time: nearly three times as many, according to the *Maternity Rights* survey. There has also been a rise in the numbers of women going back to the same employer: three-quarters now do as against a third in 1979. We know less about what happens next. We know that the proportion of women with children under five in the (paid and recorded) workforce is the highest it has been since 1945. But that statistic hides a great deal of variation: women who stay at home at first and come back to work later, women who go back after maternity leave but then don't stay, or move into part-time work. In Julia Brannen and Peter Moss's study of women in the late 1980s who had young children and who worked full time there was 'a steady movement out of full-time employment into part-time work and periods of non-employment'. This was influenced by problems with childcare and at work, but 'most significant of all were the tensions engendered by coping with motherhood and employment – the feeling of being on a constant treadmill'.[20]

The follow-up research to the *Maternity Rights* survey which Susan McRae is currently working on shows more positive change. It suggests, she says, that 'women in higher-level occupations, particularly professional women, now have less difficulty in maintaining careers over the period following childbirth. And that is at least something – twenty years ago they wouldn't have been there.' But possibilities depend on being able to afford to pay for childcare, and for women at less well-paid occupational levels "their options haven't changed as much."[21]

These patterns are significantly different for single mothers, who are less likely to be working now than in the past, and less likely to be working than other mothers. Women with younger dependent children are also still much less likely to have jobs than women whose children are at school, and women with three or more children are also much less likely to be out at work. The women most likely to return soonest after childbirth are at either end of the class and opportunity spectrum: professional high-earning women, who have more to lose, and very poor women, who have least choice.[22]

Returning to Work

How you see the earlier return of women to paid work after childbirth, and indeed most facts about women and work, depends a lot on your point of view (and your own life and choices). This was illustrated for me when the *Maternity Rights* study was published. I got three press releases about it. The Employment Department (who funded the research) was unreserved in its welcome for 'the fundamental change that has occurred over the past decade in provision for women returning to work after childbirth'. They highlighted the number of women returning to jobs with salaries at the same level as they left: 'a particularly significant advance for equal opportunities'. The Policy Studies Institute (which published the research) described it as 'a revolution in the position of working mothers' and highlighted the increased proportion of women who now qualified for statutory maternity rights and who had made use of them over the 1980s. But they also pointed out that there was little growth in the same period in provision by employers to help mothers remain in employment. The EOC (which also funded it) said the study showed maternity rights were inadequate, especially in the private sector, and called for reform. The survey showed, they emphasised, that 40 per cent of women did *not* qualify for the right to return to work.

In 1988 the issue of women with young children working was brought centre-frame by an Employment Department (ED) report *Employment for the 1990s*, which unleashed upon an unsuspecting world the concept of the 'demographic time bomb': that because of a drop of more than a million in the number of school-leavers, the work of women currently at home with children would be needed. The report said: 'Employers must recognise that women can no longer be treated as second-class workers. They will need women employees, and must recognise both their career ambitions and domestic responsibilities. This will involve broadening company training policies, much more flexibility of work and hours and job-sharing, to facilitate the employment of women with families and help adapt to their needs.'[23] It sounded good, though women who had spent most of two decades campaigning for women's right to work promptly pointed out that treating women as cheap labour wasn't what they'd had in mind – and some argued that, after all, this 'wasted resource'[24] wasn't exactly doing nothing at home. Still, it was nice to be wanted. The EOC began a high-profile campaign to open wide this window of opportunity and argued that a business case could and should be made for equal opportunities. The CBI investigated businesses' approach to childcare provision and the *Financial Times* ran a series on how 'career-minded families' dealt with childcare. New organisations founded include Employers for Childcare, a forum set up by British Airways, Shell UK and others, and the Working Mothers Association (which became Parents at Work in 1994).

Very few companies did much more, though some did and their number is slowly growing. When I asked Joanna Foster in 1993 for an estimate of how many British firms there were with good family provision she suggested 50. Late eighties predictions that 'For the first time in years, jobs will be chasing workers instead of the reverse'[25] proved wide of the mark as unemployment rose again in the early 1990s and stayed high until beginning to fall in 1994. Not even the young people who were supposed to be in such short supply have found jobs waiting for them. 'Issues which employers have been happy to leave as problems for individual parents are now top of the boardroom agenda,' I wrote in 1989. 'However there is as yet rather more talk than action …' In most cases that's as far as it went.

Though some few far-sighted employers have proved exceptions, recession meant shelving plans to extend 'family-friendly' policies in many cases. 'Equal opportunities just dropped right off the agenda when the recession came' said a spokeswoman for BIFU, the Banking and Finance Union. But if a number of good ideas were mothballed because of the recession, women's employment continued to increase throughout it and despite it.

In all, the time bomb was a damp squib – although it did contribute to changing attitudes and created an impetus for information and policy discussion. 'It may still be ticking,' an ED spokesman said dubiously when I asked in 1993, but he seemed unconvinced. (It peaked in 1995, after which the 16–19 population rises again before levelling off at around 2000, although at a level still lower than in 1971.)

Childcare is still mainly left to women to sort out unless they work in certain offices of some banks or for an unusually enlightened company, in some departments of the civil service, some local councils and some colleges. There has been growth in some areas in private day nursery provision, and that is continuing, with a large US firm expanding into the UK. The Employment Department told the Employment Committee that there had been an increase in 153 per cent in the number of nurseries, almost all privately run and funded, and a 40 per cent increase in registered childminders, between 1988 and 1992. Harriet Harman's analysis shows that since 1985 the 'childcare gap' – the difference between the number of places available, which has increased slightly, and the number of children under five whose mothers are in work, which has almost doubled, has widened by an estimated 400,000 missing places. The majority of parents depend on relatives for childcare, especially grandmothers.[26]

'Family friendly working' is patchy, the Employment Committee found, and childcare 'is a mixed bag of provision by a variety of different agencies. 90 per cent of childcare is unsubsidised.' So only a quarter of working mothers use formal arrangements such as nurseries and childminders. On average paid-for childcare costs a quarter of women's earnings. There has been no expansion in publicly funded nurseries for the children of working parents (as distinct from children 'in need').[27]

A comprehensive overview of research on employment and family life published by the Education Department in November 1994 confirms that 'managing the relationship between employment and family life including eldercare continues to depend heavily on household resources and social networks (especially close female relatives)'. 'Family-friendly' employment practices 'are not widely available', they say, and depend more on where you work and the employer's discretion than family need. 'It is also increasingly clear that the introduction of formal policies needs to be accompanied by other changes (for example, in organisational culture) if these policies are to be fully effective ... Mothers are more likely to be using "flexible" or "family friendly" practices than other women or men ... at the workplace, family responsibilities are regarded as a women's issue.' The costs and benefits of policy options in mediating work and family conflict have not been fully explored, the report says.[28]

Despite major social and economic change government policy has been to re-emphasise the private nature of childcare and the decisions parents make, and that, if the need was there, the market would provide. This has meant more people have suffered adversely because of change than needed to. There is also concern about the quality of care in some new private day nurseries. Some pioneering 'partner-ship childcare' schemes have been developed with local enterprise agencies, employers and local authorities combining forces, and these provide a useful model as well as good provision for families who are lucky enough to live nearby, but not many do.

I'd been intermittently paying attention to the Employment Committee hearings on mothers in employment throughout 1994 and it seemed that they were heading for a painful dilemma: almost everything that everyone told them pointed inescapably to the need for coherent social policies which take seriously parents' need to care for their children and participate in paid work. And for a national strategy on childcare rather than piecemeal, profit-driven development. But that would fly in the face of current absence of policy and this was a Tory-dominated, male-dominated committee.

They resolved the dilemma in favour of the truth: that this country urgently needs to support working mothers and their children. Women with young children working, they say, is 'a permanent change in the pattern of employment' but in the UK 'women receive little state support in performing this complicated feat of juggling'. There is discrimination at work and 'women's difficulties ... are exacerbated by the fact that it is still fairly unusual for fathers to play a full role in the care and development of their children'. This means women 'are still forced to make difficult decisions about having and raising children or pursuing or furthering a career'. The Report says: 'whether they work full-time or part-time, women are at every stage constrained in their choices by the UK's provisions on maternity pay and maternity leave; by the availability of childcare; by the structure of the benefit system; by the availability of training; and by employers' attitudes to flexible working.' The Report recommends the extension of statutory maternity pay to women earning below the NI threshold; a minimum entitlement to family leave of five days for all employees and a statutory right to paternity leave. They recommend 'that the Government work to increase the availability and quality of childcare.'[29] Now that may seem commonsense, but from a document bearing the House of Commons' forbidding stamp this was revolution!

Although childcare (and, though less so, provision for elderly dependants) is higher on the political agenda than ever before, it is, as Bronwen Cohen at *Children in Scotland* argues, poorly understood. 'It's thought of as a simple, single issue. Actually childcare is one of the most complex policy issues there is.' Childcare must meet children's needs for care and education, parents' needs and economic requirements, particularly in economic development and job crea-tion. There are also newer cultural arguments, seen for example in the Gaelic playgroup movement, and childcare has a role in addressing racism. 'We need' Bronwen argues 'a greater recognition of childcare services as fundamental to society as a whole rather than being "special need" provision. And the long-term individual and eco-nomic effects are far more significant than is usually realised.' The need for more and better employment provision for people with caring responsibilities and for a national policy on childcare is more evident than ever.

Taking the Strain

In the absence of co-ordinated support for working parents it is women, children and families who are making the adjustments and taking the strain. The move of women with children into the workforce has not been matched by any shift of men back into the family. The conflict is the greater because we want to do our best by our kids and we want to live decently, even well. As Penelope Leach comments, 'because working and parenting are seen as separate functions there is a continual conflict between their demands'.

There are 'huge social and economic pressures on families now', Joanna Foster, chair of the International Year of the Family, said when I talked to her. 'Trying to balance paid work and family responsibilities is still extremely difficult for both men and women. The workplace culture is premised on men as breadwinners with wives at home. Traditionally the culture of most workplaces has demanded that we leave our family concerns right off-site ... Everyone, but especially women, just coped, at a high price.'

But she believes things are changing now, that 'economic as well as social arguments are providing a strong case for changing the corporate and organisational culture'. An emphasis on skills and creativity and a realisation that productivity is linked to personal life is important: 'the return on investment in people, as well as in plant, is now an issue'. And demographic changes mean 'that an increasing number of employees, men as well as women, will have caring responsibilities for dependent relatives'.

Her approach parallels the kind of argument we are now hearing from the European Commission about reconciling work and family responsibilities. The 1994 EC White Paper on Social Policy suggests a framework directive on reconciling work and family life, and a new EU-wide network has been set up to share good practice. It is interesting to see arguments which began in the women's liberation critique of women's unpaid domestic labour and men's absence from housework and childcare now articulated and presented by the European Commission. Ideas about reconciling work and family responsibilities are 'at the heart of the challenge to post-industrial society,' Social Affairs Commissioner Padraig Flynn has said.[30] Some question what the argument has lost *en route*, but the argument that what is at issue is not actually about women only, but about how people and societies reconcile work and family responsibilities is important. It emphasises that the real issue is how *people* with children, or other dependants, meet their needs both for gainful employment and to care for them, now that the way of reconciling those responsibilities which has been most common since 1945 no longer works for most people.

There are specific limitations in the equal opportunities approach: a risk that equality becomes 'a women's problem' and the solution a 'mommy track', and because the emphasis so far has been primarily on enabling women to work in paid employment structured around men's lives, rather than paying equal attention to the other side of the division of labour. However, the 'reconciliation' argument holds a risk of eliding how much what's at issue in practice is still about women, and women's real lives. The line is a fine one to tread. There is also a danger that the ideas of reconciling work and family treat the world as if it is made up, like Noah's ark, of well-matched male/female pairs. A cold wind blowing through the world economy also limits individual families' room for manoeuvre.

Our own policy processes lag a long way behind Europe. The UK Government is engaged in spoiling tactics on a range of measures aimed at supporting working parents: the directive on maternity leave and the protection of pregnant workers which was finally passed last year was weakened by the UK. Britain was the only country to oppose the proposal on parental leave – refusing it was described by Michael Portillo as 'a triumph'. The exemption from the Social Chapter which John Major negotiated at Maastricht has a whole raft of specific consequences for women.

Social policies to support people with family responsibilities in work have been thought through in exhaustive detail over the past twenty-five years. Nor are they theoretical; we can see them in practice in the Scandinavian countries and by some good employers in Britain who offer more than the state requires of them. The question now is one of political will: not how can it be done but *why* don't we do it? The market philosophy and conflicted feelings about women with children working of the British party of government since 1979 is part of the answer, but it has roots in a refusal at a deep level of real equality. That is changing, but very slowly.

In the introduction to the second *Maternity Rights* report W.W. Daniel, who carried out the earlier research (in 1979), comments on a 'surprising' lack of change. Despite the larger numbers of women returning to work, and for the same employer, 'little more seems to have been done by employers to encourage them to return to work.' The demand among women for improved childcare facilities, for more flexible working arrangements and enhanced maternity rights had increased substantially. But what women actually did, how they managed, hadn't changed noticeably since 1979. 'It is likely that the principal influence behind this change has been a major cultural change among women, that has been accelerating steadily over the past twenty years,' Daniel writes. 'Employers have found little reason to provide added inducements for mothers of young children to continue working. In short, employers have been able to meet their need for more women to return to work simply because a steadily increasing number of women want to return.'

It creates a serious double-bind. Margaret Thatcher's comment in 1988 is worth remembering. She shrugged the question off, saying that 'women have always made and will continue to make provision for childcare'. Because women are good at managing, because women and families are finding solutions, one way or another, well – we can go on doing so, can't we?

And we did, and we do – but in part because of that there is change in the air again. Three factors affect change and pull against each other: the financial pressures on people with young children which means two incomes are needed by most; women's continuing aspirations and need for economic independence; and the pressures of the contemporary workplace. The kind of harsh choice Joyce Macmillan talked about may be re-emerging for a new generation of women.

Maternally Correct

The debate about 'working mothers' never really goes away. About every five years, I reckon, the media rediscovers a 'return to maternity'. One such flurry was around Maeve Haran's *Having It All*, a blockbuster in which the heroine, a high-powered television executive, like the author, jacked in her career for the sake of her children, like the author.[31] Like her Paula Yates drew other mothers venom by extolling the virtues of stay-at-home motherhood while flirting with rock stars in a TV studio at a time when real stay-at-home mothers were filling lunch boxes. It broke through the surface again when Penny Hughes, head of Coca-Cola in Britain, 35 and cited as one of a new breed of able, successful corporate women, gave up her job and £250,000 salary to stay home with the baby she was expecting in early 1995. 'Coca-Cola boss says motherhood is the real thing,' crowed the *Daily Mail*, describing hers as 'a classic dilemma of our times'. Not quite: most women who face it have neither her opportunity to have built up savings nor as good a CV to wave when they come back.

Her decision was much discussed, though she herself refused interviews. 'Working mothers are as familiar with feelings of guilt as they are with exhaustion,' said Jeremy Paxman, introducing a discussion on BBC TV's *Newsnight* in November 1994. 'Such a high-profile decision reopens all the old arguments about the conflicting demands we put upon women.' Then he interrogated a cheerful woman solicitor about her 'remarkable' lack of guilt. It marked the transition of the topic from women's mags to feature pages to serious news. The other woman in the discussion, there because she was making a decision to stop work, said wistfully, 'You can't have it all – that doesn't mean I don't want it all.'

Much of the media attention exposed how little we seem, still, to understand the issues around women, childbearing and work. The choice isn't just between executive burn-out and staying home watching *Play Bus*, though the decision to wouldn't be easier even if it was. Although I've talked about the growing understanding of reconciling family and work as a social, indeed Europe-wide, challenge, some of the arguments still put seem more 1970s than 1990s. The focus, still, is on the individual woman's decision, as if it were a free one. The father's role is not subject to the same scrutiny. While mothers' employment has been much examined, the recent review of research on families and employment notes, we have 'far less information on fathers' or 'their preferences and attitudes to their own employment'.[32]

The Institute of Management survey in 1994 which showed the number of women managers had fallen for the first time in twenty years was considered surprising by very few commentators, since the pressures on managers and the hours they work seemed weekly to intensify. A 1990 study of recruitment to management practices in forty-five companies concluded that 'informal and unaccountable' practices reproduced race and sex discrimination. And a 1994 study concluded that 'stereotypical views held by male managers of women playing secondary or support roles' were common.

In Helen Wilkinson's 1994 report for the think-tank Demos on young women and men she comments on a decreasing interest among young women in marriage and children and says that women are resentful of the slow pace of change: 'The mismatch between a culture of high aspirations and institutions that are failing to deliver is causing acute strain,' she says; 'the optimism of younger women over the age of 25 wanes a little – a product perhaps of encountering obstacles'. She goes on to say: 'The costs of women's caring role in trying to reconcile career and home is well documented. In the light of these experiences it is no surprise that younger women are emulating the distant role models of successful female managers and are being much more circumspect about when and whether to have children.'[33]

An *Independent* editorial soon after Ms Hughes's choice became public commented: 'In the relentless search for efficiency, there appears to be less time for activities that are not directly geared towards work productivity. So producing babies has become more of a handicap than ever for "career" women.' Nevertheless, it concluded by saying that for middle-class high-achieving women this was a personal not a social matter: 'There is little the Government could or should do. These are not exploited low-paid workers but educated and ambitious women who are making their own choices.' Yet another no-win situation – were they low-paid and unambitious they would after all get no more support, from the government or the *Independent*.[34] There was no comment that middle-class men might also have to choose – because they don't.

Analysis by the Family Policy Studies Centre (FPSC) in April 1995 of the OPCS projections of increasing childlessness, and the flurry of press and public comment around it, also suggested a greater polarity, a re-emphasised need to choose. Greater career problems and opportunities were seen as contributing to greater childlessness, alongside the cost of childbearing and the failure of society to be child- and family-minded. This is a change policy-makers should be alert to, Ann Condy at the FPSC argues: women may be involuntarily childless 'not because they are infertile but because they are forced by a variety of circumstances to delay or forgo childbearing'.[35] The British Organisation of Non-Parents emphasised the need to support the choice not to have children as socially responsible. They have also said that women show they are serious about work by not having children. An important factor in increasing childlessness, Lady Howe, who chairs Opportunity 2000, commented 'is that many women do not believe it is viable to combine having a successful career with having children.' Although some companies were introducing measures to help women combine work and family responsibilities 'such arrangements are still not available for the great majority and employers alone cannot be left to address the issue'.[36]

A changing climate of opinion and possibility is reflected in employment statistics. The number of women who told the Labour Force Survey they were 'economically inactive' because they were looking after families, which had fallen steeply since the question was first asked in 1984, rose again in 1991 and 1992 and although it fell again in 1993 it remained higher than in 1990. The number of men who said they were looking after families had more than doubled since 1984 but was still tiny in comparison to the numbers of women.

Policy and Politics: a Serious Double-bind

Senior management and politics are the two areas which emerge again and again from studies as hardest to combine with bringing up children. Harriet Harman is a conspicuous exception among senior political women in that she has young children; famously, she was seven months pregnant when she first became an MP in a 1982 by-election. What makes that possible, she says, is having a London constituency so she can see her children every morning and night. Less than half as many women MPs have children as do women on average. Women managers are also less likely to be married or have children than their male counterparts: in one study they were twice as likely to be separated or divorced as their male colleagues, and if married more likely to be in a two-career relationship and thus less likely to be able to draw on a spouse's undivided support.

Angela Eagle, Labour MP for Wallasey, has had the useful and at times frustrating role as a member of the Employment Committee as it, for most of 1994, examined issues for working women with children. The very positive and useful report which followed their deliberations in March 1995 was due in no small measure to her input. She says she regularly goes to meetings where she's the only woman and understanding of women's issues is minimal, but shrugs and says it's just something you learn to put up with.

How individual experience matters in policy development was made clear to the committee by Diane Abbott MP, who is a single parent with a young son. 'Because out of 650 MPs, 600 are men, it is very hard to get men to take the question of childcare seriously, but I assure you, if all of you had to get up at six, dress a two-year old, give him his breakfast, tidy the kitchen, get a two-year old to nursery, and come in to work, you would be less concerned with the narrower points and more concerned with the question of policy.'

Angela Eagle has been interested in politics since she was very young and made her first political speech in the 1970 election campaign when she was nine. She joined the Labour Party on her sixteenth birthday, along with her twin sister. 'It is what I've always wanted. I like helping people in my constituency. I like being able to say what I think, having a platform for that. I like being a role model, it's tremendously satisfying.'

Did she think she would have children herself? 'It would probably be impossible in this job – you'd have to find an amazing man anyway.' Being so conscious of the difficulties 'would make deciding difficult – and I don't think I'd find it possible on my own. But who can predict?

'This job is very much full time – there are tremendous pressures on your time from all directions. There's a whole job to be done in the constituency and then another here – it's hard to see how children could possibly fit into that.' It's no different, she said, from the conflict that any career woman has: 'and women in Scandinavia didn't have'. The members of the committee had gone on an eye-opening fact-finding trip to Denmark and Sweden. 'We met women in parliament there who just didn't have the conflict we all take for granted,' she said, a little wistfully. 'It shows the extent to which social policy could change things. It shows you what's possible – safe state childcare, now second and third generation women in full-time careers, and women having two or three children, not forced to make a choice.'

Neelam Bakshi was, when I interviewed her, a regional councillor in Strathclyde, the Scottish region centred on Glasgow, a role which because of the region's size and sizeable budget is very demanding of time and energy. She also works part time for the Inland Revenue and is the winner of the first Emily's List award for women in local authority politics. Soon after I spoke to her she lost the nomination for her seat in the reselection process for the new unitary authority. A number of women councillors have also lost seats to senior male politicians and this has caused a lot of anger, particularly in Neelam's case since she was the only Asian woman councillor.

Her daughter Ambika was seven when Neelam won her Maryhill seat but already a political veteran. When she was a baby and toddler Neelam had continued the political commitments she had begun at university, campaigning in a general election and then becoming chair of her local Labour Party branch. 'I would just take Ambika to meetings with me, she'd sit at the end of the table with crayons' – it's clearly a warm memory. 'She got quite choosy about which meetings she would go to! I think for women in politics the younger you go in the harder it is to choose between family and politics. I was in the fortunate position that I already had Ambika and I'm grateful because if I hadn't I would still be wondering when I could.'

She seemed deeply weary when we talked. 'Family life, a decent working life, some sort of economic independence – add on top of that the attempt to do something in the public world, to create change and to act politically ... and it's a killer.' Ruefully she adds: 'but I'm not sure how much I'm tired because I'm a woman and black and how much I'm tired because politics does that to you anyway! It doesn't matter what you do, you can't satisfy everybody and people always notice the meeting you didn't go to – and they notice the battles you lost, not the ones you won.'

Isobel Lindsay is a veteran of many political battles. She has been active in politics since her teens, with CND and the Committee of 100, became a SNP councillor in Glasgow at 25 and stood unsuccessfully for Westminster on several occasions. She is Convenor of the campaign for a Scottish Parliament. But it is attitudes to married women working that have changed most in recent years, she thinks, rather than to women in public life. 'Astonishingly so – whereas jump back 20 years, jump back even a dozen years ago and you'd have heard "women shouldn't be working, they should be staying at home looking after their children". *Nobody* says that now!' Isobel believes that women's role in public life has actually diminished in recent years, as a consequence of increased employment. Public life drew on the time and skills of women at home either with children or whose children had grown up. Now the idea of managing three things is too much. 'Women in public life played a minority role certainly but it was not *worse* than now.'

There was greater prejudice about the idea of someone running for parliament who had young children or was pregnant, as she knows to her cost from one election campaign in the early 1970s. But she remembers, giggling, the night when the SNP lost a crucial by-election and their fortunes began to wane. 'I saw the writing on the wall. I had wanted to have another baby but I thought really this could be a terribly crucial time in Scottish politics, and I couldn't ... That night I went and took my pills and threw them in the bin and said, good!'

Giving up either work or politics when she had children was never in question. Growing up a clever girl in a working-class home she was too conscious of the achievement of having got a good job to let go of it. 'It never occurred to me that I would not have children and it never occurred to me that I would give up my work or my politics. I saw that for a woman to take a career break meant there was no guarantee that you would be able to come back in and therefore the important thing was to try and keep it all going. I would just guddle through somehow.' And so she did, working as a lecturer at Strathclyde University, and holding a number of senior offices in the Scottish National Party. She was lucky, she says. 'I managed to have all three children without missing a single lecture. I didn't want them to say, "We've got all that extra work because of her having children." The timing was fortunate. Yes, you felt you had to prove something.' Her husband was 'supportive – though not in terms of doing lots of work around the house – his work was very demanding … But at least we could go to meetings together.' There was family help from her parents at weekends, a neighbour did childminding: 'it worked out fine'.

The Third Option

Women are finding their own ways around the obstacles which still stand in the way of women seeking to combine bringing up children with a satisfying working and/or public life. Those who have support and formal policies in their organisations to back them in so doing remain a minority, though a significant one because they provide paths for other parents and other firms to follow. And, logically, it is only women who have the support and saleable skills to carve out their own solutions who can do so. But more are finding resourceful and imaginative ways round specific problems. This fits well with the functional and intellectual flexibility we are now being told the modern workforce requires of us, yet it is not usually part of discussion of the 'working woman's dilemma'.

It was one of the things I talked about with with Reena Bhavnani, who described herself as having 'a half-foot' in City University, in London. She is self-employed, doing training and consultancy work on women's employment issues. She has worked independently for almost ten years. It fits in well with being a mother – she has two children Anil (6) and Anjuli (4) – though that wasn't her initial

99

reason. 'I don't like organisations very much ... It is very flexible but it is not part time, it is more than full time because it can't be anything else, really. But yes, the flexibility is wonderful.' Her first child was born when she was 39 and it is this possibility of delaying childbearing that she identified as the main personal change for her, something she didn't feel she could have even a decade earlier. 'I would have felt that there were some starker choices to be made ... whereas it was possible to leave it, feeling that it had to be right time and that it wasn't yet ...

'I like the work do. I am very busy, very stimulated. I feel that my work has an impact. I feel proud of that and I love having my two children. I have a partner who is very supportive, who loves his children and will spend lots of time with them so I am able to go away, I am able to do lots of things.' Though she worries that by doing so much 'I can't do things really well. I would like to do my work really brilliantly and I want to spend time with my children and my partner and see my family and cope with this and that – I just feel I can't do everything and I wish I could.'

Although she recognises that the tension between love and work is still an issue for many women it has not been so for her. 'The process of emigration ... does something around how critical it is to be able to survive and therefore how important education is and that if it didn't work out in other ways I could still do this work, that was really important. The question was not about whether I could combine being a woman and having children with my work but that I would always have something – something that would ensure economic and emotional independence. That was very strong for my parents. They felt with three girls, and the kind of stereotypical views that people have of women of South Asian origin, it was drummed into us really strongly how important it was to do well here.'

Marian Bell may be an economist who can tell you what interest rates are likely to be doing a year from now, but she says she doesn't know the cost of a loaf of bread: 'I never do the shopping.' She and her husband, a psychiatric social worker, share domestic tasks and the care of their two young children, both working full time but with an overlap in hours. She has the higher salary. Her partner's mother comes to look after the children, Zoe, five, and Catherine, two, for the main part of the day. Marian works from 7 a.m. to 3 p.m.; these hours are possible because the main part of her job is commentary and analysis 'to set them up for the day', which means mainly early morning meetings and assessing data which has come in overnight. She emphasised that she had been supported by management in making the arrangement.

'If I hadn't got this I'd be working much longer hours. Certainly people doing similar jobs are working much longer hours, and if I was a trader it would be harder. Yes, they really do arrange to be woken in the night.' When I asked her whether it would be possible to do her job part time she laughed and said, 'My colleagues think I do anyway – because I do eight hours and go home'. Yes, being a mother slows her down in career terms. 'But you can't have everything. I really enjoy my job, that could easily become my whole life. And I really love my family and that could become my whole life as well, and what I have is a compromise where I manage to have two worlds and two lives'.

As women, we have to create our own models as we proceed. 'There are an awful lot of people doing an awful lot of small things differently which all adds up. More women, more variety of people and more ways of working, in terms of the way things are structured and the hours worked, the more alternatives become available then the easier it becomes for other people.' The key to sanity, Marian reckons, is good time management and accepting you can't do everything, but she does worry that 'because you're fitting two very different things into one day means that you can't do either of them properly, perhaps. I'm not sure I spend enough time with my children and I'm sure I would be achieving a lot more at work if I was able to put more time into it. It *is* tiring. But I think that's the price you pay – of course it's worth it. You have to pay the bills and I'm lucky that I'm in a job that I enjoy so much.'

She reckons she is 'fairly confident'; not by nature but she has become more so. 'I know what's important to me, what's really important to me. Perhaps having children gives me more confidence – at the end of the day work isn't the most important thing to me, so it gives me the confidence to go out and do things at work.'

What is very good, Neelam Bakshi said, 'is the growing awareness that the choice is not whether you're a mother but what kind of mother you want to be – instead of being told, "Well there's only one kind of mother and that's the sort that stays at home and looks after the child until they go to school." It's opened out the possibilities. The last time I went to London my daughter said, "You know, Mum, I don't really like you going away – but then I think about what it is you're doing and it's OK." '

Some of the same themes are still apparent: the woman who is back at her desk/on the studio floor a few days after birth and shrugging it off; women who find both lack of childcare and the opposition of their men means that they have no choices. For economic and personal reasons the need to choose between work and having children is being re-emphasised in the 1990s. And more women are not having children, some of them because it seems to mean giving up so much they have worked for. But we take for granted now that women will play a part in the public world as well as the private, and most do. We know that work and love shouldn't be opposing choices, even if in practical terms they still may be for many women.

Many women are facing real, everyday difficulties and greater pressures. But more are finding ways round them – gaining from our multi-faceted lives and contributing more because of them. Many women are refusing the polarities and finding new and creative ways round the obstacles which still stand in the way of women seeking to combine bringing up children with the rest of their working lives. It's a workaday version of what American philosopher Mary Daly calls 'the transcendental third option': refusing either/or and carving out something else altogether.

Chapter 4

From Richer to Poorer to the CSA

I felt like an anthropologist at the 'National Bridal Fair'. For while we talk about new women and new men and theorise the 'post-modernist, post-feminist sexuality of the video generation,'[1] here in the Scottish Exhibition Centre you felt it could have been any time in the last fifty years. Marriage may be drifting out of fashion but if you do it – at least for the first time – it means serious money and ritual clothing. Held as well at the Alexandra Palace in London and the National Exhibition Centre in Birmingham, these are the trade exhibitions of the wedding industry – turnover £7.5 billion according to *Wedding and Home* magazine. Dresses of embroidered tulle and silk dupion are only the start: then there's the veil, the lingerie, the hosiery, the flowers, the shoes (hand-embroidered, for prefer-ence), the rings, the necklace, the bracelet, the bridesmaids' necklaces and bracelets ... Though such variations as the sinister Salome are available (bra in hand-beaded gold silk tissue and ivory chiffon harem skirt) the Victorian silhouette and symbolic shining white – or at least cream – remains dominant: prices from £400 upwards.

You could hire a white Belgravia Landolette with the number plate VOW 1. Or a photographer good at brides with just a tasteful inch of cleavage (fully inclusive, £595). You can sign up for a Nutri-Metics International Makeover, only £5. Or collagen treatment for ageing skin. In the Ladies two women, mother and daughter, were scrubbing off their makeover with exclamations of disgust. Outside two young women were trying on veils, incongruous over their jeans and leather jackets. The Slimmers stand was right next to Celebration Cakes. (*Relate* didn't have a stand.)

The people who come through the door are counted in 'bride' numbers, as in 'we expect 1,500 brides at Birmingham ...' What do grooms want? I asked, after a long explanation of what the discerning bride would be looking for, from an undoubted expert. 'Oh they choose the cars and well, mostly they nod a lot and grunt a bit.'

Mainly women came, some with a man in tow but more often mothers and daughters. The average outlay on a wedding now (again according to *Wedding and Home*'s 1994 survey) is £8,000. That's why you need 'peace of mind with wedding insurance', though you can't get cover just for changing your mind. Perhaps it isn't surprising that 1993 saw register office weddings outnumber church weddings for the first time: at least it saves on cash and effort.[2]

For all that nobody *intends* otherwise, how many couples really mean 'till death us do part' any more? 'Till something serious, perhaps. Fewer couples make such vows. Marriage is no longer taken for granted. The rise in cohabitation has been one of the strongest social trends over the past twenty-five years, particularly since the early 1980s, and accounts for some – but not all – of the drop in the marriage rate. Now more couples live together before marrying than not, but few do so permanently. Whether that is now changing again, and how different living together is from marriage, are questions of some interest. But most people still do marry and most who haven't still expect to, although there is conspicuous confusion and ambiguity about what marriage is for and what we should expect of it.

'Marriage today is regarded as a partnership of equals,' Lord Keith said in October 1991 when he and his fellow Law Lords confirmed (for England and Wales; Scottish law had already been changed) a married woman's right to refuse sex with her husband. And that is what most couples now say marriage should be. As Penny Mansfield at One plus One says, since 1970 both legislation and a changing climate of opinion have altered how we see marriage: 'an expectation of equality between men and women in public life, reinforced by legislation, soon became transformed into expectations of equality in private relationships between men and women'. But how true is it in practice?

There is a continuing difference but also considerable confusion about how the husband's and wife's roles are now seen. New perceptions are needed, but how are they to be created? L. B. Rubin wrote in 1983: 'We know that the old ways are not for us, but have no clear picture yet of what the new ones will be. We know there's a new vision of masculinity and femininity, but can't figure out how it fits each of us.'[3] A decade earlier expressing such uncertainty would have been against the grain of the times: we *knew*. A decade or so later the question is still as relevant, and the answers – except for a minority of couples who have consciously chosen a traditional division of labour – no clearer. There are issues around defining what a successful marriage is now, and what's better for you, what's better for the children, which cause real conflict and were not as significant even ten years ago. People are making modern marriages work or not – and the question of equality, or at least perceived equality, is writ large across the divorce statistics.

Good Wives

Little Women has been remade for a contemporary sensibility, but are there still Good Wives? When Cherie Blair, one half of a conspicuously egalitarian couple, made a public display of wifely admiration after her husband's first party conference speech a *frisson* of alarm ran through women in the liberal newspapers of the land. (Soon afterwards there was concern in the less liberal papers about whether Cherie really wears the trousers, which should have reassured us.) What's expected of a wife, at least as publicly expressed, has changed relatively little. The appeal of being single or cohabiting is described precisely *against* the perceived wifely role. 'You don't have to cook, clean, serve others' sexual desires, propagate, affiliate or placate if you don't want to,' *Cosmopolitan* declared, in a celebration of 'single power'. 'There must be more to life than the struggle to cook and intermarry.'[4] More than 'the tepid pleasures of the marriage bed,' says Linda Grant, in *Sexing the Millennium*: '... taking a walk on the wild side is the way we differentiate ourselves'. 'I made it clear to him that I wasn't just some wife and mother,' said a woman lawyer, of someone she wanted to impress.

'I like my own space, I can do what I want, when I want,' Amanda Ward, a thirtysomething painter and illustrator told *Cosmopolitan*. 'I can do what I want and go where I want. I never have to think "Perhaps he won't like it",' said 23-year-old law student Liz Moore. What was striking about the *Cosmo* women interviewed on the advantages of being single was that, though these were the affluent, assertive young women you'd expect the magazine to feature, the descriptions of live-in relationships they gave were almost word for word the same as the descriptions single mothers I've spoken to, in infinitely less advantageous circumstances, gave of the relationships they'd left.

Some of the reasons women give for cohabiting rather than marrying – independence, being able to go out and do what you like – strongly suggest that wifeliness has yet to be given any new egalitarian definition. One cohabiting woman told Susan McRae: 'I always feel if you're married you've got to do what your husband tells you, whereas if you're living together you can go out and do your own thing without asking permission.'[5] To take the role of wife is sometimes seen now as a conscious gesture against a prevailing egalitarian orthodoxy. Part of the appeal of fundamentalist Christianity is an appeal to 'traditional' sex roles; some couples put the words 'to honour *and obey*' back into the wedding service. How many busy women haven't sighed: 'What I need is a wife'? You have to say 'wife' rather than 'partner' or the idea wouldn't work. Wife still equates to self-effacing values. The wife's is the supporting role, her task to reflect her man at twice his size. The trouble is, as someone said, he reflects her back at half of hers.

I grew up surrounded by good wives. They were like Martha in the Bible story, bustling and self-righteous with immaculately scrubbed doorsteps and even the backs of their cupboards, should you care to look, proclaimed their spotless virtue. But without a minute for such subversive, time-wasting things as feelings or, goodness me, ideas. But, as I also noticed as a child, all their hard work and goodness didn't seem to get them very far. Theirs was the sort of work that had to be its own reward, for it brings little other outside heaven.

The public/private split depends on the work of the good wife. But who else will do it? As Penny Mansfield broke off to say, 'people *do* need to be cared for'. A good wife will not only deal impeccably with all of life's little problems, most of which require the skills of union negotiator, light engineer, educational psychologist and systems analyst, but pretend that none of it was any bother.

It is important not to to let women's work be invisible, especially what has come to be called 'emotional housekeeping'. It's easy to overlook it and – unlike who does the washing up, which has been the subject of numerous surveys – no one measures the emotional work women do: making the world go round, oiling the interpersonal wheels at home and at work. Like housework, if women go on doing it more or less adequately, then men won't try – but if we stop, things are liable to get messy; messier than maybe we can stand. There *is* a general ideal that support and care in a relationship should be reciprocal – it's just that mostly women are better at it. Few women I've spoken to, wives, ex-wives or researchers, seem to believe it can genuinely be so, though they recognise that some men are trying.

Towards the end of Fay Weldon's novel *Affliction*, written after the end of her own marriage, the main character, a beleaguered wife, talks about 'the gap … the space between the world as it ought to be, and the world as it is; between what you think love and marriage and babies is going to be, and what it turns out to be, and its proper name is Disappointment'.[6] 'The gap' is the site of many of our troubles: women, Weldon thinks, fall into it often, pushed by men. *Affliction* is a book about women and men and power, and the destructive power of therapeutic ideas and techniques in unscrupulous hands. Weldon suggests that therapy's currency is about filling that gap; that we are increasingly using therapy to try to make our lives and our expectations of life line up, when we had better settle for a more robust acceptance of life and love's limitations. Expectations of egalitarian relationships have only widened that gap, made it more conspicuous, less 'natural'. Weldon's gap should be named after her – it is a geological fault in human relations.

In early January 1994, a month of political scandals for John Major's government, Lady Caithness, wife of a junior minister who was reported to be conducting an affair, committed suicide. That she was, on her parents' account, so distraught over the possible end of her marriage that she killed herself could not be other than deeply troubling. It seemed a nineteenth-century tragedy cutting across the truisms of the twentieth. She was described by her parents as 'a totally supportive, loving wife. She was the ideal that the Conservative Party believe in and only cared for a true family life.' Perhaps our times get the political scandals that best illuminate them. This death seemed to crack open the political use of marriage and the family. Lady Caithness was described as loyal, sweet, gentle, self-sacrificing, dutiful ... Her mother said: 'My daughter supported her husband as a politician ... My daughter wanted everything for him'.[7] Isn't that still what wives do? Faced with marriage breakdown, how then is a good wife to hold on to her self-respect?

Soon afterwards a *Network First* television investigation looked at 'Women Who Kill' – five women who have killed violent partners, including Sara Thornton and Emma Humphreys, who was imprisoned when she was 16 for killing a rapist whose violent jealousy was the nearest thing to love she had ever known. It was insightful, heartbreaking. All but one of these women had tried to be good wives – to men who in any other circumstances would have been recognised as monsters and locked up. These were women who had stayed despite appalling cruelty and humiliation. Serious threats were the main reason they hadn't left; so was lack of help. But their investment in the relationship and the identity it brought was also part of why.[8]

In summarising the reasons why women don't leave violent men, Professor Rebecca Dobash emphasises that the factors they must consider are no different from those facing any woman considering divorce: economic reasons, whether they have dependent children, where they will live; the way a woman's identity may be wrapped up in being a wife and mother; the social pressures to keep trying for the sake of the children; all the encouragement to blame ourselves for relationship problems; and the remorse and promises not to do it again, which they want to believe, as we all would. Only the threat of even more severe violence is different. Battered wife syndrome is a controversial concept because it pathologises what may be a reasonable response to unreasonable circumstances.[9] But I wondered at the time if something similar happens to good wives after years of self-effacement and serving the needs of others. Perhaps we should posit 'good wife syndrome': its causes and consequences may rarely be so extreme, but there may be an equivalent incapacity to recognise what is happening to your self-esteem and capacity to think and act for yourself.

If all domestic violence was as extreme and as visible as that which receives media attention or has been the subject of a Scottish Office campaign of social advertising, and the Women's Aid *Stand by Your Man* film, there would, in a sense, be less of a problem. No police officer would dismiss it as 'just a domestic' or any GP accept 'I just walked into a door, doctor.' Everyday violence is not just about 'battering'. There is no clear line to be drawn between kinds of violence against women and children. Emotional violence and systematic intimidation and control of women, sexual attacks and child sexual abuse are all familiar parts of domestic violence.[10] Rape in marriage is a crime; child abuse is a crime; they go almost wholly unreported and when they are, both have minimal conviction rates.

It is immensely important that domestic violence should be finally, very visibly, on the agenda. But one woman told me how 'for years I suffered from emotional abuse and dismissed it as "not that bad". When I finally got to Women's Aid they welcomed me with open arms and confirmed that I was truly abused. I had felt so much a fraud because the black eye and cracked ribs were missing.'

She feels strongly that the message must be: '"All altering of behaviour through fear is abuse." Fear comes in so many ways. Emotional abuse is the most potent because even the victim can't recognise it if the internal logic of the abuse has been set up carefully – and it is.' When she tried to talk to her husband he said, '"But I never laid a finger on you." Hundreds and thousands of men say that.'

Few marriages exhibit power relations which are as extreme, or as dangerous but the extremes can reveal values that underpin more ordinary relationships. Inequality is now a major reason for marriage break-up: while most women now expect equality in marriage, very many men expect continuing dominance, or at least a kind of routine priority to their needs and acceptance of their view of things – the liberal rather than authoritarian version.

'Equal Enough'

Penny Mansfield has been looking at the lives of a group of couples who married in 1979.[11] Most of them have children now 'and there's not a lot of equality,' she says. 'Some couples claim to be 50/50, but when you look at the detail of who does what, they're not.' Couples who come closest are those well enough off to buy in help, 'with money to paper over the cracks'. Fairness is the word she prefers to use because what is crucial in whether a marriage survives or breaks up, she argues, is the couple's own idea of equality and the 'fit' between it and what actually happens: how near they get to the degree of fairness and sharing they expected. It's more, she says, about 'wanting to be equally valued, so it's not so much the detail of who does the washing up as a sense that what I contribute and what you contribute are of equal value'. Ideas of what's fair are a movable feast (one woman found it in him bringing her tea in bed on Saturdays and Sundays: 'one more cup of tea than my mother ever got') but at whatever level it's usually viable, she says, until there are children, which 'completely upsets the structures on which that fairness has rested'.

As this and other research shows, the idea that marriage should be a partnership of equals is widely held. In practice people need to settle for 'equal enough'. A lack of fairness or workable equality is almost inevitable, given the structure of working life and the way in which we organise bringing up children and other caring tasks.

'Children exacerbate the issues you have to deal with anyway. So if these things haven't been thought through or you're not very good at communicating or managing conflict then the arrival of the baby exacerbates that,' Penny says. Equality, understood as each partner doing half the breadwinning, half the domestic work and half of caring for children, is almost impossible to achieve because of the way the world works. 'It is difficult to get an organisational structure that makes it possible to live that way. So you work out what you can do within whatever constraints apply. Marriage and parenthood are different institutions, and parenthood works to reassert traditional divisions of labour between the sexes.' For both parents to have a full-time job can bring immense strains, and the most common compromise is for the woman to work part time. 'But then it's easy to fall back into the old pattern. It's very frustrating for couples trying to put egalitarian ideas into practice.'

The ideas have grown faster than the structures that could support those ideas. So there seems to be a double contradiction in marriage now: between the expectations of men and of women and between expectation and reality.

Living Alone

The increase over the 1980s in young women living independently is striking, as are the lower rates of childbearing I looked at in the last chapter. There has been an increase in the proportions of all young adults living alone, sharing with others, or remaining at home with parents, but these patterns are more marked for women.

Population Trends reports a 10 per cent fall in the number of young women married or cohabiting between 1981 and 1991 and an almost corresponding increase in women in their twenties living as head of their own household. The fall in the proportion of women in their late twenties living in couples with children is even steeper. The proportion of women and men living outside a family unit has also increased for ages 30–49, but not as steeply.

In 1991 just over half of women aged 15–29 were married or living with a man compared to more than three-quarters in 1979. The number of unmarried women aged 30–45 rose by a startling 70 per cent over the 1980s, which the rise in the actual numbers of women in the age group only partly explains: just over three-quarters of that age group were married in 1991 against 85 per cent in 1981.

The increasing number of young women living alone or outside couples is part of a wider tendency to live either alone or in smaller groups. Average household size in Britain is steadily becoming smaller – more single-person households, fewer households with five or more people. In 1971 18 per cent of households consisted of one person; in 1993 this had risen to over a quarter. There is a clear increase in people living alone among virtually all groups, though Pakistani and Bangladeshi people are much more likely to live in larger households. Women over pensionable age are still the largest group of one-person households, and that is expected to continue. Elderly women, particularly those aged 75 and over, are more likely than men in the same age group to be living alone.

Another increase, in women and men in their mid- and late twenties remaining in the parental home, is commonly ascribed to economic difficulties but also shows a move away from formal marriage, which has only partly been replaced by cohabitation. This statistical analysis points to a striking 'postponement or rejection of marriage by young people'.[12]

Living Together

But which is it? Cohabitation has become a hot topic among social scientists. By the early 1990s about 70 per cent of heterosexual couples lived together before marriage, and almost all did before re-marriage. Marriage rates are falling fairly steadily and although part of that is due to more people living alone there has been a dramatic rise in couples living together. In 1979, the year that the General Household Survey first collected information on cohabitation, only 3 per cent of single women aged 20–49 were cohabiting, whereas more than a quarter were now doing so in 1989.[13] In the 1960s one in four remarriages was preceded by a period of cohabitation, today about 90 per cent are. Asian women are an exception to this, and other black women are also less likely to be cohabiting than white women. Couples are most likely to live together in London, and least likely to in Scotland.

As one woman commented, in a generation or so the dominant wisdom has reversed. 'Our parents' generation saw living together outside marriage as wrong; we would worry more if our children did not.' Kathleen Kiernan and Valerie Estaugh, in their research on cohabitation, report that only 18 per cent of under-35s would advise a man or woman to marry without living together first. But if cohabitation has become usual before marriage, most couples either marry or break up after an average of around two years.[14] This may not be the case in even five or ten years' time: the still recent pattern may be changing again as more couples continue to cohabit when their children are born.

Although there have been earlier periods when informal or social marriage has been common, with assorted rituals and colloquial names for it (for example 'living tally' in Wales and 'living over t'brush' in northern England), this marks a significant change in the twentieth century and raises interesting questions. Are marriage and cohabitation becoming equivalent – the Scandinavian pattern – or has cohabitation become a prelude to marriage, as in America and Australia? It may be that the greater caution about entry into 'permanent' partnerships shown by those currently in their twenties reflects the economic uncertainty of the 1990s, a decade that shows similarities to the 1930s. This suggests delayed marriage rather than rejection. In either case, is this significant in terms of how people relate? Are cohabiting couples more egalitarian?

Greater acceptability of pre-marital sex is, of course, a precondition for increased cohabitation, and pre-marital sex is now more common than not. But when in contemporary times did it become so? During the 1950s and until 1965 it's estimated that less than one-third of women had sex before marriage. (The poet Philip Larkin seems to have been right – sexual intercourse *did* begin in 1963). During the latter half of the 1960s that proportion increased although it remained under half, but 'during the 1970s the figure increased dramatically so that by the end of the decade the great majority of young women had experienced sex before marriage – 80–90 per cent'. It was not until the first half of the 1970s that the pill became widely available to single women although it was increasingly used by married women from the mid-1960s.[15]

It is probable that the proportion of couples who live together but who never marry is growing. Pregnancy or deciding to have children has been a key reason for moving from cohabitation into marriage. The steep increase in the numbers of couples having children without marrying strongly suggests it is a lessening reason. But, as both Kiernan and Estaugh's and Susan McRae's studies of cohabiting show, couples move at all stages from cohabiting into marriage, and some do so even when their children have grown and left home, which makes the picture hard to read.[16]

As cohabitation becomes common, marriage becomes a decision. A couple cohabiting in the 1970s were not only likely to be unusual but to have made a decision *not* to marry. In the 1990s it may be just that they haven't got round to it. That it 'hasn't seemed important' to marry seems a greater social change than does principled opposition to marriage.

Analysis of 1991 census data by Fran Wasoff and Janet Sultanan suggests that the small number of couples who don't marry on the arrival of children is concentrated into two very different groups: the very poor and the well-educated and fairly affluent.[17] This pattern indicates, Fran Wasoff suggests, 'that marriage is still very much an economic contract – women who don't need it and women with nothing to gain from it don't bother with it'. The majority of cohabiting couples with children have significantly lower incomes than married-couple families, are more likely to be on benefit, and are more likely to be unemployed. Inheritance and property law and pension regulations favour married women, as did maintenance arrangements until the Child Support Act of 1991. Even where large estates are not in question it may be that marriage remains an economic transaction still most often practised by those with something to transact.

Susan McRae's study makes clear that children's security remains a very important reason for marrying. But she also says: 'Cohabitation, and in particular, motherhood within cohabitation, challenges the long-standing ideal ... that has depicted marriage as the best – or only – place to have and rear children.' But is it a *very* different place to rear children? Only a small number of the mothers in McRae's study were long-term cohabitees and of those only a fifth were against marriage on principle. For them questions of independence and the feeling of marriage as a trap figured large: 'if I want to leave I can just leave', as one woman said. But how far this greater *sense* of freedom is realistic for women with children is emphasised by an ambivalent answer one woman gave: 'I just feel more independent not being married. It would be easier to go if things went wrong. No, actually, it probably wouldn't be any easier now that we have a child ...' The group for whom it is easier are high-earning professional women – not a high proportion of mothers, but a group who are slightly more likely to be cohabiting.

Many people believe a less traditional domestic division of labour, and power, is more likely in cohabiting couples – but this seems to last only until they have children. Germaine Greer has argued that 'Because the commitment in cohabitation is under continual negotiation most aspects of the relationship are more equitably handled.'[18] Kathleen Kiernan's evidence is that cohabiting couples were more egalitarian than married couples when childless, but once they had children the two groups 'were indistinguishable'. Susan McRae found that 'children have a greater impact on household organisation and marital harmony than the legal arrangements that bind, or do not bind, couples to one another.'

The differences between cohabiting and married couples may be more conspicuous to statisticians than on the street where they live. A couple where the man makes the financial decisions and the woman does the washing and picks up the children from school, for example, does not suggest any sort of social revolution, even if they aren't married.

The Housework Gap

What fine talk about equality in relationships mainly comes down to in the end is housework. The domestic division of labour has been the subject of a number of studies. Like attitudes to equality in marriage, they almost all show a shift in attitudes which is not fully followed through in who does what: rather more couples nowadays seem to think male participation is a good idea than actually manage to put it into practice. While most couples now say domestic work should be shared 50/50, most actually only manage 75/25. Also consistent, in most attempts to examine who does what at home, is that men say they do more in the house than their wives/partners say they do.

What men's share of domestic work is still considered to be was made wonderfully clear in the unusual *Ginder* v. *Ginder* court case in April 1994, in which a disabled woman sued her husband so that the insurance would pay compensation. Mrs Ginder had been badly injured trying to rescue a child who had crawled out on a garage roof and had been able to do so because of a faulty window latch. The Ginders had what was descibed as a 'traditional' division of labour: she looked after the house and three children under six, he did the DIY. She had asked him ten times over three months (sounds familiar?) to fix the lock on the window through which their child eventually, dangerously crawled. Mr Ginder said in court: 'we had an agreement that she would deal with the nappies ... and I would deal with the sink'.[19] How often does the average sink need unbunging?

There is a wider spectrum of division of domestic work in male/female households now. The more traditional division at one end contrasts strongly with those couples who try to share equally in domestic work at the other. The latter group has grown while the former has shrunk, though the second-group, when it can, often depends on paid help to bring standards up to what 'a good housewife' might aspire to. There are clear generation differences as well as considerable differences according to whether or not there are children. Most people are ranged along the middle ground – weighted towards the woman doing most. Even if she doesn't do it all, she organises it all. Women dealing with undomestic men face two big problems, just as you do with children: the first is that the effort of getting them to do it falls to them, the second is that 'it's quicker if I do it myself'.

But if the gap between what people say and what they do is often considerable, nevertheless a traditional division of labour is now seen as right in only a minority of households, whereas in 1970 it was an almost unquestioned norm. Who does what in the house remains closely related to hours of work, and pay. A greater domestic role limits many women's options in paid work, just as men's longer hours of work excuse and limit their participation in domestic work and childcare. Where the woman works part time, research shows that the domestic workload of women is usually no different from that of the full-time mother and housewife. What unemployed men say about their inactivity suggests, Paul Gregg says, that family roles are 'almost unchanged'. Kate Sandham found that unemployed men did more with children, but not much more domestic work.[20] I talked to Judy Aitken about that; she is a single mother and community activist in Drumchapel, an area of Glasgow with very high rates of male unemployment and even a scheme to teach men to cook and eat healthily. She thought it naive of me even to ask: 'well maybe *some* do – the odd one … ' Mainly though, she and others indicate, male unemployment creates more problems for women than it brings them an additional hand around the house.

The greatest signs of change are reported in families where both partners are working full time. But, according to evidence given to the International Year of the Family parliamentary hearings, even in such families women still do almost all of the domestic work almost three-quarters of the time.[21]

The historian Rosalind Mitchison summed up women's changing lives in two words: 'Washing machines!' Looking at various studies of domestic work, Patricia Hewitt concludes: 'women in Britain and most other industrialised countries are doing less housework than they did 30 years ago and men are doing more', but she also notes that women, even if they are working outside the home, are still doing more than men.[22]

There are clear differences in the tasks men are more likely to share. Shopping and washing up are most popular, across the whole of Europe. Taking children to and from childcare comes next – but only a quarter of men regularly cook or clean. Even in Denmark, with its egalitarian attitudes and high rate of women out at work, researchers find that sex roles are more conservative in families with young children, with women in about half of families solely responsible for cooking and cleaning; only in a third did women and men share these tasks.[23] An increase in egalitarian attitudes can actually make this situation feel worse: not only are you the one who picks up the socks from the bathroom floor but you feel you are uniquely pathetic in doing so ... And how come other women's men are so wonderful? (But is it true?)

Hope over Experience?

In Britain, though most people still marry, the marriage rate has been falling since the 1970s and despite a slight increase in the early 1980s and again the early 1990s it still is: in 1993 the number of first marriages was the lowest recorded this century. Divorces have more than doubled since 1970; 1993 saw the highest number of divorces ever in England and Wales though not in Scotland. Nevertheless, Britain has the second-highest marriage rate in the EU. Part of the reason is that most men and women who are divorced subsequently remarry, even though the rates of remarriage have also declined sharply. In 1971 one in five marriages were remarriages; in 1991 there were fewer marriages but more than a third involved at least one previously married partner.

Headlines like MARRIAGE UNDER STRAIN have to be understood as strictly relative. You might equally plausibly argue that marriage is proving resilient. The statement 'Marriage ... is in decline: over half of today's 25-year-olds have cohabited with a partner compared with 1 or 2 per cent 25 years ago', in a newspaper report of the British Household Panel survey in 1994, needs several pinches of salt. A high proportion will go on to marry that same partner; one in seven within a year, according to the survey in question.[24]

Age at first marriage has increased steadily and there are many fewer teenage marriages, but British women still marry on average younger than women elsewhere in the EU, and Asian women marry earlier than other British women. The overall average age at which women first enter a partnership has not changed as much because of the time people spend cohabiting first.[25]

The proportions of black women who are married is generally much lower than for white women and is just under 40 per cent of women in their early thirties. Among Asian women, marriage rates are higher. Early marriage is much more likely for first-generation Asian women, and Asian women born in Britain have marriage rates similar to white women of their age.

Divorce rates, like fertility rates, have to be described as 'the divorce rate so far'. Comparing the number of divorces in a year with the number of marriages is not strictly meaningful, since there is no actual connection. 'They may,' Fran Wasoff comments, 'tell us something about the social landscape but not much about the likelihood of individual marriages ending in divorce.' For people marrying under 30 the rate of divorce within twenty years of marriage has quadrupled over the past three decades and the proportion of partners divorcing for a second or third time has also risen steeply.[26] Divorce actions are overwhelmingly brought by women:[27] however, a legal settlement rather than informal separation is usually in the interests of women with children, particularly in terms of house ownership or tenancy. Using that fact to argue that women are voting with their feet needs some care. (It may be true, nevertheless.) Women are almost always the parent with care when children are involved. Children are involved in around half of divorces.[28]

Divorce is now part of social patterns in a way it was only beginning to be in 1970. 'Divorce is now "normal" and is as entrenched a social institution as marriage', as a recent Scottish Office report said.[29] Divorce law was liberalised in 1969 and 1984 in England and Wales and in 1976 and 1985 in Scotland. Mores and attitudes have changed to cope – reflected in the rather tortuous process by which the Church of England is moving towards allowing remarriage for divorced people, as the Church of Scotland and the Methodists already do, and further reform of English law.

One in five children born in the early 1970s is estimated to have experienced the divorce of their parents before they were 16. Almost one in four would do so if the divorce rates of the late 1980s continued, according to 1991 estimates which were also used by the IYF. Highly relevant to any discussion of divorce must be the fact that half of fathers lose touch with their children after divorce.[30] But the predicted increase may never actually come about. You have first to marry in order to divorce; the increase in cohabitation necessarily has an effect on figures for divorce if not for overall relationship breakdown. The higher age at first marriage is also relevant: divorce is strongly linked to marrying young.

Rates are no longer rising as steeply, however. The Scottish rate has been consistently lower than in England and Wales and has fallen slightly in recent years from a peak in 1985. The most recent figure in England and Wales was the highest to date but the increase since the mid-1980s has been much less steep than it was before that and the number of divorces fell between 1985 and 1990 before rising slightly again.[31]

Divorce has very different financial consequences for women and men and plays a major role in increasing family poverty – nor is this changing very much now with more women in employment.[32] As I've said, the proportions of single mothers working decreased over the 1980s despite increases in married women with young children working.

Most working married women depend on other family members for childcare. When most work that 'fits in' is low-paid the poverty trap creates a serious disincentive to single mothers working, particularly if that working future may not feel very secure. And maintenance has not been a significant part of most single parents' income.

Freer to Leave?

That women are now more willing to leave men they think are bad for them or their children was one of the two big changes which were most often mentioned by women I've talked to. (The other was more opportunities but more work.)

Judy Aitken talked about her own life. She is, as I've said, a community activist in Drumchapel in Glasgow and a warm, confident woman who knows her own mind. It is difficult to imagine it when she says there were months when she was too depressed even to bother to get dressed, let alone leave the house.

Five years ago Judy was on trial for attempted murder; she stabbed her alcoholic ex-partner while defending their youngest child: 'I would let him batter me, but not the kids.' It was, she now says, a turning point: 'it got me to look at life in a different way – I've never looked back.' She got a two-year suspended sentence, broke up with her man and, with the encouragement of a local health visitor, though she took some persuading at first, became involved with the Community Health Project. She was a single mother with one child when she met her partner and a few months after he moved in with her she found she was expecting. 'He was beginning to drink more often than usual and giving me the odd slap'. She threw him out and, 'realising what kind of a situation I was in', asked for a termination of the pregnancy, 'but being a parent already I couldn't go through with it'. She took him back and the violence got much worse. Still, she had another baby. 'You may think that is odd, but if you are living with an alcoholic you live in a love–hate relationship. When he's sober he is fine. When drunk he's an animal.'

Drumchapel, like most estates, has its good and bad streets. At the edge of the city, dominated by three great grey blocks of high-rise flats like giant standing stones on the rough hillside, there is a kind of exposure to the elements, a lack of shelter from whatever life brings. The project was formed because the estate has such serious health problems: life expectancy of five years less than the Scottish average and ten years less than the affluent neighbouring suburb of Bearsden, a perinatal mortality rate twice the Scottish average and a rate of hospital admission in the first year of life twice the Glasgow average. Poor, damp housing is linked to the high number of childhood respiratory problems. Women trying to bring up children there 'either get angry and get active or you go under,' Liz Lamb, the health visitor who works with the Project, thinks.

Getting involved in the Project, Judy says, saved her sanity, perhaps her life. 'I was going through a bad time. I'd always got depressed but it was getting mair frequent.' She had been given prescriptions for tranquillisers but had never wanted to take them, having seen other women become addicted. 'Coping with the kids and his drunkenness all took a toll on me. I never went anywhere, he was drinking day and night. I was just stuck in the house with the kids and him.' As important as anything was that as a volunteer at the project she could use the crèche, or the project would pay childminding costs, giving her both a break from the children and renewed purpose. What made the difference was 'people – knowing they were involved in all the same problems, people round about you. Well I suppose you could work that out sitting looking out the window – but it was being part of the human race again.'

One in three families in Drumchapel is headed by a single mother and poverty, loneliness and depression are endemic. When the project carried out a pioneering community health profile in one part of the scheme, with local people themselves doing the research, they commented on 'the amount and intensity of human misery we uncovered and how willing people were to talk about it', and the frighteningly high incidence of various phobias and serious depression (among 38 per cent of respondents). There was also a very high incidence of stressful life events, including sexual abuse, bereavement, domestic violence and marital breakdown.[33] The street on which the survey was centred, Kendoon Avenue is sometimes called the Canyon because of its high buildings and the traffic rushing through – more than twice as many women live there as men.

'I don't see much equality,' Judy says. 'I see women working long hours for not much money. Women having to go out to work because men haven't got jobs and coming back to dirty dishes, dirty weans and dirty houses.' The problems caused by unemployment and so many women bringing up kids on their own are the main things that have got worse: 'that's not much forward, is it?' But surely women being able to leave difficult and violent relationships is better? 'But it's all to do with strength in the end.' Her ex-partner's violence made her stronger in a way, Judy says; strong enough to leave. But around her she sees women who can't manage it. 'There's a lot of women stuck indoors, staying with violent men, without the strength to break away.' Her biggest concern is that there is so much less for young people: 'no jobs, no benefit'. She hopes her own elder daughter will stay on at school – 'she'll no' make the mistakes I have'.

Joyce Macmillan and I went to see a play written by another

Glasgow single mother, Frances Corr, put on by a semi-professional theatre group, themselves mainly single mothers. It gave a vivid picture of how it feels with bored and energetic kids 'stuck in on a Sunday 12p in your purse and it's raining'. But still 'the crucial change *is* women's willingness to leave men who they feel are bad for them,' Joyce said afterwards. 'It seems to me that there is a huge assumption which is almost stronger among working-class than among middle-class women that something has changed – that women have got rights they didn't use to have.'

'Women are just not putting up with lousy relationships any more, they're not putting up with men who are violent, they are not putting up with men who are completely unable to meet their emotional and sexual needs,' says Ellen Kelly. 'Women are not putting up with things they used to,' Penny Mansfield agrees. 'Women are recognising that they have a right to a certain kind of life, they are not going to carry someone who doesn't give them something in return.' That used to be economic support. But if you don't have to marry to bring up children, 'marriage has to leave you better off – it's got to be good enough for you to see you're getting something out of it'.

'What's changed for women today? The freedom to leave – that's the big change,' said Frances Corr. 'Twenty years ago you just didn't do that, did you? I don't think women had time to think, they just got up – not everybody had washing machines, you could spend all day washing or cooking, no time to think. You knew you were gonna grow up and find a man and get married and have kids – and now it's throwing us all into confusion because we are finding that women wanting things differently disna' fit into what is convenient, the convenient family unit, somebody bringing in the money and somebody bringing up the kids ...' What hadn't worked for her was 'this stifling domestic thing – nothing was your own, not even your bed. I lost myself altogether ... I found myself again by leaving. People say you're being selfish – but at the end of the day it would have been bad for the kids if I'd stayed. Kids watching violent scenes – not at two and four. I have that wee cosy fantasy – but in reality it would have been worse for them. People know that when they decide to leave – all you're looking for is some kind of peace.'

That women are now more likely to leave their men was

mentioned repeatedly when I asked women about change. It is undoubtedly true, yet an argument that seems to put the decision, the choice, and therefore the responsibility, squarely on women's shoulders. It's rather more complicated than that, I think.

Discussion of divorce is polarised: either, it seems, it's feminism and women with fancy ideas at fault or it's feckless fathers unwilling or unable to stick around – but that's probably the women's fault too, as succinctly summarised in a comment in one *Sunday Times* article: 'Women are more independent, men are more emasculated.' The liberal orthodoxy is expressed in a comment from the think-tank Demos: 'the main driving force behind the weakening of the old-style nuclear family is neither social mobility, irresponsible individualism or recklessness. It is the gender revolution, the transformation in the position of women, their life opportunities and choices.'[34]

Well, yes and no. Women's economic dependence within marriage, male behaviour and the refusal of many men to adapt to the changes women are making in their lives must all be brought into the frame. Women who would have preferred to stay if only they could have, and women who have been deserted must not be ignored. Even recklessness, fecklessness, individualism and social mobility all play a part. Even if women are leaving they may still dream of a decent man, one who'll take his share of responsibilities. Susan Galloway, an Edinburgh councillor and community activist who is a single mother with two teenage sons, said that women bringing up kids on their own in the scheme where she lives 'are making the best of limited choices. They probably see themselves as mair independent minded than their mothers – as much as you can be when you're struggling on Income Support. But I think a lot still have an idealised romantic view that one day they'll meet the perfect man who'll whisk them off to a nice three-bedroomed house and a Marks and Spencer chargecard and take all the responsibilities off. I still have that – that one day somebody'll come along and wheech everything off my shoulders!'

'The main reason there are so many lone parent families here is because there are so many abusive men,' says Judy Aitken. 'They are violent or drunken or on drugs – it means massive problems for relationships. And poverty, unemployment – that's why people split up.' Women, taking almost all the responsibility for bringing up kids, still have a clear purpose even if not an easy life, 'still have to worry about their responsibilities. The men don't, they've got nothing else to do, they can't face the next day ...'

Joyce Macmillan commented that 'women defending themselves and their children against really unsatisfactory domestic situations – it really is an epochal change.' But the paradox of this change is that it's not just about changes in women's employment, although it's often presented as if it was. Because a lot of women who are exercising that right don't have much money, don't have good jobs or any jobs, don't have any support beyond the social security system. It is about rising self-esteem – albeit recovered often at the point of desperation. Women see themselves as having as much right to work and likelihood of working as men, even if in their own case that may scarcely be true. Even if they are struggling and trying to keep their kids together and only working a few hours at the supermarket checkout.

If it was only fear, economics and the probability of social opprobrium that kept women in some marriages, was that really better? If women are able to say: 'I won't put up with this', then that seems to me an advance, though it is won at a cost to the individuals concerned, including – though not always – the children involved. If Income Support is an incentive to leave, what sorts of circumstances are we talking about staying in? If a lot of break-up is due to the changing aspirations of women, Penny Mansfield says, 'I don't see that changing – so are men going to be able to respond? What's also crucial is whether people are prepared to work through the difficulties of modern relationships ... Nothing will change until men change – and until we change our approach to difficulties in a relationship.

'There is a loss of guidelines and certainties and boundaries. We are seeing a redefinition of marriage in terms of what women want, which is partly about redressing the balance – but men find it threatening. Women are better at managing change; men are terrified by it.' Where the consequences of change, and divorce and separation were writ large is in the furore that followed the introduction of the Child Support Act.

The Dad Tax

The protester carried a placard which said it all: DAD TAX. And underneath, confusingly, I AM INNOCENT. Of what? What had innocence or blame got to do with it? But in his mind they had: and hadn't most of these angry dads done only what society seemed to allow – love, marry (or not), have children, but when it wasn't working out, move on? Only someone changed the rules.

The Child Support Act and Agency is the most significant state intervention into sexual politics since divorce was initially liberalised. It has been the first serious attempt to intervene in the changing family and as such has brought further change to women's lives. It is about saying the state will not pick up the tab, but also that parental responsibilities continue even if the parent's relationship does not, and irrespective of 'fault' in that break-up. When the Bill went through parliament it was unusual in having all-party support. *The Times* (not untypically) welcomed it as 'a sane though modest step'. A year into operation and all anyone could agree on was that it was a mess. Children, divorce and money – it was bound to be inflammatory. But not *this much* trouble, surely.

Fathers' and second families' organisations multiplied and marched on the CSA from one direction; a women's group who disagreed that families need fathers attacked from another. MPs were inundated with complaints, CSA staff were threatened. One Parent Families, although with increasing reservations, was the Agency's only friend. After just over a year and a half of increasingly besieged and increasingly incompetent operation, and various smaller bones thrown to the absent fathers' lobby, the DSS in January 1955 announced twelve changes.[35]

'Parenthood is for life,' Margaret Thatcher said in July 1990, introducing the intention to set up a maintenance agency. 'Legislation cannot make irresponsible parents responsible. But it can and must ensure that absent parents pay maintenance for their children.' In the event, it couldn't – at least not via an Act and an agency made law unusually rapidly and designed in such a way as to give it no real constituency of support among those it directly affects.

If, as was repeatedly argued, mothers and children on Income Support were able to keep the first £15 of maintenance payments (as they are on Family Credit) before the pound for pound clawback from their benefit, then single mothers, and the children in whose name this was being done, would have been a bit better off and resistance to the Act would have probably lessened. (Ninety-six per cent of funds collected in the Child Support Agency's first year went to the Treasury.[36]) But the DSS and Treasury stood firm. More than the loss of cash (an arguable amount, given the additional costs of recouping maintenance which followed from the Agency's unpopularity) it seemed the government thought any advantage to the 'parent with care' would be an incentive to them to stay on benefits and not seek work – an idea which increasingly became a social policy obsession.

'The whole process will be easier, more consistent and fairer,' Mrs Thatcher said, introducing it. 'Our aim is to give the lone parent back her morale and her confidence.' In practice only a small minority of parents with care stood to gain anything, and most were worse off. The White Paper claimed the proposals would 'serve to advance the welfare of children'. The major children's charities and the Child Poverty Action Group found that instead the Act was contributing to rising child poverty. Four other reports which monitored the CSA's first year all concurred that it was making a difficult situation worse.[37]

Among continuing problems is the requirement, with a 20 per cent penalty for non-cooperation, to name the father unless 'good cause' not to is claimed. Guidelines which say that demonstrable risk must be taken seriously have been heeded in some areas but in others women who have suffered violence in the previous relationship have been put under pressure to co-operate. In general, Marie Cairns at One Plus in Glasgow says, CSA processes and interviews have brought 'a tremendous increase of anxiety and uncertainty' to single mothers' lives. 'It means the possibility of totally upsetting their whole lives again, and their children's lives.' In her experience, CSA officers have been unable to grasp how vulnerable many women feel: 'If your only income is Income Support, you're completely at their mercy, you really are.'

The children's charities are worried because of ill-effects on relationships between former partners, between fathers and children and between 'first' and 'second' families, all of which are crucial to children's well-being. 'In contrast to the (at best) very uncertain financial gains ... the emotional *costs* for both the children and their mothers were unmistakably clear.' Where previous relationships had been difficult – not unusual for separated couples – research commissioned by the charities found 'these difficulties were exacerbated by the advent of the CSA'. It has meant reopening old wounds and increasing the adversarial feelings in separated parents.[38]

The Act defines what matters most in the father's role as paying up: no change there. A large part of the problem is that many men – most, probably – simply can't afford to support more than one family. 'No father should be able to escape from his responsibility and that is why the Government is looking at ways of strengthening the system for tracing an absent father and making the arrangements for recovering maintenance more effective,' Margaret Thatcher said in January 1990. Unwilling 'return' to the family, reducing the father's role to a financial obligation (important as it undoubtedly is) and basing a parental relationship on compulsion, is hardly likely to be other than damaging. If the anger shown by the protesting fathers is any gauge, the family problems which may result from the new measures will hardly be a gain for the child. The children's charities' research found that 'hostility against what the Agency stood for tended to be directed against the mother'. To some children the CSA has brought final loss of contact with fathers who have moved away rather than pay.[39] And since the CSA arrangements for 'shared care' are rigid they may actually discourage some absent parents from having children for holidays and weekends if they see that this is not reflected in maintenance as assessed.

One key change in January 1995 – deferring 'indefinitely' the middle-income cases which would have come within the Agency's remit in 1996 – was an attempt to evade vote-losing middle-class male anger but at the expense of a small group of working women who might have benefited and now will not do so. It made clearer than ever, despite continued talk of 'moral principle', that the government's primary concern is to cut the cost of welfare. Even 'new' single mothers with jobs, who stood, in theory, to gain, were soon disenchanted, finding that long delays and complications made it hardly worth their while – 'six months' hassle for £3 a week,' as one woman said. 'I made a big mistake in getting a part-time job in the summer and I applied for Family Credit' another woman explained. This automatically triggered a CSA reassessment of the court maintenance award cutting the agreed payment considerably. 'All the CSA has done is to support him and leave us shattered.' The family is now on I.S. Her story highlights not only the Agency's limitations but its failure to achieve the government's own purposes.

But these were not the main problems highlighted by most critics. Two searing reports from the Social Security Select Committee, a damning account from the Ombudsman and a National Audit Office report found almost *half* the Agency's assessments wrong. As One Parent Families said, rather sadly: 'The Ombudsman overlooked the real failing of the CSA – that it is not delivering regular, adequate maintenance to lone parents and their children.' The argument was dominated by the absent parents' lobby and all but two of the concessions the government made were to it.

There were genuine grievances: in particular the failure to take account of 'clean break' deals, and the lack of positive incentives to co-operate. But at the height of the campaign you could be forgiven for cynicism. Three-quarters of absent fathers weren't paying maintenance when the CSA was conceived: the ranks of protesters now included those who could do so self-righteously. Some of the protesters' claims were exaggerated or unsubstantiated, which led to real problems in distinguishing 'can't pay' from 'won't pay'. As the chaos of the CSA's operation became evident, non-cooperation spread: DSS sources were reported as saying many fathers were refusing to pay but that the CSA was not acting for fear of the outrage that would result. This was rewarded by the decision in late 1994 not to pursue the 350,000 cases which had been on the CSA's books for more than six months.

Although the Agency made some serious mistakes its operation has hardly been helped by an average of forty formal complaints a day and harassment by some campaigners. The government now expects the new appeals procedure to be swamped.

The absent parents' campaign had major media support: nothing about the Agency was too trivial to attract the attention of the hacks. That the CSA makes 'impossibly high cash demands' was the core of the argument. But in many of the cases which were publicised, with lots of fathers happy to tell journalists the details of their family budgets, you could only conclude that they didn't really know how much it costs to look after kids. Whether the new maintenance rates were unreasonable depended entirely on the point from which you viewed it: £100 a week, for example, is going to be missed from a pay packet – but it is not a lot of money to support a couple of kids and a person at home looking after them.[40] Maintenance had been too low – the average weekly payment was £30 – which is part of the reason why demands jumped so steeply. The idea that it is unreasonable for a father to pay a sizeable share of his income, after housing costs and those of a second family have been met, to support his children tells us more about what we see as reasonable for a father than anything else.

The protests revealed a double standard: when he says he can't afford to pay, the child's needs *don't disappear*. The assumption is that the mother will pick up any slack: he can't manage, she will have to. One woman made the direction of concern clear: the courts, she said, 'always looked at whether he could afford to support the children. No one has ever asked me once can *I* afford to bring up two children on my own.' Much has been made of the fact that fathers can no longer afford to visit children from first marriages: a wreath laid at the door of CSA HQ in one demo said: 'In memory of the daughter I once knew. The CSA say paying maintenance to the Treasury is more important than seeing you, sweetheart.' Was it ever, from the child's point of view, a *choice*?

No equally forceful, effective voices have been raised to object to thousands of women and children living in poverty. A great deal more passion has been generated by the men who are now having to pay more than they think they ought than about the children living on the breadline. There had been real problems, but fairness for two-family fathers rapidly became an issue in a way that fairness for lone-mother families has never been.

But if the anger of absent fathers was considerable, there was little incentive for anyone else to actually support the proposals – Ros Hepplewhite, first head of the Agency, talked about social justice and equality. Resistance was, she said, to 'a cultural change. Many people in the past have not seen paying maintenance as an ordinary financial obligation, but as if it was to some extent optional. If they have paid anything at all they have seen themselves as entirely responsible parents – but in reality they have been pursuing a lifestyle they could only afford by passing most of their responsibilities on to the State.'[41] But there was a further shift which makes it hard, even so, to see the Act as progressive – a reversal of the recent trend in which women have moved from dependence on the financial support of individual men to dependence on benefit as a stepping-stone to greater independence once their children were no longer in need of full-time care. The Act brought a serious erosion of a woman's right to benefit, to which she would be entitled if she was single and childless. If the maintenance contribution is greater than the allowance within Income Support for the children then it continues to be subtracted pound for pound. This reinstatement of women's economic dependence on men from whom they have separated is humiliating and regressive and has nothing to do with equality; yet it has gone virtually unremarked.

For women who want a genuine 'clean break' there is no longer that option. Any support through the benefits system she seeks in bringing up her children will trigger CSA intervention into her affairs and family life. Women no longer make the decision about pursuing maintenance (as they could do under the previous 'liable relatives' regulation): the Agency does.

But the inequities and failures of the old system had become accepted. Introducing the Act meant a massive reversal of the tacit social acceptance that a father's responsibility was contingent, a mother's natural – that fathers paid up/stayed involved if and only if they wanted to. Good fathers did so, perhaps, and those who didn't were hardly approved of: but compare that to the difference in public perception of good and bad mothers to see how relatively little weight it holds. That more than two million children in single-parent families in Britain were getting only 10 per cent of their support from maintenance payments revealed a widespread refusal to care, financially and otherwise.

'If men wanted to pay for their children or see them they would be doing so,' one woman said to me, wearily. She was worried that her ex would want more access now he was being pursued for maintenance. 'I'm afraid he'll raise their hopes and then vanish again.'

As the Child Poverty Action Group says, 'it is still early days to examine the Act's full effects. The truth is that the Government has planted a time-bomb and its full social and political impact may not be felt for some time.'[42] That sexual and family morality would be affected was not to be doubted: but how? Some men might feel a greater commitment to remaining with a partner and children. Others might just ensure their 'flight from fatherhood' took them further away. Some women might decide that the trouble of trying to leave was greater than the trouble in staying. Some might be frightened away from claiming benefit and into low-paid or illegal work. The government has now reduced sharply its forecast for the growth in the number of single parents living on benefit. In January 1995 Peter Lilley told the House of Commons Social Security Committee that although the number of single parents on Income Support had been expected to grow by 100,000 a year for the rest of the decade, revised estimates now were for 20,000 a year fewer. Lilley said the CSA had played a role, by 'unearthing fraudulent claims' and floating some mothers off Income Support. He also commented, ambiguously, that 'it also seems to have resulted in slightly fewer people being in the position of being single parent families'.[43] It may have more success, and sooner, in changing behaviour than even Messrs Lilley and Burt had dared hope.

The whole sorry saga lifts the lid off the idea of the modern egalitarian marriage. Overwhelmingly fathers were absent and mothers 'with care'. I asked the CSA if they could tell me the proportion of parents with care who are women, which an informed guess puts at around 99 per cent. 'We don't collect the figures in terms of men and women,' a spokeswoman said, with what I suppose passes for political correctness, 'but as "absent parents" and "parents-with-care".' However, since in the population in general 10 per cent of absent parents are women 'we would expect our client base to reflect this'. The use of gender-neutral language only serves to hide a deeply-gendered reality. If women and men were equal in this country, if there was equal pay and opportunity at work, if we had good systems of child support and better ways of reconciling work and family, if most men took genuinely equal responsibility for their children, there would not even be an issue.

The principle that fathers should play more of a part in their children's lives after separation was supported by almost everyone – including many more single mothers than had been expected. High rates of divorce and separation with their consequence of poverty for children demand new measures and new policies. We needed to create a climate in which maintenance is not a readily evaded joke but an accepted obligation. Clearer and more consistent ways of setting child support levels were overdue. Yet in practice it was an unprecedented disaster. Divorce, when children are involved, leads to poverty – which is not right, but it is *not better* that this should impact almost entirely on the women and children concerned. Men are beginning to have brought home to them the financial consequences of divorce in a way women have known for years. There has always been a 'mum tax'.

Part II

Family Values

Chapter 5

Thinking about Families

1994 was the United Nations International Year of the Family and in the media it was clear that change in the family had become synonymous with 'the family in crisis'. The headings rapidly became familiar: 'single mothers, absent fathers, home alone kids, teenage pregnancies', to quote the introduction to a BBC debate on the family for IYF. Lack of discipline, poor school results, casual divorce, child crime ... Well-marinated prejudices were given an outing.

Other important questions about change have not been on the public agenda. They centre on the possibility of more equal relationships between parents and children, between women and men. To what extent has male dominance within the family been eroded, or are heterosexual relationships predicated on it still? Are single mothers more accepted? Is it easier and more socially accepted to live in a lesbian family? Or to choose not to have children? In other words, do women really have more choices, more freedom of manoeuvre in forming families, or not doing so?

Is it harder now to leave a difficult relationship, or easier? Is it any easier for couples who have separated to create workable ways of parenting which do not depend on their having a 'traditional' relationship? Are what social scientists call 'consensual unions' emerging as a new, more egalitarian form of relationship? Why do so many people marry for a second and even third time? Why are many more young women reluctant to marry?

You must, in this emotionally and politically charged arena, begin with definitions. Pretending that 'the family' is essentially one thing, or easy of description, is where the political debate starts to go askew. 'Family' is not a straightforward description of households or kinship patterns. Meanings range across a spectrum from those sections of the women's and gay movements which cannot use the word without the postmodern equivalent of waving garlic, to the veneration of Mum, Dad and two-point-whatever kids double-glazed with a thick layer of sentiment. Both ends of this spectrum see the family as the basic building block of society, either positively as an anchor, source of stability and responsibility, or alternatively as source of most of our personal and social problems, the place where patriarchal/capitalist values are inculcated. It is, as the theorists say, 'contested terrain' and the image which that phrase brings to mind, of charging willy-nilly across it wielding ideological lances careless of what we trample underfoot, is not inappropriate.

At one end the 'Family Right' believe the Conservative government has betrayed true family values. For example, Richard Whitfield of the National Family Trust believes, 'No culture has ever survived unless it has safeguarded the relationship between men and women for the procreation of children ... The neglect of children goes across all social groups.' He thinks we don't address it because of 'a crisis of moral courage among people in the know'.[1] Similarly Adrian Rogers, director of the Conservative Family Institute, lists cohabitation, rising 'illegitimacy', abortion and divorce and reported crime 'at record levels and rising', child neglect, truancy, under-age sexual activity and teenage drug abuse all as social trends which 'emanate from the breakdown of the family and the failure of men and women to live together and supervise their children effectively'[2].

Margaret Thatcher once, memorably, called hers 'an ordinary married family'. 'A nation of free people will only continue to be great if family life continues and the structure of the nation is a family one,' she told *Woman's Own* in 1987, showing a matriarchal tendency not otherwise apparent. And, famously, in what became known in Scotland as 'the sermon on the Mound', she said: 'there is no such thing as society. There are individual men and women, and there are families.'[3]

Scottish Office Minister Lord Fraser was sent out, shield in hand, to a conference on 'Changing Families' organised by Family

Mediation, Scotland in October 1994. 'Marriage still provides the best form of relationship for parents and children' he said firmly and 'the responsibility for bringing up children lies with the children's parents ... the state should recognise the privacy of family life and intervene only to the minimum extent necessary.'

'Few can doubt that the family is in trouble,' the leading ethical socialist, Professor A.H. Halsey, wrote in the *Sunday Times* in March 1993, casting his hat controversially into the ring. 'Nobody can doubt that parliament and people are now casting around for solutions to what is seen as a problem of endemic disorder, rising crime, intrusive squalor, spreading welfare dependency, collapsed community ...' He supported their editorial assertion that the nuclear family 'needs to be preserved and nurtured'.[4]

Tony Blair, in a televised interview in July 1994 immediately after he was elected leader of the Labour Party, made his family credentials clear, if not exactly coherent: 'There is a limit to what public policy can do, but it is important we recognise the family as the essential, stable social unit, and we attempt to do whatever we can to allow the family to develop in that stable framework.'

It's worth noting that the debate around 'the family' mainly ignores family forms and functions that do not include dependent children. All the media discussion I've looked at equates the family with bringing up kids. This may be part of a contemporary redefinition, though if it is, it is in opposition to the direction of population change.

Then there's added confusion because the word family is routinely used to mean one type of family: 'family breakdown' reserves it for what's seen as the unbroken sort, the Mum, Dad and kids variety. That 'family' equals 'heterosexual' was made very clear when the dubious notion of 'pretended families' was enshrined in law in Section 28 of the 1988 Local Government Act. The usage, 'the traditional family' is becoming commoner where the word 'family' would have been used on its own before, to differentiate it from the conspicuous others at the door.

Feminism, as its political historians Vicky Randall and Joni Lovenduski say, is almost by definition agin the family, although little has been said in public on the subject in recent years. Socialist feminists Michelle Barrett and Mary McIntosh, in a thoughtful if idealistic analysis, see the family not only as a primary site of women's oppression but as fundamentally anti-social: 'the family embodies the principle of selfishness, exclusion and pursuit of private interest and contravenes those of altruism, community and pursuit of the public good.' And, they claim, 'As a bastion against a bleak society it has made that society bleak ... in monopolising care it has made it harder to undertake other forms of care.'[5]

The International Year of the Family, very sensibly, ducked this one: 'There is no definition of a family,' they stated firmly.[6]

Playing Happy Families

I am happy to use the word family, mainly because my children have reclaimed it for me, and made me think harder about it. I live in one, and it is something I write about, in part because in so much of the public debate around the family the voices of women bringing up children are absent. Of course I use it inclusively. The habitual honeyed glaze over the term creates problems – like 'community' it has an overwhelming symbolic meaning. That, and its use as code for conservatism means you have to clear away a lot of fog.

The ideology of the family gets in the way of family life: it is hard to avoid trying to live up to phoney, manipulated images. In a close parallel to the way our own breasts or thighs or noses can only be inadequate in a world of airbrushed, pin-up perfection, so it's hard not to measure yourself against pervasive images of family life, with the same built-in failure. It is striking how persistent the tendency to mythologise family life is, how potent those myths are and how little changing. Despite everyone's knowledge that family life can be a mixed blessing, despite the commoner habit of cohabiting and the familiarity of 'reconstituted families' as they seem now to be called (an unfortunate phrase which makes remarriage sound like the more dubious sort of sausage), a 'proper family' must still approximate to the one which sells cornflakes rather than to the one we live in.

As Fiona Mackay said, people retain a well-developed capacity to hold contradictory positions: on the one hand, yes, marriage is the best place to raise children, but on the other, 'my Mary was right to leave Bill and she's doing a wonderful job bringing up the children on her own ...' Joyce Macmillan described it as a 'double culture – I think people do see marriage and a happy family life as one of the few remaining ideals. It is something that people dream about and advertise in the papers for – but it doesn't stick to the reality of modern life.'

It seemed symbolic when viewers of the BBC's *Good Morning with Ann and Nick* in June 1994 chose as their 'model family' a divorced single mother with a five-year-old daughter, a boyfriend who stays at weekends and an ex who lives 260 miles away and sees his daughter a few times a year. According to the programme's producer the viewers chose not only who they thought was the most attractive family but also the one they most identified with.

Yet when Julia Brannen and Peter Moss carried out their interesting and detailed study of how families with young children and two working parents organised their lives in the late 1980s, 'normal family life' was still understood by the women they talked to as the breadwinner/homemaker model – even though they themselves in dual-earner families were now actually the norm. Family life may be changing in significant ways, they say, but it is still not represented in new ways. For example women often minimise the importance of their earnings and give priority to their husbands' work, even in those few cases where they earned more. 'In the face of change, ideologies of family life are notable for their emphasis on stability and continuity,' they say.[7]

The family is an everyday icon, selling chicken nuggets and floor cleaners alongside messages of how to live. Images of happy family life still tug powerfully at the purse strings. Christmas focuses with a vengeance the dreams and delusions of family life: I went shopping and began to share the palpable anxiety; worried women in the aisles-full of glittering gifts. As it becomes less of a spiritual festival it beams hard in on ideals of happy families. Every image is riddled with nostalgia, holly comes from the tree not the supermarket and red-cheeked children make snowmen in defiance of global warming.

People have never before been so surrounded by imagery of what and who we are and might be, how we live, might live. The template is almost convincing – the warm, glowing house with 'real mums' making frozen chips (but what, I want to ask the copywriter, do unreal mums do?), and well-brushed, well-behaved children who are gloriously happy.

That last bit's the real killer. But children who sulk don't sell Sindys. Those women scurrying along Princes Street today are only trying to organise the kind of Christmas that in reality needs a team of professionals to set up for you – the designer decorations, added variations on turkey, and party scenes blessed with the harmony that in my experience only a gifted nursery teacher can achieve. As the merry tills ring, we buy hard – to replicate an event designed from half-flickering images of happiness. Charles Dickens was chicken-feed. Never before have family images been so professionally presented, so consciously manipulated.

Forms of Change

Changes in the family are a major and highly contested issue for the 1990s and the new century, central to the broad demographic, social and economic changes in Western society, both a cause and a consequence of women's changing lives and expectations. In so far as change is about, or includes, an erosion of male authority in and through the family it is resisted, though that resistance can be well-disguised.

Change may serve to disguise continuity. Patterns *are* changing, particularly if compared with the 1950s. But that change can be, and commonly is, overstated and oversimplified. It is characteristic of every generation to use idealised images of family life in our grandparents' time to compare with life today. The variety has always been greater than social mythology implies, but the family was also at its most stable in the experience of the pre- and post-war generation, from 1930 to the mid-1950s: 'half a century when family life probably showed more signs of conformity and outward stability than in any previous century for which records exist,' social historian Michael Anderson said. That is the 'grandparents' genera-tion' for the age groups from which most decision-makers come.

Diversity is the central characteristic of families today, Fran Wasoff, social policy lecturer at Edinburgh University, emphasises, even if one form is still in the majority. 'People move in and out of different family forms over their lifetimes, all the time thinking of themselves as part of a family.' The main conclusions of a new, detailed survey of British households is that change is a major characteristic of family life today: 14 per cent of the households studied experienced some change over the year, though children over 16 leaving home was the main change reported. 'Lone parent households were also especially likely to experience change as new partnerships were formed,' the survey says.[8]

A plausible liberal argument is that 'there is no such thing as *the* family, only families'. But if it is important to emphasise diversity, none the less 'the family' still has a major cultural presence, influencing social policy and commerce. We cannot sweep change under the carpet in that way. Change in how families are formed is often exaggerated, but it matters – perhaps most of all to women.

The control and manipulation of women's fertility and the circumstances in which we bear and bring up children are fundamental to all forms of authoritarian government. In democratic societies this is true primarily for marginalised women and those defined as deviant, but in no society are these wholly within the woman's control. It is the common ground of such disparate creeds as Islamic fundamentalism, Roman Catholicism, Chinese communism, and the Protestant fundamentalism which is influential in the USA and arguably a growing force in Britain. Possibly the *only* thing they have in common is the need to control women's fertility and child-rearing, whether by making abortion illegal – as in all Catholic-dominated countries outside Europe, in Ireland and, in effect, Poland, and most Islamic countries – or by forced abortion and sterilisation, as in China. To insistently situate the family outside politics, apart from society, separable from community, is itself a political statement.

Questions of definition and description matter, not least because of an urgent need for social policies which recognise and support 'the family' in its diversity. Can you have, as Shere Hite suggests, a democratic family?[9] The phrase 'dysfunctional family' which has slipped from therapy-speak into the broadsheets implies that we know what a functional family is. How far is 'functionality' dependent on the oppression of women, as many feminists would argue? Is it something inherent in family structure that leads to abuse? Can you have a (heterosexual) family which does not carry and reproduce current social meanings of sexual difference and male superiority/the authority of the father?

These questions, which feminism raised, had scarcely begun to be addressed before they were swamped by the 'family breakdown' debate, 1990s style: the focus on 'broken families', among other things, serves to imply that unbroken ones have no comparable problems. It is a powerful counter to women's aspirations for change to imply that those very changes are antithetical to the well-being of those she cares for.

It is no longer enough, nevertheless, to say that the family oppresses women. It's true, but what is *also* true is that for many women family life is something we have aspired to, in practice, and that it embodies values and a sense of identity. Women have wanted committed relationships, have wanted marriage, have wanted children. So either you reckon that an awful lot of women are deluded and self-deluding, as some women's liberation writing suggested, or you recognise that these are available if imperfect ways of meeting real needs.

And – the robust question – for bringing up children and caring for others in need of care, what other choices do we have?

We need to ask those questions again and we need to ask new ones. We need to recognise that the family is the major site of violence towards women and children: we must never forget that women are more likely to be killed by a partner or ex-partner than anyone else. We cannot forget that for children 'stranger danger' is the smaller part of the problem.

But we need to acknowledge that the family is also a place of comfort, power and refuge. This is something black women have said, arguing that the feminist concept of patriarchy cannot be unproblematically transferred from white to black male–female relations and that families provide an important site of support and resistance against racism in society. Although not consistently and undifferentiatedly, most women face hostility and discrimination and will feel the need for refuge. Whether, black or white, we always get it is another matter.

Just as our sexuality is, a source both of pleasure and danger, of power and vulnerability, so our relationship to the family is characterised by a similar tension: a source of pleasure and power, but also of danger – extreme, to the person, habitual, to the sense of self.

Thinking about families has to recognise this dual reality: that the family is a site of power and powerlessness, agency and restriction, happiness and oppression, identity and loss of selfhood. To focus on security and pleasure is to minimise male dominance and to further marginalise those many women whose experience is very different; to speak only of violence and oppression ignores women's experience of agency and love and choice.

Figures, Facts, Attitudes

The facts and figures of family change have become familiar: since 1971 the number of single-parent families has almost tripled; one in five families is headed by a single parent, nine out of ten of them women. Marriage is not what it was. The number of people living alone has grown rapidly. Most mothers now work outside the home as well as in it: in the mid-1980s the breadwinner/homemaker family became a minority form. Change indeed. On the other hand, women are still left holding almost all the babies – more are because of the steep increase in women bringing up children on their own (though we can't make the assumption that they had any less responsibility for their kids in a two-parent family).

Despite women's growing economic independence most women with children remain economically dependent on men: this is increasing because of legal and welfare changes, especially the creation of the Child Support Agency. Women, even women who are economically independent, remain within marriages characterised by bullying and inequality. Most people still marry even if they don't stay married: social pressure to be part of 'a neat couple' remains considerable.

'What do I call the woman my son cohabits with – my daughter-out-of-law?' Michael Anderson asks. He poses a set of questions for which in the past there would have been clear answers, often prohibitive. 'When in a relationship is it acceptable to sleep with someone, and how should couples signal consent? A student going home with their boyfriend or girlfriend – how many know in advance how their parents will feel about their sharing a bed? Do you commiserate or congratulate a woman on the day her divorce comes through?'

'If a man comes to live with a divorced woman who has children, does his mother become their grandmother? Can he, himself, be their stepfather if there is no marriage? If there is a marriage, does he, the stepfather, remain part of the children's family if their mother divorces him?' Penelope Leach and Patricia Hewitt ask, with similar purpose, in their report to the Social Justice Commission.[10]

We might add, can a girl be bridesmaid at her mother's wedding? What, if you see little point in engagement, do you say when two men announce theirs? It suggests a new parlour game, but these questions are about more than modern etiquette and sharply focus family change.

The crucial, hard to answer question is: what do we now think families are *for*? It would have been easier to answer twenty-five years ago; a lot easier fifty years ago. The primary function of marriage in maintaining a successful household economy has faded; there is a sociological and popular consensus, as far as I can see, that emotional satisfaction, love and romance, is what marriage is now about. But for how many women has that *really* been the main factor?

The answer to Michael Anderson's first question is partner. 'Partner', meaning spouse or spouse-equivalent rather than business partner, has come unusually rapidly into usage in the early-1990s, a sign of both linguistic need and social readiness. (It now appears on some bank credit card and loan application forms.) Spouse, I suppose, feels too old-fashioned, boyfriend/girlfriend too transient and teenage. Partner is a way of recognising long-term lesbian, gay and unmarried heterosexual relationships and of creating equivalence. It is also useful in the way Ms is – whose business is it anyway? (Since he works in Scotland Anderson could also use the phrase 'bidie in', meaning someone you live (bide) with, as a warmer alternative to the distinctly technical cohabitee.)

The answer to all of the other questions is that it depends rather more on the people concerned and what they want and how they get on, and less on compulsion – which has both positive and negative aspects.

Measuring Changing Lives

It seems important to say that I am writing this book in the middle of the pleasures and problems shared by most 'working mothers': 'women who juggle their lives', in *She* magazine's slightly smug phrase. I want to say so not because family relationships and work problems sometimes seemed like a conspiracy against my ever finishing this book, nor to bemoan my lot, but to allow reality to creep in. A final text usually shows little of the smudges and sometime despair. Writing this has been characteristic of most women's everyday experience of trying to get something done against a chorus of demands, of trying desperately to work out a decent balance between your own needs and those of kids, partner, mother, friends ... In family life chaos is less a theory than an ever-present threat. Children only come out in spots when you have a crucial meeting and sprain their ankles the day *before* you go on holiday, never the day after you get back. Tears and tummy-aches about going to nursery or school occur when you are most preoccupied and have least patience. There are times when trying to make things more equal seems more trouble than progress. Crises in my partner's life, money crises, flu, washing machine breakdowns ... One week there was a disco in the room I use as a study. I had the idea of a meta-system, rather like *Cold Comfort Farm*'s asterixes for passages of particularly purple prose. It would go something like this: * this was written after I had a row with my partner, ** this was written in the dental hospital waiting room, *** I began this in the café while Katie was at gymnastics but lost the notes ... You get the idea. Most of us have a domestic life. Yet we are supposed to pretend otherwise, or at least that it is a smooth affair, a matter of design decisions and dinner parties, an appropriate background to the proper business of life, which is of course work.

But this afternoon my children have gone out with their father to shop for clothes in the January sales, leaving me to try to think about the changes in family life that this is one small illustration of. Because that isn't such a big deal any more it illustrates change. A generation or so ago a father shopping for socks and tights and sweatshirts with two girls would imply a special reason why the mother couldn't: that she was ill or neglectful. As fatherly involvement nowadays it would still, I think, rate as more worthy of comment than going to the museum or playing football. (And, as they said when they got home, the changing rooms in Tammy Girl do not yet accommodate this social shift.) Parents who fully share practical responsibility for their children remain unusual, at least as much because of the economic underpinnings of family life as for reasons of belief and intent. Parents who try, who at least *think* sharing practical care is best, are no longer unusual.

In a broad European Commission survey of social attitudes published in 1991 people in all the EU countries were asked which of three arrangements of domestic and paid work corresponded most closely to their idea of a family: an egalitarian model with both parents having equally absorbing paid work and sharing household tasks and looking after the children equally; a family in which the wife's work is less absorbing than the husband's, and in which she takes on more of the household tasks and looking after the children ('the middle option'); and a breadwinner/homemaker family.[11]

In Britain the 'middle option' is how most people now live; in several European countries breadwinner/homemakers are still the majority. But the egalitarian model was the majority choice (41 per cent supported it), 29 per cent supported the middle way, and a quarter went for the 'traditional' option. The change in attitudes so measured is not equivalent to a change in behaviour. It is none the less striking evidence that there has been, as Kathleen Kiernan at the London School of Economics comments, a 'marked change in norms regarding the equality of women, and men's responsibilities in the family'.

Families made up of a breadwinner father and full-time home-maker mother plus children are now less than half of families with children in the UK, and families with children are a slightly smaller proportion of households (51.4 per cent as against 55.7 per cent in 1971). But seven out of ten births take place in marriage, and eight in ten children live in a family headed by a couple, three-quarters with their married natural parents. Two-parent 'original' families are four times as numerous as one-parent families, who in turn are almost three times as numerous as stepfamilies. There are important variations. For example, Bangladeshi and Pakistani households are much more likely to consist of couples with dependent children. The proportion of births to single mothers varies considerably across the country. There are also significant exclusions: lesbian mothers and any sort of gay families are not revealed by current statistics. But the myth of the nuclear family has been, if anything, too well eroded.

Facts about family change can be expressed in different ways to show different things, depending on what you pick out and compare with what. A cluster of myths, old and new, adhere to them. Figures are commonly used to highlight 'the crisis of the family': that one in three children is born outside marriage, for example. I've just used the same figure the other way round to highlight the continuing dominance of conventionally formed families.

I wanted to go back and look again at some of the broad statistics – with the particular advantage that material from the 1991 Census was becoming available. I piled volumes of tables and charts ever higher around me in the library, I talked to demographers and statisticians. And it all got more and more and more complicated …

Demographers are reluctant to commit themselves. They prefer the certainties of what they creepily call 'an extinct generation'. Fertility rates and marriage habits can fluctuate dramatically and at any one time change may seem to be more striking than it may be at the end of the period. Current low fertility is a good example of why caution is needed: fertility rates may be misleading when many women may be delaying having children rather than not having any at all. People who are cohabiting have an irritating habit of getting married just when they might seem to safely fit the category of long-term bidie-ins.

Journalists, however, are allowed to speculate, and although my major caveat is that the two-parents-plus-kids family remains more dominant than public debate would allow, population and other social statistics confirm a widening trend towards greater diversity and autonomy which, although there are significant differences between ethnic groups and also regional differences, crosses class and most social divisions. Fewer women having children, smaller families and a 'pervasive trend'[12] to living alone: the pattern seems to show more independent living for women at all ages. But that independence is cut across by greater caring responsibilities. It is part of a continuing move to individuation which is double-edged for women who have such responsibilities.

The 1980s and early 1990s, for younger women particularly, was a time of increasing change. 'Lonely career women' or 'sophisticated femmes seules'? – there were competing stereotypes. Lone parent families became not just a measure of diversity but themselves became more diverse. And there are an estimated 10,000 communes in the UK – both 1970s survivals and newer, mainly middle-class green households. New tribes and travellers broke most domestic conventions, though sex roles seem remarkably resilient.

Sufficiently uncommon to cause social awkwardness in the early 1970s, the glamorous divorcee could sell Volkswagens by the nineties. Though not many shops selling wedding dresses have been forced out of business there has been a weakening of social norms around marriage. A growing tendency to cohabitation-plus-kids shows at least a shift in the timing of marriage and may also presage a greater rejection of marrying at all. 'Shotgun weddings', common in the 1970s, have become almost a curiosity of social history. Four times as many conceptions outside marriage were followed by marriage in 1971 than in 1991.[13]

Since the social climate encouraged secrecy it isn't possible to say how many children grew up in lesbian and gay families in the 1960s and 1970s. Changing social attitudes mean more such families feel able to live on their own terms, or closer to their own terms, although far from all can. Writing in the lesbian magazine *Diva*, academic, author and mother Elizabeth Wilson says her subjective impression is that more and more lesbians are deciding to become parents, and that is an impression confirmed by a number of women I've spoken to. The impact of the women's and gay movements has been significant in allowing lesbian mothers and gay fathers to be open about their sexuality. But prejudice against lesbians may be stronger when they are mothers. The tabloid press remains eager to take up the case of outraged fathers, from a Scottish father of two daughters, John McKendrick's 'amazing-round-the-world mission to rescue them from his lesbian wife' to the limited weak complaint of 'gay dancer' Silvio Gigante who donated a syringe-full of sperm to a lesbian couple but 'didn't think it would work'.[14]

Elizabeth Wilson says wryly of an article in the *Independent* in September 1994 that it presented her and her partner (who were not named in it) as 'responsible, law-abiding professional women ... and even if we could never reach the exacting standards of heterosexuality, we were a jolly good second best'. The *Independent* article itself said that all names had been changed and was accompanied by a photograph of two women and a child taken from the back. The message was that openness was not an option, contradicting the acceptance in the text.[15]

Under the 1988 Children Act lesbian co-parents have been legally recognised. In July 1994, in a Manchester case which attracted national attention Mr Justice Douglas–Brown said that since the welfare of the child was his paramount consideration: 'the evidence pointed overwhelmingly to making a joint residence order.' The Lesbian Custody Project reported a number of other lesbian parents in England who had applied successfully for residence orders under the Act in early 1994. The legal position in Scotland is less clear and has yet to be tested. It is also now possible, though often difficult, for lesbian couples to foster and adopt.[16]

In September 1994 the Court of Appeal dismissed the case of one father who sought to overturn a residence order because his children were living with their mother and her girlfriend. The court ruled that being a lesbian did not make a mother unfit to care for children and this was 'not the sort of case in which the court could interfere'. A number of court cases in the 1970s showed that, contrary to most resolutions of contested custody, if the mother was a lesbian custody would go to the father. That has changed, but Rights of Women, the feminist legal collective, says it still depends a lot on the judge's prejudices and on class, ethnic background and how much the mother is seen as 'feminine' and 'respectable'. They advise women to be sure to get a good solicitor who has experience of lesbian custody cases. Stonewall say custody is more likely than five years ago, but lesbian mothers are still put under pressure. Some still think secrecy is safer.[17]

Estimates of 'reconstituted families' suggest they are around one in fifteen of families with dependent children, and that around half of stepfamilies also include children from the new partnership. The proportion is smaller than the amount of attention paid the issues of creating stepfamilies would suggest. Most are married-couple stepfamilies and a sizeable minority cohabiting stepfamilies. About three-quarters are natural mother/stepfather. Particularly interesting is that the proportion of stepchildren now is not so different from the figure of 5 per cent estimated for several earlier historical periods and has not changed as much as might be expected from the increased incidence of divorce and childbearing outside marriage.[18]

Family change in Britain forms part of a wider European pattern which, while not consistent from country to country shares many characteristics. Average family size fell throughout the European Union between 1970 and 1992 and European Union birth rates are the lowest ever recorded. But interestingly, in the prosperous countries of north-west Europe birth rates are rising again. The recent rise, by a quarter in the case of Sweden, follows two decades of low birth rates and there are questions about whether this is due to the policies which make it easier for parents to combine work with raising a family, or catching up by women who have delayed having children, or both. In contrast Spain and Italy now have the lowest birth rates in the EU, closely followed by Greece and Portugal. Germany is also among the lowest.[19]

The Greying Population

The greying population is almost always presented as a problem. As psychologist Dorothy Rowe says in her recent book *Time On Our Side*: 'like children, the elderly are not given a voice in defining their condition'. (This has been equally true within the women's movement.) But we are seeing an increasingly determined attempt to redefine age – ideas of the 'third age' and the 'young elderly' have growing currency, and ageing feminists are determined to refute the stereotypes of older women. If Germaine Greer's image of a serene if lumpy figure walking on the skyline with her dog ('just think, you can never know how happy she is') does not have quite the style of Keith Richard's declaring at 50 that you have to be old to *really* rock, it is perhaps more achievable. (Though Tina Turner gives hope to some of us still ...) Dorothy Rowe reports, encouragingly, 'that our fears about growing old are greatly exaggerated'.[20]

The 'greying population' is a major change affecting families and society, and affecting women most (even if a lot doesn't show – more henna these days than blue rinse). Greater longevity has brought changes in inter-generational relationships and in perceptions of age and is also credited with a role in divorce since 'till death us do part' is an awfully long time – now an average of close to fifty years. Many fewer people now die in childhood and young adulthood, and the elderly, especially elderly women, have a considerably extended life expectancy. There are now more three- and four-generation families and today's children are the first generation in which significant numbers know their great-grandparents. Many people in their sixties today have parents alive and needing care.[21]

This matters most to women, first because women are many more of the elderly, and because more women spend more of their time caring for elderly people, both professionally and in the family. In 1991 nearly 16 per cent of the population were 65 or over compared to 13 per cent in 1971 and this proportion is projected to rise to almost one in five in 2021. Men are slightly less of sixty-somethings than women; there are about two-thirds as many men as women in their seventies; but almost three times as many women as men in the over-eighties, the age group which has increased most steeply. (In comparison, under-16s were a fifth of the population in 1991 and a quarter in 1971.) There is even a steep increase in the numbers of centenarians, most of whom are women.

Is there, as predicted, both because of the ageing population and because of the changes in the welfare state and NHS, an increase in dependency and in women as carers? Or are more elderly people able to live independently?

Both are true. Although there is a historical shift away from elderly people living with their children, Michael Anderson argues, 'it is clear that much of this shift towards separation of aged people from relatives is due to the fact that old people wish to and are now more able to remain independent'. Health and appropriate support are crucial factors, and both are class and income related. A frighteningly high proportion of elderly women live in poverty; many living alone are at great risk. But many also choose to live alone and in a generation of women who fought for the vote, had greater access to higher education and to some careers, many are continuing a doughty independence in old age. Research also suggests, against the stereotype, that more old people are supported by extended families than is generally believed. Michael Anderson thinks 'a higher proportion of old people are now in regular touch with at least one of their children than at any time before 1945'.[22]

Only about 4 per cent of over-65s are looked after in institutional care. The main carers of older people are families, specifically daughters and daughters-in-law. Nearly one in five carers are themselves aged 65 or over. And nearly a third of carers who care for the sick, elderly or handicapped for more than 20 hours a week also have children under the age of 16 to look after.[23]

Between 1985 and 1990 there was an increase of almost one million people in Britain with caring responsibilities. An estimated 3.7 million adults say they are bearing the main responsibility for the care of someone and 1.4 million adults are caring for 20 hours or more a week. This increase is likely to have continued, and grown steeper, both because of the growing numbers of the elderly and the legislative changes euphemistically called 'care in the community'. Men are almost as likely to be carers as are women but men are less likely than women to be solely responsible for caring or to be caring for such long hours, and they are most likely to be caring for their spouse.[24]

Among carers looking after a spouse, 65 per cent say it would be impossible or difficult to arrange a two-day break, and 70 per cent have not had such a break since they started caring.[25] For some women, caring for their children is followed by looking after their parents or parents-in-law, followed by caring for a husband grown old. You only hope someone will care for them – but it isn't guaranteed.

These are changes which deeply affect most women's lives. Yet we face the same change-but-no-change paradox. What they will mean is less clear now than it seemed to many commentators twenty and even ten years ago. Most women are still taking most of the responsibility for bringing up children, and everything that goes with it from bringing them up wrongly (psyches to criminality theories) to hanging out the washing to running the PTA, helping out in cash-starved primary classrooms, and feeding them, the cat, the dog, the hamster and the pot plants. Women are still taking primary responsibility for caring for disabled and elderly family members – alongside teenage and young children: the 'sandwich generation' is a difficult reality.

'Marriage is still the central platform in the 1990s,' Kathleen Kiernan said when I spoke to her. She is chary of making predictions. 'It's important not to make simple generalisations. It is quite complicated. Which bits are in transition? Which bits are static? It's very difficult to say which direction we're moving in.' In the mid-1980s she had posed the question whether the status of marriage was losing its traditional significance. 'But some of the changes are so recent that they may not have fully run their course,' she had written.[26] What does she think now? 'It's still unresolved – there are still no answers.' The major changes of cohabitation and an increase in births outside marriage are 'relatively recent and dramatically quick. It's hard to say what will be the case in even five years.'

When I talked to Michael Anderson he argued that despite changes in marital and conception patterns it seemed that 'most people are seeking to replicate traditional family behaviour – they may not marry but they set up partnerships using the "standard" model'. Most children were being brought up that way. 'And what do people do if their marriage breaks up? They try to replicate it.'

None the less: 'I would not like to predict what family statistics will look like in 2005 – even 2000 perhaps.' Cultural and economic factors can be of rapid influence, and, he argues, 'the biggest change is not demographic but has everything to do with "family morality". Compared to any earlier generation we have an extraordinary lack of certainty about family life.' There is, he thinks, less a crisis of behaviour than 'a crisis of certainty … in so far as we don't know how we are *supposed* to behave'. In the past most people lived their lives in communities and social networks which were fairly homogeneous in terms of values. 'People did not always obey the rules – but they knew what they were.' The perceived crisis in the family comes 'not from breach of clearly understood and shared rules, but from a sense of confusion over what the rules should be'.

Social scientists are wary of venturing forecasts. But such an even-handed assessment implies an equally serious possibility of these trends going into reverse. Put like that the question becomes, *what would it take?*

A great deal. Family certainties largely worked because they fitted with social and economic need. They were supported by tough social sanctions and practical constraints. None of the conditions that supported the breadwinner/homemaker family in the post-war years exists today 'or will exist in the future', Penelope Leach and Patricia Hewitt argue. 'Even if unemployment is drastically reduced ... employment patterns will be very different from those of the 1950s. Women are not going to give up their right to paid employment in favour of renewed economic dependence on men, and nobody is going to abandon their right to end unhappy marriages in the divorce courts, or to live together without getting married at all.'[27]

A more uncertain society creates choice and confusion in perhaps equal measure. It means both the opportunity to move towards a less rule-bound, more nuanced, more personal and less oppressive morality but equally, particularly when change is feared and resisted, a dangerous vacuum of values. In the 1950s women regardless of background could expect to have married by their early twenties.[28] We can now see that as historically specific and unusually rigid. That doesn't make it any easier, always, to know what we ourselves want.

Not long before beginning research for this book I wrote about belated attempts to bolt this stable door at the 1993 Conservative conference: 'This is a time of transition, a time of change in family patterns and how we live and expect to live, alongside the greatest changes in working life since the Industrial Revolution.' Everything I have learned since has made that clearer. But the discontinuities are writ larger than the continuities, always: what is expected of women as mothers, as daughters and wives and partners, at the centre of family life, has changed least of all. What *is* changing is how women feel about it and whether we are prepared and able to act on those feelings.

Chapter 6

Managing Mothers

Talking to me about motherhood, Usha Brown reminded me that she had contributed a short story to a book about women in Scotland in the 1980s *Grit and Diamonds*, written when her children were young. Through the specific experience of a black woman in a white world, it tells us about how alienated so much of our experience of motherhood has become.

> They arrived at school. Her son ran off to join his friends, her baby daughter wanted to be carried. The Black woman swung her up on her hip, and breathed in the people, the life, the activity. She tried to make the pleasure last as she smiled and talked and walked home with the other mothers.
>
> The Black woman understood loneliness, but not isolation. She had always had people around her. Not necessarily the ones she wanted, but there had always been people. When the Black woman talked or dreamt about her childhood it was a world where people spilled into each others' lives, where there were always noises, smells, colours and movement. Poverty and luxury sat cheek by jowl in an untidy, tragic, fearful, vivid, contradictory, comic, people-filled world.
>
> The Black woman and her daughter went back to their house alone.[1]

Becoming a mother has an extreme tension at the heart of it: it is both a very ordinary thing to do and utterly extraordinary. Most women do it, and beginning the process is not usually difficult or even meaningful. It begins a life, it changes your life. It is routine, attended by more undignified attempts to pee into small bottles than is surely truly necessary, and by its own sentimental, commercial verses in pink and blue. And it is to participate in the very core of life.

There are consequent tensions to negotiate in everyday life, deep fractures running beneath women's everyday experience of mothering. As Ann Oakley has written, about 'a mismatch between motherhood as moral ideal and motherhood as social reality. What mothers are supposed to be is very different from the resources and positions they are allowed to enjoy.'[2]

You would give your life for her, but you wish, desperately, she would leave you alone for just five minutes. It brings emotional intensity and banality in equal measure. It is power, more than you ever asked for, the limits of which are tested by the average toddler ten times an hour; and powerlessness, because to protect her you need to change the world. It is a skilled and necessary job which attracts no income and minimal recognition. The fractures are jagged, dangerous, they can catch you and cut you badly; equally you may evade them, sit in the sun and find it all comes easily.

The dichotomy between the good and the bad mother influences how we see ourselves and are seen. Bad mothers get it wrong and are subjected to public hatred: the mothers of the boys who killed Jamie Bulger; mothers who go on holiday leaving their kids 'home alone'; mothers who leave; sad Julie Kelley, stealing a baby to keep the regard of a man who patently wasn't worth it. Good mothers, however, are only as they should be.

The argument hasn't moved on much in the last twenty years and the same contradictions are expressed. In 'Leaking From Every Orifice' Claire Dowie's one-woman show about motherhood, she warns that 'motherhood is crap – undignified, damp, terrifying, exhausting and ruinous to life and relationships'. And she delivers this message with a grin of contentment. American writer Jane Lazarre called the conflicted feelings of motherhood 'the mother knot', noticing that women would say they wanted to be with their children and to be free from them at the same time.[3]

Isolation, but without the 'space' of being alone, and unending tasks and demands but without recognition of their intensity, characterise caring at home for young children today. Low self-esteem is, for so many women, as much a part of caring for young children as changing nappies and mashing bananas. This contradictory reality has intensified as the dominant world for women too has become paid work rather than home and community. There just aren't so many people around in the daytime. Women and children live in suburban and estate ghettos, apart from the adult world except on occasional, managed occasions. And then you feel you have nothing to say, that the world is going on somewhere else without you. 'In nine years I've never properly talked to any of my neighbours,' one woman said to me. 'It's not that they're unfriendly, it's just everyone is working all the time.' 'There's a whole city around you and you're so lonely,' said another mother of two little girls. In an Edinburgh project in which health visitors were to counsel women with post-natal depression at home, the women were asked to arrange one (daytime) hour a week when they could be visited but someone else would look after the baby. Many of the women had no one they could ask, even for one hour, even for a reason like that. In her study of how parents cope with crying babies Sheila Kitzinger found that many mothers felt completely cut off: more than a third were alone with a crying baby for between eight and twelve hours on weekdays and a further third for four to eight hours a day.[4] Maternal depression is frighteningly widespread.

There's no mystery about why women get depressed, say Judy Aitken and Liz Lamb at the Community Health Project in Drumchapel. 'Stuck in the house, no money, screaming weans 24 hours a day,' says Judy. 'Lack of money, poor housing, nowhere locally to go with children, nowhere you can afford to go,' says Liz. 'And practically no childcare. There is a nursery but you can't just go along and say you need childcare. You need a social work referral – things have to be pretty drastic. There can't be much prevention – things have to be at crisis point.' It is a curious disincentive to coping, of course.

But women in Drumchapel share problems with the other new mothers she visits in a more prosperous part of the city, says Liz: 'isolation, anxiety, it's very similar. The difference here is the *bleakness* and that claustrophobic feeling, the quiet desperation of day-in day-out poverty, not seeing any light at the end of the tunnel.' Isolation is compounded for many single mothers. 'Only the postman ever came to the door,' one woman said. 'I wanted to ask him in for coffee, for someone to talk to. I used to so look forward to going to Mothers and Toddlers, you'd've thought it was a big night out.'

In many areas community links have weakened and organisations for young children and their carers fold up for lack of volunteers. Ironically, it is in some of the most deprived areas that women's community networks are most active: in women's health groups, food and nappy co-ops and wider community and welfare rights organisations which women with children, mainly, keep going. The Play Group movement is an important social link for many mothers as well as their children. And mothers are the mainstay of parents-teachers associations, environmental groups and the National Child-birth Trust. But the kind of female networks that mothers of young children create to socialise and for support are less easy to sustain when there are fewer mothers and children around, and are much harder to link into for women who also work outside the home.[5] The only way to end the everyday isolation becomes through paid work.

The Continuing Role

Even so, woman's role as mother, at the centre of family life and at the centre of social anxiety about the family, has remained least changed through a turbulent twenty-five years. And least changed *despite* the rapidly increasing participation of women with young children in paid employment, the decreasing time spent by most women out of the workforce when their children are born, and the greater acceptability of the 'career mum'. Our sense of the mother's role has been given a different colouring perhaps, but the weight and direction of responsibility and expectations have not changed.

Mothers are supposed to be what they always were: there. Say mother, assume love. Assume availability, physical and emotional. Madonna and child, the perfect circle. Patient, giving, never putting yourself first, wholly reliable. Not *sexy*. And it's true – there are times, many times, in the middle of the night when they're newborn and late at night when an anguished teenager wants to talk, when you don't put yourself first, it wouldn't make sense. (Though learning, and remembering, that you can is, I suspect, the art of survival.)

If anything, the circle of mother and child is tighter, the

expectations of women as mothers are greater as we approach the end of the century. Women's expectation of independence creates new pressures because it is not compatible with the dependence of young children, and the economic dependence which still often comes with having them. Higher standards for parenting also bring pressure, as Julia Brannen and Peter Moss noticed in their research, even that 'in order to be a good mother, it was necessary to enjoy it.'[6] We say 'I'm not a perfect mother' – it wouldn't occur to us to say I'm not a *perfect* journalist, or banker, or very much else.

Today the conflict of interests between women's autonomy and their children's needs is more conscious and ideals of motherhood are tempered with a little more practicality. But just as out-of-work men tend to become more macho rather than try gender role-swapping, so women who have children and who work outside the home may re-emphasise motherly virtues in compensation. Out at work, even with excellent childcare, you're still their mother full time whatever else you do. Being a mother is only just beginning when the 'career break' ends. *Of course* it's interesting and stretching and heart-warming and fun. But not all the time. And all the time is when you've got to do it. Is there any choice but to try to do it well? But is that ever truly possible?

New Complexities

Bringing up children has new difficulties it didn't have twenty-five years ago. There is a lack of social space for young children and their carers; stress and strain because society is now so ill-adapted to the needs of children. Children cannot play in the street safely, they must be escorted and chauffeured everywhere. A recent study showed that nine out of ten journeys to school that children make are by car; twenty-five years ago they walked. As well as changing the nature of childhood this also means an additional role for their parents. Most people believe that children are more in danger than they have ever been. Ten thousand children a day try to ring Childline, although it can answer only about 3,000 of the calls.[7] In a more dangerous world motherhood is about responsibility and blame in equal measure.

Good mothers cope, with everything. 'Normal' mothering is both idealised and accepted as stressful. This can be endorsed by social work practice: behind much social work and child protection theory are cultural assumptions that good mothering comes naturally and that the needs of mothers and children are complementary. Only 'failure to cope' is recognised. 'Mothering is a difficult enough job without the impossible ideal of good mothering – and yet when a mother is having most difficulties we impose this ideal on her,' argues Vivien Nice, a social work teacher in London.[8] Janette Forman at the Women's Support Project in Glasgow talked about how women are afraid to admit there is domestic violence 'for fear of how they'll be seen by statutory services – she'll stay for fear of being seen as a bad mother and losing her children.' Where there is sexual and physical abuse of children by fathers, 'women are damned if they see it going on and damned if they don't. Women I've worked with who have reported it found themselves judged – why is this woman reporting this, what are her ulterior motives? And if the woman *doesn't* report it or leave she's blamed for putting her children at risk. It is an evasion of naming male abuse of power. There can be more anger and suspicion directed at the woman than at the man who was the abuser.' The absence of legal means to exclude a suspected abuser from the home focusses social work practice on the mother.

'Home-made Jam from Mom is Really Bottled Love'

That was a line in a gift book that caught my eye. Fortunately most women know the realities of love are not so trite.

Josie Henderson, a single mother living in the Scottish Borders, talked about the good things about being a mother. In a difficult time, what kept her going? 'They do. Though in practice it's the minutiae of Seth's standard grades or Ellen being ill – you're involved in that progression of their lives so you don't think about how you're going to cope because you're just doing that ... Five years ago, when their father had first gone I remember lying in bed, I was terribly tired and I thought *how on earth* am I going to cope, it's just not possible. Now, well I've moved on from that – it's because of the children ... With the little ones it's just that incredibly open love. With the older two the relationship is more complex. It's fun. Well, it's not all fun – but there's a lot of humour in our house that there wasn't before.'

Usha Brown moved to Britain from India after a short visit to London where she met her husband. 'I was 21 – we met in November and married in May. If my daughter did that!' She remembers how badly she missed the extended family in which she had grown up when she had children of her own, in the isolating, white world her story in *Grit and Diamonds* describes. 'Joint families are wonderful for small children – as a teenager there are more problems, perhaps. In the nuclear family one person has to provide such a large amount. My mother's family were quiet, gentle. The women mainly didn't have paid jobs (though her mother was a doctor) but ran households – busy people doing worthwhile work. My father's family were never silent, a huge rumbustious family – lots of discussion, lots of ideas, and prayer. I miss it a lot.'

Here, 'it was always you and the children trailing along – no space, not even to go to the toilet on your own, and making a cup of coffee was a major manoeuvre. Constant demands, no space for yourself.'

Frances Corr talked about how the way mothering is not valued lies behind the idea that single parents are not contributing to society. 'We are – but motherhood is trivialised so much, given the amount of work and effort and responsibility that's involved. It isna' something you get home from – I didn't know what had hit me, you were *in* all the time, they were *always there*.' You see the conflict of needs, Frances said, 'down town every day, a woman and kids standing at the bus stop and she's screaming at the kids – that sums it up to me. She can't even go to the shops by herself. And people judge you on that' – she points a fake gun – 'but they see the stressed-out scenes in public, they dinna see the nice wee moments at home.' The conflict because of lack of resources and childcare is a problem for the children too, who need more in their lives than one tired woman can give them.

'The responsibility is awesome but because you take it on you get a lot out of it,' Josie said. 'I think that mothering allows you to develop yourself. You have to question yourself, you need to be reflective. It connects you to the spiritual dimension.' She doesn't think that is as possible if you're also out at work: 'you just don't have the same time to think if you're working and mothering because you're just too busy coping. I think I'm much more defined as a person and much more self-aware than I would have been.'

She feels pressure 'to get a direction'. 'But I want to argue that mothering as a primary occupation is valid.' At a recent PTA conference she'd attended she'd begun a conversation with a nursery school headteacher who'd asked her, 'And what do you do?' 'I said, "I'm a mother" and she said, "Well I'm a mother and so's she and so's she – what *else* do you do?" I felt really put down. Well I have four children! It was rather defensive of her but all the same if it was an engineering conference maybe I'd've had to justify why I was there as a mother, but this was about education!

'All I ever really wanted to do in life was have children,' she says, though for a long time she felt she couldn't admit that. She thinks we're still uncomfortable with talking about the importance of what mothers do. 'It hides an incredibly rich world. There's nothing more important than relationships and people. Why do we value things rather than people? There's all that invisible joy and pain and hurt – the joys are so secret.'

Joyce Macmillan described women with children as in conflict with the main direction of the culture: 'Motherhood strikes me as a kind of secret society, which I'm standing on the fringes of. When women have children their priorities are not then the priorities of our dominant culture.' She talks of a group of women she knows, youngish middle-class mothers at home. 'It's as if these women are quietly sustaining a completely different way of life. They share the frustrations of that experience but they also share the intense pleasures of it. Those pleasures are not culturally public any more.'

Conflicting Needs, Changing Lives

Penelope Leach's most recent book *Children First* is a passionate polemic about how society neglects the needs of children and those who care for them. The way that the need for paid work and caring are pulling against each other, pushed by poverty and creating strain, is a strong theme. She argues that in comparison to other and earlier societies, only in the post-industrial West is responsibility for the daily care and long-term upbringing of children left entirely to parents – often lone parents – without any viable support system. 'Whatever their individual circumstances, Western parents can seldom take support networks for granted, nor are we searching for new ways to ensure them, because it suits the individualistic ethos of post-industrial societies to regard the whole business of "starting a family" as parents' alone.' And having a child 'shatters illusions of ungendered equality'.[9]

So does she think much has changed? She believes the shared area within which women and men operate interchangeably as parents has expanded enormously in this last decade, but what hasn't changed is that 'for women playing under male rules, babies are a severe embarrassment ... Stereotyped sex roles are rightly seen as social straitjackets. But our determination to be rid of them, and the resulting modern expectations of mothers and fathers, may offer a liberty that is only illusory.'

There's a sense abroad, I said, that we've tried equality as parents and failed. She very much disagrees: 'we've scarcely tried – and we've not failed either. More and more young women are saying they don't want to live like men have but they don't want to give up what they've achieved at work either, so I have a sense of change – but at the same time a lot of parents are very poor and very broke so there is a very long way to go.'

There always has been pressure on some women to go back to work soon after giving birth: 'in the last century it was about their children's survival'. What's new is 'a kind of pressure that's not just about money, but that awful sense of the world getting away from you, and that bringing up children is not really worthwhile work. So many women seem to have had the worst of both worlds – going back too soon and then quitting work altogether when the baby was six months or a year old – which is so tragic, they had gone through the very worst ...' Women should have a real choice, she says, angrily: 'if women say they don't want to go back that soon – and they do – we ought to listen to that. If we're going to leave it all to the parents then at least we ought to listen to what they think ... It is so desperately important – why do people have to make such dramatic choices? It's like saying, do you want to eat or drink this year – well I'd like to do a bit of both, thank you.'

'It's hard to talk about without sounding as if you believe "biology is destiny",' says Fiona Mackay, 'but having a child really changed how I saw the world. If you grew up in the 1970s and were reasonably high-powered in the 1980s there was a kind of glib expectation that you would have it all, and somehow having a child, a family, was devalued, you did it *as well as*. I suppose I was just hit by the realisation that this was a very big thing, physically, psychologically, emotionally. And that it *should be* a big thing, it *should* change things. That it was damaging for it to be denigrated – "I'll just clear a space in my Filofax to fit in a baby" '.

It changed things not just in practical ways but in how she understood the world and feminism. Trying to fit women into men's reality is unsatisfactory for women and very unsatisfactory for children. The illusion of equality in my relationship collapsed at the same time. I realised we were only as equal as he'd allowed us to be and he was quite happy to leave me holding the baby. It was still his choice – I couldn't choose for him to be an equal parent. And after we divorced and he wanted to be more involved, I couldn't choose for him not to be either. He could come in and out as he wanted to. I couldn't.'

'Motherhood changed me completely,' Usha said. 'Nothing in my life made a bigger difference, not even changing countries, moving to Britain. All the pressure and the isolation made me grow up in a hurry – no sleep, baby needing feeding ... All my certainties had gone – it took away my confidence for a good long time. Society's view of me changed completely – before, I was a sassy young black woman; afterwards, a dumbwit.' She mimics a health worker articulating clearly: 'Now, Mrs Brown ...' She had studied politics and economics at university in Madras. It was an exciting time, 'the world was changing, I was definitely going to go and lead a revolution – the seduction of ideas ... The kids stopped me and grounded me, which I realise has been very good for me. At 22 I had no understanding of what a woman with children's life was like. Having kids provided something to base my ideas in, I could no longer be purist.'

'We Never Thought of Ourselves ...'

The double-bind on women as mothers may pull less tightly and less conspicuously perhaps, but is still very much part of our lives. The message is: make home life work but don't let the work show. Changing roles have rewritten some of the lines but not thrown away the script. If anything the 'working mother' gives the double-bind new life. The message is: be well-organised and you can have it all. So many women have said to me: 'He'll do his bit, as long as I organise it.' 'The demands of managing the dual-earner lifestyle' relies mainly 'on the hard work, organising skill and sacrifices of women,' Brannen and Moss say. Mothers reorganised their time to cope with the extra demands, 'getting up earlier, going to bed later and cutting down on social life and leisure activities'. Many women handled the demands of a dual role with 'increased efficiency and productivity. While this produced benefits ... there were also costs. Most of these were carried by the women – in employment, personal stress and tiredness and in reduced time for themselves.' They also say that most still felt there were advantages both for themselves and their children, nevertheless.[10]

In the early 1980s the 'working mother's' cultural significance was marked by a small crop of how-to books with titles like *How to Survive as a Working Mother* and a wave of advice in the women's magazines. Dr Miriam Stoppard, we were informed, planned her menus three months ahead. If only women would become efficient enough to juggle work and home, no one else need worry. 'She has to work faster and more efficiently in the home,' advised Shirley Conran, and 'She has to be twice as efficient outside it because people expect her not to be.' There was the bestselling author with *six* children. The single mother who gave dinner parties with a choice of puddings. Didn't these women ever suffer from self-doubt, or even flu? No, said Mary Kenny firmly: 'successful women have excellent health and so do their children'. Margaret Thatcher's children were reported only to have had chickenpox at weekends.[11]

Trying to get ahead of it all – planning, laying breakfast the night before, starting the Christmas presents in September, spending Sunday afternoons cooking suppers for the freezer ... folding the birthday paper for recycling. (Recycling! It means you can't even throw out old Coke cans any more. But who has to send them to *Blue Peter*?) Housework is something children increase in large measure even as they take away any time you might have to do it in. And then have the nerve to wish wistfully for a nice tidy house like their friend's Mum achieves. (And she works, and she ...) 'Don't hassle me, Mum!' 'Mum, where's my boots/homework/book/lip-stick ...? Yes, I'll do it *later*. Mum – *don't* tidy up, come and play with me!'

With the denigration of the traditional housewife's role comes the message that we are not to waste our lives on cleaning and tidying up. But *someone* has to do it. Now there's an added twist: we can't just be competent, we're supposed to be fulfilled. We have learnt that self-sacrifice is neither healthy nor wise. We are reminded that we must make time for our own lives and interests and will be the better mothers and wives for it. The question is *when*.

A generation or so ago a mother was told her greatest wish must be her children's health and happiness; their fulfilment was hers. That message has not faded, just gone underground. Guilt comes with the territory. It collides head-on with the newer truisms of a balance of needs. No one else has taken over much of the practical and emotional work of bringing up children. So you end up feeling guilty for not paying attention to your own needs as well.

The skill of women who 'combine roles in a seamless way' is recognised and rewarded in *Good Housekeeping*'s 'Women of the '90s' award. If Superwoman was a construct of the 1980s, she has yet to be replaced, it seems. In a thousand British homes she is alive and well and juggling determinedly. The prize seems to be for not dropping the plates. Winner in 1994, Dr Catherine Pickering, GP, mother of three, in the past two and a half 'extremely challenging' years had moved house and job three times, which included settling her children into new schools. 'Life for women in the '90s is about compromise, determination and choice. I have chosen my family, and compromised my career to preserve this – but I've been determined to keep my work going.' I don't suppose you'd win if you said your priorities were career first, family second – but since the three house moves were at the behest of *his* job that's apparently still OK for her husband.[12]

I don't want to knock it – it is important that the need for 'balance' is recognised in such highly public ways. These are women seen as 'getting the most out of life – home and work, family and the community, personal growth and leisure'. Good for them! But the idea that women *take it on* is still significant, making most of it seem voluntary. This allows the division of responsibilities to rest much as it always has, and suggests unrealistically that wifely dependence is still financially an option.

Of these role models for the 1990s, the runners-up are a 'police officer, mother of three, keen cook, dressmaker, decorator, gardener and keep-fitter' – that's only the first, not all of them – who also plans to start her own business, and a wife and mother of two young children with ponies, who is also a vet and serious mountain climber: 'my goals this year are to improve my computer skills, have lots of fun with the family, a new wardrobe and a blooming garden. Reading this you sink into a corner: 'So why can't *I* manage?' Combining roles is one thing, the demand that we do it seamlessly, with conspicuous success, rather ups the ante.

The Format for Success

She magazine has identified and built a readership on working mothers since its relaunch in 1990. Its editor Linda Kelsey 'is a *Cosmo* girl who has grown into a *She* woman,' Ginny Dougary writes. 'In Nat-Mag speak this means she is no longer a single girl looking for sex, but a mother, a worker, a lover, and, most definitely, a woman.' Kelsey was the first woman editor in the company to be pregnant on the job: 'I set a good example. I was very healthy. I worked up to three days before Thomas was due. I was aware that I was setting a precedent.'[13]

When she came back to work she realised there was no magazine for women like her even though in advertising circles family life was seen 'as a major yuppie concern'. It was hard to get the format right: if they put a baby on the cover, sales dropped; a slightly harder edge detectable at first has softened. The magazine seems now to have settled into a successful format: a very few tasteful babies and charming toddlers and a mix of gloss, celebrities and endless advice – Less concerned with the nitty-gritty of managing success at work and in motherhood alike, *She* presents images of it – providing you're young and attractive, naturally.

But for all that motherhood is supposed to be fashionable in the 1990s (a curious idea really, since it happens, fashion or no fashion), a spot check of *Marie Claire* and *Cosmopolitan* confirms that they feel no need to market to maternal women. *Lots* of sex but no images of motherhood – and no childbearing hips outside the cosmetic surgery ads. The equation of pre-maternal youth with freedom holds.[14] If women once protested the limitations of being seen only in terms of their potential or actual motherhood, now most of the positive images of womanhood you see are at variance with images of motherliness.

The best portrayal of maternity's dark side I have read is the monster-mother in Anne Fine's novel *In Cold Domain*. In her bitter musings Fine explores how motherhood can go sour. 'She was just a husk. The Herculean task of suppressing all her unmotherly responses had drained her till there was nothing left.' The sheer hard work of raising a family, on this account, squeezes it dry of the joy which should power it. The children can't turn a cartwheel without being watched: '"Don't go back in, Mum! Look at me! Look at me!"' Can't grow up without coming back for more.[15]

'Like some dreadful form of allergy, it had got worse and worse, until she could hardly do anything at all, without resenting how much being the linchpin of a family ruined it.' If power corrupts, resentment corrodes. 'What *mistakes* women made, attempting to atone for each and every small ungenerous impulse with ludicrous offers of further self-sacrifice. The trouble was that no one could ever truly imagine how very long, how very fine, the wheel of life was going to grind ... Over the years, she must have told herself a hundred thousand times: *relax*. Enjoy your children ...' This mother is called Lilith. Only the Eves of this world are pictured in *She* and *Good Housekeeping*.

I thought about this one day on holiday. It looked wonderful when we got to the beach, and it was hot and not raining or sleeting or snowing or anything you might expect, and I hadn't forgotten the swimsuits or the suntan lotion of the correct factor (nowadays you don't just feel guilty if your pallid kids watch telly all day, you also feel guilty for letting them play in the midday sun). But when we sat down on the sand there were these little black bugs which crawled everywhere, horrid ones that got in your hair, and spoilt everything.

Which was all my fault. Even I somehow believed it was my fault. Good mothers, *other* mothers, carry insect-repellent in their baskets. Along with plastic spades, Elastoplast, raincoats, sun hats, wet wipes, kitchen roll and emergency food and drink supplies. But I hadn't.

'And it's *hopeless* for rollerblading here,' they cry accusingly. 'I've never been here before,' you say pathetically, 'how was I to know? I made no promises.' But somehow, in the script they have, we did.

Invisible Mothers

What is striking, when you start to look for it, is how much we don't know (and haven't felt it important to find out), about women's experience of motherhood. It is unprecedented in the contrast between its human significance and the absence of research attention paid it. In an age when even the wedding cake commands a cultural history, the small number of books seeking to come to grips with the history, sociology and politics of mothering illuminates a conspicuous absence. The only sustained attention is within psychoanalysis, resulting in as much confusion as enlightenment, and within the psychology of child development where the mother's experience is sometimes researched as a necessary by-product of understanding the child's but her 'insider perspective' is rarely considered.[16] Most feminist accounts to date have been from the perspective of daughters, not mothers, and daughters who felt betrayed at that.

When my children were babies I bought everything I could find to read on mothering. The books are still mostly only partly read. Which I put down to not having had the time, but I now think is also because nothing offered me what I was looking for, analysis which was both hands-on and reflective.

There *is* a literature on motherhood of course: by far the biggest category is advice, the mother and baby books, now even including how to mother your *unborn* baby. Mother as agent, as an active, thinking being, fully participative, as it were, in her own role, hardly appears. There is a practical issue: few hands-on mothers of young children have the time and energy to write about it – although I know a lot of mothers who've intended to. Perhaps too you need a certain distance – but by then you have forgotten half of how it feels to have the responsibility of very young children. Mothering is both central and curiously invisible.

Mothers have been a problem for second-wave feminism. Twenty-four-hour nurseries, free contraception and abortion on demand: three of the first four demands of the women's liberation movement paid attention to motherhood, but with the emphasis on freeing women from its burdens. They have not been met, and young women are beginning to reiterate them.

A failing of 1970s feminism, and a reason why it alienated so many women or seemed irrelevant to them, was that it did not adequately address the sheer centrality of mothering to many women's lives. Indeed it was concerned precisely to protest against, and deconstruct, that very centrality. If it was seen as a movement by and for young, untrammelled women that was partly, though not wholly, true; something 1990s feminism, at least in its public face, is repeating. Changing attitudes within feminism to motherhood can to a great extent be explained because, as Sheila Rowbotham says, 'women have very different attitudes to motherhood when they are 20 than when they are 30'.[17] But feminism, whether truthfully or not, has been seen as colluding with a devaluation of the mother's role rather than resisting that.

Many of the women central to the development of the women's liberation movement in Britain had young children, and their feminism grew out of their difficult lives as mothers at a time when fifties thinking was a restrictive hangover, so many presented that experience very negatively. For the first time there was a space to express the dark and difficult side of mothering. Their message to younger women, explicitly and implicitly, was: don't have children, it is selfish and foolish. To be a mother was a trap, who could choose that? Janet Ree, writing in Micheline Wandor's collection *Once a Feminist* (interviews with women who were at the first Women's Liberation Conference at Ruskin College, Oxford in February 1970) catches the tone of the times. It wasn't that the women's movement was *against* children, 'but what I did pick up as being really primary for women was to be yourself in your own right. And for mothers that meant not falling for the so-called myth of motherhood.'[18]

My daughter Rebecca was born in 1980 when that mood was beginning to thaw – part of what's been called 'the latterday feminist baby boom' – but, even so, I recognise that mood very well. To have a child was choosing oppression. I wanted a T-shirt over my bump saying 'A Woman's Right to Choose'. Joyce Macmillan remembers how 'the wave of feminism in the 1970s very strongly prioritised not letting your potential be sidelined because of the fact of woman-hood'. It was understandable, as she says, as a 'reaction against the 1950s and the sidelining of women's talent – My generation of women came to maturity on the crest of that very powerful impulsion and what people said to us was, don't get caught up in it, do what men do, get a good career – don't let anyone tell you there are things you can't do, and the only thing that will stop you from doing them is getting tied down with children. And a lot of women did that – with the vague assumption that either if you did all that you wouldn't be bothered with something as trivial as having a family life anyway, or that it was such an obvious and natural thing to do that it would somehow look after itself.'

Nor was this only a middle-class pressure: the early 1970s, with full grants and meritocratic beliefs, saw the largest group of young women from working-class backgrounds going into higher educa-tion so far and the pressures on them to make good, not be tied down, were, if anything, greater. A generation, too, raised on state orange juice, free school milk and high expectations was secure enough to demand change. Economic changes in the 1970s, the growth of unemployment and the first major wave of graduate unemployment, allied to discrimination in the job market were also powerful disincentives to trying to 'have it all'.

For those women who were indeed young and untrammelled everything about how motherhood was seen and constructed was alien to the freedom held out to us. Shulamith Firestone was one of the first to articulate what was then repeated severally: 'the heart of woman's oppression is her childbearing and childrearing roles'; she explored ideas of liberation through the eradication of this core biological difference. Nor was this new: Simone de Beauvoir in *The Second Sex* had written that woman's 'misfortune is to have been biologically destined for the repetition of life'.[19]

Lee Comer's pamphlet *The Myth of Motherhood* (published in 1972) makes uncomfortable reading now, because of how woman/mother-blaming it is, because of a refusal to recognise that mothers themselves may make resistant meanings of motherhood. The 'myth' is that mothers are more essential to their children than anyone else who cares for them. In any case 'most of what goes on under the guise of good parental care is an elaborate rationalisation of gross possessiveness'. The mother 'concentrates all the care in herself instead of sharing it with others'. (Chance would be a fine thing!) 'Women have embraced the mythology so wholeheartedly that it is they themselves who constantly reinforce it.' By refusing to see ourselves as dispensable as mothers we create neurotic dependence in our children: that dependence is then seen as normal.[20]

The alternative, she asserts, is for 'several warm, friendly people' to look after the child, responsive to its expressed needs but aiming for a child who lives 'in a totally independent and self-reliant way'. The possibility that the child might tie itself firmly to Mother's apron strings rather than acting as the tough stray of her vision is not explored. Rather, 'we have to learn to disengage ourselves from the children we care for, liberating them from the pressure to conform to our image of them.' Later arguments around collective and commune childcare make this seem a less than radical statement, but it illustrates the thinking which led to much, essentially ill-informed, idealisation of Russian, Chinese and kibbutzim models, and to some collective childcare in communes and similar settings, often rather more difficult in practice than in theory. The influence of the alternative psychologists – of whom the best-known was R. D. Laing (theoriser of 'the schizophregenic mother') – was considerable.

Also popular at the time were anthropological studies of the family and maternity in non-Western cultures – making the useful point that European norms are not universal, but of limited value to anyone negotiating family life in late twentieth-century Britain. There was a similarly naive idealisation of the extended family – which can be oppressive in different ways.

These responses can now be understood as belonging to a specific historical period. As well as a reaction against the post-war reassertion of family values, this generation was also the first to be able to easily get and take for granted effective contraception (with the worries and drawbacks of the pill still in the future) and to have to learn how to handle that very significant change. Motherhood was no longer a virtually inevitable part of women's lives but attitudes were still conditioned by a recent past when it was.

Sheila Rowbotham defends the women's liberation movement against claims that it was anti-motherhood. 'The change really was that it became possible to express the negative aspects of mothering, without feeling such a sense of failure ... Feminists have maintained that motherhood as we know it contains both oppressive and fulfilling elements ... have insisted that motherhood must be freely chosen and socially transformed.' She also points out that the early women's movement was linked closely to practical organisations like claimants' unions, Gingerbread and Mothers in Action.[21] Feminism began in the 1980s to accept that there might be powerful reasons to want to have children which weren't just media and in-law pressure – although many of those explanations were put in psychoanalytical terms which suggested that wanting to have children was a kind of cultural difficulty or personality failure rather than rational.

'Maternal revivalism' was equally reactive. More significant as an argument in the USA than here, it presented motherhood as power which men have sought to control and was a classic attempt to revalue women's specific contribution to society as women. It had dangers, which British feminists were quick to spot, of a revived biological determinism. 'As a total political concept this leads to a dead end,' Sheila Rowbotham says crisply: 'It results in an idealisation of motherhood which confines women again to a separate sphere as nurturers.'[22] And indeed to celebrate the traditional nurturant qualities associated with motherhood seemed unlikely to liberate mothers from the burden of expectations and responsibilities. Nor, however, was liberation through childlessness or a radically minimised maternal role much of an advance. The either/or between maternal revivalism and stating that women's relationship to children is, or should be, no different from that of men is a false and unhelpful, if persistent, opposition. If 1970s feminism saw only oppression the newer feminism seemed only to see positive experience and values in motherhood, which hardly fitted life as most mothers lived it. Swinging between downgrading and idealisation was only confusing in the search for a newer, less oppressive identity as mothers.

Mixed Messages

If the earth mother made something of a reappearance in the 1980s, the 'mothers with briefcases' became an icon of the age, glossier in image than reality perhaps but at least offering a sense of what was possible. Each year in the 1980s and early 1990s thousands more women found ways of negotiating work, education and family needs. They have a public identity now even if no more public support; that mothering was more multi-faceted than had previously been allowed is acknowledged, even if there is very little practical back up. There are articles like 'A Working Mum's Guide to Potty Training' in popular magazines like *First Steps* and glossily presented advice on dealing with employer prejudices ('make sure you break the news positively, know your rights and explain your plans to return clearly and assertively') alongside advice on breastfeeding and fashion spreads modelled by real, and really stylish, mothers-to-be. No more floppy bows which were mysteriously supposed to disguise your state: 'maternity frocks are just not my style. I like to wear clothes that show off my bump... ' (The acres of discovered advertising represented by ever-increasing variations on disposable nappies, buggies, car seats, pregnancy vitamins and courses in 'prenatal stimulation' has had not a little to do with the increasing positive profile of pregnancy and early motherhood.) Being a mother – a middle-class mother anyway – developed a more assertive identity as mothers at work 'came out' as such, and some mothers at home emphasised the importance of their role. Education as play ('They think they're playing. You know they're learning... give your child a head start when they go to school'), and at its extreme 'hot-housing' children's abilities, added a professional dimension to mothering. And yet another layer of guilt.[23]

Young women now are given quite confused messages. On the one hand a continuing strong insistence on education, autonomy and self-fulfilment, on the other overwhelming, sentimental messages about family life and romance. It is not expressed as a priority but for many young women having children *one day* still feels, as Joyce Macmillan said of the 1970s, such an obvious thing to do 'that it would somehow look after itself'.

Ten years after graduation four times as many mid-1980s women graduates as men graduates have not had children. It is only when motherhood *can* be freely chosen that a choice not to is also truly possible. Jane Bartlett argues that more women now make that choice, but the extent to which her interviewees see work and motherhood as militating against each other and presenting impossible strains makes me wonder how genuine it is, still. The climate of continuing 'vehement' prejudice against child-free women as well as the family and social pressures to have children she writes of suggest a less than easy context for choosing. In media discussion of the OPCS predictions of greater childlessness those who argued the pleasure of being 'childfree' were noticeably defensive and showed that it still feels necessary to put down maternity to refuse it.[24]

Success now means achievement in work *and* women's traditional concerns, not either/or. But the message that motherhood is a trap for ambitious women is still strong. The girls who leave school early and without qualifications are also the girls who get pregnant younger than average, and are held up to other girls as an example to avoid. They are seen as no-hopers, with few other choices. (Some of those 'no-hopers' actually show remarkable resilience and resources against the odds.)

The convergence of equality, autonomy and minimised-maternity is a construction of feminism assertively revived by Naomi Wolf in her 1993 book *Fire with Fire*, not so much in her rejection of the idea that 'women's higher nature comes from their maternal capacities', with which I would agree ('niceness' has always been a trap). But in blithely overlooking the part that childbearing and rearing plays in most women's lives – which there's still rather more to than the 'melting feeling around chubby babies' that she admits to. She sees it neither as pertinent to her analysis nor, we must assume, likely to add any serious layer of complication to the thrusting goals she identifies: women taking and using power, engaging in mainstream politics, and amassing and using capital. 'Power feminism' is 'centred on money and work' and 'real change for women depends on a willingness to engage with power... democracy... and money.'[25]

Although self-worth is at issue, self-worth in the rarely glamorous role of mother is not. The issue of children is to be neatly resolved, as ever, through subsidised childcare. Its absence is one of four burdens that Wolf recognises as remaining for women. 'Now that reproductive choice and the right to a wage are minimally secure in the democratic West... democracy puts our fate squarely in our own hands.' If we don't shift those burdens 'it will be because women at some level have *chosen* not to exert the power that is their birthright'.

Writing in the USA, a country without statutory maternity rights, with an equal pay gap as wide as our own, where the poverty of single mothers is worse than in the UK and the rate of teenage pregnancy is higher than the UK's and where the 'year of the woman' still leaves the proportion of women elected representatives in power lower than in most European countries, Wolf's talk of democracy is actually misleading.

In a recent article subtitled 'Is "Difference" the Future for Feminism?', to which her answer is a lengthy but resounding 'no', the French feminist Christine Delphy also weighs in against 'the maternal demand' and argues that an approach based on the difference of maternity is not compatible with women's demand for common treatment/human rights. Even to recognise the different role maternity plays in women's lives from paternity in men's is, she seems to think, the slippery slope 'to the home, a strict division of tasks, and a separation of spheres between men and women'. It may be extreme, as she suggests, to say that maternal values are so good they should inform all aspects of life, though if it's a choice between that and patriarchal values I know which I'd want. To say that the attempt to revalue mothering means 'the obligation to be a mother thus remains the most important thing in life for women, this time in feminist guise' is a defensive conclusion which doesn't hold.[26]

Equality and Difference

How much does feminism's ambivalence about motherhood matter? The intense arguments passed most women by. Questioning why we do or don't have children was a luxury to many women – and would still seem so. Delphy, for example, may be held in high regard in feminist theoretical circles but I doubt many women quote her as they slip in their diaphragm.

Despite *or* with the help of feminism, a lot of women are quietly getting on with new ways of living and seeing themselves as mothers. Feminism, sociologist Tuula Gordon argues, can provide protection against the myths of motherhood and suggest ways of understanding the contradictions of motherhood in a society that devalues it; women will thus be 'in a better position to exercise their responsibilities towards their children while enjoying their children as a positive experience'.[27]

Yet postponed motherhood has now become widespread in all social groups, an unprecedented change since the early 1980s, and concern that more women won't have children is rising. Birth rates tend to fall in times of economic insecurity; they also dipped steeply in the 1930s. But the impact of the message that freedom for women means not having children has been considerable. Not least because women can look around them and see that it is often, if not inevitably, true. But is freedom, or liberation, or autonomy *all* we want?

Feminist discussion of motherhood remains important as the only discourse which takes women's experience as central; the only approach which has even begun to think through motherhood as experience and as politics. But a consequence of that unresolved feminist debate has been an absence: where a public voice *supporting* women as mothers and fighting for social support was badly needed, there has been next to nothing. And while feminism and the feminist-influenced Left was digging itself out of several corners, the New Right was rewriting the agenda.

Motherhood creates a dilemma for feminism which has been played out in the swing between 'equality' and 'difference' arguments since at least the 1850s. It seemed that women could challenge male rule *either* by seeking to enter a male world *or* by stressing our difference and unique sphere of activity/perceptions/values. Equality, understood as between women and men and expressed as 'equal opportunity' and 'equal treatment', has been an important tool in creating legal and institutional change but in using it we have needed to dismiss or diminish differences between women and men. Women's worth has been measured along with men's as 'productive' beings outside of the home and, as Fiona Mackay argued, 'insight and experience arising from the part of their lives spent in caring work is negated'. At its extreme, 'equal treatment' has been used to argue that maternity and parental leave discriminate against workers without children.

To focus in reaction on 'difference', however, is to over-emphasise it where it really doesn't matter. It also seems to open the door to biological determinism and even to excuses – that women aren't up to it, after all. (See for example the 1992 collection of essays, *Equal*

Opportunities: A feminist fallacy.[28]) To create structures to accommodate women's difference can serve to underline it: the 'mommy
track' at work, in the current social climate, makes it seem that fertile
women are problematic workers. In the main arenas of the argument
for equality, maternity, children, and even warm-hearted feelings
have come to be seen only as handicaps.

Acknowledging 'difference' without disadvantage, Penelope
Leach thinks, 'will not be easy to achieve... Many women believe
that within establishments that are still overwhelmingly male, any
assertion of sex differences is inevitably interpreted as an admission
of female weakness. Many mothers believe that if they openly
acknowledge differences between their own and their partners'
parenting relationships and roles, they risk handing men a gift-
wrapped justification for reasserting their economic dominance and
freeing themselves from domestic roles'.[29]

'As long as both sexes battle for position in a male game-plan,' she
says, individual women will 'keep their heads down while hanging
on to whatever position they have achieved, and some will believe
they are winning. But the position of all women will remain
precarious until they insist that societies alter the game.'

Whether it intended it or not, a feminism with the objectives of
equality and greater personal autonomy for women presents mothering as an obstacle. But it is too easy to blame feminism, or even the
'wrong sort' of feminism, for something which has much deeper
roots. The energetic women's movement in the 1960s and 1970s hit a
problem which had equally tripped up the first wave of feminism this
century. It only reinforced – or was unable seriously to challenge – a
mainstream perception that being a mother was different from, was
giving up on, the rest of life.

Although motherhood nominally has high status in Britain you
only have to do it to realise that it doesn't really. Anti-mothering and
anti-child feelings are embedded in our culture. In so far as the most
successful current of feminism has seemed to devalue mothering it is
because it was superimposed on that embedded strand which does
so. And some change is simply easier to effect. Revaluing and
changing the conditions of mothering – because the roots of
disadvantage to women as mothers go so very deep and are so
interwoven with its joys and advantages – is much more difficult than

opening the workplace more fully to women, especially when you could rely on those of them with awkward baggage like children mostly to sort their problems out for themselves.

A decade or more of feminist arguments has shown that women's care of children lay behind job segregation in the workplace, lower earnings and economic dependence, and lack of a voice in public life. Which was true. And all of those arguments concluded with suggestions for how the world might change to resolve this. But very little of it happened: because these were major changes to which there was covert and overt resistance, and because of the political/economic climate in which the demands were made. Without achieving those changes the arguments seemed only to reinforce how hard it is to have kids and the rest of life too.

Care Now, Pay Later?

Two main trends can be isolated. The first is that a feminist analysis based on equal opportunity has taken hold, and has been successful because, and in so far as, it has gone with the grain of social/political change. This has meant an emphasis on those aspects of equality which least recognise difference, in apparent happy conjunction with market philosophy, primarily its fierce individualism. (I have not seen any sustained attempt by right-wing feminism to link ideas of women's liberation to market theory, though it is at least interesting that the two political theories with the most impact in the past twenty-five years should draw equally liberally on the rhetoric of freedom. Curiously enough, women's freedom is a subject on which those who hold the virtues of deregulation supreme are remarkably quiet.) At the same time it fitted the needs of the labour market.

Secondly, and partly in consequence, there has been a widening gap between women who have children and women who don't. It cuts across other differences – so that there will be, for example, differences between two high-flying women lawyers depending on their family responsibilities, and differences between women who work in a retail chain, as well as differences in life chances across class and ethnicity. This has been both a social and, more measurably, an economic gap. Friendship can be more difficult for mothers and women without children. Writer Liz Heron talked angrily about feminists 'melting into motherhood'.[30] Joyce Macmillan talked about her feelings of 'almost a complete culture clash' between her and women at home with children. Conversely, women with young children talk about a lack of sensitivity from child-free friends to how demanding their lives now are. Some women find it's hard to keep up friendships with women without children of their own. 'You need *very* understanding friends if you're working and bringing up children', Kirsty Wark says. 'When you're not working you need to give time to the kids. My women friends are incredibly important to me but I see hardly any of them now. The good friends understand.'

The widening economic gap is one of the main negative changes of the past twenty-five years. The widest earnings gap is between women with dependent children and other workers. The 'opportunity costs' of childbearing have been variously calculated: Heather Joshi, the economist who has done most work on this, has estimated that having two children reduces a woman's average lifetime earnings by a half. As she drily observes: 'foregone earnings as a result of parenthood is a price of this pleasure and privilege which is paid by women and not by men'.[31]

The pay gap between women and men is now largely a result of family responsibilities (although it changes with age too). The average pay of single childless women is over 95 per cent of that of single childless men; but married mothers earn, on average, only 60 per cent of the pay of married fathers. In a detailed analysis of the gender gap in pay, economist Jane Waldfogel found that the gap between women with and without children is 22 per cent and that the 'gender gap' for mothers is twice as wide as the gap for non-mothers. The technical language she uses is revealing: she talks about 'the estimated size of the child penalties'.[32]

Her research was done on a group of women who were 33 when interviewed in 1991, busy with 'career-building and family formation'. They are particularly interesting to look at since they are the first true 'equal opportunities' cohort. They turned 17 in 1975, the year the Equal Pay Act came fully into effect. 'As such they also delineate the limits of equal opportunity.' In comparison to variables like education and experience which might also be expected to explain the gender pay gap, she says, 'by far the most important factor by age 33 is family status'. This has not changed since the 1970s but has increased in effect: 'as women have narrowed the gender gap over time, the relative importance of family status in explaining the gender gap may have increased'.

There were improvements in work status and pay for women with young children during the 1980s, but they fell very unequally. Alongside the rise in the proportion of mothers of dependent children out at work and in full-time work, the 1980s saw a rise in the proportion of them in higher-status, better-paid work. Nevertheless, women without children still had a better occupational profile at the end of the decade. A Warwick University study in 1994 confirms 'the continuing contrast between the labour market situation of women without and with children'. Women without children living with a partner, and younger single women, made up most of the increase in women moving into management and professional occupations, the study says, and it predicts that this will continue. Its evidence suggests that if the younger women marry and have children 'many will find it difficult to sustain the type of employment available to them before they have children'.[33]

Employment rates over the 1980s rose fastest for mothers with fewer and younger children, white mothers, mothers living with employed partners and with higher levels of qualification, as well as those living in East Anglia and the South West. Employment grew slowly or fell among mothers with no qualifications, lone mothers and black mothers. Mothers with a qualification above A level were already more likely to be employed but over the 1980s they became much more likely to be – almost twice as likely as other mothers. And those working full-time were four times more likely to have professional or managerial jobs than mothers in part-time work.[34]

This reinforced the polarisation between families with two earners and none, and between families with two full-time earners rather than one and a half – in the former the woman is more likely to be highly qualified and more likely to have gone back to work soon after childbirth.

Most research concludes that women maximise their earnings by using maternity provision and staying in the labour market and with the same employer over childbirth, and that expanded childcare (meaning more opportunity to work full time) is also crucial. It is also clear that the longer the 'time out' the higher the economic penalties. (Though that difference recedes over time – once women go back to paid work there is some 'catching up'.)[35] This may maximise earnings but at what personal cost? But refusing the dominant model of achievement and autonomy also has penalties. Many, probably most, women with children *want* to play the major part in bringing them up – what we don't want is for that to be at such unreasonable cost.

The absent father is not uncommon; the absent mother is close to a contradiction in terms. Fathers who leave do so 'with relative impunity' says Rosie Jackson in her book *Mothers Who Leave*, but mothers who leave are damned.[36] When family commitments are seen as contingent the defining connection becomes that of mother and child. It is bringing up children today that really is 'for better, for worse'.

I was struck, looking at various accounts of motherhood, by how 'dispensability' and 'specialness' seem to be key concepts both in tipping motherhood off its pedestal and reclaiming it. Among other things, we need a feminism able to say that what we do as mothers *is* special and valuable, but it's not all we do, and not all of us do it. (And we do it in different ways.) Not new or earth-shaking things to say or apparently so *very* difficult. Feminism's dominant account has emphasised one half of the tension – that it is a very ordinary thing to do, adding that it is a socially constructed thing to do, and (in effect) downgrading its importance to the individuals concerned and to society. We need now to negotiate an equal tension: to recognise that maternity engages the deepest feelings of many women (both positively and negatively) and is very significant in most women's lives, not least in its time demands but also emotionally, intellectually, spiritually. But we must do so *without* accepting biology as destiny, without elevating nurturing above other important human skills and without again presenting as deviant those women for whom this is not true.

The central challenge at the end of the 1990s is one which faced us at the beginning of the 1970s: how to allow women bringing up children to participate fully in the rest of human life as well.

Chapter 7

Single Mothers,
Shared Problems

A summary of current arguments about single motherhood was usefully provided by the *Daily Mail* in July 1993: 'Just who is to blame?' it asked four writers: one said feminism, another said the mothers, the third said the welfare state and the fourth said feckless fathers. (It *assumed* blame.)

Attacks on single mothers are not new: they have been variously seen as a charge on the parish, as unchaste sinners and in the newer secular language of the 1950s and 1960s as social misfits and neurotic. By the early 1970s it was not so much having sex outside marriage that was seen as reprehensible as the failure to use contraception successfully or to have an abortion which 'labelled them irresponsible'.[1] But as the cost to the Exchequer of single parent families dependent on benefits grew in the 1980s and early 1990s, so has the vociferousness of condemnation, albeit in several guises.

The 'problem' of single mothers dominated policy agendas and became the family issue on which access to the media was possible. Although domestic violence has had more public attention than in the past, questions about the prevalence of child abuse in the family and the relationship of power, violence and the construction of masculinity have been – despite Robert Black, despite Frederick West – displaced.[2] The political use of the family (meaning the male-headed family) has an effect on most women's lives but it is single mother families against whom its force is most fully directed, and, within them, against women who have never married.

Most discussion of family change has presented it as a consequence of women's increased autonomy. Living alone in a run-down council flat with demanding children and never enough money is a funny description of freedom. None the less, as so many single mothers have said, you wouldn't do it if it wasn't likely to be better, even so. Judy Aitken said, 'without him it was a lot easier. He was mair problem than four kids together.' Frances Corr put it this way: 'to take it to extremes, it's like somebody escaping from a concentration camp and finding themselves in the middle of nowhere. It's like that, it's getting out of something that's absolutely desperate because you've got to get out but you still find yourself somewhere that's very, very hard ...'

Single Mothers in the Eye of the Storm

Public debate about single-parent families raises questions which seem to me about two things: 'family values' versus women's independence, and the role of the welfare state. In the political arena both operate to different degrees. Most ministerial attacks on 'women who have been kissed' have been understood to presage further action on the perceived need to prune welfare spending, but the sub-text is always women's behaviour and potential autonomy.[3] Bringing up children on our own, possibly even choosing to bring up children on our own, is felt as women's freedom going too far. Although the motivations of an individual single mother may be very far from anything recognisable as defiant, rebellious or even particularly positive (she may have gambled on a sexual relationship becoming committed and lost, she may be 'looking for love', she may simply have not managed contraception), she is nevertheless the focus of a struggle for the survival of male authority.

Open season on single mothers was kicked off, publicly at least, by a speech by the Welsh Secretary, John Redwood, in Cardiff in July 1993 which received very wide publicity. There had been, we now saw, a brief window of decency between the time when a Divorced Woman suffered social stigma (still the case in the early 1970s and of course always the case in some pockets of society) and now, when if she has children she is a drain on the state and mother of most ills. Come back the Fallen Woman, you have a necessary role.

The police promptly reported that for the St Mellon's housing estate which so alarmed Redwood there were 240 injunctions preventing fathers returning home. Redwood's speech coincided with an announcement in the House of Commons by Peter Lilley that Britain faced an unsustainable £14 billion rise in the cost of state benefits by the end of the century. Labour MP Frank Field, who chairs the Commons Social Security Select Committee shares this concern with the limits of welfare, and its role in encouraging women to leave or do without men.[4]

At the 1992 Tory Party conference Peter Lilley had revealed his 'little list' on which 'young girls who get pregnant just to jump the housing queue' figured high. It was a myth Mrs Thatcher had also favoured, although research has shown it has no significant basis in reality. In a speech to the party conference in 1993 Peter Lilley singled out those mothers who never married and specifically excepted the majority of single mothers. Widows and the divorced 'deserve not our blame but our support', he said, but named unmarried mothers as undeserving. (It gives an added meaning to 'better to have loved and lost ...') 'Are policies accidentally undermining the family?' he asked. There were 1.3 million single parents, 'many against their will', but the fastest growing group were 'those who hold it to be politically incorrect to uphold the traditional family'. This emphasis was shared by the *Sunday Times*. 'The problem is not single-parent families; it is *a particular type* of single parent ... unmarried mothers.'[5] (My italics – divorced mothers, after all, might be nice but redundant women once married to newspaper leader writers or Government ministers.)

In a speech in June 1994 in Birmingham Peter Lilley again expressed his alarm at the rise of births outside marriage, outside 'any stable union between the parents'. Contentiously he linked lone parenthood to domestic violence and child sexual abuse, as cause rather than consequence. 'As a result of divorce, separation and illegitimacy, some two million children are brought up by a lone parent and some half a million families are stepfamilies. Violence between men and women is a growing concern ... The physical and sexual abuse of children, particularly involving household members who are not the natural parent, is an even more disturbing phenomenon.' Sexual abuse of children by stepfathers *is* a disturbing problem but Lilley turns a reality, in which many women leave men *because* of violence and abuse on its head to suggest that violence and abuse occur because they leave or because they haven't married in the first place. (We have in fact no evidence that domestic violence and child-abuse has increased, only that more women refuse silence.)

This was not a consistent attack however, even from within the Cabinet. Virginia Bottomley argued that 'We are too quick to condemn a minority of parents; too slow to praise that great majority of parents who discharge their responsibilities well.' And she asked 'do we really want to retreat to the days when many women were economically oppressed into unhappy relationships?' The Scottish secretary Ian Lang has also argued against stigmatising single mothers as has Tory MP Alan Howarth, who said: 'Punitive policies would hurt the children as well as the parents, and make no sense either morally or economically'.[6] However, the reshuffle in summer 1994 left right-wingers in charge of all of welfare except health.

Needless to say, none of the attack looked at single fathers. Their numbers are small and they are less likely to be on benefit. The apparently egalitarian and increasingly common usage 'lone or single parent' has a gender neutrality which has little meaning in practice. Unemployment, which has left those communities with least choice and least mobility in a situation of economic emergency, is conspicuous for its absence in a debate which prefers to focus on the more promising subject of women's sexual behaviour.

I talked about this with many women, including several members of the One Plus writers' group in Glasgow. As might be expected, the group are both articulate and angry. We talked about poverty and the depressing sense of its endlessness: 'that hopeless feeling that it's going to go on for ever ...' Of isolation and lack of support, and 'being treated like a scrounger'. We also talked about feelings: the hurt, the rejection, the sense of failure, of achievement, of relief.

'It's better,' Donna Callender said, 'making your own mistakes than waiting on him coming through the door to tell you what you've done wrong. Not wondering should I make the dinner, should I lock the door tonight, has he got his key, is he coming at all?' And, she said quietly, 'you can think for yourself'.

You need, Audrey Gabriel emphasised, to make realistic comparisons. 'Most women are on their own with the kids all day whether they're single parents or not. Are you any the less burdened if you have a man coming in at 5.30 and out again at 7?' Donna took up her point: 'It's a different sort of stress waiting on help and support and not getting it. You're entitled to it – but it only makes you angry.' Expectations which are continually disappointed were worse: 'If you know that these things aren't going to happen, you can live with that'.

'Well, you're conned,' says Frances Corr wearily, 'conned from the word go. The message is get married, have kids, live happily ever after – well, it isna' like that.' 'You're seen as a failure,' Audrey says. 'You feel within yourself you're a failure,' Liz Crawford says.

Audrey has bright, dark, anxious eyes. The poem she read was saturated with depression. But she says: 'OK, I was skint and homeless. But I'm glad I did it. I've developed more as a person, I've discovered I can cope even if it is a struggle. I'm happier now.'

There are much the same stresses as there ever were, but worsened by an erosion of community: 'People having a hard time themselves needing a scapegoat.' Liz is a widow with four children, though previously she had been separated from her husband, who was violent and had a drink problem. For twenty years when she was married she wouldn't tell anybody she had problems: 'now I'm relearning the process of living, I'm enjoying myself ... Yes, there are new difficulties but at least you can get on and deal with them – you have a wee bit independence.' She is a nurse, a strong, assertive woman who laughs a lot. She took her husband back when they found he was dying, of an illness which had contributed to his behaviour.

With poverty and unemployment and so many people's lives getting harder, more fragmented, people are looking for somebody to blame, Liz thinks. She talks about when her husband was so ill: 'nobody came near. There's no sense of community now. It's more anger. Oh she's a single parent [*pointing*] but I saw her out *two* nights last week ... People's attitude, single parent or not, has changed – they're not interested.'

Continuing Stigma

Single mothers, especially single mothers on benefit, are at the sharp end of social, family and employment change and in the eye of a storm relevant to all women. Not only have there been predictable attacks from the Right but recently, and perhaps more significantly, there has been a shift in the liberal middle. The attacks have consequences for single parents in policy and practical outcomes, and more immediately in terms of their self-esteem.

You would have to be very strong indeed not to be affected by the persistent message that you are failing your children. As Sue Robertson, director of One Parent Families, Scotland commented, even if threats to change the benefit rules for single mothers come to nothing they frighten women and make their lives, already hard enough, feel besieged. A changing political climate will also have an effect on current practice even if there is no specific legislation. (For example, when the Child Support Act was being discussed but well before it became law some social security officers in Scotland were already putting single mothers under greater pressure to name the father of their child.)

'It's a propaganda war,' Frances Corr said. 'It punishes you for a situation that wisna' your fault in the first place. It's our fault kids are delinquents, we're scroungers, parasites, expecting too much – even though you know it's not true it gets to you. There is a lot of hostility, you can get sucked up by it.' 'You're already fighting to bring your kids up decently – but with that press you start wondering. It puts an added pressure on a job already difficult,' Donna said. It pushes you on to the defensive: 'If you are having any difficulties with your children, with discipline or anything else, then that's something you shouldn't be punished for but offered help with. But you don't want to ask for help, for fear of how you will be seen.'

Things are worse now for single parents than they were even eight years ago, Frances thinks: 'you used to be able to apply for money to get a washing machine for example, now they just say, "the budget's finished".' 'Money's the biggest pressure nowadays,' Liz Crawford said, to firm agreement. 'You're expected to do the impossible. And the kids, they see their pals getting things they haven't. You want them to be the same as all the other kids but you know you can't do it.'

Their comments were repeated by other single mothers. Poverty in a materialistic society is hard to handle, for children especially.

Judy Aitken, for example, talked about 'lack of money, poor housing, nowhere locally to go, nowhere you can afford to go. And next door's got £50 trainers and they're always off out somewhere.'

Siobhan Harkin is an unlikely rebel: a gentle-faced woman in her early thirties she has a daughter of nine, conceived during a short romance with a man who went back on his promises. She has a gift for quirky, personal poetry. She is convinced things are a lot worse for single mothers now. Her own mother was divorced when Siobhan was three and she remembers a lot of help from people when she was growing up: 'even the lollipop man used to look out for us'. Now she feels like a second-class citizen. 'My neighbours, none of them would even think to help out.' Her daughter's father, in nine and a half years, has 'taken her out for one day – although we're on good terms now'.

The increasing number of single mothers is a clear example of the complexity of assessing change. Women seem to be gaining greater freedom yet more women face the poverty most single mothers have to cope with, made harder as a consequence of changes in Income Support. The more single mothering is presented as harmful to children and society alike, the more it's implied that a single mother's lot is necessarily miserable, the more women may feel they should stick by their marriage. Though, as Frances Corr said, 'if this is supposed to be a deterrent it's not working. It couldna' be worse but people still get pregnant, people still separate from their partners … Yes, it's getting so difficult for us, but you don't see women looking at that and saying, "I'll not get pregnant then," or "I'll just stay with him then." It disna' work like that, it's no' human.'

She remembers the misery of the time when her own marriage split up, her worries about how it would affect her two boys, and the semi-derelict house they first had to live in – even so she *had* to leave, she says. She has wide, abstracted eyes and a calm, considered way of talking. But there is a deep sadness about her and something dead in her quiet, almost whispering voice. To afford to pay a babysitter makes a huge difference. 'I sometimes get in a state of panic when the weekend approaches. A night out would keep me going …' But it's having to ask all the time: 'I'm so tired of it now – living your life on favours. Phoning people, going round them all, asking them could they maybe babysit – trying to hide the desperation in your voice so they don't feel bad when they say they can't.' There have been a lot of low times, she shrugs. The turning point was in 1990 (when her boys were four and eight) and she got a housing association flat.

'The thing that really gets to me is when people suggest you're not trying, you're sitting sucking up the country's money. We do contribute to society – we're bringing up the next generation – people don't want to understand.' Because it's seen as your choice, there is a dismissal of how hard it can be, she says. She wrote a play for the Lone Rangers, *The Phone Box*: 'a typical day in the life of a single parent – at that point my life was taken up with standing in phone boxes trying to get through to the social security and housing, that was my entire day.' Four more plays followed, two for theatre companies, beginning a more positive cycle. 'A little bit of money, I can afford the after-school club, a bit of space. But I'm still on the bru – I'm not earning enough to rely on it.' She still feels trapped, 'and it's what happens to your mind when you're trapped. Then you get the chance to go out, there's nothing stopping you, and you're afraid to go out, you're wanting to go out and not able to do it.' Having the play on was exciting. 'It's such a good feeling when people can relate to your stuff. My head was in a spin, so much attention! I mean I've been on my own for years with not one person to listen to me!'

But: 'Money and nothing else – that's what gives me hope. Nothing more romantic than that. Nobody can be happy when they don't have enough to live on, it's as basic as that. You're helpless without it – because you can't get out to help yourself. You know what you need, but you can't do it. People say you mustn't be negative – if you were more positive you'd find a way out. That's no' the reality, not if you're on the bru. If there was any way out you'd find it, you'd no miss it, if there's any chink of light, you'll find it. It is a trap, that's why it's called the poverty trap, it's real.'

Author and researcher Debbie Taylor told me that in her work in developing countries she had become conscious of single mothers 'standing slightly apart, always, from everyone else – and they do stand apart, they have broken the rules or had the rules broken for them. They're out on the edge, challenging the rules of patriarchy – if reluctantly, almost always.'

The journey she took, which she wrote about in her book *My Children, My Gold*, living with seven single mothers in seven countries she learnt about the women's resilience but also the odds they faced.[7] 'They're the canaries in the coalmine, if you like – whatever it is, it hits them first.

'Good girl or bad girl' – she emphasises that those would not be her terms – 'it makes no difference. Widows are treated just as badly as women who have never married.' In Uganda, Scotland, China, Australia, Egypt and Brazil their worlds were very different but 'they had so much in common – the difficulties in hanging on to accommodation, mainly, and sexual harassment – the idea that if you'd been with one man you were available. That was true even of the Christian middle-class Australian woman.' The conspicuous difference was around the shame thing – where there's a lot of single motherhood then the women turned less to men for their sense of self-esteem ... If they were able to drop the burden of reputation then they had a much better time of it.' And female kinship ties, to sisters, aunts and grandmothers, provide a workable and emotionally rich alternative to a man-centred family, she found.

The Skewed Picture

To write about single mothers as a separate category of mothers is already to falsify the issues, to skew the terms in favour of a New Right agenda. It is false because it obscures the connection between the circumstances of single mothers and all, or most, mothers. The poverty of most single mothers is a consequence of women's economic dependence, particularly when we have children, and of our failure as a society to value the work of bringing up children. The idealised family and ideals of mothering make bringing up children harder for all women in whichever kind of family. And on some level the attacks are about creating/re-creating a deep division between 'good' and 'bad' mothers, between good women and the immoral and undeserving.

There is a crucial line to be drawn between recognising that many single parents have a hard life and presenting them as a social problem because they are on their own. Most public discussion manages to ignore the happy and successful single parent families – after all, they're not supposed to exist.

The routine listing of single parent families as an indicator of deprivation in an area is something that particularly angers Penny Taylor, a BBC journalist and the single mother of a 15-year-old daughter, Rohse, born when Penny was in her early twenties. 'It's a common cliché and meaningless,' she says. 'OK, so many lone mothers live in run-down flats and on benefit – first we need to ask why, why it's *made* so difficult. And secondly, it's not true of all of us.' Penny is outspoken, outgoing and energetic. There have been hard times – 'money, really'. When Rohse was a baby the only job Penny could get was as a cleaner, taking the baby with her. But it's been immensely rewarding: 'looking back, there are so many positive things ... not many problems really'.

There is both more public and media prejudice she thinks *and* more social acceptance. 'But there is an intense horror of women managing on their own. Many more of us are managing fine – but you'd never know it. The media has a single-track image and so have some social scientists. The idea of happy and successful single parent families mustn't be allowed.'

A similar point was made by Josie Henderson, who is bringing up four children on her own after the break-up of her marriage five years ago: Sem (16), Hannah (13), Conan (9) and Ellen (7). At a conference organised by the Parent Teachers Association she had overheard a remark by an education official about 'a problem school' with 'a high percentage of children from one-parent families on income support'. 'I thought, well that's me ... It was as if I was there disguised as this respectable person!

'I know a lot of women in the same position as me – we may not be able to give our children the material things, but we're doing everything we can to make sure they're all right. I feel that's just negated, when someone talks like that.

'I put a huge amount of energy into just keeping us afloat, into keeping the children feeling good so they'll get something out of school, out of life – which they wouldn't if I was clinging to the table at eight o'clock in the morning with a hangover, weeping and saying I can't cope.' If she could wave a magic wand it would be to create a 'more realistic' financial basis for their lives, 'nothing else – it's not in terms of relationships or just being on your own, it's the economics that introduce the difficulties.'

Facts ... Facts ... Facts ...

If, during the 1970s, a big change was the increasing number of single parent families created by divorce, now (and since the early 1980s) it is the increasing number of babies born out of wedlock, to use a phrase with a certain poetic accuracy. The number of women who marry because they are pregnant has dropped away dramatically. Indeed in Susan McRae's study of cohabitation a number of women who had later married their child's father said they hadn't married earlier *because* they were pregnant: 'I didn't want to get married when I was pregnant because it would have seemed I was pressurised into it', and 'I felt ... it was the wrong reason to get married at the time.'[8]

Between 1971 and 1991 single-parent families increased from one in thirteen of families with children to one in five, a proportion which has stayed roughly stable since. Most – then and now – are woman-headed. The proportion of male-headed single parent families has fallen; they are more visible but still unusual; one in six single parent families was headed by a father in 1971 and it is now one in ten. A family form which had been uncommon became so common– although clustered in cities and areas of poorer housing – that at least stigma on grounds of difference alone could not survive. In many school classrooms the notion that Mary stays at her dad's at weekends, John has two dads and Tim hasn't any, is so familiar that the sense of being set apart is scarcely an issue any more, at least among the children themselves. And, especially significant in a time of greater social and economic disparities more generally, the experience of life as a single parent is one which crosses class, even if specific dimensions of it (housing particularly) do not, or not often.

The breakdown of marriage continues to be the major route to becoming a single-parent family. But always-single mothers, the smallest group in 1971, have been a growing proportion, as various government spokesmen have been eager to emphasise. Most single mothers in the 1970s got that way as a consequence of divorce; at the end of the 1980s the proportion of divorced and separated to single/cohabiting single parents was close to two-thirds to one-third. Now just over half of single parents are women who are divorced or separated.[9]

Births outside marriage had stayed stable for all of this century at around one in twenty of all births, with small but conspicuous blips for both world wars.[10] They began to increase from the early 1960s and now account for one in three of all births. The steepest increase in extra-marital births was between 1983 and 1988 (when there was a rise of almost 10 per cent) and the rate of increase has since slowed to just under 7 per cent (to 1993). In comparison, the number of divorced lone mothers almost trebled between 1971 and 1981 but that was followed by a more modest rise during the 1980s, reflecting the trend in the divorce rate.

Because the category 'single mother' includes women who previously cohabited with the father of their children, and women who are unmarried but living with a partner, this creates a persistent misrepresentation. Statistical habit which continues to emphasise marriage creates a distortion in the measurement of family change. And an unknown number of mothers recorded as single will be living in lesbian couples. Of births outside marriage a much greater proportion, now around three-quarters, are jointly registered by a mother and father and over half of them are living at the same address. Comparing 1971 and 1991 data on single mothers shows that although in 1971 pre-marital conceptions were much more likely to be followed by marriage and in 1991 more births were to single mothers, many more children in 1991 were born to cohabiting couples.[11] There are significant differences according to ethnic group, with high numbers of Afro-Caribbean mothers single, but very low numbers (just over one in ten) of Pakistani/Bangladeshi mothers single.

A further important qualification to any analysis of two- and one-parent families is that it will give a falsely static picture. As Penelope Leach and Patricia Hewitt say: 'Statistics can summarise some of the realities, but real life is even more complicated because it is not static. Children who start life living with their two parents may later become part of a one-parent family and, later still, part of one or more step-families.'[12] In Jonathan Bradshaw and Jane Millar's study for the DSS they comment on the 'complexity and volatility of the actual processes of becoming a lone parent'. You can become it more than once; or there are single parents who later marry or cohabit and thereafter separate; or someone may marry, divorce and *then* have children as a lone parent. A high proportion of younger lone mothers remarry.[13]

So who are the *really single* mums? There are two strong stereotypes: the disadvantaged teenager and the older single mother, independent and choosing to go it alone. Both have some truth, but both are a small minority. Single mothers are most likely to be aged between 20 and 34 – 84 per cent of never-married mothers who live alone with their children are in that age group according to a 1993 study,[14] and 76 per cent of births outside marriage in 1993 were.

Contrary to popular perception a very small proportion of single mothers are teenagers: less than 5 per cent are. But – not surprisingly – the younger the mother, the more likely it is she will be unmarried: in Scotland nine out of ten mothers under 20 are unmarried and almost as many are in England and in Wales. However, this is as much about the very steep fall in teenage marriage as it is about teenage pregnancy, in which there has been an overall decrease: between 1970 and 1991 the rate of women aged 15–19 giving birth almost halved, both because the conception rate for that age group has fallen and because abortion has become more frequent for that age group. Women under 20 are much less likely to have children now but they are much more likely to be single if they do. (In 1981 just over half of teenage women who had babies were married, in 1993 15 per cent were.) It has not been a consistent fall: teenage conceptions and pregnancies rose during the 1980s before falling again for the first time in 1991, a fall which has continued to 1993 and which the Family Planning Association (FPA) believes is continuing for both over- and under-16-year-old mothers. But teenage pregnancies are still very high in Britain compared to other European countries, and parts of Scotland have the highest rates in Western Europe.

It worries me that we almost always talk about teenage pregnancy now as a social problem – though it is a measure of change that we do so. In the 1970s it was well within what was seen as normal and desirable – providing they had a man in tow, that is. But, again despite the stereotype, most teenage women giving birth are 19 (twice as many as 17-year-olds in 1991, for example). Most teenagers can be as good mothers as older women, given the right support – and *all* mothers need more support.[15]

The worry is whether teenage pregnancy prevents young women from having lives and choices beyond motherhood. Delaying motherhood has clear advantages in work and educational terms. But the decrease in teenage births, although it is across social class, is markedly less steep among poorer girls. Girls in deprived areas are much more likely to get pregnant and less likely to have an abortion than middle-class girls. As new Scottish research underlines, most teenage mothers have limited life chances before they become pregnant as well as because of it.[16] Most have very fragile chances of improving their material circumstances or working lives by waiting. What we really need to be asking is, why does life offer them so little else?

The same research shows that availability of contraception and confidence in seeking it out are both limited and more services designed for young people are badly needed: sex education is described as inadequate, 'piecemeal ... and not set firmly in the context of inter-personal relationships'.

Even for those teenage mothers who *do* fit the Ministerial stereotype, why should anyone wonder, if young people live in a culture of sexual freedom and sometimes pressure, that babies will result? Won't presenting teenage mothers as always unable to cope only make their lives harder and confidence lower?

The older, independent single mother may be a modern stereotype but she has some reality. Births outside marriage for women over 30 trebled during the 1980s, accounting for nearly half the overall rise in the number of births to women in their thirties (although the numbers are still much lower than for extra-marital births to women in their twenties). For this age group, in the 1980s the likelihood of marriage following conception has halved, and the small but increasing numbers of women having children in their forties include a high proportion who are single. But again the way of counting misleads: a higher than average proportion of births outside marriage to older mothers were jointly registered by parents living at the same address; women having first children in a second relationship are also part of this changing pattern. For women over 30 there has also been a decrease in the proportion of conceptions leading to abortion, which suggests that women are finding it more acceptable to have a child – whether inside or outside marriage – at these older ages.

A Threat to the Nation's Welfare?

A number of contemporary themes were already familiar in the early 1970s. 'Unmarried mothers are still seen as a challenge to society, to our accepted ethical and religious concepts and to the institution of marriage itself,' Margaret Bramall, then director of the National Council for the Unmarried Mother and her Child, told a conference in June 1971. The terms used at that time – 'unmarried mothers', 'fatherless families' and 'illegitimacy' (which ceased to have any validity in 1987 as a result of a seventy-year campaign) – were noticeably different however, and a number of 'experts' had what now seems an uncomfortably charitable, condescending approach. The idea that single mothers themselves might be the best analysts of their position, unlike doctors and social workers, had yet to come.[17]

But mother and baby homes were still usual and placement for adoption, now unusual, was common – at around a quarter of single births. An understanding that the mother might feel 'deep grief' was beginning to be expressed, but there was chilling 'expert' discussion about the advisability or not of a mother who plans adoption seeing her baby after birth.[18] The steep fall in the number of babies available for adoption at the same time as the social stigma for unmarried mothers eased tells us something about how genuine a choice that was, as do women's own accounts.

The problems single mothers faced in 1970 – accommodation, social isolation, lack of childcare and dependence on Supplementary Benefit, 'hostile social attitudes' – are reflected in what women say today. A study from 1976 begins with the words: 'It is all too easy to generalise about those difficult decisions which others have to take without an understanding of their circumstances' and says that single mothers 'have for all too long been the victims of a society whose policies have often been determined by opinion rather than by knowledge.' It is still true.[19] The difference is that the stereotyping and misinformation with which policy development is now dogged take place at a time when the post-war consensus on the welfare state is increasingly under threat.

The Poverty Trap

The likelihood of single-mother-headed families living in poverty is something I mentioned in the previous chapter. The facts are shocking, so worth enlarging on. Single mothers are twice as likely to be in the poorest 10 per cent of the population than their numbers in the general population would suggest; three-quarters of children living in single parent families live in poverty. DSS figures show that three-quarters of single parent families were living below half average income in 1992 against less than a third in 1979.[20]

One major consequence is poorer housing: 60 per cent of single parents live in council housing compared to 20 per cent of two-parent families, and they are more likely to live in the poorer-quality public housing.[21] There has been a recent increase in single parent families living in bed and breakfast accommodation because no alternative can be found.

Since 1980 single mothers are less likely to have jobs than they were (only four in ten are employed, half in part-time work). Those who do have jobs are very likely to work short hours and be low paid: the average earnings of women with dependent children are lower than those for other women, and those of single mothers lower still. A 1994 DSS report shows that just under a quarter of all single mothers work more than 23 hours weekly and even those who work full-time are typically low paid.[22] Of single mothers with jobs, a quarter spend up to half their pay on childcare. Childcare has a very direct alleviating effect on family poverty. Equal pay would of course have an even more direct effect.

Three-quarters of single mothers live on benefits; One Parent Benefit was an advance but its value was eroded when it was not inflation-proofed in 1991. Social security cuts, alongside spending cuts by local councils, have affected lone mothers and their children badly. Not only have the targets set by the Finer Committee in 1974 never been seriously attempted, but successive pruning of budgets has worsened a never-good position. Such is the social climate that we rarely protest about this any more. In particular the switch from Supplementary Benefit to Income Support (in 1988) was a 'simplification' which made life harder for single parents. The Social Fund and the loss of an automatic right to grants for household equipment has hit single parents particularly hard since they are often long-term claimants. At the end of 1994 it was reported that more than a million applications a year for loans from the Social Fund which met the fund's criteria are being rejected because it has insufficient money.[23]

The loss, also in 1988, of the childcare allowance in Supplementary Benefit, and the loss of a graduated earnings disregard in favour of the formula sum of £15 all meant a reduction in single parents' opportunities to escape the poverty trap. These policy decisions made it harder for single parents to be independent of the state at a time when they were being blamed for their dependency.

Most single mothers would like to have jobs, according to the DSS's own evidence, but lack of childcare and the poverty trap make it either impossible or against their interests.[24]

The Welfare Trap

While policies influenced by punitive thinking have been considered by government, the specific substantive consequences of the latest round of attacks on single mothers amounted to, by the time of writing (in spring 1995), one thing: help with childcare costs for people on Family Credit. While this measure is not without its complications (the way the disregard works favours the better-off within that group rather than the poorest; and more low-waged work may not be the best answer to many single mothers' problems) it is none the less a welcome and positive measure. At the 1994 Tory Party conference it seemed that plans trailed the previous year had been derailed. The reasons why are instructive. The first proposal to follow the declaration of intent at the 1993 conference was homelessness legislation for England and Wales. The unworkability of these proposals was such that there were over 9,000 objections from within the housing profession to the initial consultation paper and only one organisation in favour: the Conservative-controlled London Boroughs Association. No legislation was introduced for 1994–95 although the intention may be revived in the forthcoming housing white paper.

So has that sound and fury signified precious little? Yes and no, is the short answer. The long answer is inevitably more complicated. But it is genuinely difficult to cut benefits which are already at the bone.

I also think that the attempt to portray single mothers as the immoral, undeserving poor has at least partly failed because of public response, or lack of response. That the attacks struck a muted chord (apart from with *Telegraph, Sunday Times* and *Express* leader writers) was partly for demographic reasons – with more than a million women at any one time single mothers who won't be keen to identify themselves as 'the problem' and many more people whose friends, daughters and sisters are single mothers, that's quite a lot of people/voters these days. It is simply harder to characterise a large group as 'other'.

Alongside the old myths a newer, alternative one is perhaps taking hold, of anguished single mothers working heroically against the odds – this version is courtesy of the Archbishop of Canterbury – which may be neither accurate nor, in the end, helpful either.

Creating the right policy to support single parents without disadvantaging other parents living in poverty is genuinely difficult. The Social Justice Commission's fairly beneficent proposals for 'an intelligent welfare state' make this evident when you stop to think about how they would work. The present benefits system is, as they say, 'all too often part of the problem' and the welfare system they favour, for very good reasons, is social insurance based, but as such is necessarily connected to paid work. Credits for people taking time off to care for children or others in need of care are intended. But without any costings it is hard to see how it would work in practice – and in practice expensive details like that are often the first to go.[25]

Returning to work *is* different for most single parents. Combining work and bringing up children can be harder for parents doing it on their own, and especially so for those looking after children upset by a painful relationship breakdown. We need to think about *what* work. A treadmill of low pay plus loss of benefits like school meals will scarcely be better. Opportunities for training and education would meet many single parents' longer-term needs much better: but the additional costs of studying, the unavailability or cost of childcare and the absolute maze of trying to work out funding are all serious disincentives.

The Finer Committee in 1974 got it about right: a Royal Commission set up by Harold Wilson to look at the needs of the growing number of single parent families, its report is considered one of the major social documents of this century. The 230 recommendations included a benefit adapted to fit varying work, whether full time, part time or none, something the Social Justice Commission also recommended last year, and collection and guarantee of maintenance plus a tax-credit scheme. In 1975 Margaret Bramall at OPF wrote: 'If the Report of the Finer Committee is implemented, the lives of most one-parent families will be revolutionised. If the Report is shelved a tremendous opportunity to help over one million children will be lost.' It was lost.[26]

Structures to support a proper balance between work and family life *for everyone* would mean that the needs of single parents can be integrated and met, rather than treated as a social problem. Comparison of how single parents fare in countries with a high degree of support for all families with young children and those which target support for single parents makes this clear.[27] Such support for working parents even encourages the kind of self-reliance politicians call for.

Although much of the discourse around single mothers suggests a resistance to changing women's roles, the welfare dimension is critical. It is the stated context of government discussion: a cabinet paper leaked to the *Guardian* in November 1993 said: 'The primary objective of any measures taken will be to reduce the burden on public expenditure caused by lone parent families.' A less narrow analysis would include the costs incurred by *not* supporting poor families, in terms of health and poor life prospects, and the converse gains of ensuring a decent upbringing for all children. Welfare cuts which affect children, no matter whose, are no sort of saving except in the very short term. Indeed the small (at point of delivery) sums spent on people on Income Support bringing up children offer a remarkable return on investment – though the return would be greater if the investment was greater too.

But myths of 'dependency culture' and the growth of the 'underclass' have more influence on how policy is developed than research findings and longer-term thinking. The parallel between the notion of *deliberate* single motherhood and *deliberate* unemployment – people who 'decide to be idle and to live off others', in Michael Portillo's words – is worth paying attention to.[28] By focusing on and stigmatising one group you may legitimise or disguise cuts that also affect others; by creating an agreed category of undeserving poor you justify dismantling a system. There is a kind of slippage: first, criticism is explicitly focused on teenage single mums on benefit, then that characterisation comes to stand for all single mothers, then it slips from single mothers to all claimants. The severe cuts in unemployment benefit introduced in the euphemistic Jobseeker's Bill, cutting entitlement by half, from twelve to six months, came almost immediately after public discussion had expected, and protested about, cuts to single parent benefits. The proposals on council waiting lists were described as ending priority to single mothers but they have no such priority (though any homeless people with dependent children have), and would in fact remove the requirement to offer permanent housing to any category of homeless people.

There is of course a tried and tested alternative to some of the growing welfare costs of single parents – publicly funded, high-quality childcare. It is only part of the answer, but an important part. It would be expensive, but at least two detailed studies now show that the cost of childcare can be significantly offset by economic (as well as social) gains.[29] But catch the government spending serious money so those shameless women can dump their kids and go off and enjoy themselves stacking supermarket shelves.

In the 1970s legislation laid down the preconditions which make it easier to move out of bad relationships, and increasing women's employment and self-esteem has also played a role in that. Social change has meant pregnant unmarried women now have a range of options. But as the tide of change has in consequence grown stronger there has been no serious attempt to follow through in any positive way and some attempts to create barriers against it. Single parents and their children live with the results of policy failure and a more general incapacity to respond to change every day.

Chapter 8

Family Ties and Boundaries: the need for a new debate

If the return to traditional values was a strong Conservative theme of the early 1990s, the whole rise of Conservatism in the last quarter of the century can be understood as an attempt to resist social change of which the changing roles of women are seen as the major part. 'Back to basics', for example, the campaign unleashed on the world as an attempt to provide John Major's mid-term government with some sense of direction in late 1993, was a clear expression of end-of-century resistance to change. The rot, according to this line of thinking, set in with the 1960s and has been continued by 'fashionable opinion', social workers and teachers and apologists for crime, people who, according to John Major, in his speech to the 1993 Tory conference, believe 'the family was out of date and that it was far better to rely on the council and social workers than family and friends'.

In 1993 John Major promised to lead Britain back to a traditional Conservative morality based on self-reliance, decency, the family and respect for the law. It was as a revealing coda to its public pronouncements that his government was thereafter hit by a series of sexual scandals which illustrated the underside of family values that women have always known about – known about as the mistresses kept in secret, the secretaries discreetly driven to private abortion clinics. Major explicitly appealed to people as bewildered and disturbed by 'a world that sometimes seems to be changing too fast for comfort, old certainties crumbling, traditional values falling away

... And they ask where is it going, why has it happened and *above all, how can we stop it?*' (my italics)[1]

How indeed? By April 1995 and the departure of Junior Minister Richard Spring after a 'three-in-the-bed romp' described in great detail in the *News of the World*, the government had lost seventeen ministers 'for non-policy reasons', as it is put.

Resistance to women's independence and shoring up fatherly authority have, for most of the past twenty-five years, coalesced around the idea of family values, with partial effect, though it has been neither as coherent nor as successful an attack on feminism as some accounts suggest. Zoe Fairbairns published her novel *Benefits* in 1979.[2] It's what might be called social science fiction – an account of the manipulation of fertility and wages for housework in a future in which feminists and a new political party called 'Family' glare balefully at each other over the dying body of the welfare state. It rapidly ceased to seem a very distant future. It is now seen, she says with some amusement, as a novel about Thatcherism although it was written under a Labour government: 'it's about sexual politics, not just party politics ...'

The politics of the family does not divide neatly into Left and Right. In a key speech in the ending of the post-war consensus which brought Margaret Thatcher to power, Keith Joseph, her fellow architect of the move to the Right, described family life and cultural values as being undermined by permissiveness and collectivism and claimed (*pace* John Major in 1993) that 'socialists want to take responsibility from parents'.[3] With arguments that would surface again in the early 1990s, if in more careful language, Joseph notoriously identified the threat to 'the balance of our population, or human stock' because 'a high and rising proportion of children are being born to mothers least fitted to bring children into the world ... they are producing problem children'. This eugenic dimension drew a great deal of criticism and is credited with ruining his political career. Would it now? (The main policy thrust of the speech – that teenagers should be encouraged to use contraception, which horrified other right-wingers – is now part of government health policy supported by a wide consensus.)

Family policy in the 1980s was marked by contradiction and ambiguity and cannot be straightforwardly understood as about

restoring the authority of the patriarchal family. It emphasises, as do
the difficulties the Major government has faced in putting rhetoric
into practice, the complexity of family change and policy. As Vicky
Randall and Joni Lovenduski argue, 'Despite the rhetoric, little was
done under Mrs Thatcher directly to sustain the family, traditional or
otherwise. Moral conservatism clashed with liberal ideas about limits
to state intervention and individual freedom, and with economic
priorities.' Although there was no support for measures to help
women with children into work there 'was no serious or consistent
attempt to turn the clock back and to drive women back into the
home'.[4] There was much rhetoric but few actual victories for the
moral conservatives. Clause 28 of the 1988 Local Government Act
which sought to prevent the 'promotion of homosexuality' by local
authorities is a conspicuous exception, perhaps because it was cheap
and a chance to get at Labour local authorities. Even so, this
legislation is now widely considered unworkable, if effective in
allowing and encouraging the expression of prejudice by some
councils and councillors.

In July 1990, in a speech to the 300 Group which campaigns to get
more women into parliament, Mrs Thatcher sought to defuse the
continuing internal Tory Party argument over working mothers by
insisting there was no straight choice for women between working
and staying at home and that it was no part of the state's role to
dictate the balance of responsibilities between them. 'There can be no
single solution that applies to everyone: family and economic
circumstances are so different, and so are temperaments and
aptitudes,' she said. 'Yet no matter how hard you work or how
capable you are, you can't do it all yourself,' she went on, before
spoiling those sensible words by saying that what working women
needed was 'a treasure'.[5] And wouldn't we all love one – but who is
the treasure's treasure? It sets in stone a division between women
who work for decent wages and women who work for them to make
it possible, at lesser wages.

The Thatcher Years saw the launch of the Conservative Family
Campaign in 1986, and a handful of similar organisations. Aiming to
get back to 'traditional' Christian and moral values, at its launch the
CFC declared the family under attack from 'too easy' divorce, social
security and tax which 'promotes unnatural arrangements', sex

education, the arts 'and, fundamentally by the undermining of the role of the man, the father, in society today'.[6] The CFC has called on the government to use tax policy to encourage mothers to stay at home. Similar arguments have more recently been made by Patricia Morgan, senior research fellow at the Institute of Economic Affairs, a right-wing think tank with a particular interest in social policy. In *Farewell to the Family? Public policy and family breakdown* she argues that government policies on tax and benefits have discriminated against families with children generally, but particulalrly against married men with non-working wives and in favour of single-parent families. This, together with rising male unemployment, is destabilising the family and creating a 'warrior class of unattached and predatory males'.[7]

Sex, Lies and Single Mothers

The assertion of 'family values' may not be new, but it is more dangerous, both because of the link to public expenditure cuts and because there is a growing centre-left/right consensus around 'the decline of the family'. This is that the increase of unmarried women having children is a consequence of welfare and damaging to the children and society, as expressed in John Redwood's seminal speech in July 1993. 'Do you want to be married to a man or married to the state? Freedom yes, but there have to be some basic rules.'

The *Sunday Times'* house sociologist, American Charles Murray, has provided ballast for New Right attacks on single mothers here and in the USA. He sees Britain as dividing into the 'new Victorians', middle-class, educated people 'concerned about children and community' and 'the new rabble': low-skilled, dependent on welfare and the black economy, with 'high levels of criminality, child neglect and abuse and drug use'. This is true of 'lower-working-class communities everywhere'. In massaging such prejudice he speaks to potent class-based fears; the disadvantaged become 'other', with different desires and sexual habits from decent people. This is a division likely to be fuelled by the growing insecurity of the middle class. Murray has caused massive controversy recently in the USA by the (still further increased) racism and eugenicism of his social analysis in his new book *The Bell Curve*. 'Illegitimacy,' according to Murray, is the best predictor of an 'underclass', a shabby concept which neatly blames those who live in worsening conditions for those conditions. Eliminating single mothers is therefore the solution: 'I favour eliminating benefits for unmarried women altogether'. The 'latent economic penalties of unmarried parenthood' (he does not of course mean parenthood, he means motherhood) are as 'natural' as extra-marital sex, he insists.'[8]

That those 'natural' penalties have included destitution, child death and child prostitution – in Britain in the past, elsewhere in the world today – or separating mother and child and compulsory adoption, is not something he allows to cloud his vision; nor is the effect of intensified pressure on young women to end extra-marital pregnancy in abortion. If unmarried women need state benefits to bring up children they should be offered instead 'a really excellent adoption service and orphanage system'.[9] Murray's thesis is based on unproven assumption and mainly American data; nor is his appeal to history accurate. His interventions into British debate in 1989 and 1994 were paid for and promoted by News International. It is pernicious, dangerous, immoral nonsense – promoted by some of the world's most powerful men.

Similar tough solutions have been proposed by British social theorists, including withdrawing benefit, re-creating mother and baby homes and compulsory adoption of babies of teenage mothers if the father is not involved. Options for cuts discussed by the DSS in the autumn of 1993 and again in 1994 were reported to include curbing one-parent benefit (then £6.05 per week), limiting amounts paid to separated couples both of whom claim benefit, and introducing benefit limits to discourage women from having more children while on benefit. An end to automatic entitlement and the idea that benefits should be made conditional on behaviour has a growing credibility.[10]

The control and manipulation of women's fertility is a characteristic of totalitarianism. I do not suggest our society is fascist, but that we have to be careful in those areas where we begin to create a common ground.

Murray's ideas also have a parallel in a convoluted argument in *Families without Fatherhood* by two ethical socialists, Norman

Dennis and George Erdos. This book was proudly, even triumphantly, published by the right-wing think-tank the IEA, who think that 'decent people' have been betrayed by an intelligentsia-led attack 'on all the taboos that protected family life ...' Theirs is a deeply nostalgic account of the values of the post-war respectable working class. Since it's the section of society I come from I am not as ready to dismiss an appeal to it as are some commentators. It's just that the world isn't like that any more. The institution of marriage, say Dennis and Erdos, was safeguarded by 'mothers and fathers, who sometimes made a harsh and cruel example even of their own daughters ... Much pain came from breaking the rule; pain to many more would come from weakening it.'[11] Fallen women and their babies must be sacrificed for the greater good. Ethical doesn't seem the right word for this sort of socialism.

The communitarian ideas influentially argued by another American sociologist, Amitai Etzioni, have much in common with ethical socialism. Etzioni is published and promoted in the UK by Demos, the high-profile 'new middle' think tank who, with *The Times*, organised his much-discussed lecture in March 1995. He also believes that self-interest and 'the rights movement' have led to the breakdown of the traditional family and morality; making divorce much harder, at least until children are grown-up and dissuading women without partners from having children, is part of the answer.[12]

Tony Blair, early in his campaign for leadership of the Labour Party, was keen to show he would be as strong on the family as he had, as shadow Home Secretary, been on crime. Not unreasonably – while Tory rhetoric on the family has been loud, economic policies since 1979 have made life harder for poorer people, among whom a growing proportion of families must be classed. In his first full-length TV interview after being elected he 'declared himself four-square behind the family', as the *Daily Mail* saw it at the time. A 'sensible position' on single mothers has become a measure of probity and soundness on contemporary morality, in itself a consequence of an agenda set by the New Right.

In his acceptance speech when he won the leadership, in July 1994, he put creating a world for decent people to raise families in high on his 'mission of national renewal'. He also talked of women's need to work and said that men were learning 'that they have a responsibility for sharing the burdens of family life to let women do so'. It was an important, even historic, statement. But he alarmed and worried many women, single mother Labour party members among them, when afterwards, in the television interview, he said that while 'the vast majority of single parents do not choose to be single parents, if they do I personally don't agree with them in doing that'. He went on to say that 'Rather than stigmatising single parents, I would like to see a situation in which those single parents are able to bring up their kids and, for example, go out and earn a decent living. But if what you're asking me is, do I believe that it is best that kids are brought up in a normal, stable family, then the answer to that is, yes.'[13]

Blair's message that the economic individualism of the right and social individualism of the far left are equally to be rejected was further developed in a *Spectator* lecture in March 1995, described as an 'audacious raid behind enemy lines'. And the following week, Blair (a man who wants to be a good Dad to the nation) angered some women activists at the Labour Women's Conference in Derby, by emphasising that 'Labour is the party of the family in Britain.' (It would not have been difficult to say 'the family in Britain in all its contemporary forms' if he had *wanted* to be inclusive) while body-swerving the difficult issues that might entail.[14]

Ethical socialism has gained a new impetus from Tony Blair's success but his personal definition of it, set out in a rather bland pamphlet published in 1994 does not tie it as closely to ideals of the traditional family as others do. Whether the more pragmatic, feminist analysis of family change advanced by Harriet Harman, Patricia Hewitt and Anna Coote in *The Family Way* and Harriet Harman's book *The Century Gap*, or the Christian socialist emphasis on new/old family values will win the family policy heart of New Labour is a question that remains of considerable relevance to women voters.[15]

Consider the children

The growing concern that divorce is damaging to children has been the explicit impetus behind reform of the Divorce Law in England and Wales. Plans for 'go-slow divorces' will mean replacing 'fault' grounds with a sole ground of irretrievable breakdown proved by the passage of a 12 month 'period for consideration and reflection'. During this period the couple would be encouraged to seek marriage guidance and there will be an increased role for mediation as outlined in the December 1993 Green Paper *Looking to the Future*, which begins with the unambiguous statement 'The Government is committed to marriage and the family'.[16]

The White Paper has been praised as likely to reduce conflict. The Chancellor, Lord Mackay, said he wanted 'to reduce the bitterness, hostility and sense of injustice which so often surrounded divorce'.[17] Waving a legal and money-saving wand won't do it. The only way is by reducing conflict between women and men in relationships: which would mean social and economic equality, equal expectations of marriage, and an end to violence in families. A key assumption in the Green Paper was that couples divorce in haste and their children repent at leisure. Yet the evidence they rehearse shows that the 'cooling off' period which is already provided for by the option of a no fault divorce after two years (when it was introduced in 1969 it was expected to become the majority route to divorce), has not been a popular option: three-quarters of divorces are sought on the grounds of adultery or intolerable behaviour (and take an average of six months to go through). In *Looking to the Future* the Government made clear it wanted divorce law change which would ensure 'that saveable marriages are saved' and would 'encourage people to think hard about the consequences of divorce before making any irreversible decision'. That a compulsory cooling-off period will 'reduce the trauma for the children' has yet to be demonstrated – unless it leads to the mass changing of minds the government dreams of but this side of Hollywood does not seem strictly likely. Uncertainty and raised and dashed hopes bring their own pain. Why 'consideration and reflection' will be encouraged by making divorce slower rather than by adequate additional funding for counselling and guidance is not clear.

Mediation plays an important role in creating better settlements in children's interests but the emphasis on 'a neutral third party' can mean sidelining the need for legal advice. Sometimes divorce is adversarial *not* because lawyers like a fight but because real differences have meant the parties *are* adversaries. There have been cases where women have been attacked by ex-partners they met for mediation, and one woman was killed.[18] Mary Watson, a woman now separated from a violent husband said to me: 'Everything's supposed to be done for the children, but it's not as easy as that. I've come to *hate* Family Mediation – the Courts seem to think it works miracles but it's only made things worse for us'.

Deciding to leave a violent relationship is often difficult and women can be bullied or frightened out of acting. Removing the possibility of almost immediate divorce where there is violence or abuse will be dangerous. The Chancellor promises 'better protection for domestic violence victims' during the compulsory twelve-month period but since police and legal protection is not sufficiently effective even now this may be an empty promise. Violence is a factor in a high proportion of divorces: we don't know in how many but in Millar and Bradshaw's research for the DSS the man's violence was a factor in 20 per cent of separations, and the main reason in 13 per cent. Violence was identified as a factor in a majority of divorce actions brought by women on grounds of unreasonable behaviour (grounds rarely used by men) in Scotland in the early 1980s.[19] There is no other research which would confirm that, but the extent of domestic violence makes it hardly surprising.

It is revealing how rarely the difficult subject of domestic and sexual violence is allowed to intrude on public discussion of 'the changing family'. There is a kind of collusion in not recognising that the numbers of women escaping bullying and violence against them and their children is a major reason for the increase in single parent families. What was almost wholly unspoken has begun to be spoken, but there is still massive denial. Sara Thornton has said: 'domestic violence is very hard to put across in a Court of Law because it has nothing to do with laws. Domestic violence is about pain and power and control ... Is it any wonder that people don't want to see it?'[20]

We may exaggerate the extent to which it is possible to talk about it even today and the intense pressures and constraints on women who suffer violence within ethnic minority communities have only begun to be addressed. One of the most important aspects of the Zero Tolerance poster campaign from the perspective of women who have suffered domestic violence, has been the public acknowledgement of its reality.[21] It is not to deny women's power in the family to recognise how much more vulnerable we can be, and how legal and social structures reinforce that. Violence aside, the determined emphasis on the *form* of the family skews all discussion of divorce. Most debate and research is locked into the question about whether life in a lone parent family is worse for children than life in a loving two-parent family *as if that was the choice on offer*, as if it remained a realistic alternative for most lone mothers and their children.

We *do* need to talk about quality of care, about committed parents and 'good enough' parenting and what enables it. There are problems for some children after divorce but their cause is rather more complex than recent debate allows, and 'two loving parents' is not a magic formula.[22] A full set of grandparents, several involved uncles and aunts and committed family friends would be better still. Is a child with two parents but no other close relatives worse or better off than a single parent's child who has close relationships with aunts and a granny? Dividing families into two and single-parent so insistently is artificial and unhelpful.

There is a kind of radical commonsense gloss to recent discussion. *Times* columnist Janet Daley, for example, says: 'Since children are enormously demanding of time and attention, then having two people around to do it is likely to work better than having one.' I would not disagree, except to say that unless you start to talk about which people, and what the relationships are like, this doesn't mean much. If an unsupported single mother has less chance of being in a position to look after her children well, so has an unsupported mother with a husband. Melanie Phillips (columnist in the *Observer*) is an exemplar of the shift in the liberal middle and seems to see herself as a lone battler against a new orthodoxy. 'A relationship with one parent is unhealthy' she asserts, and that, though imperfect, two-parent families 'are the model of a healthy society'. This is a common silliness. Families are not a model of society, they are *one* of the groupings which *make up* society.[23]

'Only the ideologically blind believe one parent is better than two.' a *Guardian* editorial declared.[24] Well no, actually, there is a proportion of cases where it is straightforwardly the case that one parent is better than two, those where violence and abuse has occurred. The absence of a male role model is routinely advanced as a central problem: sometimes the male role models available are ones for whose absence we might better be grateful.

'We must not be afraid of stating that it is better if at all possible for children to be brought up by both parents', as Norman Fowler, a man famous for wanting to be with his family, put it. Afraid of whom? Similarly Peter Lilley talked about the ideal of stable family structures: 'but for a long time it has been taboo to restate that ideal. People who did so were sneered into silence.' Patricia Morgan at the IEA inveighs against an apparently all-powerful 'anti-family establishment'.[25] It is curious that feminism is rarely named in these diatribes against 'the fashionable consensus'. Perhaps that would be to allow its ideas too much power. This overlaps though with the forceful anti-pc debate.

Despite Conservative rule for fifteen-plus years, despite the Conservative allegiance of all but four national newspapers, the hegemony of the sneering classes is apparently undisturbed. We are living in a 'soft-hearted, soft-headed liberal culture'[26] – which is curious since we've lived under Thatcherism and post-Thatcherism for so long. Funny thing, lots of people condemn child neglect and drug abuse and terrorising old ladies, even intellectuals and social workers. Even people who seek to *understand* social problems also sometimes have a sense of right and wrong, although John Major believes the two are incompatible. But moral high grounds are occupied not by pushing through hard arguments but by creating false opposition and implying through your own principled condemnation of rape, burglary and scrounging that your opponent thinks them excellent ways to behave.

That two parents are better than one is the answer to the wrong question. We need instead to ask what supports committed care for children? Why is it that so many men don't want to cooperate with women in bringing up children? What is many women's experience of relationships and male behaviour that they prefer to go it alone despite the penalties that occur? And for any generalisation you can only add – it depends which parents. Political discussion of lone motherhood is strikingly out of touch with life as it is lived.

Social policy has to be backed by real understanding of change rather than wishful thinking about normality and stability. Support for single parent families is not some nice liberal extra but integral to a society in which relations between women and men are truly equal and sex roles no longer constrain possibility: an equal relationship can never be built on unequal power, nowhere else to go.

To pick out never-married mothers for specific disapproval is to go along with a quite successful social myth which by emphasising women's choice and the apparent redundancy of men serves to excuse and explain men's disaffection from family life. If the real concern is that 'comprehensive benefits and free housing' reinforce 'the illusion that anyone can have a baby at any time regardless of their means' as Tom Sackville believes then couples on the dole who have children would logically also be in the firing line. (Perhaps they're next.) Civil service advice is that there is 'little clear evidence' that higher benefit rates for lone parents encourage women to have children on their own.[27] Women who have children on their own from the outset are a minority of single parents – and to describe even them as having made a positive choice would be hazardous.

It would make life easier if having babies were so simple. There is much talk of 'deliberate' pregnancy, and there are a few single women who go out and find a man with intent, certainly, and some who seek AID to do so (although there has been an attempt to end this). Even so, not very many do. The point at which choice comes into it for most women is when you discover you are pregnant. Let's be very clear: if by saying that single motherhood is wrong it creates a climate of increased hostility for women who decide to continue a pregnancy outside marriage then we are eroding choice *at that point*. Which means increasing the pressure on women to have an abortion. I believe 'a woman's right to choose' is a practical and morally important position: but it is as wrong to pressure a girl or woman into abortion as it is to compel a woman to carry and give birth to an unwanted child. It has to be a *viable* choice.

As it does at the breakdown of a relationship. Most divorces are initiated by women. To assume that means those women chose to bring up children on their own doesn't follow: a legal settlement is usually in the interests of the parent looking after the children. But at that point a woman's right to choose is equally important – to create what seem to her the best circumstances in which to bring up children even if that may only be a choice between the fire and the frying pan, even if none of the options is what she might have freely chosen.

Civilising the New Rabble

The absent father – 'deadbeat dad' in the USA – started to come strongly into frame in the mid- to late-1980s and was part of the thinking behind the the Child Support Act. It is on the surface of it the converse of the focus on the faults of single motherhood. The 'families need fathers' strand in this suggests that the threat of women's disaffection from men feels very real. But it can also be seen as a response to a challenging redefinition of the father's role, not just as provider but also carer. An argument articulated within feminism since the 1970s, that fathers should play a full and equal role in bringing up their children, is now coming from a rather different perspective. We can date its arrival in the mainstream to Peter Lilley's Birmingham Cathedral speech, which, if the Tory press is a measure, hit the spot. *The Times* ran a leader in June 1994 headlined 'FECKLESS FATHERS: Men have to learn to take responsibility'. The problem was named as deliberate single parenthood, but 'Mr Lilley is right to see the fathers as part of the problem. If a young man is unemployed (perhaps even unemployable) and is prepared to make no contribution either to the cost or to the care of the child, then it is not surprising that the mother should prefer to live on her own. To have the father in the household would be as much of an additional burden as an extra child.'

The Times continued, 'Becoming a father ... is one of the most civilising rites of passage for young men. Encouraging active fatherhood is one good way of reintegrating young men into a society which is widely seen to be disintegrating ... looking after children should be seen as an acceptable alternative to employment in a world in which jobs for women are easier to find than jobs for unskilled young men'. *The Times* also suggested a more flexible benefit system which could allow both parents to engage in part-time work without becoming worse off, which is indeed badly needed.

It is a measure of the changing discourse and influence of some feminist ideas, so why am I suspicious? Because looking after children is not almost the same thing as working on a building site.

Because of the almost complete absence of a culture of committed fatherhood within current constructions of masculinity. Some men are doing it anyway but they do so in a cultural vacuum, with little public presence or voice. Instead fathers are called for as a guarantor of functioning families and a better world. 'Families need fathers, communities need fathers,' Charles Murray declares. At stake 'is the survival of free institutions and a civil society ... How are males to be socialised if not by an ethic centred on marriage and family?' 'From the missing father flows the missing community ethic,' A.H. Halsey has declared.[28]

It is taken as quite natural that men will defect from the family and its 'onerous tasks', its 'heavy risks and responsibilities' unless persuaded/coerced otherwise. Sex is the 'tantalising prize' which will do this, 'unavoidable parenthood' what comes with it. I am reminded of Margaret Thatcher's ringing cry that 'No father should be able to *escape from* his responsibility.' Fathers 'protect their partners and their children from their economic and cultural disadvantages' say Dennis and Erdos, which is not a statement many single mothers in Drumchapel or St Mellon's would take very seriously. Even boys not doing well at school is now explained because they are 'growing up in communities deprived of the civilising role of father.'[29]

Civilising? All things being equal, of course it is good for children to have responsible and loving fathers. But they aren't equal. And some of the most marginalised, desperate communities in Britain, rather than benefiting from civilising fathers, are made more dangerous by the recreational violence of men and boys.

The intense anxiety is because the authority of the father over his family has traditionally been a validating symbol of all the larger social forms of authority, of law, society and religion, and has in turn been validated by them. 'This authority is in its very essence male,' argues writer Sean French, one of the few men to publicly discuss such issues, speaking at a conference for IYF, which was of the very few public forums to address fathering; it was attended by women, mainly. When politicians call for the return of the responsible father they are also calling for a return of a whole system of authority. 'A good father is a good thing, a bad father is a bad thing,' French went on to say, and that 'this might seem tiresomely self-evident' except that the right-wing had begun to talk as if 'he simply needs to be there, like a totem pole ...'[30]

The argument that women must civilise men is rather like the advice on sex which used to be given to young women: men would get carried away, it was our task to keep their urges under control. It easily slips into woman-blaming. Nor is there any awareness in this argument that recognition of women's equality might have some part to play. Men who want to be central to family life in new and better ways must rewrite their role in it and learn to accept equality. Without that the costs for some women of socialising men are now too high to be worth paying.

Women and Children Last

Feminism has challenged the automatic linking of 'women and children'. In the real world the connection is an abiding one. Arguments about the neglect of children and family crisis have in recent years been presented from within Conservatism and con-strued as an attack on women's freedoms. These are none the less real issues which feminism needs to address – and more than defensively. The notion of a feminist family values is going too far for credibility, but it is crucial that radical women have a stronger voice in creating policy that affects family life: policies which recognise that it is women who do almost all the work of bringing up children and caring for other dependants and look at what we need to do it better and less oppressively *without* accepting that we must do so and without giving up on sharing those responsibilities.

We need seriously to raise the question – what can women/ mothers do in the face of such *social* neglect of the needs of children? At the same time as arguing that children are not women's responsibility only.

There is both an overlap of interests between women and their children and a conflict of needs. Growing independence, especially expressed by working-class women, will necessarily create cracks in a social fabric predicated on women suppressing their needs and pretending men know best. 'The best interests of the child' are very often not the best interests of her mother – though the child will rarely be better off if the mother is worse off. It is a conflict which can't be magicked away with concepts like 'quality time' and even, though of course it would make a gigantic difference, more childcare.

There are genuine problems of transition as well as exaggerated fears. They are painful every morning when a woman leaves a child in care she knows is not very good, because it's all there is. They are horribly difficult when she must choose between a job which takes her away from a vulnerable teenager for long hours, or both of them living on an insecure pittance. They are heartbreaking for a woman who must decide between leaving her children alone during the school holidays or losing the job which keeps them. These conflicts are writ large at divorce or separation in decisions about custody and access: the child's right to be in touch with the father is in thousands of cases in direct opposition to the mother's need to make a new start. It hurts when a child comes back difficult and 'acting out' from a weekend with Dad. It is hard to manage when a father may or may not turn up on Saturday, depending on whim or whether you've been polite enough on the telephone, arranging it. This conflict is made very clear in proposals to increase unmarried father's rights in the Scottish Children's Bill, which may go further than the current legal position in England and Wales in which (since the Children's Act) an unmarried father can have equal parental rights and responsibilities by means of an agreement with the mother.[31]

The growing articulation of children's rights, which I agree with in principle and have argued for in public, too often ignores what that means in practice: for women. How do you square that circle? Even the long-term solutions are not easy. New arguments that the needs of families must be made central to the legislative and political process (for example, in the IYF *Family Agenda for Action*)[32] are important. The impact of social, welfare and economic change on children, the elderly and those who care for them needs to be a central part of decision-making, not least at the Treasury, not an ill-thought-through consequence. But as these arguments are put more strongly there is a risk that the realities for women as mothers become subsumed again within the family.

Again it comes down to the difference between long-term policy and immediate strategies: yes, we need clear parental rights and responsibilities which are taken seriously by both parents. Yes, we need proper, co-ordinated and well-funded childcare; yes, we need

paternity and parental leave, and career-break schemes. And mediation and parenting contracts. In the meantime, in their absence, what
do women do?

The conflict between women's aspirations and their continuing
role as primarily responsible for children leads directly to an acute
personal *and* theoretical dilemma: between demanding that men and
fathers play an equal role in caring for children, in families, in the
community and as childcare professionals, and recognising that some
men are not to be trusted with children. This is true not only,
although most crucially, because of the prevalence of child sexual
abuse in the family and professional childcare, but also in a less severe
way in terms of the quality of care children may receive from men
whose upbringing has not fitted them for tasks requiring sensitivity
and patience. Childcare, as is quite commonly argued, *is* good non-
violence and sensitivity training for men, but if that is at the
children's expense? As my younger daughter says, we need to 'get
real': whatever the theoretical position these are problems which
need to be solved by many women today and tomorrow.

Rights and Duties

The tension between rights and duties, between individualism and
commitment, is a dominant contemporary theme. Although I think
it has a sub-text which is about resistance to women's changing lives,
the questions raised need to be addressed, and in new ways. The
unstable mix of change and continuity (caught even by the blunt
measure of statistics looked at in Chapter 5) creates a central
contradiction in everyday experience: the rhetoric of personal
freedom is pervasive yet the constraints of family life cut across it
continuously.

The argument that carried away by 'rights' we forget obligation, is
one which has increasing credibility. The search is on for a
reconstructed relationship of the individual to family and society. A
strand of feminist thinking has contributed to the tension; the social/
perceptual change which has underpinned greater sexual and personal freedom for women is part of a possibly unstoppable process of
increasing independence, everything from decision-making and
transport to living space. A woman's right to choose: her body, her

bank account, her slimmer's chocolate drink, her car. (In the ads it's *her* car: in real life women are much less likely to own a car than men are, and have less access to family cars.)

If only it were that simple. Declarations of independence and rights may have been used to express women's demands but they don't describe how more than a minority of women live. The relationship of individual freedom to obligation has always been, with some few exceptions, cast differently for women than for men. Indeed in the early 1990s it was possible to 'lose' two million citizens, mostly young urban men, from the Census – a 'disappearing' which is not credible for women of that age group. Male personal freedom is less threatening to the social fabric.

The social order is seen as breaking down; the rules no longer work. But the basic rule that once you've had kids you try to stick with them is not one many women break. Woman's role at the centre of the family, as I've argued, has if anything been re-emphasised.

That there is a crisis of the family and society which is about shifting priorities/behaviour on an axis of collective/individual responsibility is accepted now by Left, Right and Centre. Group bonds are seen as undermined; 'moral individualism' holds sway. The 'new political settlement' must have duty as its cornerstone, Tony Blair argued, setting out Labour's aims and values in March 1995. Personal responsibility had been reduced to the 'narrowly acquisitive and destructive', he said; without duty 'freedom turns to ashes'.[33]

'The old moral vocabulary of rights and duties, mutual obligations, sin and virtue, sacrifice, conscience, rewards and penalties, could no longer be translated into the new language of desired gratification', writes historian Eric Hobsbawm in *Age of Extremes*. Practices and institutions 'that linked people to each other and ensured social cooperation and reproduction' have been 'reduced simply to expressions of individuals' preferences.[34]

These statements may be true as an analysis of social and political discourse. Whether they describe many women's lives is less clear. The woman crossing the city twice a day to clean and cook for her crabby and infirm father cannot be described as acting out of moral individualism. The woman who checks up twice a day on the elderly couple next door, wondering what she'll find when she opens the door – wouldn't she rather stay in and watch *Neighbours*? The woman who cares 24 hours a day for her husband who has Alzheimer's, who dribbles, shouts and no longer even knows who she is, cannot be described as acting on preference. Nor can a 13-year-old going home after school to look after a mother with AIDS. People who run food co-ops in Easterhouse and pensioners' groups in Meadow Well are not 'narrowly acquisitive'. Keeping a community group alive in North Benwell, an area of Newcastle from which some residents have fled in terror, isn't done out of 'desired gratification'. To describe the life of a single mother on benefit as irresponsible is to distort the meaning of the word. People caring in difficult circumstances from a sense of duty and decency, and, if they're lucky, love, are exercising individualism in a very limited sense.

Taking responsibility does not divide on straightforwardly female/male lines. I would not want to slip into the temptation of saying that women, especially mothers, are everything men are not, and vice versa: that where men are competitive women are co-operative, where men are violent women are peace-loving. To fix those characteristics so firmly to gender is a counsel of conservatism, and possibly despair. Women's characteristic life experience, however, is to have both more caring roles and skills. In hard-pressed communities women and older people, mainly, are building supportive networks against tremendous odds. Caring and constructive roles, in new tribes, decaying neighbourhoods and families of all sorts, fall to women more often than men and this is one of the things that has changed least in the past twenty-five years. 'The cultural revolution ... can best be understood as a triumph of the individual over society, or rather, the breaking of the threads that had woven human beings into social textures,' Hobsbawm writes.[35] That may be accurate in terms of class mobility but unless you think the thread which ties mothers to children not terribly important, it isn't for most women.

Etzioni, the 'communitarian' sociologist, puts the 'parenting deficit' at the centre of his analysis of the 'daunting social and moral issues' we face. 'This is not the women's fault,' he says, since fathers left children and home to go to work first. Then 'in the last twenty years many of the mothers joined them and they were sent back a few nannies and babysitters'. So 'children are neglected. Children come home to liquor cabinets and TV sets and they are not good sources of values.' Since he doesn't suggest a way to reverse the Industrial Revolution the attempt to disguise the focus on women's changing behaviour as causal is not very successful. Children in single parent families 'are left without a proper home' but two-parent families are also culpable, Etzioni says: they 'come home exhausted with a briefcase full of work and have no patience and energy left for their children' and they 'invent various rationalisations'. That coming home exhausted with still more work to do might not be a result of personal choice is not a point he labours.[36]

Speaking in Edinburgh in March 1995, ethical socialist A. H. Halsey called for a balance between freedom, equality and community and said that family should not mean 'two hedonistic adults plus that high-grade commodity called a child' but something closer to how an African might understand it, in terms of 'all those who have kinship obligations to each other'. Outside such dreams the balance is not so easily achieved. Unless we fully understand how gender functions to shape possibilities for women and men in relation to children and other caring responsibilities then we cannot create solutions which are other than woman-blaming in practice. This was something Professor Halsey acknowledged, I think inadvertently, when he said: 'I'm all for women's equal chances, but not at the expense of the children.' The arguments for them are so deeply embedded in our culture that no one need say 'I'm all in favour of men's equal chances, but not at the expense of the children'.[37]

Halsey spoke of the 'time robbery' which children today suffer from – a contemporary cliché which a social scientist, you might have hoped, would be wary of. Although there are certainly immense pressures on families with young children parents may be spending *more* time with their children now. (Various studies suggest women spend less time on housework now and more time with their children and that fathers also spend more time with their children than they did.'[38]

It mattered less it seems when families held only one hedonistic adult, and one who supported him. The 'problematical self-centredness' Dennis and Erdos deride is a rather good phrase to characterise many men in the past. 'The consequences of unbridled selfishness' were rather less at issue when they were hidden behind net curtains. 'The individualist doctrine' that Professor Halsey decries was not a problem, it seems, when the only individual to be considered was Father.

The public lectures of these concerned fathers and grandfathers are conspicuous in their failure to address questions of how we might encourage the involvement of fathers. The economic and cultural changes that would allow and encourage men to become more active and responsible in caring for their children or in the low-prestige work of maintaining community campaigns and organisations is not a subject which seems to excite them. Destructive and dangerous behaviour by young men in many communities is not, as writer Bea Campbell observes, 'a problem with no name' but it might as well be.[39] That a culture of masculinity which valorises authority and resists emotion and cooperation might also be at issue is a subject which is curiously absent from this discourse.

The Right Questions for the Wrong Reasons

Nevertheless the emerging discussion of the purpose of politics and the economic and social crossover that is being attempted, is important. Some of the right issues are being raised, if for the wrong reasons. The clear statement that neither the individualism of the Right nor a centralised state offer a way forward is useful. The notion that many women are, could be or even want to be free-standing autonomous individuals does not bear much examination – could any society function on that basis? But that shouldn't mean non-negotiable dependence or limited personal power either. We need more cooperation; we depend on each other for our well-being; we need, in Etzioni's phrase, 'a well woven society'. But not at the expense of narrowing women's lives: we need to square the awkward circle of women's greater independence and caring responsibilities which no one else takes on. We need to think about how economic change and community fragmentation are increasing inequality. We need a new political settlement. But none of this can be effectively addressed without looking at how gender functions in families and society to create divergent choices for women and men.

You cannot pretend that 'parent' means mother or father evenhandedly; cannot wave a wand and create equality with words, you only obscure inequality. Nor can you talk about families as if male/female power relations weren't at issue any more, or about communities as if different people and interest groups did not have greater access to power within them. If you talk about responsibility and duty in the abstract without talking about women and men and the different way most still live then those who already take responsibility for children and other people in need of care feel defensive and unrecognised, and those who have never seen cooperation and care as their responsibility anyway aren't likely to change.

The family and community link that Tony Blair makes is important and an important distinction from the Family Right. 'There can be no artificial line drawn around the home. Families live in local communities, which are in turn part of a larger society,' he said in a 1994 speech to an IEA conference, with implicit reference to Margaret Thatcher's 'sermon on the mound'.[40] The uncritical conjunction he makes between normal, stable and two parent, and family as standing for something cosy, commonsense and decent rather than authoritarian is simply unrealistic – there are cosy and decent families but there are as many which are authoritarian and repressive. Communities aren't always cosy either: they can be coercive and limiting. They may gain cohesion by presenting some members as 'other': racial harassment and discrimination is rife in some 'communities'. People who break the unwritten rules can suffer quite badly. Today's communitarian thinking downplays the ways in which communities can also be about conformity and control. Whether they were ever as warm and supportive as we now pretend is dubious.

Questions about community and responsibility *matter* – perhaps most to women who have caring roles. '*Of course* it's a conflict,' Penelope Leach said when I talked to her, 'but it's really about the needs of parents and others – we have to see some redistribution of resources from non-parents to parents and from men to women. I don't see a solution as long as children continue to be seen as the responsibility of women only, because it's seen as a women's problem – and men are good at leaving women's problems to women.

'Children have a right to have their needs met. If you don't do so you create a multiplying circle of disadvantage. But you won't do right by children unless you do right by parents. There are similar kinds of problems in every post-industrial country I've ever been in – and there are bits of solutions being tried. But I don't think people are looking very urgently at these problems in this country and the people whom they affect most, parents with young children, have the least time to involve themselves in the political process or anything else, so have no voice.'

We listen instead to men who are detached from the world they prescribe for; this discourse spins away from the reality of homes and schools and families it is supposed to be reforming. Children *are* being short-changed. Whether they are being *more* short-changed is debatable, although poverty is clearly a serious concern. (We do not know, however, what claim children and women have ever actually had on 'the family wage'.) Good fathers may do their best to make an equal contribution to family life. But gendered structures of work and pay underpin what is possible; families cannot create more equal relationships in a social vacuum.

Change carries risk. Families which are changing are vulnerable; people are vulnerable when the old rules don't seem to work but there is no encouragement to find new ways of living. But people are vulnerable when more rigid rules hold, if and when they break them. During times of change women and children in weaker positions may face those risks most. But women and children were at greater risk when violence was a family secret, when sexual abuse was unspoken, when there was nowhere to go and no one would acknowledge it was happening. Silence and ignorance were not better. More women's voices are needed in this conversation, and more than defensively.

'People need rules which we all stand by, fixed points of agreement which impose order over chaos,' Tony Blair believes. 'The problem,' Amitai Etzioni says, 'is not that the old society was laid to rest but that we did not replace it with any new set of agreed values.'[41] Creating authentic equality between women and men seems a value-laden goal to me; so is building new sorts of families which work for all their members in fair ways. But this is not agreed, it is resisted. Many men, and some women, find it profoundly threatening.

Women need recognition and support for what we are trying to achieve, not new rules.

Family Problems

While a swirl of debate and counter-accusation about single mothers and social breakdown has dominated public discourse, the problems which many families face have worsened and little or nothing has been done to help. People bringing up children do face new and difficult problems – plus some which stretch back into history. Shift the focus from women's waywardness and issues partly obscured by this obsession come into frame: inequality in relationships and taking responsibility; the isolation of modern families, allied to mounting pressures on parents; immigration law, which has broken up some families; domestic violence and child sexual abuse. And poverty. These are serious policy issues which need to be urgently addressed, and addressed in new ways.

The tension between a nostalgic ideal of family and the fractures, patch-ups and pressures of the world we live in has sent mixed messages to parents: we are intensely important and we aren't doing it right. The arguments focus on individual behaviour at a time when there is a failure to support the majority of families. (But then, the good family pays for what it needs up-front, not through taxes.) Delinquency is presented as the fault of parents, and their allies in social work and education. Michael Howard, Home Secretary, in a speech to the Institute of Directors in April 1994 gave a useful summary of this argument. 'The failure of some parents to give children proper values and the ability to discern right from wrong; the failure of some schools to instil discipline and respect for authority: clearly those failures do create conditions in which crime and law-breaking can thrive'.[42] A culture of cash for questions and council houses for votes, of arms sales to dictators, in which the men who run once-public utilities vote themselves huge wage increases while cutting services to customers and the wages of those who deliver the service, on the other hand, has apparently nothing to do with it.

Immigration law is another of the issues which is conveniently ignored when 'family breakdown' is the subject. But for some families British law forces them to live apart and it traps many women in dependency. The 'firm but fair immigration policies' which John Major is 'determined to retain' (as he told the House of Commons in February 1995) mean parents separated from children and from each other. Being 'firm but fair' means deporting women and children when they are no longer seen as property of a man, widows and mothers of British nationals among them.[43]

After a European Court of Human Rights decision in 1985 that immigration rules for spouses discriminated against women, equality was achieved by removing rights from men rather than enhancing rights for women. The law now applies equally; the practice, since applicants are required to 'satisfy' officials that they qualify, is biased. No one really believes the 'primary purpose' rule (meant to exclude anyone who marries primarily to come to live in Britain) or the 'twelve month rule', operates in the same way for women and men or for black and white people.

The removal in 1981 of the right to British nationality by birth in the UK, which means that some babies are born stateless, has affected women and children in cruel and unjust ways. New immigration rules which came into force in October 1994 have removed established practices with respect to long residence, common law relationships and the interests of children in family breakdown. Further restrictions have virtually ended the right of unmarried daughters between the ages of 18 and 21 and widowed mothers under 65 to join family in this country, under the guise of 'sexual equality'.[44]

In August 1994 Church leaders called for the threat of deportation to be lifted from over a thousand families who had lived in Britain for more than five years. Most of the families whose stories are told in a pamphlet by the Churches' Commission for Racial Justice have children who were born in Britain and who have known only this country as their home; these are families who have lived in Britain for around ten or in two cases twenty years. And they 'do not know from one day to the next whether or when the police and immigration officers may come to remove them'.[45] In many of the cases the problems occurred after breakdown of a marriage. This institutional racism continues because of the silence and indifference of the white population, and the kind of myth which has clear parallels with how single, working-class mothers are seen. The construction of people from certain countries as a problem bears no connection to the contribution they make and role they play and wish to play.

The Economics of 'Family Crisis'

The gap between rich and poor in Britain is wider in 1995 than at any time since 1945. Families with young children are now more likely to be on the wrong side of that divide than they were 25 years ago: worse off in real as well as relative terms.[46] Poverty and the erosion of public services is exacerbated by isolation and underscored by a climate of individualism and insistent consumerism. Political and economic failure has demonstrable consequences for many families – they are, of course, problems which also affect homeless old men huddled in shop doorways, old women in hostels, redundant middle-aged men and single women stuck in low-paid, dead-end jobs. New pressures no longer affect only the most disadvantaged. They are pressures for people in work, working longer hours: Mum going out the door for a 'twilight shift' as Dad comes in, just about managing, but seeing the social contract on which their efforts depend eroded and derided, and facing new worries about their kids' education and health care and services for the elderly.

While the vulnerability of single parent families significantly contributes to child poverty, unemployment is a much greater cause and low pay a major cause. The largest group of children growing up in poverty live with both their unemployed parents. There is a growing gap between families with two earners and families with none which the current structure of benefits pushes wider. (Between 1975 and 1993 the proportion of two-adult households where both adults worked rose from 51 per cent to 60 per cent but the proportion with no earner has also increased from 3 per cent to 11 per cent.)[47] Benefits no longer meet the realistic costs of bringing up children. Having children is now understood in Britain as one of the life crises that creates poverty, along with illness, unemployment and old age.

You can see what 'child poverty' means on any measure in the poor areas of the West of Scotland: in Glasgow's 'priority areas' poverty is etched in people's faces, the sense of hopelessness is counted in drug abuse, and young women with children look ten years older than they should. For most children growing up in poverty it will affect their whole lives: 'People in poverty can get caught in a vicious circle', Save the Children Fund in Scotland say. 'Ill health and poor educational attainment can reduce future employ-ment and earning opportunities, which increases the risk of being in poverty, which in turn impacts on families' health and children's education.[48]

It means damp, overcrowded housing and inadequate heating and a lack of warm clothes and bedding. It means poor physical and mental health, insufficient food and a poor diet. It means 'not being able to make ends meet and getting into debt.' 'Getting depressed – money is a constant problem, just juggling pennies and going from shop to shop wondering what you can afford. I just live worried all the time.' It means 'worrying about the kids ... worrying they'll turn to drugs or vandalism ...' 'Dreading your child saying his shoes hurt or needing money for extra – any unexpected invitation is a nightmare.' It is not just about survival but whether you can take part in ordinary, everyday activities which most people take for granted. Managing to make ends meet becomes a full-time occupation. Above all, as several women said to me: 'It's the coping all the time that gets to you ... constant pressure and worry about how you're going to manage.'[49]

UNICEF's first *Progress of Nations* report in autumn 1993 said that progress for children had slowed and in some aspects reversed in the UK and the USA since 1970 as compared with ten other industrial-ised countries. On four key indicators, infant mortality, government spending on education, teenage suicide, and income distribution, much poorer EC countries (as well as Japan and Sweden) show up better – emphasising that relative wealth is no indicator of the absence of child poverty.[50] Income distribution and social priorities are. Countries like Greece and Portugal are much poorer overall (as European Union figures show) but their families with children are not. In some countries the balance of disadvantage is tilted away from families with young children, in this country it is tilted in their direction.

Compared with most of the countries UNICEF works in we are rich yet they describe children 'living in a poverty so severe that their basic needs for adequate nutrition, basic health care and education are not met'. In the 1994 Report they say: 'Progress for children in the industrialised world can no longer be taken as a given' yet 'the proportion of a nation's children in poverty is or should be a litmus test of progress'.[51]

This is a reversal of what a society with a future needs; evidence, if evidence were needed, that Britain does not value children. But you can test that statement any day by trying to get on a bus with a buggy, by taking children out for a drink and discovering the legal apartheid of age (which persists *despite* licensing changes supposed to make pubs more civilised, family-friendly places). On an individual level it is tragic; on a social level it is a kind of slow suicide. The recent Quentin Tarantino film *Killing Zoë* is well named: *zoë* is the Greek for life. If we celebrate violence in our popular culture and we don't value maternity and we don't value children, ultimately we will cease to value life.

That is where the real problems for families lie. Not in a crisis of certainty, not in a crisis of behaviour, not in what women are doing or in what women want. Yet the general, loose consensus remains that the family is in trouble – because mothers go out to work, and mothers won't put up with or can't keep their men. Because of the decline of the extended family. That consensus needs to be taken apart.

The past twenty-five years have been described as 'a social revolution'.[52] I think a better description is 'half a revolution': we need now to complete it. Feminism, cultural change and education have changed women's expectations; social and legislative change has meant marriage is not necessarily for life. But we haven't followed through. Policy will not work unless the reality of family change is paid more attention to than dreams of the self-reliant two-parent family. Gendered constructions of social and family life have to be taken fully into account. The CSA, for example, is a disaster mainly because of the failure – or refusal – to understand or even begin to address the inequality of mothers and fathers in Britain today and the complexity of change in families. Divorce law reform is likely also to create more problems than it solves.

We need new social provision that underpins the complex responsibilities of bringing up children in a changing world. We need to think harder about how we can support 'children in need' as a consequence of changing family patterns and in 'traditional' families alike. This would begin by recognising that for families of all sorts there may be problems at one time or another; and that for all parents the caring role must be combined with economic responsibilities. The way we approach social policy through crisis-intervention reinforces an increasingly divided society. We need a broad-based supportive network offering all children the best possible start in life: a continuum of childcare, and provision for children in need of additional care; a continuum of protection and support; and of education, play and participation. We can't achieve this without at the same time looking at women's lives, and making workable equality a priority.

Crisis? What Crisis?

I don't believe the family *is* in crisis. I think people with caring responsibilities are having a harder time carrying them out because of economic decline and mismanagement and the cutbacks in welfare. But I also think family life is getting better *because* of what women are doing, because of the ways in which women's lives are changing.

Mothers working, for example. Certainly there is a mismatch: there are women with young children working who would rather be at home, just as there are women at home who want to be working but can't, for all the well-known reasons. There are women working for wages which should be illegal, and then coming home and doing the same work for no wages at all. But most women's work is positive for their families. It is important financially, first of all. Women's income plays a major role in keeping families out of poverty.[53] Women working may not have changed domestic division of labour much yet, but it has begun to. If, in a materialist world, work means more self-respect and independence for the mother, then her children are more likely to treat her with self-respect and her daughters will learn it from her. And it does no child any good to have a mother as a personal servant.

Good relationships are not based on inequality, on repression and subordination. If women won't put up with men's destructive behaviour, that too must be better, even if it's hard. Some men are changing too, but an awful lot still believe that women were put on this earth to meet their sexual, social and domestic needs. Sexual and domestic servitude won't end unless and until women refuse it. Do we really want to argue that it is better for children to grow up watching inequality and the dominance of one human being by another?

Because women can get away, because more women feel there is more they won't put up with any longer, more children are being moved out of violence and into safety. It may not be easy to leave: but women staying and suffering is not going to end male violence.

EVERY CHILD A WANTED CHILD was a slogan of the early 1970s. That is closer to being true now in this country than it ever has been. With the sense that a fulfilled child-free life is possible comes a greater possibility of a positive choice to have children. And it is a consequence of better availability of contraception and of safe, legal abortion, even though 'choice' may be more complicated in the real world than on paper.

Also immensely important are the ways people are learning, slowly and painfully perhaps, to handle family change. Stigmatising those who are doing so, and labelling them failures at the outset, doesn't help. Given the public discourse around divorce, stepfamilies and new families, it's hard to feel that your own attempts to make a 'reconstituted' family work, or keep a consistent relationship with children with whom you no longer live, or to be more egalitarian, are other than exceptional, against a sad and sorry tide. Yet there can be, at best, a kind of recast extended family, with some of its complexities but some of its strengths. A new partner may be a glad and immensely enthusiastic step-parent; a grandmother may play a positive role when the children stay with their dad at her house. Several women have commented to me that separated fathers now have a closer relationship with their children than they had in the 'intact' family.

We should not make too much of such possibilities, perhaps. There are young people who sleep out in a graveyard not 50 yards from where I'm writing this who are the rejected of 'new families' – though some runaways are the rejects of 'old families' too. But children (for whom the numbers of adults who are interested in them and love them has a fairly high upper limit) may be learning, as is commonly said, that relationships are contingent; they may also be learning that you can pick yourself up and start again and make things work.

As for subversive feminist ideas – well, at least some of them would go a long way to ensuring that those women who are caring for children do so in better circumstances, are more highly regarded for it, have some choice about doing it and have at least the chance of enjoying it – which is good for children as well as their mothers. Feminism has been seen as anti-family by definition, and if the family is understood as cementing male authority, it undoubtedly is. But there are also elements in a feminist analysis of the family that are crucial to any positive rebuilding for the future.

Perhaps the greatest challenge at the end of a century of change is to rewrite the relationship between woman and family and community: reconciling individual choice with new community and social structures, reconciling contradictory needs for individual freedom and a shared life. That is a task which has begun.

Part III

Old Problems, New Possibilities

Chapter 9

'Young Women Today ...'

I've lost count of the number of times that women of my generation have said to me, 'Young women today think they're equal – they're in for a shock.' Or words to that effect. I might have accepted that as expressing a certain weariness, except that I remember being told the same thing in 1971. 'You young girls don't know anything yet,' Maggie, a woman in my first women's group, used to say, with all of the wisdom of her five or so additional years. 'Just wait until you've got kids.'

She had three and she was right. Would she still be? As I've argued, the divergence between women with and without children has widened over the past twenty-five years, meaning that it is around 'family formation' that the strongest inequalities now cluster, particularly if women have limited educational qualifications and work experience. The most public articulation of the 'young women today' argument has been in response to Helen Wilkinson and Naomi Wolf's conceptions of 'genderquake', which met with both an enthusiastic reception from many young women and scepticism of the 'young women today' sort from some older – and some younger – women. Since the equality they celebrate is primarily that of young, untrammelled, well-educated women, it underlines this divergence.[1]

You can no more generalise about young women than any other women. Work chances for young women with recognised skills have never been better, though unemployment for their age group is also at a very high level. Current ideas about relationships put a high premium on equality and negotiation, but pressures on relationships are intense. For every young woman enrolling in medical school there is another trying to build a life without a job or (if she's under 18) benefits. Sitting in class next to a girl contemplating a career in astrophysics is another just waiting for a prince in a white GTI to take her away from it all. On the one hand there are confident, well-educated young women striding out to take on the future; on the other whole streets of young women alone with their kids in dump housing estates. But as Helen Wilkinson and others argue, many more young women are determined to take the chances they have – and many women who themselves face poor work prospects and disadvantage are determined that their daughters won't.

'It's Going to be Different'

'It's going to be different for our generation.' It is something many young women say. And: 'It's our turn now.' Irene Roberts intends to be a managing director of a large company, make lots of money *and* have lots of children. A dark-haired, tall and self-assured young woman of 17, daughter of an equally assertive mother by all accounts, 'our generation will change it', she believes. Few of her classmates in the fifth year at an Edinburgh comprehensive are as sure of what they want but they will almost all go on to higher education and are making choices between architecture and psychology, politics and maths. 'It's not that I want to throw my weight about,' Irene added. 'But when I'm 60 I want to think *I did that*.' Sadia Majid comments that she would find it difficult to take 'a male job' for family and religious reasons (she is Muslim) and is conscious that this sets her apart from the others in the class; she plans to study psychology at university and has no more wish than the others to 'settle down' young. Girls in the same school without either their confidence or prospects are just as keen, from what they say, on independence.

So many younger women today seem to me clear-sighted and impressive. They take their lives seriously, though that doesn't stop them having fun. They know what they want – 'a life on their own terms', in Ellen Kelly's phrase, and see no reason why they shouldn't

get it. Though they also understand that it may not be as straightforward as all that.

'You just have to look at the statistics for who does what jobs and
at women in parliament,' Anna Sommerville said, to see that there
isn't equality. 'I don't think until we have experience of trying to get
into these positions that we'll see what it's all about, really.' 'We're
not equal but we're heading more that way,' says her classmate, Anna
Harkiss (who is thinking of doing 'something managerial'), to nods
of agreement.

Catherine Kay studied science and is deeply committed to the
radical environmental movement and part of the Rainbow Tribe; she
helps run the Rainbow Centre in north London. What's mainly
changed for her generation, she thinks, is 'that we were encouraged
to think there were no obstacles. OK, you find the obstacles are still
there but encouragement has a lot to do with whether you give up
and go along with the mainstream or whether you go for it anyway.'
Science at University meant always being in a male-dominated
group, but 'it didn't seem to matter as much ... *Because* we took some
things for granted that was a step forward – and then you can say,
actually women and men are very different but we can work well
together, and that difference enhances rather than takes away ...

'What *hasn't* changed? Men are still in power and still trying to
play the game on their rules – businessmen, politicians ... We want to
challenge it on a really deep level – we're saying we don't want to play
your game *at all*.'

The changes in how young women see their lives are tied to class
and advantage, if not straightforwardly. Changing attitudes show up
most clearly in girls' school performance, and girls are doing better in
poorly resourced inner-city schools as well as the independent 'top
girls' schools' which scooped the top places in the league of A-level
results in 1994. Young women and men leaving school at 16 share
poorer prospects, and job segregation is still pervasive, but young
women's unemployment is less in most regions – particularly so
comparing young black women and men. Girls' wider horizons are
not confined to any one group, though where they can fly to may
depend on where they take off from. Young women with the odds
against them have achieved most of all: women from Bangladeshi
communities in London, for example, who have very high levels of

educational attainment. A higher proportion of Indian, Chinese and Asian women aged between 25 and 29 are educated to degree level or over than white women in that age group.[2] 'I feel so proud of young black women: their confidence, their sassiness,' Usha Brown said. 'I'm proud, because I know what they have to deal with – society stacked against them and their families. I think they're wonderful.' 'Young women seem so much cooler and wiser than I was,' Bea Campbell said, about the girls who live on Tyneside housing estates.

Changing expectations are evident in everything from girls' exam results to whether a young woman marries when she gets pregnant. 'Girls of all backgrounds are putting more value on academic achievements than ever before,' Sue Sharpe found in 1991. 'A sea-change is underway in younger girls' attitudes,' Helen Wilkinson argues, quoting research from the University of Exeter: 'schoolgirls now have greater self-esteem, are happier than their male peers, are more ambitious, are more likely to want to continue in education and are less likely to want to start a family when they leave school than boys. Above all, perhaps, girls are much more positive about the future'.[3]

A more circumspect account comes from research for the Health Education Authority, published in May 1995. They found a traditional split in the factors that affect young teenagers' self-esteem: girls, they say, 'worry more than boys, have less self-confidence and are very concerned about their appearance and being liked'. The report's editor, Helen Brown, said: 'This research clearly shows that girls and boys are still brought up to have different expectations of themselves and the outside world', though this was more the case for working-class than middle-class girls. They found that 'girls approach the future with a clear sense that they are likely to have to choose between or manage the balance of work and family goals. A common solution to this dilemma is to reduce the world of work to a more manageable, less demanding, less "male" set of options.' Girls (in all social classes) complained of being expected to do housework when their brothers weren't, perhaps one reason why 'the possibility of having a fulfilling career *and* a wonderful family is seen as an unattainable ideal'. Yet the report makes a familiar assumption which needs to be questioned: why should wanting to be liked or look good mean you won't become a doctor or engineer? Or 'male' options be seen as more demanding?[4]

The report makes the important point, however, that 'crossing over' to non-traditional options 'seems to imply the need for unusual strength of character and determination'. Liz Spencer and Sally Taylor's 1994 research for the Employment Department also notes that women felt you had to be unusually determined to enter a traditionally 'male' occupation – a valid perception which needs to be taken more into account. There were also 'notions of appropriate levels of aspiration which applied to men and women, and which depended partly on social class and partly where people were placed in the education system', and not always straightforwardly: they quote one woman who went to a 'very snobbish school ... when I said I wanted to do nursing they were horrified ... Why not medicine?'[5]

The 18- to 34-year-olds Helen Wilkinson calls the 'first post-equality generation' value autonomy, work and education more than family or parenting, she says. It is not surprising that young, ambitious women today don't see family and children as a priority; it doesn't mean it never will be. 'It's difficult to imagine getting married and having children,' Anna Sommerville said. There were lots of other things to think about first: 'When I'm older I'll probably feel differently but I'm interested in getting on with my own life just now. I want to be happy, I want to make money, I want to have my own flat.' Rosie Thomson is in the same school but leaving soon to take up a job at the hairdresser's where she already works at weekends. 'I think you should think about your career first before children,' she says. Maybe she would like to have children, but not until her late twenties anyway.

They take for granted personal freedom and independent decision-making, and are right to do so. But the difficult economic climate, Sue Sharpe cautions, may mean 'girls will eventually find that the economic and personal commitment involved in further study and/or the reality of unemployment may lead to them making many compromises in their career aspirations'. She says relationships and children may come more strongly into the picture if work proves disappointing, 'may assume a primary role through necessity rather than choice'. Recent Scottish research[6] shows how high unemployment among young women who leave school at 16 and early pregnancy are closely related and, according to the FPA, a similar pattern holds elsewhere. Younger women, the Employment Dept research reports, 'felt under dual and conflicting pressures: to stay in education or take further training qualifications; but on the other hand to "grab the first job that comes along",' a dilemma which was marked in areas of high unemployment.[7] Expectations of independence and equality may leave young women less prepared for what happens if and when they are mothers, either on their own or when, as Penny Mansfield's work shows, relationships hit the rocks of a division of work and care still underpinned by deep layers of gendered assumptions.

But they may also find new ways round old problems. Another difference in the ED study between the younger and older women is that 'the birth of children was not seen as marking an end to their career'. Whether they intended to stay in work or not, they knew they must 'keep their options open'. Sue Sharpe says that to girls at school at the beginning of the 1990s, the world of girls in 1972 seemed a century away. 'For myself, researching their ideas and hopes at both times, their lives did not appear so far apart.' These girls knew 'that nothing can be taken for granted, especially in employment and marriage'. But when they have children, she thinks, their expectations and hopes 'are likely to come up against exactly the same barriers as their predecessors ... Young women may be more aware and determined about their lives and aspirations, but they look forward to a future in which they are likely to end up juggling work and domestic life like their mothers before them.'[8]

But as more women, the mothers of today's schoolgirls among them, learn to juggle and find ways of resolving the dilemmas of work and children, new pathways are cut out. Knowing that nothing can be taken for granted may sharpen both knives and wits. Women mainly find and manage the solutions themselves. Clambering over the barriers creates the 'exhaustion and guilt which arises from a series of conflicting demands,' as the Employment Committee report describes it.[9] Young women know that – they can see in their mothers' lives that it isn't easy: they notice that their mothers do most of the housework even though they're out at work as well and that their work is less prestigious – and they've learnt from that.

The HEA study concludes that 'parents aspire to happiness for their daughters and success for their sons'. But the ED study found that parents often supported their daughters in whatever they wished to do even if they gave them no active encouragement, and for some women 'their parents had been quite ambitious on their behalf. This was true in the case of mothers who had been unable to pursue opportunities, who regretted earlier decisions or the direction their life had taken; and conversely, for mothers who had been able to achieve a successful balance between career and family life.'

A useful perspective comes from a broad-based study of academically successful Scottish school-leavers and first-year students in 1971 and 1981 which looked at girls' changing expectations over that decade. In 1991 the study was narrower (for funding reasons) and the questions about how girls saw themselves and their future were not asked – a pity, yet the evidence is all around us that the change they saw by 1981 has continued. In 1971 'selection and socialisation processes' were channelling able teenage girls into a secondary-school track of academic underachievement. Gender-related occupational values and intentions were formed because of educational tracking rather than causing it, the study said. By 1981 there was much less divergence between young women and men in 'the clarity and quality of their occupational ambitions': young women were more certain about what they wanted from work, and wanted more from it. There were strong changes in both belief and intention, 'major change ... in men's and women's expectations about women and also the expectations that each woman is likely to have for herself. Qualified women have become more ambitious, educationally and occupationally, and more men and women are now prepared to accept such ambitions as legitimate.'[10]

However, the study notes that in 1981, despite major changes in women's intentions, they wouldn't necessarily become reality. That would depend on 'the opportunity structure and ... the resolution of conflicts between work and family'. We now know that for that generation 'the opportunity structure' was not purged of discrimination and that conflict between work and family for many women has continued. We also know that many more women have stayed in the workplace while their children were young, particularly those well paid enough to afford good childcare or who were able to create flexible ways of working. We know many have postponed having children.

As Helen Wilkinson says, young women 'are now having to resolve complex choices without clear precedents: balancing work and home, coping with more fluid identities'. But if many constraints remain, as Sue Sharpe says, 'whatever the practical realities of their future lives, they have absorbed assumptions of equality and independence, and the ability to support themselves'. Women with greater self-esteem, women who want more from life and have been told they are *not wrong* to want more, are likely to become *mothers* who want more. They are likely, too, to have the support of more women of their mothers' generation and, maybe, more men of their own. They may still face resistance and face problems men their age do not – but their aspirations are less likely to be against the grain of the culture and they are less likely to be isolated in them. There *is* precedent. Many women are combining work, politics or creative endeavour with fulfilling relationships and bringing up children, even if few have the supportive structures they need. The pathways marked out may not be without thorns and bumpy patches. Some of the same constraints facing young women now are no different from the early 1970s and 1980s, but they face them, I think, better armed.

Destinations

Many of the messages young women get from popular culture are underlaid with themes familiar from the whole post-war period. In the railway station, next to the destination board, Helena Christensen is stretched naked but for a boa across a giant poster: the film's title *Prêt à Porter* becomes a play on 'ready to take away'. The fastest way to stardom is still to take your kit off: Elizabeth Hurley in *that* dress – and the other one … The same mantras: 'two women out of three have combination skin', solemn advice to 'use eyelash curlers before applying mascara', beauty tips from the super models. The same anxieties.

In the public images of women sex is what sells; the beauty myths still have power. Even over those who sell them: Kate Moss in an interview with Alistair Mackay for *Scotland on Sunday* said she had been reluctant to strip for photographs. 'But it's really difficult when you're young and you're on a set by yourself and you have the make-up and the stylist and the photographer all telling you "Come on, it's fine, don't be such a prude."' Did she feel exploited? 'At the time … in a way … Like when I was really young I didn't really want to show myself but I was pushed into it … but they were friends of mine, they were just doing it for their art.'[11]

In the preoccupations of younger women in the 1990s the lines have only partly been rewritten. Model boys pout and look sexy in the shower and the agony columns tell teenage girls things their parents never knew. The magazine section in your local newsagent's is a scarcely muted hymn to the female orgasm. But there are powerful pressures which bring new versions of old problems. Young women must negotiate what Sue Lees accurately describes as 'the savage chauvinism of male youth culture'.[12] Body consciousness in women has if anything intensified: images of desirable femininity are impossibly thinner *and* impossibly curvier. Though there may be more possibility of refusing it, it's hard to forget sexual vulnerability in a world papered with female bodies on display; you can only learn to shrug it off.

How we see ourselves and how that is mediated by the images with which we are surrounded is much harder to measure than the number of women judges or even how work is changing and housework unchanging. The messages about what we should look like – how much can women now dismiss them, how much do they matter? Looking at part-time employment figures and different kinds of childcare is straightforward compared with trying to think about feelings and bodies, about sex and sexiness – but it matters as much and underlies the decisions young women make, or feel they can't make.

It's on a kind of feedback loop: if things are going well in life women (at any age) are more likely to feel good about how we look, however minimally we match up to airbrushed public ideals of womanhood; conversely if we feel good about how we look – hard when the commercial success of the beauty industry depends on female doubt – we are better prepared for the rest of life.

Thinking about such things only deepens my sense of paradox.

Women are more sophisticated in the ways in which they are manipulated – but we buy the face creams anyway. 'We've come a long way,' as the cigarette ad told us – and at the age of 15 girls are now more likely to smoke than boys. How young women negotiate messages and meanings may have changed, but the attributes of desirable femininity in the 1990s have much in common even with the 1890s, only you show more of them. (And against any reasonable prediction the *bustle* has been reinvented.) Push-up bras are 'worn with confidence and irony' (how you wear a bra with irony puzzles me but then I don't work in advertising) but the cleavage is as competitive as ever. The 'Or are you just pleased to see me' line which sold Wonderbras in their thousands was, according to the ad agency concerned, 'talking to sassy, confident women'. How silly of me to think she was saying 'Hello, Boys!' Between them the Wonderbras and the Ultrabra have boosted British bra sales by a third – to a £385m industry.)[13]

There's a wider choice of who you can look like – as long as it's not your unadorned, unprofitable self. From the growing range of strictly scientific ways to erase them we can deduce that wrinkles are no more acceptable than ever. If there has really been a 'revolution in sex roles' why are we still supposed to be young, firm and beautiful or the nearest approximation we can manage to that? When and why does pleasure slip into obsession, vanity become anxiety, compulsion – tragedy: the ex-'beauty queen' who died while undergoing plastic surgery in pursuit of a girlish body; girls who starve themselves into perpetual childhood.

But messages *are* changing – in very mixed ways. The visual clichés are subtler: outside the shampoo ads, which seem endlessly to rework Rapunzel, women get men to do the hoovering, 'the cleverest woman in the world' chooses washing powder, and big strong men cuddle tiny babies. Men get more of it directed at them than ever: now as well as girls undressed everywhere there are boys undressing. Clairol's 1995 hair-colouring ad campaign, for example, is an appeal to the sexually adventurous: 'I like my hair like my men. Great to look at and easily changed.' The market in sub-*Cosmopolitan* reading for teenage girls (which extends to the pre-teens too) is a magazine-world success story which subsists on a chirpy version of the big sister mags. The obsessions of *Just Seventeen*, for example, are boys, 'boyfs' and more boys, make-up, advice and sex. Compare *New Woman* (though you could be forgiven for not noticing) which headlines sex, beauty, advice and men. *Just Seventeen* has a regular feature of 'chicks on life, love and everything'. *New Woman*'s cover line is 'life, love and you'. Relative newcomers *More* and *Cosmopolitan* may be a world away from the traditional *People's Friend*, but the latter had the highest circulation of any British magazine until overtaken by *Good Housekeeping* in 1994.)[14]

A cursory examination of teen mags would enlighten those who were shocked when barely pubescent girls waved 'Shag me, Mark' posters at Take That concerts. Recent cover lines have promised advice on 'what really turns *him* on' and 'how to be a super lover'. There are no boys' magazines which give equivalent advice. Half of *Sugar*'s readers who replied to their sex survey in February 1995 were having regular sex and half of non-virgins had first had sex at 14 or 15; 16 per cent had lost their virginity with someone they'd known for a week or less. But it's not just the same thing, more explicitly. The *Sugar* survey, while being determinedly accepting, has clear messages about the age of consent, the connection between promiscuity and STDs and HIV/AIDS. *Sugar*'s view is that 'spur of the moment' sex with someone you hardly know is not 'the most fulfilling or the safest way to begin a healthy sexual relationship'.[15] The lead sex story in April 1995's *Nineteen* carries a strong message that you can't tell a lad's sexual history from his appearance: 'for your sake you need to know'. A feature 'Feel Like a New You?' in *Just Seventeen* is about hairstyles and make-up but also trying things out: write for the school mag, try a fake tattoo, read Sylvia Plath, watch Keanu and 'fight for what you believe in', all cheerfully mixed in together.[16]

For a young woman growing up not sure it's boys she fancies, though, there is still little easily available advice. In March 1994 Health Minister Brian Mawhinney banned – because it was 'distasteful, even smutty' – a planned HEA sex information book for teenagers, *Your Pocket Guide to Sex*, which, as well as the troubling 'colloquial language' included information on lesbianism and homosexuality.[17] Sex education in schools has been opposed by organisations like Family and Youth Concern and parents now have the right to withdraw children (arguably those most in need of information) from lessons. Sex education guidelines remind teachers that they may be aiding and abetting under-age sex if they offer individual advice to young people without informing their parents. Section 28 means they may also be acting illegally if they give supportive advice to young gay people. What can be said and to whom has been an ongoing skirmish, with open warfare around HIV/AIDS on the secondary science curriculum, 'Mars Bar parties' and Nick Fisher's guide. He said he was writing for young people surrounded by images of sex and who 'continually talk about these things but may not really understand them'.[18] The highest teenage pregnancy rate in Europe and the highest rate of abortion for girls between 14 and 17 is evidence that he is right. In Holland and Denmark, where there is greater openness and sex and relationship education is well funded and less contested, the incidence of unplanned pregnancies is low.

Mixed messages come from public images of real women too. Kate Adie, Oprah Winfrey, Helen Mirren in *Prime Suspect*, Ruby Wax and (oddly enough) Patsy in *Absolutely Fabulous* were the assorted set of 'leading role models for women' identified in research for the Broadcasting Standards Council in 1994: strong women all (well, maybe not Patsy) and women who challenge boundaries. But the research also showed that personal appearance remains important in recruiting women to before-camera roles in media in a way that it isn't so much so for men and that in speaking roles across a range of programmes men still predominate (70 per cent, and 82 per cent in news programmes).[19] Strong and creative women in pop and rock music are much more to the fore – and nowadays they *survive* – though the industry's decision-making structures are male domi-nated and unashamedly sexist; women bands must still be sexier. But if rock music still has its fair share of men holding guitars in a suggestive manner, PJ and Duncan hymn 'going all the way' and Marianne-Faithful-type drippiness is not exactly a thing of the past, successful women from Shampoo to Björk and Echobelly manage how they are presented, and appeal to fans because of it. Though more-than-decorative women are *still* seen as a novelty in the business, some say: Tanya Donelly from Belly told writer Amy Raphael 'My vagina doesn't come into my guitar playing and my singing ... I want to get to the point where women aren't treated like

… giraffes. It shouldn't even be interesting at this point that I'm female and I do this.'[20]

kd Lang broke the mould: a 'big-boned gal' and strong woman, as the first major female star to evade all the stereotypes she is inestimably important for lesbians but affirming for all women. As Leslie Bennetts observed in *Vanity Fair*, 'this is not a male fantasy object. I think she would jam the radar.' Her biographer Victoria Starr quotes kd saying: 'I'm gonna swagger, and I'm gonna have fun up here and I'm gonna be sexy, and I don't have to look like Dolly Parton to do it.' Although kd plays with androgynous images, she told *Vanity Fair*, 'I really pride myself on being 100 per cent woman, but with this great luxury of pulling from both sides.'[21] Even images of glam older women have made a reappearance (despite Isabella Rossellini at 40 being deemed too old to advertise Lancôme) looking like themselves, not like Joan Collins.

But some changes are hard to reconcile with images of more equal, more personally powerful and assured women. 'Aesthetic surgery' is one of Britain's few growth industries, for example (and an inadequately regulated one). Though women buying a *Baywatch* bosom have been joined by men trying liposuction and buttock moulding (a dubious sort of equality), it's estimated that nine out of ten people who seek out cosmetic treatment are women, and nine out of ten operations are done to reverse the effects of ageing.[22] The advertising at the back of women's magazines offers an ever-expanding range of options with explicit pictures of before and after stomachs or tactful references to 'the enhancement you are considering'. Alongside them medical finance companies offer loans to pay for it.

How we expect women and men to look and behave *is* changing, undoubtedly. There are clubs (like the Love Boutique in Glasgow) where *everyone* dresses like a tart, and occasionally men wear even rather ordinary skirts (well, *very* occasionally), girls have crew cuts and pick up men – how can I doubt change? But we are surrounded still by templates of ideal masculinity and femininity: 'secondary sexual characteristics' reign, images of smiling, curvy, *available* women are everywhere, with laddish lads and lean and handsome, commanding men. Notions of appropriate masculinity and femininity still form the social climate in which we live – but *what* exactly and *how?* No one I think would assert that sex roles are divided just as they were even ten years ago or that young women and men are not challenging them. The idea that female equals passive and not very good at maths cuts little ice today – certainly not with a class of averagely assertive schoolgirls. But when the film *Natural Born Killers* is described as 'emblematic of masculine fundamentalism' we don't say, well I thought the violence was rather *girlish*, actually. When told about 'the season's feminine dresses and shapely suits' we don't think square shoulders and straight up and down is what's meant. (Though you do get some rather funny constructions: an M&S bra, for example, described as 'a feminine bra for the fuller figure'. What would a *masculine* bra be?)

Barbie and Ken may not be taken seriously now but prescriptions of male–female difference are writ large across how we dress, our social roles, ways of talking and expressing emotion. Drag and gender-bending do not contradict but depend on our knowing those rules. (Gender diversity was celebrated by a man in a frock interviewed on television: 'masculinity and femininity are ideas, they're not real things,' he said. 'They're a fallacy, a construct ... I get closer to people as a woman, I earn more as a man.' Those reactions and that income seem real to me.)[23] The more people talk about sex and gender (*especially* psychiatrists) the more apparent it is how completely confused we are, and how eager to assert essential male and female qualities that we also know can't be neatly pinned down.

Girls' and boys' toys, seen in the 1970s as among the most straightforward stereotyping to challenge, are pinker and bluer than ever. (Actually, for blue read black and tech.) There's Fairy Princess Sindy and Ninja Warrior Action Man; Polly Pocket has a Tiny World Cottage, her male equivalent Mighty Max Dread Heads have 'doom zones'. (Is someone trying to tell us something about the future of masculinity?) Sindy may have a mountain bike and Barbie goes to the office but Action Man has a 'hi-tech crossbow and concealed dagger'. (In a kind of full circle there are now *Baywatch* Barbies, made to look like the women who look like her.) Even Lego, monument to Danish design skills and egalitarianism in plastic, has introduced a pinkly clichéd domestic scene for the 1990s (complete with baby and newish man); Lego Technics, for 'adventurous builders', has packaging which is coded 'girls keep out'. Then again, the argument has changed too – should we worry more about girls' nurturant and communicative toys or boys' competitive and destructive ones?

Language is a subtle barometer: think of how awkward 'women and men', not 'men and women', seems still (though to say so is to leave yourself open to accusations of being PC). Masculine has its links with machismo but they are looser; the interesting difference between how we use 'masculine' and 'feminine' is that although both have a prescriptive role, something to be achieved and lived up to, masculine can also be used quite neutrally to mean male, being a man, as well as to approve (or not, as the case may be) of someone's manliness. 'Feminine' has no such neutral usage: 'feminine' doesn't mean just being a woman, it means being a certain sort of woman.

Fragmented Femininity

Though powerful messages about sexuality and sexiness, femininity and possibility, affect young women now as they have in every generation since media gained culture-wide coverage, I would not argue that their effect is the same nor the message the same. Femininity can be more *fun* than feminism has found it possible to acknowledge. It too has fragmented. Three important strands contradict general assumptions about women's independence how-ever and are strong evidence for continuing low self-esteem. Endemic eating disorders; the sexual double standard; and the high rates of teenage pregnancy and growing rate of young women with HIV/AIDS all illuminate the darker side of femininity.

The diet industry and its shadows, anorexia and bulimia, have both grown over the past twenty-five years. Slimness is a core obsession of our age: £66 million worth of slimming foods were sold in 1993, more than double the amount sold in 1990. Profits from the diet industry multiply but obesity has increased in line with them. Some form of eating disorder is more usual than not among women in this country, and obsessive exercise shows related patterns. We pay it attention when it gets out of hand but some degree of on–off dieting or 'restrained eating' among women is so common as to be normal. It exists in a vicious circle of cause and effect with low self-esteem, emotional disturbance and depression.

There is a contradiction at both a personal and a social level between our sense of young women as confident and achieving and the pressures, confusion and unhappiness that manifest themselves in eating disorders – particularly anorexia and bulimia, which have increased at all ages (and have shown a small increase among young men) but are much more common among teenage girls facing the contradictions of womanhood. A major research study on teenage growth norms which is under way in Edinburgh has found that even among young women who gave no apparent cause for medical concern their diets were worse nutritionally than at any time this century, giving real reason to worry about their future health. I asked the director of the study what he saw as triggering anorexia: 'low self-esteem, unhappiness, sex roles – the boys hit out, the girls internalise it'. In girls' and women's magazines 'biologically impossible women' are the norm. Girls as young as eight diet; there are seven-year-old anorexics.[24]

'The diet industry,' observes Marion Hetherington, a psychologist with a particular interest in eating disorders, 'depends on diets not working in the long term.' Controls on industry advertising are weak and diets are a wonderful product: when they don't work we blame ourselves. But there is also, as Marion says, a groundswell of women rejecting skinny chic, and ideas like National No Diet Day have been been taken up enthusiastically.

To think about eating disorders, depression (much more common in women than men) and tranquilliser addiction and to admit how widespread these problems are is to open the way to uncomfortable questions about women's lives which are supposed to be part of women's past, not present. More women are more assertive and more confident: but there is a down side too. We need to be more honest about the prevalence of these problems. And ask difficult questions about what it is about the requirement to be feminine that is so very damaging to women.

Cycles of dieting and self-reproach are not recognised as a mass neurosis because they are still close to desirable feminine behaviour. The Princess of Wales was used to sell it. Week after week, in women's magazines and in some newspapers, she was praised and presented as an example for dieting, working out, for going blonde. We know now the unhappiness that was hidden in the fairytale. There is, not surprisingly, a relationship between being in the public eye and an obsession with appearance, including a disturbed body image. The Princess must, in therapist Susie Orbach's words, 'manage the split that all women feel in a public context that is terrifying'.[25] For those women who embody the images of femininity of an age, there always seems a price to be paid.

If the media have a key role in sustaining the monarchy and in manipulating projections about them, so too are they big players in the continuing process of defining woman's role in relation to men. After a decade in which uppity women had hit the headlines the virgin princess was a newsman's dream. She had won her prince, it seemed, through the very qualities women had just begun to try to throw aside. Between her engagement and the 'wedding of the century' the Princess lost 28 pounds and was consequently described as beautiful. She was presented as femininity personified: purity, beauty, goodness, devoted motherhood. Well yes, there was a nasty patch when Di the shopaholic had a public appearance but then she had another baby and so redeemed herself in the tabloid eye.

When the story that their marriage might end first began to break we saw, for the first time, photographs of the Princess looking not pretty but angry. The qualities first seen as the essence of her charm – her modesty, her dependence, her girlishness – were used to show her as sad, naive, neurotic. The same photographs used to show us how slim and beautiful she was now showed us she was thin and sick. After her separation from the Prince she became game for two 'photo scandals', when she was photographed topless in Spain and exercising in a health club. If the commercial pressures are certainly extraordinary, the sub-text is about power. Beauty and sexuality are things to be bought and sold, controlled and traded. The Spanish picture agency boss described the pictures gloatingly, describing a posture of subjection and with the calculating objectivity used to talk about porn. The gym pictures emphasised vulnerability and sexual access. It is as if she is punished by the men of the international media for being so important to them in the first place.

That one of the most advantaged women in the land should be subject to sexual harassment on such a scale suggests that no matter how rich and privileged you are the only way to escape sexual exploitation is to be ugly. And then they'll ridicule you for that. The photographic pursuit of Diana is emblematic of the ways men punish young and sexy women for the power they can have over them. Most women know how flattery and seduction can turn to derision very easily, that put-downs are to be expected however carefully you say no. The rewards of conforming to our society's definition of the feminine are considerable, at least in the short term. But the first price to be paid is unwelcome sexual attention; the second when you realise a trap has been sprung.

Tarts and Teasing

One of the things that angers many young women most is the double standard in sex: there is a fine line between being a slag and sexy which may have been redrawn but its contradictions are not a lot easier to make sense of. Assertions of sexual power and openness rest awkwardly alongside the continuing sexual double standard. 'Reputation' still matters, women are still at risk for behaviour that a young man would be admired for and can walk away from. And after puberty public space holds the permanent threat of sexual harassment.

'Slag' and 'slut' mean much the same as ever. When she interviewed 18- and 19-year-old women in Glasgow in 1992 (both university students and working-class women) Jenny Kitzinger found them, 'acutely conscious of the dilemma they face when trying to attract men without "going too far"'. What counts as 'going too far' may have changed; the central dilemma hasn't: between being sexy and looking like a tart, between being a tease and uptight. Though, Jenny says, an attractive girl who has a lot of sexual encounters which *she* controls is less likely to be seen as a slag by other young women than one who allows herself to be used. 'The distinction between acceptable femininity and unacceptable sluttishness' is made in a different place, but it is 'easily crossed'.[26]

'Men's attitudes to women have not kept up with the dramatic changes that have altered women's lives,' Sue Lees believes, after studying young women and men's lives in London in the 1980s. Girls 'may go to nightclubs or parties but the problem of getting home unscathed is a fear they routinely have to contend with'. Girls must daily navigate their way through the contradictions of 'the system of gender domination. The overall effect ... is to shake their confidence in themselves and can lead to depression, eating disorders and other disturbances.' Girls are criticised if they behave as adolescent boys do, 'but by conforming to models of correct femininity, girls do not escape criticism, nor is this a solution: they are seen as old-fashioned, straight and dull.'[27]

The same double standard on sexual behaviour is used effectively in the courts by lawyers for men accused of rape: juries still believe in it enough to find the 'crime' of a woman going with a man enough to exonerate anything he might then do. She is not seen as a 'deserving victim'. Yet 'women raped by acquaintances,' Sue Lees argues, after research for a forthcoming book, 'find the experience even harder to come to terms with than those raped by strangers. They feel betrayed, not just by the men but by their own judgement.' The increase in reported rapes, legal professor Jennifer Temkin believes, may be because 'women now no longer accept the stereotype which has served so many so well – that rape is a crime which is only committed by psychopaths leaping out of the bushes after dark'.[28]

Extensive research on rape trials has shown how prejudiced attitudes to 'good' and 'bad' women are manipulated in the legal system to allow offenders to get away with it and that 'acquaintance rape' has a very much lower rate of conviction (rape and child sexual abuse have very low rates of conviction in any case). A senior police officer told the (justly) award-winning programme *Dispatches* that 'they rape again because they believe – rightly – that they can get away with it'. 'Whether you get a rape conviction,' Anne Davies of the Metropolitan Police told the programme, 'is nothing to do with whether rape occurred or the circumstances of the case, it has a lot to do with how the jury perceives the woman.' The programme presented the results of research (led by Sue Lees) which shows why rape has exceptionally low rates of conviction. In rape cases where the victim knows the attacker two out of three are acquitted; the legal changes meant to prevent the victim's sexual history and character being brought into the case are evaded through both ignorance and collusion. 'I was on trial, I was being judged for what I am,' one woman told the programme; she echoed the feelings of women who have spoken to researchers and rape crisis centres throughout Britain. The woman police officer who accused a fellow officer of rape in a widely publicised case in early 1995 said afterwards that she felt as if 'my whole character, my whole soul, was being judged and found wanting'. She now intends to work as a counsellor with women in rape cases: 'I'd never taken in what it is really like for the woman who lays charges, how badly you're treated in court, how your life gets turned upside down, especially when it involves someone you know and care about, someone you trusted.'[29]

Research in Scotland where the 'sexual character' legislation is stronger than in England and Wales found it is also only partly successful. The intention of the legislation (introduced in 1976 in England and Wales and in Scotland in 1986) was 'to break the link between sexual immorality and credibility and to outlaw the notion that because somebody was sexually promiscuous they were also a liar'. But women were asked questions about their sexual conduct in half of the cases studied, either because the legislation was ignored or because lawyers asked the judge to waive the rules and he did so. Lawyers 'were adept at employing cumulative questioning' using non-sexual character evidence as the building bricks in the construction of a 'bad sexual character'. 'You are often out late? You drink regularly? You were wearing a low-cut dress. You are an unmarried mother? Where were your children? Do you often go to this type of pub? You went to a disco alone? You were happy to get in a car with a strange man?' It should be generally known, the study concludes, 'that the defence routinely tries to besmirch complainers, to call them liars, to bring in irrelevant evidence, to seize on any aspect of their sexuality that can be found and to construct motives for false allegation'.[30]

The poor funding of provision for victims of rape is the same double standard, writ institutionally. The rape crisis centres are funded and recognised in a way they weren't in the mid- and late 1970s when the first were set up, but still on a shoestring. 'Like any other voluntary organisation in this country we don't know where we're going to be after next April,' Lily Greenan at Edinburgh Rape Crisis Centre said. 'We just keep going but we haven't been able to expand or develop.'

'All of us have waiting lists for face-to-face counselling which we didn't use to have,' Lily Greenan said. 'We're a *crisis* centre but we can't offer a crisis service beyond a telephone line and one immediate meeting.'

'In the seventies,' Sue Lees says, 'the Rape Crisis movement had a major impact on the community and police responses to rape. Yet in the nineties, services are underfunded and skeletal, and few women receive the help they need.'[31] The way Rape Crisis is funded is typical of how support needed for women victims of violence is now recognised, but grudgingly. 'There's a pressure on us to be less than overtly feminist. We tread a fine line, we go on saying what we want to say,' Lily Greenan says. 'Some of our demands are being met and it's not because the politicians have changed, because they're mainly the same men as they were fifteen years ago, but because the public agenda has changed: there's more awareness of the extent of sexual violence and how wrong it is. It's a curious time – all the right things are being said now but does it have substance?'

Seizing the Time

Uttering a curse to undo or claim its power is a form of well-proven magic, Marina Warner observed in her 1994 Reith Lectures, exploring the myths of our times. 'Former misogynist common-places are now being seized by women; in rock music, in films, in fiction, even in pornography, women are grasping the she-beast of demonology for themselves. The bad girl is heroine of our times, and transgression a staple entertainment: Madonna flexing her crotch with her hand, singing "Pappa don't preach".'[32] She is displaced as contradictory icon now by Courtney Love, who declares her defiance in terrifying images of vulnerability.

Ideas of women as passive and only wanting to please, you'd think could hardly survive a decade or more of images of women as predatory (in film especially). Ann Summers parties sell vibrators and penis rings, the Chippendales on tour and male strippers at hen parties allow expression to female raunchiness (though there has been less space to explore what uncommercialised female sexual expression might be). In marked contradiction to this is the reality of young women who protect themselves neither against HIV/AIDS nor pregnancy because they either don't want to be seen to be 'asking for it' or can't acknowledge their sexuality sufficiently to make preparation.

The spread of AIDS among women and the numbers of unwanted pregnancies suggest that the Cosmo Girl approach to life and love has yet to have the impact on young women's lives it is claimed to have. Neither would be occurring if women were able to put their need for safety and sexual pleasure before anything else. Emphasising intercourse as 'the real thing' is as much a problem as not using condoms is in limiting the heterosexual spread of AIDS. Almost a third of women with HIV in Britain by 1994 were aged between 15 and 30.[33] I talked to Jan McClory of the Women and HIV/AIDS Network about this and it was not until I was walking home that I realised it was St Valentine's Day. Roses and chocolates and red hearts in the shop windows were an ironic backdrop to a morning spent finding out about the impact of HIV/AIDS on women. But not irrelevant: Jan had stressed how traditional romantic and sexual attitudes have a lot to do with the growing risk to women.

'Yes, there are young women who are assertive and sexually confident – but I also meet an awful lot who are not,' she said. 'These are young women who say "I'm not bothered – I do it because he wants to". And "I'll lose him if I don't". They are not young women brought up in some remote traditional community – these are young women today.' *Sugar*'s survey also suggests many young women are having sex because of cultural and/or boyfriend pressure. Social commentators spin theories of post-AIDS sexual behaviour – what's harder to find among young heterosexuals is much real evidence of it.

A double standard: nice girls as passive, condoms as not something to keep in your handbag, boys to be humoured and pleased – plenty of ideas about sex today seem sadly familiar. I have never forgotten what an HIV-positive woman said to me a few years ago: 'He disna' even care if I'm *comfortable* – how can I get him to wear a condom?' It is hard to understand why a woman stays in a relationship that apparently offers her so little, let alone risks her health and life. Dangerously low self-esteem is perhaps the one characteristic that most HIV-positive women share. More and more young women will put their health and lives at risk unless they insist on their own safety.

In heterosexual intercourse women are more at risk from infection from a man than vice versa (around four times as likely). Misinformation about the risks is also a problem.

'We are not building the confidence in young women, the skills, the ability to negotiate what they need,' Jan believes, 'partly because our society is so hypocritical about sex.' You need, she says, first the information but then the confidence and communication skills to put it into practice. 'It's about holding your ground – it's about the whole balance of male–female relations. It's very difficult and there are such pressures on young women around sexual behaviour, because it's expected of them, the status of having a boyfriend ... I meet women who do not feel in control or even that they have any contribution to make to a sexual encounter other than to be used.'

Similar messages about girls' sense of self-worth are the key to limiting unwanted pregnancies, the FPA says. They talk about the pressure of 'oh well, my pals are doing it'. One in five young people now has sexual intercourse before the age of 16 in a sexual culture which encourages sexual adventuring but not the open discussion which is needed for safety and real choice. Not all teenage women who get pregnant didn't want to be, but for many it is a consequence of living in a society that promotes sex but not the self-esteem which would ensure its safety.

Going for contraception still means acknowledging sexual activity in a way that 'getting carried away' absolves. For the women who most often get pregnant when they are young, living in disadvantaged communities and often unemployed, images of sex, consumption, glamour and fun surround them: the only part of the glossy package they can actually get their hands on is the sex. Some young women told Sugar they'd first had sex 'to get it over and done with'.[34] Sexual freedom may not have created much more space for young women to discover what they want and when.

Social messages about sex are 'confused, complex and contradictory' a 1995 study concludes.[35] 'You may know the score, but there's a big jump between that and feeling you have the right to say no, or to insist on a condom,' says Jan McClory. Women are dying because of social hypocrisy about sex and because of inequality – because of their lack of power to ensure safety in sex.

Contemporary Realism

But if young women 'think they're equal', isn't that at least half the battle? Even if they think, more realistically, that 'equality is won – well almost', isn't that a thousand times better than seeing a status quo of limited opportunity as either natural or unavoidable? I would not pretend that there are no traps for the unwary but the confidence and common sense of so many younger women now is an achievement of feminism.

Part of the assertiveness of 'we're equal now' has involved, or has been claimed as, a rejection of feminism and has led to sporadic soul-searching about why feminism doesn't appeal. (But are we talking about disdain, incorporation, or in Carmen Callil's phrase, that 'feminism is in the water supply'?) A central concern is that if feminism is seen as history rather than relevant it means that gains are being lost: 'most of my friends see my interest in politics as weird' says Natalie Brown, 'it's depressing if we're going to have to make all the same arguments again'. Questions like the need for women-only meetings and for women's officers (for example in student unions) are re-fought. 'I worry about young women today,' Cynthia Cockburn said, 'because their circumstances and reality of life are going to make them angry and unable to accept a lot of what's going on, but they're going to have to do it individually, there isn't the collective support for them – and that can be dangerous. Women are driven by their circumstances to be stroppy but the collective stroppiness of the women's movement isn't there for them to be supported by ...'

But I see no evidence that if many young women don't see feminism mattering it is because they want to live like some latter-day Lucille Ball. Rather, they take for granted things their mothers couldn't in the same way as women in the 1970s took for granted the vote. A friend of mine has a key ring which says 'Girls can do anything'. (Her own daughter is now a priest.) I was going to get copies for my daughters. Then I realised they'd shrug and say 'we *know* that'. We know as a society that 'Girls *can* do anything' – even if we are still learning how much resistance there is to really letting them, or more than a few of them. If some girls say they don't need feminism it's because they're going to do it all anyway and don't see why they shouldn't. (And if feminism now seems to give the message that 'you may think you can but ...' is it surprising that many women don't want to listen?)

The profile of high-achieving women has created a disjunction between the image of what is possible for women now and what is really possible for most women. The success of some women serves to partly disguise structural inequalities. None the less, if we believe we can, doesn't that give us the energy to jump the barriers? Women have begun to believe the publicity: it can create a cycle of positive reinforcement. We can't all be Kate Adie but we needn't feel that it's impossible for 'people like us' either. Believing you can is a thousand times better than the negative messages of 'you can't, you shouldn't and maybe it's better not to try' which were whispered so seductively into so many women's ears.

I think it was James Baldwin who said that your enemy is really winning when you believe what he's saying about you. The strength of 'second wave' feminism was that it began to explore the interface between social definitions of women and the subjective experience of femininity. Recognising that change is both personal and public is to acknowledge the interaction of many factors: that the relationship between personal and political change is dynamic, that who picks up the socks, who dominates the argument in a seminar, who makes the tea at the bowling club and who runs the country all connect. Women were held back in the world 'out there' not only by discriminatory practices in employment, public life and domestic work, but also by our own sense of who we were and could be.

Discrimination has a kind of pincer movement. First there is what happens in the world and all the subtle and not so subtle assumptions about what qualities are needed for the job – to be an MP, etc. Then there's the hook inside yourself when you think, maybe it's true. The experience of discrimination creates self-doubt. You may believe you've as much to offer as the next person but by the time the next person has been chosen and you haven't four or five times it's hard to still think you've got what it takes. Ask a first-time pregnant woman several times is she *really* going to manage to cope with work and the baby – well, it's a new situation, she doesn't really know either, so maybe she had better give up ...

Nor is it usually as clear that discrimination has occurred as discussion of the issue suggests. It may even be *less* easy to be sure, now that women have made headway in so many areas: 'it must just be me'. If it *is* because different standards are being applied for female applicants they won't tell you that, after all – because you could use the legislation to fight back, or because they don't even see that they are applying different standards. ('No women applied,' shrugged my editor as he went ahead to appoint another bright young man to a senior post, but *because of* assumptions of equal opportunity he does not wonder why no women applied.)

The very lack of adequate explanation adds a twist of difficulty. How are you to know and untangle possible prejudice from your personal failings, or to keep the confidence and self-esteem to know what to do next and do it? There's often a little voice whispering, 'Maybe I'm not good enough, what am I doing wrong?' And a door closing in your face is a pretty unmistakable message, however you explain it to yourself. Even a cursory glance at statistics on women in politics, in decision-making from science to the arts, shows that doors are still not wide open. Discrimination operates by creating discouragement and self-doubt.

Another way of exploring this is suggested by American author and academic Carol Becker, writing in 1987. She believes that 'the optimism of the Women's Movement had left women unprepared for the contradictions they were encountering during the process of change'. Women who were successful often did not feel it: they suffered ambivalence and self-doubt and there was a 'discrepancy between how they appeared to the world, competent, hopeful ... and how they felt when they were alone'. There is, she thinks, 'a crisis of anxiety' among women. Many senior women she spoke to lived with a fear of being 'found out' which was objectively quite unfounded, believed they were really less talented and competent than they had somehow convinced others they were. We have, she suggests, 'underestimated the psychological complexity of the process of change and the internal resistance they would have to struggle against when they tried to undo centuries of tradition'.[36]

It is something I recognise in women I have spoken to, and we should not underestimate the personal complexities of living with change. But it has markedly lessened among younger women – is that age or is it generation? The women Carol Becker writes about are caught between fear of failure and fear of success; they are women 'who do the unorthodox' and who 'often have the intellectual sense that their work is legitimate, yet they do not have the internal permissions ... to validate their life choices'. She describes an intense double-bind. 'Women who did not grow up with an image of themselves as smart and assertive have difficulty in seeing themselves this way, no matter how successful they may become.'

I would not claim that these contradictions have been smoothed out, but if the unorthodox is year by year seen as less so they lose some of their strength. What we have seen over twenty-five years – over 150 years – is that the internal permission to achieve has become less exceptional and has lined up with social permission. Some of the barriers to achievement, at least in terms of women's family role, have not been broken down and that permission has not been offered equally, especially for less educated women. Public messages may underestimate the practical problems and the women who are role models may still be highly unusual. Expectations of equality are ahead of reality – cultural/perceptual change is ahead of economic change – but even for women in jobs that aren't bringing in much money, or who are at home or unemployed, the relationship of work and home and family is perceived differently. Not many women *are* architects or pilots: but it matters that we think we can be.

It's a cliché to say there will be equality when there are as many untalented women in the office as untalented men. Or even ordinarily-able of both sexes with equal chances. But it's also true. The ground floor matters as much as the glass ceiling, and all the steps in between. It has been harder for women, with and without family commitments, to build up work experience and consistency of the sort which provides a solid basis for less-than-brilliant men to build a working life on. Women are still more likely to have a patchwork career. Now that more women are coming in at lower rungs and being more accepted there, and taking work and education seriously, it will make a difference.

If you talk to senior women you won't find many who feel they've never faced barriers and discrimination that the men they work with don't face – though there *are* some who sail through untroubled. The secret is not in being lucky or brilliant enough never to have to face discrimination, but in having enough self-belief, and cunning and courage to bounce back, to find a new way in (or out – the numbers of women fed up with the slow pace of change and going freelance or setting up in business on their own are multiplying). It *isn't* always possible: there are a lot of good women who swallowed the disappointment and discrimination and tried again and again and gave up, or were pushed out, and it's the world's loss. But the secret is having whatever it takes to keep going anyway and find new ways round the obstacles.

If that little voice hasn't been whispering all your life that you can't do it really, then setbacks are easier to overcome. The messages that *really* get to you are those for which a slot is ready prepared. For women who grew up in the 1950s and 1960s there were many more cultural messages that they weren't as good – as men, as 'proper' fulfilled, feminine women – messages which were the prime impetus of Women's Liberation. As a movement it may have created its own dead-end, but it rolled over and squashed a lot of those messages on the way. For women now – at least if they believe they are equal, and some of the people who matter to them do as well – it's less likely that the same conflicts and deep reserves of self-doubt can be manipulated and reinforced. It doesn't mean they won't face difficulty and discrimination but at least they may not believe it. 'It's going to be different for our generation' is what women who were in their teens and early twenties in the 1970s said too. We weren't wrong, even if it wasn't so *very* different. When young women say, 'Our generation will change it' they may be right.

Chapter 10

Even More Equal Than Others

'It is a pitiful performance by boys that now requires a radical rethinking of attitudes to equal opportunities. The question is: have girls had it too good for too long while society has complacently accepted that boys will be boys?'

What the *Sunday Times* (in June 1994) was talking about was an excellent performance by girls: that girls were more likely to get top-grade GCSEs in all but three subjects and almost twice as likely to get an A grade at GCSE English as boys. That summer for the first time, girls in England also achieved better overall success rates at A level than boys.[1]

In summer 1994 a new myth took wing, or whatever it is that myths do. This was that while girls were now doing wonderfully well in school boys were doing terribly. I'm not about to argue that if boys are doing worse than they were we shouldn't be concerned. But they're not, unless comparison with girls is your only measure. The achievement, as measured by exams, of all school pupils is improving throughout Britain. Everyone is doing better than they used to, but girls' results are pushing ahead.

Some measures now suggest girls have a lead even when they start primary school. National testing of seven-year-olds in England showed girls ahead of boys in reading; tests for 11-year-olds showed girls doing significantly better than boys in Maths and English. Girls are also less likely than are boys to leave school without any qualifications. Women are now more likely to get a first or upper-second in more than two-thirds of subjects at the 'old' universities.

And women are now almost half of university students. They were under a third in 1970 and a third as many boys left school with three A levels.[2] Yet if all girls who were qualified to do so now went on to university they would take up *more* than half the places. The male-dominated nature of higher education is something young women say they find uncongenial and old-fashioned.

Boys' 'underachievement' has rapidly become a major concern: the subtitle in that *Sunday Times* article was: LOSERS IN THE RACE OF LIFE: HOW BOYS ARE TRAILING GIRLS. If they're all doing better, is this something we should *worry* about or be pleased about? Shouldn't we be headlining the brilliance of girls rather than 'The Trouble with Boys'? But boys' problems have rapidly become a concern throughout education; a ripple of alarm ran through parliament. When boys did better than girls it was considered natural: we know now that it involved manipulation of the 11-plus results and gender quotas at grammar schools and on university courses. Some girls may have passed their 11-plus but gone to the secondary modern none the less: while girls like Bea Campbell who failed her 11-plus, have gone on to show a sharp intellect in journalism and books.

The Minister for Education, Gillian Shephard, told the annual conference of the Girls' Schools Association in November 1994 that girls were forging so far ahead at school that we needed to examine the way we educate boys. 'Of course we can take pride in girls' achievement, but there is a danger of going too far the other way. Certainly these trends have implications for how we educate boys.' The Office for Standards in Education was asked to look at the problem of boys' academic performance.

So what are we going to do about boys? But what can you expect? Think of their hormones and their low expectations … Still, surely they can find a well-paid wife to take care of them? No, those aren't the arguments I've heard either. Rather, it's that girls have all the advantages now and anyway they get there by underhand methods like working hard and being determined.

Positive action programmes for girls have not been as widespread as suggested; nor is the curriculum now tilted in their favour. Instead there has been a removal of some barriers and (whisper it) feminism has had an impact on how young women see themselves. As one woman said, 'girls have been given permission to achieve, and by

God they are achieving!' *If* there are new difficulties for boys they are not *caused* by girls doing even better. Boys with problems may need special action, but not at the cost of girls. Asian children do very well in school exams but we do not conclude from that that racism is not a problem in schools; nor should we infer from girls' exam results that sexism has been eradicated.

Comparisons between Scotland and England are interesting in this context, especially in view of the exaggerated response in some quarters about girls' advances at GCSE and A level. In Scotland girls have been doing better than boys at Standard Grade and Higher since 1984–5. The assumption that good exam results straightforwardly translate into greater work opportunity is not borne out by the past decade in Scotland where women's advances in professional and public life have been no greater than in the rest of Britain.

Current analysis of how curricular and management changes in education have affected equal opportunities shows a different pattern in England and Scotland, but in both equal opportunities practice is 'patchy' and threatened by the changes. In Scotland it is probable that those councils and schools where there is a commitment to equal opportunities will maintain it, researchers found, but where there is not there are fewer incentives now to improve matters, and 'no pressure' to do so. In England they found that the metropolitan areas which have done most are now feeling that things are going backwards because LEAs have less power and opportunity to develop policy. But in Conservative-controlled councils which had done very little so far, individual schools (particularly in areas where parents' voices were strong) were now developing policies creating 'a second, weaker phase' of equal opportunities development. On both sides of the border the ending of the TVEI initiative is regretted because of the value it has had in developing equal opportunities, especially for less academic pupils.[3] Perhaps we should wait a while before concluding that girls' academic excellence means the future is female.

The Trouble with Girls

The reasons given for girls' achievements have been an interesting display of prejudice. The GCSE results, it's been said, are because of 'bringing in course work that rewarded conscientious candidates'. When girls were doing better than boys in the Scottish Higher exam but not at A level it was suggested that this might be because the Higher was a less intimidating exam. Girls are well behaved; girls talk to each other; girls mature earlier. Hard work, conscientiousness and communicativeness are all subtly devalued. Valerie Walkerdine, beginning research into girls' performance in maths and science in the late 1970s, found a habit of underplaying girls' success, and a consistent attempt in the research literature, as well as more popularly, 'to ascribe girls' good performance to hard work, diligence and good behaviour. Boys, by contrast, were held to have the kind of potential that leads to brilliance, even if their current classroom performance exhibited no tangible evidence of it.'[4]

Subject segregation at school and university, although not as extreme as it was in the 1970s (with particular advances made by young women in science, maths and computing), still shows a continued pattern which reflects sex-stereotyping. In Britain as a whole almost twice as many women as men are doing arts degrees; there are almost twice as many men as women in science.[5] The reduction in 1993 of funding for university places in arts and social sciences, where women are well represented, while maintaining the existing levels for science and engineering, where men predominate, means more is being spent to educate male students.

It is a less marked pattern in Scotland now than in England: at Standard Grade (the equivalent to GCSE) girls are more likely than boys to take modern languages but they are equally likely to take all other subject areas, including science. The gender imbalance in subjects studied for Highers is greater but has decreased since the early 1980s, a Scottish Office comparison shows. For students on lower-level vocational qualifications segregation is much greater.[6]

One specific change which has affected girls' overall results in England and Wales is the introduction of the National Curriculum, which means girls now have to continue science and maths up to the age of 16. There is disappointment that after 16 pupils of both sexes are not keen to continue in science, and that girls are still less likely to take A-level physics and chemistry. At GCSE 'the gender imbalance in the study of the three sciences remains as intractable despite the majority of girls studying the physical sciences within balanced science GCSEs and gaining equal success to boys,' a recent report concluded. Boys still do better than girls in maths at GCSE but only by a small margin: just under 2 per cent more boys got A–C grades. Twice as many boys as girls do A-level maths, however, despite the marginal difference in their GCSE results.[7]

In the main, steps to discourage segregated subject choice concentrate on girls' attitudes and aspirations although recently more attention has been paid to boys' lower interest in languages and poorer performance in English. As things stand, girls may be making positive rather than prejudiced choices in favour of the areas in which they are taken more seriously and are not made to feel uncomfortable. Rather than decrying girls' traditional routes, we need to be asking school and university science and computing departments to consider why the environment they create continues to be unattractive to many girls. Girls still report harassment for taking non-traditional options. We need to make sure that they have a real choice, but we also need to question the value we attach to certain routes. Instead of bemoaning the numbers of girls going into the caring professions or teaching, for example, we need to question why those roles are valued less by society.

The General Teaching Council for Scotland policy document on gender in education in 1991 comments, rightly, that 'While it is perfectly legitimate to encourage girls to opt for studies and careers in science and technology, care must be taken not to regard girls as "deficient boys" who can fulfil their potential only by adopting male norms of behaviour.'[8]

Popular Wisdom

American research in the 1960s posited a 'fail bright woman' syndrome.[9] Girls now are seen as more motivated to achieve than boys. The common argument that girls might seem brighter but that was because they matured earlier has faded away as many more young women go on to university and do well there. There is no longer a contradiction between ideas of femininity and cleverness.

The idea of boys being brainier is met with ridicule by schoolgirls today. But as a girl in the 1960s I thought they were, because the world I lived in thought so. (This was a belief that survived sharing a class with a girl called Agnes who year after year swept the board for prizes.) The idea now gaining ground that there are inherent reasons why girls may be more intelligent than boys does not seem any more useful, but is interesting as a reversal of popular wisdom.

Mature Options

As I talked to women about our changing lives I was struck by how many had taken a less than straightforward route into education and work. The massive expansion in 'second chance' education at a variety of levels is a positive change which has affected women most. More women than men take up 'Access' opportunities and mature students are now more than half of those starting first degrees; their numbers doubled in the decade since 1982. In the 1970s they were still unusual.[10] As an alternative route into education it is making a difference – for young women only two years out of school coming back to get qualifications once they see what poor job chances they have without them, to women pensioners fulfilling a long-held ambition. Though some older women students are catching up on opportunities they would rather have had immediately after leaving school, others are demonstrating a different time-mix of work, having children and education which has its own benefits. There is a lot of talk about 'lifelong learning' and how the strait-jacket of school, further education, work and retirement is no longer functional: a lot of women are already doing it.

Sharon Taylor dropped out of nurse training when she was 18. She has two daughters Amy and Lucy, aged nine and six. She's an enthusiastic advocate of 'Access' projects and hopes to move on to social work training. 'It's made *such* a difference. When you're at home as a mother you tend to forget you have other gifts. I lost a lot of confidence – a lot of the women at Second Chance say that. But you realise you *do* know things and you're learning new things – you realise you're still a person.' Schemes like Second Chance in Edinburgh, which Sharon attends, and the scheme of the same name in Greenock in the West of Scotland, replicate the experience of projects throughout Britain in finding that women with young children are their most enthusiastic customers. The network of women's technology training centres has had conspicuous success in 'non-standard' students going on to work or higher education. But you are still twice as likely to study as an adult if you are middle-class and more than twice as likely to if you stayed on in education after 18, the first time round.[11]

The unexpected drop in student applications to universities in 1994 included, however, a big drop in mature students applying. It makes sense that they, possibly with more to risk and who may have dependants, are likely to be first hit by the need to think harder about the financial costs of a degree now that funding is getting tighter. A high proportion of mature students are 'women returners'. Research shows that this group, precisely the people the government was at pains to encourage back into the job market, face both ageism and sexism when they graduate and seek work. Their experience may now be having an impact on the plans of others.

Alice Brown, herself once a mature student (she did a first degree when her children started school) is now head of the Department of Politics at Edinburgh University and with Janette Webb has looked at how mature students fare at university and what happens when they look for jobs.[12] They found there are problems as well as advantages: women returners got better degree results than men returners but were less likely to find employment or to get professional or career-type jobs – almost three times more men than women got jobs in the top occupational category. Women found it easiest to get work in 'caring' professions: if they had sought to escape their maternal role through education they were finding that their best chance of work was with employers who valued 'maternal qualities' in social work and similar areas; they were seen as inherently unsuitable 'by virtue of the same attributed maternal qualities' for prestigious, high-flying careers. Employers were not however, they note drily, noticeable for their reluctance to employ fathers. This meant 'a severe mismatch' between the expectations of women over 30 who imagined themselves embarking on an upwardly aspiring career and the expectations of employers who identify 'career' with youth and a record of continuous employment. There are additional financial problems for part-time students, which more than half of mature students are.[13]

Financial problems were identified as a main constraint in a 1992 survey of women in education and training in Scotland: childcare and transport costs were the main aspects. The study showed familiar barriers: money, dependent care and discriminatory attitudes, but also 'considerable drive, motivation and energy targeted at overcoming the barriers, usually through self-help'.[14] Women talk about starting their work at ten at night when the kids are in bed. Some hit relationship problems when they spread their wings through education. One woman told me: 'I had a small baby and that was hard enough but every time I had an essay to hand in it seemed my partner would engineer a big scene or disrupt things in some way.' Another said: 'He used to always look down on me because I didn't have a degree – when I did this I thought he would be *pleased*.' Instead he left her. 'It's not what I wanted – after twenty-five years it is very hard to be on your own again. But coming to university I discovered I was OK. I could talk to people, we could laugh – I discovered I had a brain.'

When Liz Stanley left school she'd failed most of her O levels; she is now a senior academic at Manchester University. She was, she says, seen as 'a sullen, dirty working-class child who wasn't very good at doing what they wanted me to do'. But in books 'there was always a sense of there being something other – somewhere where my mind could roam in ways that weren't governed by the kinds of expectations that my parents had or indeed most of my friends had. I think now, thank God I was a lesbian! If I wasn't I'd've fetched up probably pregnant at 16, like many of my friends did, because their "other" was boys, that was the fun in their life, whereas boys weren't any fun for me'. As a teacher she sees people making good use of opportunities for 'non-standard' students. 'Adult education is being kept alive on women's education.' She talked with admiration of young working-class women in her classes, coming in through Access and similar routes. 'Many of them are quite young, women who left school at the earliest opportunity and have a couple of kids and have turned their lives around the hard way, on a shoestring: three part-time jobs and an Access course!'

'So many students are just cluttering up the place ... they don't want to be here really, all they want is the bit of paper at the end.' But the Access group: 'nearly all of that lot really *want* to be here'. Surely women like that will make an impact on the world? 'Well, they're certainly making an impact on me!'

Unequal Advantage

The young women who hit the headlines with their A-level results were mainly from fee-paying all-girls schools, followed by those from well-funded state schools. There is a widening attainment gap between them and working-class girls at schools in poorer areas. Although the proportion of students in higher education from working-class backgrounds has risen, many fewer of the latter are going on to university. Many of these girls 'who achieve so well at junior school', Valerie Walkerdine says, 'are facing no greater prospect than the dole queue. Not for them top marks and Oxbridge entry. In the postwar expansion of higher education, the worlds of girls like these did come closer together. Today, it seems, they could not be farther apart.' Recent research to back up 'value-added' league tables emphasises the divergence.[15]

In the past twenty years girls from independent schools have taken most advantage of the expansion of higher education: their numbers entering university almost quadrupled. The increase for girls from state schools in the same period was only 40 per cent, although it was higher than for state-educated boys. For boys from independent schools it was just over double.[16]

Studying girls' aspirations in the mid-1980s in south-west England, Sheila Riddell found noticeable differences between middle-class girls who had academic aspirations, and working-class girls who were both more pragmatic and more traditional in their approach: 'they were sceptical of over-simplified messages about doing engineering and science,' she says, 'no women in their experience worked in those areas.' There were penalties, she says, for being different: 'doing physics especially marked you as "brainy and a bit weird". Girls still have to contend with strong pressures from each other as well about what it's acceptable to do'. Harassment is also likely to be greater for women working in lower-level jobs in non-traditional areas than for senior and highly qualified engineers or geologists, for example.[17]

Helen Lucey is following the educational tracks of several groups of girls (in London and Brighton) from age four to the mid-twenties. She says 'in education the stark fact is that the working-class girls and middle-class girls are miles apart.' Among the older girls all but one of the middle-class girls is in higher education, of the working-class girls all but two left school at 16. But when they were four they had similar levels of ability. 'The working-class girls are no less bright but it's like they've lived on a different planet' she says. But, she stresses, the advantages are not simply one way: the pressure on middle-class girls to achieve and the levels of anxiety they expressed were worrying. 'Success and failure is seen differently in working-class and middle-class families. For middle-class girls it was unthinkable to get less than straight As. A lot of them gave no sense that they felt they were good enough and *everything* else – relationships especially – was subordinated to education.'[18]

The continuing changes to state-funded education are doing nothing to narrow the gap. Spending on education has not risen in real terms for ten years, the report of the independent National Commission on Education said in November 1993. Children from poor families are losing out under education changes that are deepening social and economic divisions. The rising cost of school uniforms, meals and public transport falls most heavily on those who can least afford it. Things we know would help – like financial support for 16- to 18-year-olds in full-time education, universal nursery education for three- and four-year-olds, and smaller primary classes – begin to seem impossible dreams as councils can't even afford to pay all their teachers.[19]

Young women who are not academically able are generally doing better than boys at their level. But young women and men who leave school at 16 without qualifications or with limited qualifications are much more likely to go into rigidly sex-stereotyped work than their better-educated peers – that's if they can find work. Youth unemployment rates are very high, though young women in some areas now find it easier to get work than young men. School-leaver destinations analysed by gender (which is unfortunately not a government requirement) in Lothian Region confirm continuing sex-segregation for young people leaving for jobs or training at 16. The ongoing *Changing Lives* survey by the Policy Studies Institute of young people from English inner-cities also shows young women who leave at 16 continuing to opt for office work, hairdressing and 'caring': over half of young women employees and over three-quarters of female trainees had done so but young men went into a broader range of occupations.[20]

The principle of opportunity through education is being discarded at a time when Britain needs new ideas and new 'people skills' more than ever before, to turn round mounting social and economic crisis and because 'thinking for a living' is expected to account for well over half of all jobs in the European Union by the turn of the century. But the changes now in funding students in higher education may rapidly mean that students without family financial support will find staying on too difficult, widening social division and blunting individual possibility. The cutback in grants and reliance on loans has been justified on the grounds that graduates get better-paid jobs, but that is less and less often true – even for once safe options like law and accountancy – with graduate unemployment a long-term reality and redundant experienced workers competing for jobs with new graduates. And because of the difficulty in getting summer jobs, the unavailability of housing benefit and Income Support creates hardship for a growing number of students.

Not even the government now expects students to be able to live on a grant. Commercial and other student debt levels have increased steeply since 1990.[21] Debt clearly restricts your options as you graduate; building up debt is a very different thing for students with families in a position to clear it for them if needed than for students from backgrounds where that isn't possible, and where debt may be culturally much less acceptable. Student loans can have specific consequences for women, especially those on long courses like medicine and architecture. They may still be in the middle of paying back a loan when they want to have children. These problems may well be reflected in the sharp and unexpected drop in university applications in summer 1994, despite record numbers of young people qualified to go.

A lot of able women I've talked to come from similar backgrounds to myself: 'ordinary' kids from council estates for whom a grant plus other sources of support in school meant a route into the sort of world our mothers could not have dreamt of. Would many of us make it now? Or even try? We are seeing the loss of not merely a fundamental equality but a major social and economic strength –

we'll feel the impact in twenty years. It is also possible that when families are having to choose which child or children to support through university – as some are – the attitude that a girl's education is less important than a boy's will come to the fore again, reversing one of the most unequivocal of advances towards equality.

When I was a student at St Andrews in the early 1970s I didn't know it was the first Scottish university to open its doors to women, in 1892. (London was the first British university to do so, fifteen years earlier, and then Durham.) Only twenty or so years ago it still felt as if you were pushing against a door that wasn't quite open. It felt like a male preserve in which we were guests who mustn't make too much noise or challenge the rules of the house. I remember the nagging feeling of not being taken quite as seriously, and the way in which my attempts to integrate my interest in women and gender with the 'proper' areas to be studied were belittled and dismissed.

The door is wide open now. Catherine Taylor is president of the Students' Union and studying geography and international relations. She reckons that as a student things are pretty much equal. Though some staff do treat women and men differently, they're seen as 'dinosaurs', she says. Where you notice inequality is in so few staff being women, and that matters: 'it feels very male dominated. It's a culture shock after school.' She had been a student representative on Senate, the governing body – 'four women and 70 men, that's when it really comes home to you'; she's planning a future in politics and grins and says at least she's getting a training in male-run institutions. In her Union role she'd noticed that no one ever comments on her being a woman except when they think she's done something wrong: 'then I'm a silly *girl*!'

The cutback in student grants went almost unprotested. Students shouted a bit, but then shouting is what we expect them to do. The possibility of students now contributing to tuition fees as well, and ideas like a graduate tax, add an impossible extra layer. The very able young person without means will still be seen as worthy of special efforts. But equality of opportunity is giving the ordinarily-able student from a less well-off background the same chances. OK, it was never as equal as all that: it was always the case that if you went to the right school your chances of going on to university were greater, and boys' chances are still slightly greater. But we are seeing a rapid erosion of the ideal that education is about merit not money, more about what you can do than what you can afford. The image of students as privileged has been out of date for years. If current changes continue it may one day be true again.

Women ahead, women behind

'You're going to sound like Eeyore – dreadfully gloomy', a friend said when we discussed the parallel themes of this chapter. It is hard to dissect the down-side of current trends without seeming to denigrate women's achievements or ignore women's efforts to resist traps laid by poverty and stereotyping. But, partly because Britain today is a more unequal society than twenty-five years ago, and also because for some women equality in income and opportunity has become a reality, or close, there is now greater inequality *between* women. The growing divergence in opportunity in education is part of a wider pattern in terms of income and resources: better living standards for some women but a growing gap between women. The opening up of opportunity has left many women behind: women working for poverty wages, old women without adequate pensions, young women without jobs, women at home with children. While such differences remain between different women's life chances we can hardly talk about equality.

When I talked to Usha Brown she gave a succinct account of what she saw as the key changes of the past twenty-five years. 'Ways of increasing women's representation – though not without a hard battle – and issues around women's health and sexual harassment which would not have emerged without feminism there talking about women and women's needs. And raising the whole question of work and what counts as work and what place it should have in our lives. The work of Women's Aid – that's been huge.' It has all been immensely important, 'but poverty still remains at the core of everything, the central challenge. If we tackle poverty we also tackle exclusion, discrimination, violence.'

The Women's National Commission (WNC) has criticised the government report to the UN conference in Beijing for ignoring the extent of women's poverty. 'Poverty is the most serious obstacle to the advancement of women in Scotland,' the independent Scottish report for Beijing also says. 'There can be no genuine development for women while they form 62 per cent of the poor,' the WNC says, in a strongly worded statement. 'The poverty of women is directly related to the status and reward attached to traditional women's roles', and women are ten times more likely than men to have very low incomes. The Commission has called for a national minimum wage, as has the EOC.[22]

Family poverty and women's poverty are tightly connected: most single mothers, for example, are poor not because they are on their own with kids but because they are *women*. Single fathers are much less likely to be on Income Support or low paid. Often women's poverty has been hidden in analyses which define poverty in relation to families or households. But in the deepening poverty throughout the 1980s in Britain women have been badly affected.[23]

This is a deeply materialist society: the capacity to earn one's own living underpins almost everything else. But because paid work has gained a greater place in many women's lives at the same time as economic change and a market-driven politics have created a workplace which is more competitive and still offers limited support to people with family responsibilities, the gap between different women's access to independence and income has widened. The divide between better-off and poor women is even wider than the inequality which has grown between different groups of men and between families. Although very few women are high earners the gap between the poorest tenth and richest tenth of women workers has more than doubled over the past twenty-five years.[24]

The division is greater now between women who have equal pay and (more commonly) *almost* equal pay and women who are low-paid and/or part-time workers and who work in the areas legislation doesn't reach. It is apparent between firms that practise equal opportunities and the firms that don't, and the sweatshops which scarcely even try to be legal. There is a division even between women working for the same companies, those with skills in demand and at promoted levels who are able to benefit from equal opportunities policies, and those at clerical and similar levels who are seen as easily replaceable. This is backed, as I've argued, by a widening division between single parents and two-parent families and between families with no earnings and families with two incomes.

This divergence between women is marked out most of all by motherhood, education and ethnicity (although there is also a widening gap between black women). Whereas twenty-five years ago you could delineate differences in income and opportunity between all men (or almost all) and all women, the patterns of inequality between women and men are now cross-cut much more than they were with inequalities between women and between men. The line now runs between *most* men plus *some* women and most women plus *some* (unusually disadvantaged) men. It is most marked in the gap between skilled and unskilled workers and between white and black and ethnic minority women.

Black women's greater unemployment and their under-employment is particularly at issue. Analysis in 1989 in London showed that black women benefited least from earnings increases of the 1980s and because of that and their higher rates of unemployment, the gap between black and white women's incomes and living standards had increased more than that between black and white men. Black women's lower wages and higher rates of unemployment also mean they are less likely to get maternity pay and retirement pensions.[25]

Double segregation at work for black women widens the gap. There is no adequate national research on black women's earnings but black workers are more likely to work in sectors which pay low wages, as are women workers, and black women workers are likely to be further segregated within their areas of work. Black women are also more likely to be working below their qualification level.[26]

Unequal Pay

The reach of equal pay legislation is not very great. Equal pay for equal work is not a radical or controversial demand – it is an old one, and has been voiced since at least the 1830s.[27] It's not a subject of media interest nor does it excite many campaigners – but pay isn't even equal where you expect it to be. Women primary and nursery teachers earn 88 per cent of the average earnings of their male equivalents; the small but growing proportion of professors who are women are on average paid less than the 95 per cent of professors, who are men. Recent Employment Department research concludes that most highly-qualified women earn less than men with equivalent qualifications. On an analysis of monthly gross pay men were significantly more likely to be in the top 25 per cent of earners.[28]

'Some women have benefited greatly as a result of the Equal Pay and Sex Discrimination Acts. Many more have not,' Aileen McColgan observes in her study of why new legislation is needed. The steady trend since 1988 in narrowing the pay gap between women and men should not be discounted, however, even if it is slow: (between 0.5 and 1 per cent each year). In some years in the 1980s progress reversed; the improvement since then is likely to reflect more women in professional and managerial work and the slow onward progress of trade union equal pay negotiations but also, less positively, an increased number of men on lower wages. The EOC argues that less daunting legislation would bring improvements: one EOC-supported equal pay case (*Enderby* v. *Frenchay Health Authority*) has been going on for over ten years. Athough the equal value amendment (introduced in 1984) has led to improvements, in its first ten years there were only twenty-two successful equal value claims.[29]

The usually quoted unequal pay figure of 79.5 per cent of male wages overstates the nearness to equality. Since it is based on comparisons between full-time workers, and full-time women earn more than women on average, it underestimates the real gender gap. It compares hourly earnings but comparing weekly earnings – in other words, actual take-home pay – shows women earning an average of £100 less each week.[30] Furthermore, the worst-paid women don't even appear in the statistics so the true picture is worse: An equal pay figure which does not take into account the most low-paid women is a questionable measure.

To get a real sense of pay inequalities you also need to look at who earns least and who earns most. Of the three million plus employees who earn below the NI threshold 85 per cent are women; of a strangely symmetrical three million or so who earn more than its upper limit, 84 per cent are men.[31] Complacency over unequal pay is only matched by the hypocrisy. No one disagrees with the principle – why then isn't it usual practice?

Special Pleading

We still talk about poverty as if it didn't have a gender. Far more women than men live in poverty – though it's seen as 'special pleading' to say so. But male and female poverty are not the same in cause or consequences. Men are better paid, are better pensioned and, married or not, are recipients of benefit in their own right. The two poorest groups in our society are single parents on benefit and the very old, and both are mainly female. Even among the 'young elderly' women are much poorer: EOC research shows that retired men between 55 and 69 have an average weekly income twice that of women of the same age group. Half of full-time women workers are in occupational pension schemes but 62 per cent of men; under a fifth of part-time women workers are.[32] Women are penalised in old age because of low pay and interrupted employment in earlier years. Some thanks we give them. Inequality in employment creates poverty in age. Women are living unrewarded and difficult lives and dying in the winter cold, because they are old and female.

As Sally Greengross, director of Age Concern, England put it: 'personal poverty in later life is the price of fertility'.[33] The high divorce rate has added a whole group of female poor who don't have access to their husbands' occupational pensions. A House of Lords amendment to the Pensions Bill in March 1995 may mitigate that problem in future, (as has been possible under Scots law since 1985) though some MPs fear it may be as controversial to put into practice as the CSA. Only women who have never married have average incomes close to men's in retirement.[34] The message is clear – if you want a decent old age, don't marry and certainly don't divorce.

Younger women now who reject more traditional roles may not find themselves better off. Casual work without pension rights and private pension schemes which may not deliver what they promised mean less of a safety net in the future. With part-time workers paid less than the NI threshold forming possibly half of all part-time workers now, this is creating a welfare time bomb.[35] 'Grey area' work where employers can avoid social or labour laws has been part of the development of what's politely called an 'ancillary employment structure'. It will have long-term consequences.

The visible evidence of what poverty means for young women can be seen daily on the streets of all our major cities. The removal of the right to benefit for 16- and 17-year-olds in 1988 has had devastating consequences for some, in homelessness, exploitation and prostitution. Eighteen- to 24-year-olds are also penalised by the benefit system and very vulnerable to unemployment: for young people outside further education the transition to independence is more difficult now than it was in the 1970s and even most of the 1980s.

Poverty and inequality are most apparent in where we live. Woman-headed households are twice as likely as male-headed households to be council tenants, and most are divorced, separated or widowed. More than half of single parents live in public housing.[36] This is not *in itself* a measure of disadvantage since council and housing association property varies considerably – some is very good. But people with less choice, and people who have become tenants since council housing has been so drastically cut back, are more likely to live in the poorest housing areas and 'hard to let' flats. The best houses are bought by existing tenants, and people with least choice take what they can get. The 1990s has seen a continued decrease in local authority housing available – plus a steep increase in repossessions, almost 300,000 houses in the early 1990s.[37]

Nor, despite a strong social myth to the contrary and legislation to encourage it, are most women with children able to stay on in the family home after separation or divorce: less than half do and the most common move is into local authority housing. Just over a third of separated or divorced women are home-owners compared to half of men in similar circumstances.[38]

Although more women live in poverty than men it's unusual to see it on the streets, while men's poverty is in-your-face. In hostels and cardboard cities the archetypal homeless person is male, but the problem of women's homelessness may be far greater than has been realised: a recent Scottish study suggests it may be *more* of a problem for women, but a hidden one. For homeless women, outside *or* inside may mean fear, vulnerability, danger. Women may be less conspicuous among the 'presenting' homeless only because they have to manage their homelessness differently. They can 'buy' a bed for the night, or perhaps not even a bed, but a drink and a bit of shelter, with their bodies. It also means that the greater dangers homeless women face on the streets and the lack of hostels they feel safe in (some women have said it is safer on the street than in mixed hostels), leads to women staying in bad situations or living with friends or relatives, however temporary or unsatisfactory that may be.[39]

Research analysing council waiting lists for the Scottish Council for Single Homeless shows that living 'care-of' is a major problem for poor single women. There is no reason to believe the problem is less severe in the rest of the UK: CHAR say that there is a lack of information but they think it is equally an issue in England and Wales. The SCSH research emphasises that living 'care-of' does not solve homelessness, but it does conceal it. It means, one woman said, 'living in someone else's house and they don't want me here but I don't know where else to go'. The worst affected women are young, under 26. For every young woman with a baby alarming government ministers there are other women of her age homeless and very vulnerable. These girls are nomads: 'moving from friend to friend to relative, from couch to floor to couch – moving on as she outstays her welcome and sleeping in closes when she cannot secure her next "care-of" address.' It means losing friends and jobs and self-respect and having low expectations of it ever being different.[40]

But it's not just young women – a particularly poignant situation is that of women who have lived at home caring for elderly relatives but because of succession rights when they die, or because the house is sold to pay residential care costs, are made homeless. Danger and social attitudes and policy create a catch 22: few homeless single people fit the categories for priority rehousing anyway, and women living 'care of' don't because technically they have an address to return to. They have somewhere to stay but no permanent, safe or secure accommodation. They are not a priority despite vulnerability to harassment, abuse and violence.

Poverty is about much more than money. It is a term which slips too easily past our eyes in official reports and polemic alike. It is about social exclusion. It is about lack of resources in every sense – poorer housing and poorer local facilities and environment and poorer health. Poverty and limited opportunity is handed on. To be poor is to have fewer resources for building a ladder out of poverty. Women fight back: campaigning for childcare and training, in community development and community employment initiatives, as trade union members. But it can be hard to persist against odds which seem never to lessen and when even small amounts of funding for community schemes take years to prise from council budgets.

Poverty is the most fundamental consequence and cause of inequality. Ending poverty is not only a matter of social justice; it must be a key component of how we understand equal opportunity because it is a major barrier to it.

A limited definition of 'equal opportunity' has meant women joining a working world governed by pre-existing male rules and value-systems designed to buttress male power. True equality would mean much more. We must (and can only) move beyond the current paradigm, beyond correcting wrongs and patching over the old structures, to wholly new ways of structuring work, thinking about education and relationships. Otherwise the inequality between women will only grow greater. There *is* change and advance in the 1990s, particularly for well-educated women. The challenge is to make it work for all women.

Chapter 11

A Working Future

The message that women now had all the best jobs began to spread in early 1994. GIRLS ON TOP! screeched the headlines. It was couched in terms of social and economic concern but the anxiety which underlay it was, 'What about the men?' 'Society is undergoing fundamental changes which are unlikely to be reversed in the foreseeable future and from which men could well emerge the losers,' wrote Victor Keegan in the *Guardian. The Times* claimed that women's greater productivity and modernity was pushing men out of the job market. 'With the job market today ... she'll be wondering how Daddy keeps his hands soft,' the *Scotsman* said in May. 'Career males are becoming an endangered species' said *The Times* in October.[1]

They exaggerated. But they typify a troublemaking perception that women are getting jobs at men's expense. The job market is seen, for the first time, as favouring women. Unemployment among unskilled men and long-term unemployment, mainly a male phenomenon, is increasing. Non-employment, men over 50, mainly, leaving the labour market and no longer looking for work has also been increasing. The Social Justice Commission comments that 'many of the one-third of a million men between the ages of 55 and 65 who are living on Income Support, early retirement pensions or other benefits would like a job'. I'm sure they would – but so might many women in that age group who are still less likely to be economically active than men but are left out of the discussion.[2] Unemployment is not seen as a problem for women. Women's *under*-employment is so usual as to rarely rate much comment. But employment for men has fallen over two decades as employment for women has increased.

So full employment is back on the agenda. Rightly so. But high rates of male unemployment and non-employment are not *caused* by growing female employment. Jobs are increasing in the service sector and decreasing in manufacturing and other areas; these are parallel not competing trends. (You don't see a lot of unemployed miners taking jobs at supermarket checkouts.) Add in people who are working but self-employed, three-quarters of them men, and that changes the picture again.

There are real problems which need to be addressed. But more women getting more jobs is not one of them, nor the cause of them. In reporting and political comment the repeated conjunction of these two trends strongly implies otherwise. 'Flexible women take over the job market' is contrasted with 'The outlook for men has grown increasingly bleak'. To call this, as Labour MP Frank Field has, 'the most disturbing of all the employment trends to emerge over the past twenty years' depends on your viewpoint.[3]

The facts about job segregation are well known: almost all women work in the service sector but men are more likely to work in all sectors of the economy. Changes in manufacturing and services have been the subject of much discussion. Different skills are needed now, summarised as 'brawn is out, flexibility is in'; since 1979 there has been a fall by a third in the number of workers with no educational qualifications.[4]

But the real alarm about women's paid employment, is about moving towards equality. Already it looks as if some men can't handle it. You never hear the argument that women should go back to the home any more, I said to Yvonne Strachan who works for the TGWU in Scotland. 'That's because they're still there,' she retorted. Even if women work outside the home they still do most of the work in it. But I wonder if we're now seeing a more sophisticated way of saying much the same thing. Before we take this much further it is perhaps important to emphasise that although women's employment rates are converging with men's and women are now almost half of employees, men are still more likely to be in paid work and working in better paid, more secure jobs with recognised skills. 1991 census figures show that men are still much more likely to be in the higher socio-economic groups than women. They show that five times as many men as women are in the professional category, and that there were nearly three men for every woman in 'employers, managers and professionals' altogether. In every age group men are still more likely to have qualifications above A level than women. Men outnumber women in the skilled-manual group also. The only category in which women noticeably outnumber men is in 'inter-mediate/junior non-manual', which includes clerical and secretarial work, where there are twice as many women as men. Women and men are in equal numbers in semi-skilled manual and there are slightly more women than men in unskilled-manual. Forthcoming research for the Employment Department concludes: 'Despite the increase in the number of women pursuing post-compulsory educational courses and gaining qualifications ... career opportunities available to qualified men and women remain unequal. Women graduates entering jobs generally have lower starting salaries and lifetime earnings expectancy'.[5]

Educated young women are getting more of the better jobs than we did twenty-five years ago, but let's not rest on our laurels quite yet. A survey for *Panorama* in October 1994 showed that some leading companies had steeply increased their intake of women graduates over the previous ten years: three of the ten companies they talked to with available records now take on more women graduates than men. (This was later reported elsewhere as 'three *in* ten leading companies' – which would be rather more dramatic if it were true.) ICL had increased its women graduate intake from 39 per cent in 1983 to 65 per cent in 1994; both Abbey National (from 43 per cent to 54 per cent) and Barclays Bank (from 36 per cent to 59 per cent) now take on more women graduates than men. (I also saw that reported as '*employ* more women graduates than men', which again is rather more than was said.) The survey also shows, of course, that despite roughly equal numbers of women and men graduates, seven out of ten of the companies take on more male graduates than female. Since we expect that we hardly notice it.

When *Panorama* used the title *The Future is Female* for that much-talked-about programme it marked the transition to mainstream current affairs of a slogan which first saw the light as a feminist badge in the 1970s. Within feminism the phrase had, in the meantime, added a large question mark.[6]

The Census of Employment on which Incomes Data Services based a widely quoted analysis of changing employment (in May 1993) shows women as a higher number of employees than men in eight counties and Scottish regions: that is eight out of 65.[7] A straight comparison of employees makes no distinction between full- and part-time work and does not count the self-employed. I have seen this information used to say that women are more likely to have jobs than men everywhere. Until you look more closely at what jobs women and men do, the hours they work and what they are paid, these comparisons don't mean very much. Although the decreasing economic activity rates of men since the 1970s are contrasted with the increasing rates for women, the fall for men to 85 per cent needs to be set against the rise for women to 71 per cent, to get an accurate picture. If you compare women and men, between 25 and 39, there is a wider divergence: figures from the last Census show that at the ages when most women have children only three-quarters as many women are in work or looking for work as are men. If you look at the reasons why people aren't working or looking for a job then those who describe themselves as 'other inactive' which is the category people at home caring for children or others are (misleadingly) put in, then in those age groups between 96 per cent and 97 per cent of the 'other inactive' are women.[8]

The comparison between male and female rates of unemployment – the male rate almost double that of female – used in such arguments is also fallacious because unemployment figures so notoriously underestimate the numbers of women out of paid work that it is distorting to use them. (Almost three-quarters of people who are not registered as unemployed and not in receipt of benefits but who are looking for work are women.[9] This category will increase with the new Jobseekers Allowance.) Male unemployment rates, after several redefinitions of who counts, are now reckoned to underestimate by about half the number of men actually unemployed. Women's always have done so.

But only people who live in Islington worry about women now, the new myth goes; 'it's men we need to worry about'. Young men are the 'new neglected minority'.

Full Employment and Culture Shock

They rarely say it publicly, but more politicians and trade unionists are linking the rise in part-time women's employment to persistently high male unemployment, suggesting that a reversal of 'the feminisation of the labour market' is needed to re-create full employment – in other words male full-time employment.

In February 1994, Labour MP Frank Field made a speech on 'the jobs revolution' which crystallised a growing argument. This revolution, he said, had 'unexpected' and 'frightening' implications; that married women workers drag wages down and part-time women workers are 'undercutting men' and a growing gap between unemployed and dual-earner families was a consequence of rising women's employment. Women were gaining 'a fairer share' of jobs but at the expense of 'the job disenfranchisement of a large number of male workers'. Field is right to protest about the low wages offered by many jobs, and he is right to say that if flexibility is to become part of the labour market then the security 'workers previously had within the firm must be replaced by security outside the firm'. But that must go for women too, a minority of whom had the security he regrets.[10]

Arguments that work should be distributed on the basis of need assume that full-timers (mostly men) must need a job more than part-timers (mostly women).' Analysing the growth of low-waged flexible work, Will Hutton in the *Guardian* said: 'Some (usually those whose partner has a full-time job) actively prefer this new environment ... But for the majority the conditions are oppressive and exploitative'.[11] Paul Gregg and Edward Balls (who went on to greater fame as the man who converted Gordon Brown to endogenous growth theory), in an influential paper for the Social Justice Commission comment that most women getting new jobs are married, with employed husbands, rather than in households where the man is unemployed, so part-time work has 'bypassed many of those in need of jobs' and changing employment patterns have 'substantially increased inequalities in the distribution of paid work across families'. But this is because the social security system does not treat people as individuals: a woman with an unemployed husband or live-in partner must be able to command above-average wages to off-set the loss in benefits. However they manage to blame women too. Neither the US nor the UK have reversed the falling trend in male employment because 'it has been matched by a substantial increase in the employment of women.' This section of their paper is called 'Danger: men not at work'.[12]

'The consequences of millions of males having no prospect of working is beginning to have the most profound effects on the society in which we live,' Frank Field believes, in common with politicians and commentators across the political spectrum. Men are disenfranchised, afraid and working illegally. (Women, of course, also work illegally but in ways which benefit men of all classes and political belief, so this does not worry them in quite the same way.) The choice therefore, as Edward Balls expresses it in the SJC essay (though again it is an argument heard across the political spectrum) is between subsidising work for the unskilled unemployed or accepting the social costs that widespread male inactivity engenders. The private sector, he suggests, might be subsidised to offer unskilled employment, 'closing the gap between male wage aspirations (or income from the illegal economy) and what the market will pay'. I've not heard any argument that the gap between male and female wages should be ended by subsidy.

Although a nod is usually made towards women's employment as 'welcome', in most discussion of full employment the direction of concern makes it clear that work means men's work. Unskilled men are seen as posing the greater policy challenge. *Real* work is supposed to be a male prerogative, with women conveniently filling in the gaps.

Long-term unemployment levels demand a serious response. But policy responses should *not equal* a determination to ensure that men retain their economic power and their priority in the jobs market and family life at the expense of women. These arguments, like some arguments about the 'breakdown of the family', draw a direct line of consequence from increased female employment through to social chaos and men turning to crime and drug abuse. Our role is to civilise them, not to compete for resources.

Contrary to what's sometimes said, some men *are* willing to take 'women's work' – though it is often perceived as a sign of desperation. The EOC reports a steep increase in inquiries about sex discrimination by men who believe they've been passed over for work in favour of women. In early 1995 the EOC carried out its first ever investigation into the recruitment practices of an employment agency (the Yorkshire-based Workforce Employment Agency Ltd) after complaints from men who had been refused jobs as packers because it was regarded as 'women's work'. The EOC found the agency had discriminated against both men and women.[13]

An argument wheeled out against women part-timers by many trade unionists in the past now has new life in the 'flexibility debate'. It comes close to the old line that married women work for 'pin money'. This argument was also used by the government to abolish the remaining wages councils: 'most Wages Council workers work part-time, contributing a second income to the family home,' Gillian Shephard (as Employment Secretary) said in justification at the time. It is undoubtedly true that some employers are happy to take advantage of married/cohabiting women's access – in theory – to a male wage. For example, in 1994 pressed to comment on a take-home pay for semi-skilled women textile workers of £92 for a 39-hour week, one mill-owner said: 'One of the things which probably compensates for it to a certain extent is that a lot of people are employed and very often this means that there's more than one member of a family being employed.'[14]

Women's wages are low, as Matilda Quiney, from the Pay Equity project, says, 'because of discrimination against part-time female workers, not because women can afford to be indifferent about their wage'.[15] It is not going to improve the position of *any* low-paid workers if women's work and wages are treated as peripheral. For this argument to go anywhere we would have to demonstrate that there is an alternative, that women without 'a male wage' coming in are seeking out jobs with better pay. For women without saleable skills few such jobs exist and for women with children but no partner there has been a reduction in employment.

A recent study of unemployment and social change contradicts the assumption that married women working drive wages down by arguing (and it's equally common sense) that women with employed husbands are more likely to hold out for decent pay.[16]

Arguments about the necessity of male employment were used in the 1930s to bar married women from employment in some areas and in the 1950s to encourage employers to discriminate against married women. Women argued at the time that persistent job segregation meant women and men did not compete for work: that 'you cannot replace a domestic servant by an unemployed coalheaver' and that both women and men were suffering from the consequences of changes in the global economy and technological change. The problem of unemployment was too great to be lessened by 'such piecemeal tinkering', they said; it would only postpone the search for real solutions.[17] They were right, but were ignored.

Unemployment is wasteful and personally and socially corrosive. Woman-blaming isn't going to help. The sight, on an estate like Castlemilk, of burdened women heading off to work in the morning, taking the children to the childminder on the way, and the men emerging later in the day to hang aimlessly and anti-socially around the street corner, is not the female future anyone has in mind. But the traditional division of labour has also been damaging. People excluded from work do need more and better training and education, and imaginatively created opportunities (like those created by the Wise Group in Glasgow, doing environmentally and socially necessary work alongside training). But women need to be wary.

Given the context in which the debate has arisen, policy developed will mean more training and skills development for unemployed men, leaving already under-utilised and poorly trained women where they are; and a short-term plaster over a much deeper, longer-term problem. The message to women is clear: threaten to riot grrrls if you want to hold on to what you've got. Become 'a problem'. It is repeatedly argued that the jobs available are not secure or well paid enough for men to have. Fair enough – why is that less of a problem for women?

Part-time, Poor Deal

The source of so much anxiety, part-time work has been the major growth area in women's employment and as such demands attention, and not just as a 'threat'. As things stand, part-time work could successfully challenge traditional conceptions of work that matters, or it could be used to solidify existing inequalities. It plays a pivotal role in current change in the workforce and in women's lives.

Most of the things which could be said about part-time work in 1970 can be said today – only more so, since there are so many more part-time workers. In 1971 15 per cent of employees in Britain worked part-time; now more than a quarter do and the forecast is that part-timers will be a third of all employees by 2001. Part-timers are more likely to be low-paid than full-time workers, and not to have the same access to promotion or employee benefits. Often they are not seen as 'proper' workers by colleagues, unions (though this is changing) or employers. Women taking part-time work for family reasons are actually less likely to have decent maternity provision and less well able to afford childcare. Pay inequality between full- and part-time workers has increased over the past decade. The proportion of men part-timers has risen in recent years and has occasioned some comment, but part-time workers are still mainly women and it's still seen as 'women's work'. Although almost half of women in employment work part time, only 9 per cent of male employees do and most men working part time are either over 50 or under 25. Part-time work is more of an issue for white women employees than for black or Asian women, with just over a fifth of ethnic minority women working part time compared to more than a third of white women (although Asian women are more likely to work part time in Wales and Scotland).

Two things are very different. The first is that part-time work's association with disadvantage has begun to be broken. Even if relatively few part-time workers are affected, new possibilities are being opened up and may become accepted. This will be more important as part-time workers become a still greater proportion of the workforce and more likely to be seen as essential workers. The second is major gains in employment rights for part-time workers, the result of years of argument and campaigning and, most recently, a hard-fought legal case.

Part-time workers are not always employed just because they are cheap or easily dispensable: the crucial House of Lords decision in 1994 on equal rights for part-timers turned on that fact. Some companies have begun to give pro-rata benefits to part-time workers and the numbers of part-time professional workers is growing rapidly, making up almost half the increase in part-time work in the year to spring 1994 (although from a low base), an increase which is predicted to gain pace. Part-time work may genuinely be the best option in meeting changing needs of an organisation, for example for longer opening or production hours. The concept of 'key time staff' in retail emphasises this. Harriet Harman quotes an estimate that by the beginning of the next century part-time workers will be a majority in health and education and more than 40 per cent of workers in banking and finance, distribution and hotels. Anne Rennie also argues that part-time jobs are gaining higher status – accountants, lawyers, personnel and marketing people are the examples she gives. 'People that it's jolly expensive to employ full time. You may not need a full-time accountant, you may need one one day a week, and companies are realising that.' Advances in well-protected part-time work tend to be in the public sector and bigger companies but not with small employers. The Labour Force Survey in 1993 showed 'a clear upward trend' in part-time management work. Part-timers are only 13 per cent of managerial and professional staff, even so.

Job-sharing is an idea whose time has come; according to its proponents it avoids some of the disadvantages of part-time work within a structure based on full-time hours and brings several added advantages. Some growth has been in teaching, though much less so in promoted posts. However, *Employment Gazette* analysis in 1994 said that only between 3 and 6 per cent of part-timers job-share: nearly all are women and they are concentrated in clerical and secretarial occupations. Half of all job-sharers work in public services.

A different kind of job-sharing is an often overlooked dimension to part-time work: people piecing together a living from several part-time jobs. It is a dimension which changes the sometimes complacent picture that increasing part-time work is about work that 'fits in' with family life: it may, but several short-term jobs may also bring several additional stresses – too little time for domestic work *plus* marginal employment. The Labour Force Survey estimates an increase of over 60 per cent in the number of people with second jobs between 1984 and 1994, with a steep increase in the past year, and research for Scottish Enterprise showed that the numbers of women in Scotland with more than one part-time job doubled over the 1980s. The TUC say second jobs are increasing much faster than main part-time jobs.[18] Liz Stanley, when I spoke to her, had been doing research with women in Rochdale where 72,000 women had lost full-time employment in the cotton industry at the end of the 1970s. 'It looked like they went back into the home because many of them didn't appear in the formal unemployment statistics – but what many of them did was to stitch together one, two, three, four jobs that were part time, casualised. So you'd have somebody who lost a highly skilled job in 1979 and she'd be running an Avon club, childminding, sewing in the home, couple of hours in a shop ...' Working-class women, as Liz said, 'have always had to tie together three pieces of string and make do'.

In March 1994 the EOC won an important breakthrough in a long-running legal case which eventually they took to the House of Lords. The EOC argued that since almost all part-timers are women, to treat them differently was indirect discrimination, contravening EU law on equal treatment of men and women at work. It meant the extension of compensation for unfair dismissal and statutory redundancy pay to part-time workers on the same basis as full-timers. In October 1994 the European Court gave part-time workers the same rights as their full-time colleagues to join company pension schemes, and to backdate their claim for the years during which they were barred.

These decisions go to the heart of crucial questions raised by changing patterns in work and family income. As Harriet Harman argues, employment change means 'the rights of part-time workers are no longer only a matter of equity for a group of workers on the margins of the labour market'. They are central to managing a change from an old pattern based on men working a 40-hour week to women and men both working a variety of different hours. As is the way of things though, many employers, perhaps most, have yet to respond to the change in the law. 'It's a real advance,' comments Morag Gillespie of the Low Pay Unit in Glasgow, 'but as usual it'll take a long, long time before most employers wise up.'

Part-time, Good Deal

The title of an article in a recent *Low Pay Review* serves as a summary of the orthodox view, on the Left and among feminists: 'Part-time work: double bad deal.' But if the disadvantages of part-time work have been catalogued, the advantages are less often seriously explored, or at best are considered an expression of lack of realism. In most accounts part-time work is presented as a poor option. Women are seen as taking 'atypical' work because they are unable to take 'typical' work; are described as 'having difficulty' in joining the full-time labour force; part-time is routinely equated with dead-end. The assumption is that any woman would choose full-time well-rewarded work if she were free to.

The Employment Department's position is that part-time work meets women's and employers' needs equally.[19] That must be challenged. And the negative account of part-time work has hard facts behind it. Nevertheless, it is a partial and problematic account for several reasons. First of all, the idea that many, if any, women *really* work *part time* is a falsehood, a description only of the 'first shift' they do. It follows from privileging a definition of work which fits the life experience most men have. Part-time work is seen as a constrained choice – full-time is not; it remains the norm. This also overlooks the different role of paid work, choice and expectations across class. The feminist/left orthodoxy has been developed for perfectly good reasons, and the arguments about the discrimination part-time workers face need to be made repeatedly. We need now to take it further.

The argument has been that what women need is full-time work with full benefits and childcare. We may: there isn't a lot of evidence that that is what most women *want*. People have a variety of reasons for working part-time: some *will* only choose atypical work if they have childcare or other constraints. Some women may say they prefer part-time work only because that is the socially-validated choice. Then there's the argument that we make our choices out of what seems to us possible. But other women find 'the benefits outweighed the disadvantages. What had started as a transition had become a satisfactory end in itself', according to research published in the *Employment Gazette* in 1993. The aim was 'a satisfactory compromise' between work and the rest of life; 'a bit more home life. You have also got your independence', as one woman put it. The large majority of interviewees said the advantages outweighed the disadvantages although older people and/or the financially better-off were more likely to feel this than younger respondents and single parents. 'The key factor was satisfaction with the "total package".'[20]

In *About Time* Patricia Hewitt writes succinctly: 'Working time is structured in radically different ways for women and for men. Put at its simplest, the time men spend in paid employment determines how much time they have for their families: the time women spend caring for their families determines how much time they have for paid employment.'[21] Most women have 'double lives', as women I've spoken to have put it, which include unpaid as well as paid work, and paid work fits in differently than both some feminist critiques and the traditional definition of work allow for. (Feminist arguments recognise women's unpaid work but assume substitutes for it as the best solution.) For most women choice and necessity cannot be disentangled. Part-time work may be less a constrained choice than a strategic one.

Most working women in relationships with men earn less than the man, part-timers significantly less so. That is not to say their income is not essential to them or their household or that their work matters less to them. Women describe what a small income offers very precisely: 'a bit of independence'. That matters. Work offers one of the few arenas in which many women can be a person in their own right, not someone's mum or wife. Women see their part-time jobs not as 'on the side' but as an important part of their lives and integral to their household economies – because they are.

Part-time work needs to be assessed not just in comparison with full-time work but as part of a 'total package'. In developing policy we need to think not just about jobs but about the way they fit in with the rest of life, as most women have to. Full-time work might also be usefully analysed that way, but rarely is.

The Dynamic Economy

Anne Harrison has three jobs. From 6.30 to 8.30 she works as a cleaner at the local primary school, which her 10-year-old daughter attends. She goes back there at lunchtime to serve school dinners.

From 5.30 to 8.00 she cleans in a day hospital for old people in the city centre. She's cheerful and pragmatic about it, says she quite likes the variety. She can fit in housework and other things in between. The biggest problem, she said, is the bus journey to her third job, and the fact that the bus service has become so unreliable since deregulation. The cleaning company she works for is a private one; it was better working for the NHS. The supervisors are tougher now, there is no sick pay and the position on paid holidays is vague: 'they said we might get them if the company does well'. What really bothers her most is that the amount of disinfectant and cleaning materials they're allowed isn't really sufficient for the job. Since it's a hospital, she reasonably argues, cleaning shouldn't be something to cut corners on. Cleaners have always been 'flexible' workers because they have to clean offices and factories when the other workers aren't there, on dawn and twilight shifts.

Anne Rennie has three and a half jobs: she has two part-time executive directorships, with Reed Employment for three days a week, which is a permanent part-time job, and the second, on a three-year contract, on the Board of Thamesmead, the new town built by the GLC in the late 1960s which is now run as a private company. She is also personnel director of the Prince's Trust on a voluntary basis and is writing a book on the changes in work of which she is an unusually high-level example. She works in two offices, at home and wherever she might be; the dividing line between work and the rest of life is fluid. At Reed the flexibility is made possible, she acknowledges, because she has senior staff who report to her and deal with the day-to-day, leaving her free to focus on 'strategic stuff, new policies, future development'. She also likes the variety and thinks there are definite advantages to doing rather different things. 'I think it means I can compartmentalise more easily – and they feed off each other, which is good too.' Good communication and good time-management are essential to making it work.

Both women are part of the same social revolution, albeit at different ends of it. It is not a comfortable revolution – or it is more comfortable for some than others, but not in a way that's entirely predictable by class any more.

More than half the working population had full-time, permanent work twenty years ago; now it's estimated that only 40 per cent do.

The number of the self-employed and of part-time jobs is growing fast. Will Hutton, the *Guardian*'s economics editor, reckons that 40 per cent of the workforce now have tenured full-time employment or secure self-employment; 30 per cent are insecurely self-employed, part-time or casual workers and 30 per cent are 'marginalised, are idle or working for poverty wages'. Charles Handy, popular theorist of the new ways of working, reckons that only one in three British workers now works 9 to 5.[22] This is what most people are talking about when they talk about the 'flexible workforce', but different people use the word 'flexibility' to mean different things: you can have remarkably confused conversations in consequence.

Two other workplace changes interact with this changing pattern. The concentration of work between the ages of of 25 and 50: from an extended education or youth unemployment at one end to early retirement or redundancy at the other. A further change, which sits ill with the others, or rather, concentrates the force of them, is increased competition, 'the relentless search for efficiency' (as an *Independent* editorial described it – whether that's really what is achieved is another matter) and all the pressures which now mean that lunch is for wimps and non-executive directors.

Anne Rennie doesn't think there's a choice about the new ways of working. 'A lot of people think this is a temporary phenomenon, the result of recession and companies using the recession as an excuse to down-size. But it's the way of the future, people need to get used to it rather than look for a career for life ... People talk of a "period of consolidation" – it'll never be like that.' Anne Harrison shrugged when I asked her if she'd prefer a full-time job; there weren't any that she would be qualified for. She'd left and looked for another job when conditions in hospital worsened at privatisation but had gone back because she couldn't find a better one. Although it began to be talked about in the early 1980s, in the 1990s flexibility in the labour market was seen as the magic solution in management theory and public policy alike. Encouraging flexibility in the labour market is possibly the only policy on which Employment Secretary Michael Portillo and the Opposition spokeswoman on employment Harriet Harman actually agree. There will be 'fewer jobs for life but more jobs in a lifetime,' Portillo says. 'But change can bring advantages ... People have more chances to work when they want: part-time, part of the year, or in more than one job.' Harriet Harman argues the case for flexibility in her book *The Century Gap*: women need it most because we are 'trying to work within a structure that prevents both men and women balancing work and family.' Full employment cannot mean what it did in the 1950s, she has emphasised in recent speeches, 'it is about jobs for women as well as men, part-time as well as full-time', and economic policy must take account of technological change, a global economy and women in the workplace.[23]

What they say *next* tends to diverge: when, in autumn 1994, figures showed that the jobs created so far by economic recovery were mainly insecure, part-time and low paid, Michael Portillo cheerfully said they might be 'the sort of work employers don't care to declare' but that was better than no job at all.[24] Much of his attack on the European Commission has been concerned to vaunt Britain's forward-looking 'deregulatory agenda' and oppose its 'job destroying directives'. Harriet Harman, when I spoke to her, was quick to emphasise that there's no sense in talking about flexibility without asking, flexibility *for whom*. 'If it's on behalf of the employer only then it means uncertainty and insecurity.'

The Employment Department's aim (stated in 1991) is 'To support economic growth by promoting a competitive, efficient and flexible labour market.' Labour's Social Justice Commission emphasised that we need to recognise that the world of work has changed fundamentally. 'Forty years ago the typical worker was a man working full-time in industry; today the typical worker is increasingly likely to be a woman working part-time in a service job.' The Commission argued for a flexibility which means 'the opportunity for people to develop new skills, take on new responsibilities and raise productivity and have a wide range of working hours ...'[25]

The European 1993 White Paper *Growth, Competitiveness, Employment* emphasised labour market flexibility; in most of the European Union states labour flexibility is at the heart of current debate, the European Network on Families and Work reported in December 1994. The Conservative Government boasts that Britain is ahead of Europe in moving towards flexibility in the workforce – as we are, both in the numbers of 'non-standard' workers and in limiting trade union power and employment protection. So much so that looking to what Britain has achieved has made a number of other

EU countries, especially those with reasonably effective systems of social partnership, very cautious about the concept of flexibility.[26]

Flexibility is a Feminist Issue

Most discussion of employment and economic issues is gender blind, ignoring how economic and labour market changes have different impacts on men and women. Although what is being reported may most affect women, we're not mentioned. The changes in banking, for example, or in telecommunications: the 'shakeout' at Mercury and 'down-sizing' at BT are not analysed in terms of gender, nor the much-discussed decline in the High Street bank or even the growth of part-time work in retail. Workplace equality *is* about access to training, about 'the glass ceiling'. But during the 1980s major forces reshaped the economic and social environment of the developed countries – trade expansion, fiercer international competition, the spread of new technologies. There have been changing trends in demand, new production processes and work organisation.[27] These changes are happening in a workplace in which gender is still a major determinant, so they have a different impact on women's and men's working lives. I was relieved when I read in the *Employment Gazette* that 'It is difficult if not impossible to provide a watertight definition of flexibility'. No wonder I had been having trouble. 'It is used as both an analytical concept to explain structural changes in employment and as a "buzz-word" for what many see as positive or exciting long-term changes to the world of work', they say. I've found it used as a synonym for deregulation, the loss of necessary employment rights and unnecessary workplace rigidities alike. It sometimes stands in for that other synonym 'down-sizing', which means giving people the sack, and 'organisational refocusing,' which often means the same thing. It can be nineties-speak for pay cuts: 'earnings flexibility'. Then there are meanings internal to work – flexible skills and multi-skilling – for example BBC reporters who now work in both radio and TV. Formal 'functional flexibility' of that sort is still quite unusual, but equally, rigid job demarcation is not widespread. Most commonly 'flexibility' means change in how work is organised, in time and in place. This is what I want to concentrate on because it has immense possibilities for people who have lives and responsibilities apart from paid work, as well as bringing new dangers. 'Flexibility' as currently used is a euphemism *both* for innovative and family friendly and for insecurity and exploitation.

A management consultant and the woman who serves in the office canteen may five years ago both have had 'proper' jobs with the firm they still work for, but though they share structural change with each other and a growing proportion of the workforce, while the consultant may have traded security for a lucrative portfolio (providing she keeps her competitive edge), the canteen worker has lost wages and sick pay. The new patterns of employment have two faces: they offer both a serious opportunity for people, parents particularly, to combine work and the other demands of life in some sort of balance. Childcare, good maternity leave, paternity leave and parental leave are all immensely important, but an authentically flexible way of working across a lifetime makes them seem like tinkering at the edges of the problem. But, as is evident from analysis of where and how and why most flexible working has occurred so far, it is also about the possibility – and reality – of increased exploitation.

To Will Hutton it is 'the economics of the sweatshop and the morality of the mill-owner'. For Charles Handy 'the fragmentation of work ... offers new freedoms', and 'the only way forward for a tramlined society, one that has got used to its ruts and its blinkers'. The job, 'that much-sought-after, much-maligned social entity is vanishing today like some species that has outlived its evolutionary time', says William Bridges, another of the emerging species of commentators on the phenomenon. We are 'no more ready for it than eighteenth-century English villagers were for jobs in nine-teenth-century English factories,' he says. (He is described by his publishers as an 'executive development consultant' and 'thriving in the post-job era'.)[28]

When you look behind the post-industrial rhetoric two things are clear: flexibility is (so far) mainly about women. And secondly, what it means isn't always as fancy as it sounds. I found Charles Handy's much-hyped book *The Empty Raincoat* useful: it made me realise that what I've always thought of as doing a bit of this and a bit of that is what smart chaps like him call 'a portfolio career'. What Handy and others are getting excited about is how a lot of women have always worked.

It's about what the European Commission calls, usefully if ungracefully, atypical work. 'Atypical' is used to cover a whole range of time patterns, not just part time, but serves as a reminder that this is not seen as 'typical', that it is defined by its difference from a norm. That norm is what most employed men do (and still do). Though in Britain at least the chances of atypical becoming more typical than typical seem only a matter of time. Another term used is 'non-standard'. L.C. Hunter and J. McInnes say in the introduction to their report on the subject.: 'What we call non-standard is broadly similar to what others have called the peripheral, marginal or secondary labour force contrasting respectively with core, central or primary labour force concepts.' In the USA they call it 'contingent' work. The synonyms make clear the relative perceived importance.[29]

Change has been driven by technology, changes in production, service sector growth and increased opening hours (Britain's first 24 hour superstore opened in December 1994). It has followed the idea and the possibility of using a 'lean' workforce augmented as necessary by temporary labour or 'out-sourcing' and increased project-based work. Competitive tendering is creating a changed workplace in local authorities, and in the NHS organisational change is having an impact as much on employees as on health care: between them they are the biggest employers of women in this country.

By far the biggest category of flexible workers is part time workers. There is some disagreement about how big a category temporary employees form or how many people now are on 'standby appointments' and 'zero-hour contracts', but they are more likely to be women too. So are homeworkers (whose numbers, as recorded, have doubled since 1981). Although new forms of flexibility are having an impact in manufacturing it is mainly a change to the service sector, and 85 per cent of women workers, and 91 per cent of women part-time workers are in the service sector. To turn that round another way: twice as many men are full-time permanent employees as women. In all but two of the categories of 'flexible work' we're talking about women. The only area in which men significantly outnumber women is self-employment. Men are also more likely to work overtime than women. Analysis of the Labour

Force Survey shows the 'flexible workforce' has grown from 30 per cent to 38 per cent of all employment between 1981 and 1993, an increase of just over two million people which affects just over a quarter of men in employment and just over half of women.

Post-industrial portfolio workers – or insecure and exploited? There's a lot of talk of new, slim, sexy organisations, but much of the reality is much more mundane: the self-employed window cleaner, the contracted-out office cleaners, the security man who is now part of Group 4. McInnes and Hunter found that flexibility was 'clustered into two main occupational groups'. The first, and smaller, group was skilled professional and technical occupations: 'Overwhelmingly these specialists were highly-paid men'. The second group consisted of four occupations with large numbers of temporary and part-time employees: packers, shop assistants, cleaners and catering staff. Only the category 'packers' included men in any number.[30]

It is useful to look at *why* work is contracted out or increasingly done in 'non-standard' ways, and at whose behest. In both private firms and the public sector the areas of work which have been subcontracted have predominantly been cleaning, catering and security. McInnes and Hunter found the critical difference in whether work is contracted out or retained to be its 'ancillary character'. Although it may be vital to the operation – workspaces need cleaning, workers need to be fed and gates manned – it is not seen as part of the main purpose of the organisation. This meant employers had fewer worries about the quality consequences of low pay.

There *has* been an increase in male non-standard work: the small but quite quickly growing number of men working part time; and men are affected through casualisation, in seasonal work, as they always have been, and in construction and related trades where self-employment is now more often the norm. Change is now also affecting middle management. The proportion of men working in flexible ways is estimated to have grown from 18 per cent in 1981 to 27 per cent in 1993. Some professional work in management, media, accountancy and computing also brings more men into the flexible workforce. Another new phrase, 'the interim executive' has been invented for it. But although it has received more attention, numerically it is very small in comparison to women's involvement in non-standard work.

Fast Lane or Twilight Shift?

Flexibility is a senior civil servant working part time when her children are young without interrupting (well, not *too* much) the smooth progress of a fast-lane career. Flexibility is shifts at the supermarket checkout 14 hours a week, a working week designed to evade the cost to the employer of employment protection (though this limit was subject to legal change in March 1994), broken into shifts of three hours at a time to avoid even the cost of tea breaks. For a woman word-processing in 'the financial sector' four nights a week, 5.30 to 9.30, it means picking up the kids from school and getting the tea ready and getting grandmother to cover the time before her partner comes in and then, after a full enough day, heading off to work. And finding that although her smallest child is at nursery school now and she'd like to change to working the same hours in the mornings, she can't because the twilight shift is organised around using the technology fully, around the machines' needs, not those of their operators.

A flexible worker may be a high-flyer at her terminal in the early hours when the Japanese markets are operating. More likely she will bring you lunch in the new hospital trust in a job which two years ago had National Insurance and paid holidays. She may be a nurse who does overnight shifts when she can get them and her husband is at home to look after the children. She may work for a large retail chain every weekend and late-night Thursdays, with job security and hours which suit her and her employer alike, or she may be a temporary worker for the same firm but at lower pay with little advance warning of when she works.

Some of the best use of non-standard working is in highly rule-governed employment like the civil service; in such settings potential disadvantage can be taken into account. Homeworking is a paradigm of flexibility: its miserable pay depends, usually, on the workers having no choice. Although there is a growth in better-paid teleworking the majority of homeworkers do piece work in manufacturing, particularly the garment industry. A computer programmer may seem to have little in common with someone making crackers for 50p an hour but much new teleworking is, like more traditional piece work, highly insecure. More than twice as many women as men are recorded as homeworkers (and that is almost certainly an under-count).

Teleworking is one of the new ways of working often put forward as an answer for people with children. But it also has a down-side: working on your own all day can make going to the post office seem like a social event. The small army of tele-saleswomen, sadly polite, telling you about double-glazing bargains with not even a gossipy coffee break to keep them going, is scarcely a breakthrough in new ways to work. The increase in women working from home risks a newer form of social isolation – though the opportunity to combine working at home and with colleagues at different times can be ideal.

Closer attention to the detail and realities of flexible working lives reinforces the conclusion of American research that flexible work schedules have the greatest potential for helping workers balance work and family demands in occupations that do not require commitment beyond fixed hours of work. 'In jobs that link worker initiative and time commitment to advancement,' Carol Wharton concluded, after studying the lives of women estate agents working on commission, 'flexibility may result in more hours of work or in sidetracks or second-class status for workers who choose to limit their involvement.'[31] Most of the higher level developments in flexible work are in precisely those areas which demand open-ended commitment such as the various forms of consultancy, media and design work and research.

Employability or Insecurity?

There is blithe talk of 'employability' as the new security. The Social Justice Commission quotes labour market expert Hilary Metcalf, saying something that is becoming orthodox: 'the increasingly competitive market has raised issues of shifting from *job* security to *employability* as the source of employment security'. Michael Portillo says 'Many people will change out of dead-end jobs that in another era might have lasted a lifetime ... people must have the self-confidence to regard change not as a threat to be resisted but as a normal part of their working lifetime ... They must have a higher level of transferable skills ... and be able to finance investment in their own training.' But that means identifying skills which are in demand, financial reserves, strong nerves and mobility.[32]

'There may be trouble ahead ...' Insurance companies were not slow to see an opportunity: developing cover 'for the life you don't yet know' (as Allied Dunbar put it). But research shows 'Britain's more flexible workforce is a more fearful one.' Fear of unemployment, stress of working hours and, conversely, less overtime, deregulation and greater general insecurity, are dragging down the 'feel-good' factor, the absence of which seemed to persistently puzzle the government (though not anyone else) in 1995. In its search for flexibility the economic system, which depends on increasing consumer spending for growth, has marked out the limits of that growth: 'the increase in labour marked "flexibility" has been accompanied by an increase in insecurity most obvious, perhaps, through the steady refusal of domestic consumer demand to pick up.'[33]

Because these changes, while offering more opportunities for employment to people who can't or don't want to work full time, are accompanied by such insecurity they may deepen and entrench divisions between flexible or atypical workers, mainly women, and core workers – mainly men. Many women and some men are using greater flexibility to balance work and family responsibilities, creating their own 'career breaks', but the changes are not primarily about 'reconciling' work and family responsibilities even if that is a by-product. We shouldn't, Linda Dickens argues, fall for 'the myth of matching needs'. 'Clearly atypical work does give some options to women with caring responsibilities ... but that does not mean it is meeting equally the flexibility needs of both employers and atypical workers. She gives evening and weekend work, variable hours and days and homeworking as examples where women are 'having to try to accommodate their domestic responsibilities around employer-shaped job packages'. 'The United Kingdom has a long tradition of allowing employers and employees, who are best placed to judge their own needs and circumstances, to determine between themselves terms and conditions of employment,' the Employment Department told the Mothers in Employment inquiry in February 1994. 'This approach has helped develop a rich variety of flexible working arrangements which have proved helpful to women wanting to combine work with family commitments.' Harriet Harman's question is relevant: flexibility for whom? While many people have arrangements that suit them, for many it is at a high cost.[34] Workplace and union rigidities *have* made things harder for employees with demanding family commitments. There could have been change which did not drive down wages and increase insecurity. The government's position is only convincing if you forget that negotiating power is rarely equal between employer and employee and choice is only a small part of the story. We need to look for better ways to create a 'fit' for employer and employee alike.

While these changes bring risk, resisting them often rests on a wish to return to the status quo. Many of the same arguments apply to all 'flexible' ways of working as to part-time work. Will Hutton in the *Guardian* began an article on current changes in the workforce by saying: 'The 40-hour week, paid holiday and occupational pensions seem such a natural part of our working environment that we have forgotten how hard they were fought for by earlier generations.'[35] Do you recognise that world of work? For most women that was never on offer. Nor is it now, except for a minority. Howard Davies, director-general of the CBI, less critically, said: 'Workers can no longer rely on jobs for life, and must be prepared to move more frequently, and cope with periods of unemployment. The future of the labour market is not going to be like the past. Womb to tomb employment, a lifetime spent with one employer, is becoming the exception rather than the rule.' But it never was the rule for almost half of the population.[35]

The full-time, lifetime employment model never fitted the discontinuous employment patterns of the majority of women, nor took into account women's unpaid work other than to see it as a problem. Some of that fight for the family wage and full employment rights was about excluding women from certain trades and well-paying jobs. When most flexible workers are women, and most 'typical' workers holding most of the remaining 'proper' jobs are men, the risk is of creating a new form of job segregation. But the old (and continuing) form of job segregation wasn't any better. Change and

the breaking up of old rigidities at least brings room for manoeuvre –
we need to use it.

Chapter 12

Contract Culture

'You're either overworked or out of work.' It's a cliché, sometimes a justification, and something that everyone comments on: that while so many people are unemployed, the rest are working harder than ever. 'We are seeing the end of an old culture' *New Ways to Work* told the Employment Committee. The distinction between full-time and all the other ways of organising work is coming to seem increasingly old-fashioned, Charles Handy says.[1] Yet the biggest change in workplace culture is not towards 'post-industrial working time' and equal opportunities but towards longer hours and a heightened pressure of work concentrated in fewer years. These are changes which have a down-side for many people but a major impact for people with family and caring responsibilities.

Down-sizing, restructuring, whatever you want to call it, means that those left within 'core' employment work under greater pressure and so do people on the periphery, freelancing, moonlighting, afraid to say 'no'. Workaholism, present-ism, presentee-ism – we bemoan them all; there's even a new phrase for the rest of life we say we're missing, 'hinterland'. And then we just get on with it. Trying to do more in less time, juggling work at work and work at home with time off (productively repackaged as 'stress management') shoehorned into a demanding schedule so it becomes just one more task.

To be ambitious is to accept that there's little time for anything else; to be conscientious has become a noose. If long hours are seen as showing commitment, especially in the professions and middle-class jobs, in many working-class jobs material pressures achieve the same end. Long hours may be a problem for senior managers but they are as much an issue for supermarket managers and joiners and especially for people piecing together two or three jobs to make a living. There are however particular pressures for high-flyers which make me wonder whether those who embrace the new world of out-sourcing, consultancy and portfolio work (and are influential in doing so) are uniquely unaware of their own vulnerability, allied to a rather short memory as to why employment protection was needed in the first place. Being able to structure time according to your own priorities is more possible for higher-level employees but allied to new technology can mean that you're always on line and rarely off duty.

At the same time I take *some* bemoaning of long hours of work with a pinch of salt – people extend work rather than go home sometimes, and work can be a kind of play too. It's a reinforcing circle: the less time you have for life outside work the less life you have and the more reason to stay on at work, which becomes all of life.

Lip-service is paid to this issue, but it is still not taken seriously. Or, rather, it is recognised and discussed but the pressures, and perceived pressures, which lie behind it are not thereby diminished. 'I don't want to live like this', people say, before explaining they can't meet you after all because there's an urgent whatever to finish. Stress and work addiction are not just features of high-pressure jobs; it is more often a problem for people in the middle grades and can be especially a problem for the low paid. Stress is reckoned to adversely affect around 100,000 people a year, accounting for 20 per cent of absence from work. Business leaders have inveighed against the cost of increased maternity rights, yet the costs of stress have been calculated as 10 per cent of GNP in Britain.[2]

At its extreme the pressures of work have led to ill-health, nervous breakdown, and in the case of a junior doctor, Alan Massie, who collapsed after an 86-hour hospital shift, death. There is, as ex-headteacher Keith Tait demonstrated in a BBC *Open Space* programme, a kind of machismo: 'People in jobs are trying to demonstrate they can cope – to admit to stress is to admit to weakness ...'[3]

Men's working hours have fallen fairly steadily for most of this century in most industrial countries, but, against the European trend, in Britain male hours worked started to rise again in the early 1980s, with long hours now common in both production and professional jobs. Women's working hours have steadily increased since 1945. Although on average women's paid hours are shorter than men's, even if their actual working day is longer, working time for women is going up as more women move into full-time work or combine two or more part-time jobs.[4] Despite this, two and a half times the proportion of men in employment are reckoned to work long hours than women. This has an impact on women's lives in two main ways: by limiting the domestic role of men, and by creating a working climate in which women must also put in long hours if they are to be seen to be pulling their weight.

By 1994 almost 16 per cent of British workers put in more than 48 hours a week, four times as many as in Germany. We work not only the longest hours in Europe but longer hours than the Japanese, usually seen as the world's pre-eminent workaholics but whose working week is now being shortened by government ruling as an anti-stress measure. Three-quarters of those who work long hours (or who do and declare it) are managerial, professional or self-employed; professional jobs now account for over a quarter of European women working long hours.[5]

One recent survey showed two out of five managers putting in more than 50 hours a week, and another showed that heads of departments in colleges worked on average 55 hours a week. Catherine Marsh found in 1991 that British fathers work the longest average hours in Europe; pressures on them to do so have increased since. As John McInnes comments, the flexibility employers rely on most is men not having (or taking) other responsibilities: 'There's nothing more flexible than a full-time man whose loyalty you can rely on in the face of domestic demands on his time'.[6]

It isn't surprising that in the 1994 Social Attitudes survey 44 per cent of people said they were coming home from work 'exhausted'. About a third of employees, according to yet another survey, would prefer to cut their working hours by about a third even with the corresponding cut in pay.[7]

The European Directive on Working Hours, which the British government has consistently opposed, would set a maximum 48 hours working week (and with lots of exceptions). Britain is the only EU country which does not set limits to working hours or have statutory rights to paid holidays. The then Employment Secretary David Hunt, speaking to the CBI in November 1993, called the growing European demand for a statutory 35-hour week 'the politics of despair'. He asked 'How can anyone seriously propose that people should be discouraged, even forbidden, from working as long as they want?'[8] Meanwhile his government was preaching a return to family values. Perhaps the family values they had in mind included fathers having little to do with their children?

Yet there are other people who want paid work who are unable to work. Caring for elderly relatives is now as likely to mean a disrupted working life and financial problems as is caring for young children. Three times as many (non-pensioner) households have no one in them in paid work now than in the early 1970s.[9] It's not so much being 'discouraged' from working as long as you want as being encouraged to work longer than you want or discouraged from working at all.

Time for Living

These pressures are still different for mothers than for fathers. And there are pressures on professional women particularly to adopt a male-model work-centred career pattern in their twenties and thirties. 'Get a life' is a catchphrase which compresses a lot. But the rewards at work still go to those people who are prepared to put work first. Women's choice has been to join in, or remain on the margins.

Short-term contracts, consultancies, homeworking and the various forms of self-employment all add a tense layer of time/money imperatives and affect all sorts of people from plumbers to caterers to playwrights and TV presenters. This is rarely creative pressure. You cannot divorce work and production from its human and social costs without also divorcing it from the full human contribution. Our roles as producers, consumers, members of families and citizens are not actually divisible.

The further away from engagement with life, the less good the art, the thinking, the decision-making – delete as relevant. An awful lot of art has spiralled off into arcane worlds where it completely fails to communicate. People in media work talk mainly to each other. 'Bottom-line' decisions notoriously evade the real issues, which usually turn out to have indivisible financial and human costs. Government ministers have not only wives but a small army of mandarins, secretaries and personal assistants between them and any discomfiting intrusion of real life.

We need to recognise that work and relationships are important to all of us, and are only put in opposition to our detriment. It's an opposition which helps make women's work at home invisible. It is important to refuse that opposition, especially now when there is some sort of myth that most of the problems have been solved. It has long seemed to me that certain professions – architects and planners certainly, shop designers, health providers and managers, civil servants, social work managers, politicians of course – would achieve improved results if women were better represented within their numbers, not simply as a matter of equality but because most women are still doing more of the caring tasks than most men and will take better, more contextualised decisions as a consequence. Creativity may be as much a function of interruption as concentration, as much about breaking patterns as following them. Breakthrough in any area is probably at least as much a function of perspective as of obsessive concentration on a central idea. Try explaining to a seven-year-old why, since we know it has damaging consequences, we are still chopping down the rainforests.

We need friendship, experience, children, art, feelings, change. We all have weaknesses as well as strengths. We need rooms of our own and time to concentrate, yes. But we most of us, women *and* men, have more complex lives than working structures allow. We need life, love, work – all of it. After a traumatic visit to Bosnia as a war artist the painter Peter Howson said, 'my whole attitude to life has changed ... It made me think about art as coming second to my family whereas before I think art came first.'[10] First I thought, but how could he have thought otherwise? But it is a false opposition, and one which is created by both the work/living patterns of our society and its concept of creativity/achievement. Neither need be first or second and each informs the other.

The Age Squeeze

These pressures are heightened by what might be called 'the 25–50 squeeze'. There is an increasing Europe-wide unequal distribution of work and unemployment so that 'working people aged between 25 and 50 are under severe temporal pressure while other categories suffer from an excess of "free" time that is imposed upon them', French academic Jean-Yves Boulin says.[11] People without jobs are more likely to be young people or over 50.

Early retirement and longer education create a compressed working lifetime, and young people not in further education have high rates of unemployment. Unpaid as well as paid work is ill-divided, with the years of greatest pressure being the years when most women have young children. It means, more than ever, that the years when most women, and some men, might either take a career break or want to 'slow-track' are the years on which your work future depends. That most women's working lives run on a different timetable from most men's is something we've known for at least 25 years but as a problem it has only intensified. With eligibility for early retirement schemes set at 50, the time in which 'women returners' have to develop their working lives is curtailed. Despite having done so much when her children were young, Isobel Lindsay talked about feeling free and able to really do more of the things she wanted to now they are grown up. 'Lots of things came together for me when the children were older ... It's going to suit a lot of women for their peak periods to be after their forties, not before. I sometimes think we should be pushing for a *later* retirement age than men.'

An Employment Department campaign called 'Getting On' was launched in March 1994 to combat ageism after a study of British employers' attitudes and policies on employing older people found 'sizeable numbers still maintain negative and inaccurate stereotypes' and there was 'some evidence of both direct and indirect age discrimination by employers.' (Encouraging older civil servants to take early retirement in the name of efficiency savings suggests the campaign has yet to reach the rest of Whitehall.) The 'early exit culture for older workers' worries the Institute of Personnel Management, who say the age group 25–35 is now consistently favoured. The general finding from many studies, the IPM say, is that younger and older workers are equally effective in most work activities.[12] There is no legal protection against age discrimination in Britain.

Moving Goalposts

Since 1970 the idea of equal opportunities at work has become part of working life, for larger private and public employers anyway. But equality gains in employment are being undercut by contrary trends not just in workplace culture but in organisation. 'Equal opportunities initiatives appear to have had little impact on real change for black women's employment patterns' Reena Bhavnani concludes in her review of research on black women at work. Policies had made some difference to recruitment in local government but labour market changes and recession meant an erosion of what slow progress there had been. 'Contract culture', privatisation and quasi-market re-organisation all have a specific impact on women's working lives.[13]

The public sector union UNISON believes that progress in equal opportunities 'has been curtailed' by Compulsory Competitive Tendering (CCT) and accompanying changes. In particular the ban on using 'contract compliance' has meant local authorities have been unable to ensure that equal opportunities policies are adhered to by private contractors who take over services. 'CCT has damaged equal opportunities for women', research published by the EOC in March 1995 concluded.[14]

Workplace change has been pushed through in discriminatory ways, with wage-cuts, poorer working conditions and loss of holiday pay affecting women workers most. McInnes and Hunter found that the hourly pay rate of directly employed staff was often defended at the expense of such measures as dramatic reductions in hours of work for women, though 'this was not seen as an option for men'. A UNISON/Local Government Information Unit review of CCT published in early 1994 found that costs have been cut by undermining pay and conditions among the already low paid. The EOC report on CCT underlined this: in the 39 councils studied there was a loss of 13,000 jobs since 1988, 97 per cent of which were done by women. In return for higher productivity the wages of male refuse collectors, for example, had risen but higher productivity among cleaners and caterers, mainly women, had been achieved through 'loss of jobs, reduction in hours of work and pay, an increase in temporary and casual work and a general worsening of their terms and conditions of employment'.[15]

In the same way, contracting out catering, cleaning and laundry in the NHS has had a major impact on low paid women workers, as has the transfer of most care of the elderly to private nursing homes where wages are on average between a half and two-thirds of NHS rates. (Although in two Scottish hospitals cleaners proved their necessity and improved their conditions by going on strike. The European TUPE regulations may also prevent some deterioration of conditions.) As the CCT process is extended to white collar work in councils (more than 200,000 white collar posts are potentially affected), and to the civil service through 'market testing', again a higher proportion of workers affected are women. The 'leaner, more focused and more competitive' civil service envisaged in the 1994 White Paper *Continuity and Change* is likely to have a specific impact for women.

Short-term contracts pose specific problems for women. So, for example, in an organisation like the BBC, which has excellent maternity and equal opportunities provision, short-term contracts which are now common may undermine them. When Richard Patterson at the BFI asked (discussing their survey of workers in television) 'how do you take a maternity break on a six-month contract?',[16] he was voicing a question that has been on the mind of many women in media. There is a parallel concern among women with children: 'how do you hire a nanny when you're not sure if you'll be able to pay her in three months time?' said one woman. 'Well, you do and you feel guilty.' New working practices introduced in ITN require some workers to do unlimited overtime whenever required, which is not compatible with family commitments that need planning ahead. The introduction of departmental budget controls in the BBC may also have implications for women because the costs of maternity leave are now borne by departments (rather than the organisation's overall employment budget) and it would not be surprising if this affected future recruitment. Although short-term contracts have been introduced in media more rapidly than most areas they are increasingly common everywhere.

Banking is a parallel case. Following a formal investigation begun into Barclays by the EOC in 1983 the major banks developed some of the best equal opportunities policies during the 1980s, and finance was the main growth area for women's employment over the decade. With recession and changing technologies came redundancies and increased workloads (followed by record pre-tax profits for a number of banks announced in early 1995). Part-time staff as a proportion of all staff in banking and finance steadily increased over the early 1990s and women part-timers increased most steeply and there has been a steep increase in short-term contract work. The banking and finance union BIFU say although they cannot give a gender breakdown of temporary and contract work, since most of it is in lower-grade clerical work they expect it to be affecting women most.[17]

The union is particularly concerned by the conditions of work for data-processing workers, an area of high-productivity and variable demand, who are mainly women doing very intensive work in what BIFU describe as 'office factories'. Much of the short-term work is at 'relatively low pay' they say and without maternity benefits and sick pay. The Low Pay Unit is currently investigating this.

Weekend and evening working in telephone banking – successful innovations such as First Direct, now copied by several other banks – has meant a rapid increase in flexible work and also in 'zero hours contracts', which basically mean an employee works when wanted. There is a telling contrast between their advertising which presents banking as fitting into people's busy, multi-faceted modern lives and the union's worries. First Direct employ mainly women for evening and night work but pay no premium for shift-work, BIFU say.

Changes in medicine are a further example. Half of medical students are women, an often-cited fact of progress towards equality. The Medical Women's Federation suggests they might be wise to think again. At their national conference in November 1994 they discussed the need to tell sixth formers the reality of medical practice in the NHS today: 'long hours, frustrations and uncertainties', and expressed fears that a two-tier health service was developing, with women with family commitments being pushed into the lower tier.

The new deal to cut junior doctors hours set a *ceiling* of 72 hours a week for 'hard-pressed posts' but many still work longer. (And if there are any junior doctors' posts which aren't 'hard-pressed' the BMA don't know about them.) This has specific consequences for women seeking to combine training with family life. 'Long hours and uncertain futures are forcing women out of hospital medicine into general practice', Dr Gillian Markham, a consultant radiologist in Liverpool, told the MWF conference. Women are now the majority of GP trainees but Glasgow GP Dr Judith Chapman said that a lack of jobs was forcing young doctors to work as assistants or locums, without security, sick leave or maternity leave.

New Priorities

Women used to complain that images of work excluded us, were of serious men doing serious things, usually with serious technology. The Employment Department's publication, *The Best of Both Worlds* (1991) aimed to convince employers of 'the benefits of a flexible approach to working arrangements' and it is very apparent whose flexibility and which workforce it has in mind: the cover photographs show twelve women and three men. As I've argued, 'flexibility', if it is only for and about women with domestic responsibilities, can reinforce the traditional division of labour.

It is clear, twenty-five years on, that a paradigm of work based on the life patterns and traditional domestic role of men can survive rapid change in the workforce. Assumptions about what real work is, and women's employment as governed and constrained by our domestic responsibilities, persist despite increased women's participation in employment and a changing world of work. The traditional division of labour now has a new twist: women work at home, women look after the kids and granny, and women work outside the home – preferably with a job that won't inconvenience the men too much.

In March 1995 the Employment Committee concluded that this country urgently needs to support working mothers and their children and that this is not just a matter for women or only for people with children but 'policy in this area is vital for society as a whole'. Usually the government waits until the ink is dry before denying the conclusions of parliamentary committees; usually it lets them moulder in the House of Commons library for several years before trashing them, especially if the conclusions are unanimous, as these were. This time it sent Employment Minister Ann Widdecombe into the fray even before the report was published to call it 'an expensive menu with no prices' which would penalise 'the very people who create the wealth and jobs' (who are never, ever mothers, it seems). It was the usual mantra: 'no regulations!'[18]

Demonstrating an equal commitment to employing men and women, the Employment Department had said, only four years previously, means showing that 'active steps have been taken to eliminate discriminatory practices in pay and promotion prospects' and 'establishing the right image of a family-friendly working environment'. How many British firms will now do that when the Government insists it's not *really* necessary?[19]

In the 1990s most women have to give short-term personal answers to questions better tackled by long-term public policy. Full-time work with a proper career progression is undoubtedly the way to get the best work – in terms of prospects and (possibly) interest, responsibility, prestige. And an income on which it is possible to live independently. Part-time and flexible work is still mainly confined to less well-paid work with skills which are not highly regarded. But 'best' can be – and in practice is – defined differently. It can also mean work that doesn't interfere too much with the rest of life, that is compatible with bringing up children, other needs and choices, which may not always be experienced as constraints.

Let's reprise. Almost half the (paid and recorded) workforce are women, almost half are working part time, and almost half have dependent children. Despite demand, few private sector employers have introduced facilities to make it easier to combine work and family responsibilities (though those that have say they've benefited). The more a woman is like a man, as Linda Dickens says, 'the closer her employment pattern mirrors his, then the better she will fare in employment opportunities and rewards. The more she differs from this male norm ... the greater disadvantages she will experience.'[20] Most research shows this very clearly. So it is women who have made the adjustments, trading pay, position and opportunity for time to manage family responsibilities. Some changes risk embedding women's work as secondary, undercutting progress in equal opportunities so far, and reinforcing the choice beween marginalised work and full-time, highly-pressured employment which leaves no time for the rest of life. It is also possible that reactions to change – fed by the idea that women are 'taking men's jobs' – will reinforce this.

But change creates opportunity as well as new problems. The advantages of the better balance many women have achieved between paid work, work in the home and community and (when there's time) the rest of life, have been considerable – in terms of functioning as whole people, in terms of a better integration of work, caring responsibilities and wider values. What *hasn't* changed, Glenys Watt said, 'are a lot of good things about women. I think we can be too gloomy – and even though women have to work so hard and are very often juggling so many things, women haven't lost that capacity to be supportive to each other, to be caring and thoughtful – and I think that women *think* more flexibly than men, most men anyway, do … Sometimes I look at successful men and I wonder what else they've got.' Changing work patterns which mean people must have the self-confidence to handle change as a normal part of their working lifetime, demand the sort of adaptability and 'transferable skills' that women are more likely, because of experience and education, to have. They are easier to manage for people with an identity over and above work. Women who 'juggle' their lives should not be seen as less committed or as constrained workers but as pioneers of a better way to work. Better to juggle than have nothing to juggle with.

Gendered Time

Although I have argued that current changes in the organisation of working time, which are likely to be far-reaching, are very much about 'women's work', it isn't as simple as core/peripheral equating to male/female any more. Some of the gendered impacts one might have expected because of traditional and persisting attitudes to men's and women's work have been mitigated *because* of job segregation. Where women have been segregated is of growing economic importance. 'Women tend on the whole to have some of the new skills that modern firms need. As these skills are now recognised' and 'as productivity in the service sector improves', the gap between women's and men's incomes could rapidly start to close, the OECD say. It also thinks there will be poor prospects for 'women employed in the lowest jobs that will eventually disappear', which is a necessary note of caution. (Though it's hard to believe that cleaning will disappear.) 'The skills increasingly required in a global economy are very different from those required by traditional mass production' the TUC say, and may be 'most likely to be found in women – e.g. facilitating staff, multi-disciplinary thinking, flexibility, non-directive staff management, participative team working, creativity'.[21]

A whole cluster of arguments suggest that women's labour market position is changing for the better. If women were ever a 'reserve army' of workers, we are not now. At work in such numbers for all but short periods over the working lifetime, women workers' importance to the formal economies of all industrialised societies is hard to ignore. The service sector, where most women work, is not only more economically important but holds most economic promise and the common equation of service sector work with low pay and limited opportunity is a gross simplification: a sector which includes education, health, banking, insurance, business services and public administration, as well as hotel and catering and the retail trade, has its share of good jobs as well as bad.

Some would go further: 'the world is on the verge of a productivity miracle in women's service-sector work, so that this may be one of the great wealth generating engines of the future' was one of the conclusions of a seminar on growth and employment in April 1994 organised in Oxford as reported in the *Guardian*. American economist Eileen Appelbaum believes that greater productivity in services should mean that a wide range of services become more affordable and this is the key to higher wages and better employment conditions. But, she cautions, 'it is by no means inevitable that changes in technology and work organisation will occur, or that they will be translated into rising productivity and rising wages if they do. In the US the phenomenon of up-skilling and down-waging is not unfamiliar in services, especially where women comprise the major part of the workforce.' Only if women workers are valued, more unionised and make sure we have better bargaining power will this happen, she argues.[22]

The increasing 'export' of data-processing and related white-collar work to the Third World – using communications technology, which means it really does not matter whether the information is keyed in in Manchester or Madras – may also bring rapid change to a sizeable section of service sector work. British Airways now has ticketing services based in Bombay; Texas Instruments, India has a staff of more than 230 software engineers in Bangalore and pays its graduate staff a monthly wage of £176, while in Britain a computer engineer can take home a starting salary of £1,600 a month and upwards. Nothing can be taken for granted.

But more people now realise that better thinking about the role of women in the workforce is essential not primarily as a matter of social justice and fairness but for economic strength and appropriate growth. Positive changes in work for women run with the grain of economic need. A European economic strategy which is high-skill and centred on quality, innovation and good service demands a skilled, educated and adaptable workforce in which well-educated and adaptable women will undoubtedly play a central part.

The key questions we need to ask seem to me to be: is 'women's work' becoming more valued? Is 'women's organisation of time' becoming more valued? And is paid work beginning to fit differently with the rest of life? Yes, maybe, and yes! The future is not simplistically female. The argument that 'women's skills' are the skills of the future depends on stereotypes of women *and* men, stereotypes which are not less restricting just because they are cast in positive terms. I would add a cautious comment that skills according to gender are never as fixed as they seem – the allocation varies according to how they are regarded and rewarded. As 'women's skills' become more in demand and better paid, men discover they have them too – nowadays using the language of equal opportunities to say so. (It is useful to remember that certain skilled jobs in printing, for example, were seen as women's work in the nineteenth century, and that the first secretaries were men.)[23] A balanced and progressive workforce would allow individuals to use all their abilities not just those permissible to their sex.

Nevertheless areas in which women have been more likely to gain skills and feel comfortable working are now valued more in the changing workforce of the First World. Communication and information management are the main examples. Women, as BT and Bob Hoskins so irritatingly tell us, know 'it's good to talk'. Keyboard skills and information management have been the basis of an area of traditional women's work which women are now well placed to develop.

'Someone who can't type his own letters and reports is going nowhere,' Anne Rennie believes; 'it's gone beyond equal opportunities now.' She thinks the way many women organise our working lives, and what we value in them, is the way of the future. 'Where influence is coming from now is different – it's coming through technology, which women are very good at. It's about information, about accessing it and knowing what to do with it. The reports I can do now are so much more sophisticated than even five or ten years ago. A man who relies on dictating to his secretary can't access the information he needs to do those things.' And newer organisational emphases on 'empowerment', teamwork and 'flat hierarchies' may suit women better, she argues.

Women are starting their own businesses or working on their own precisely because they don't want to 'work like men', Glenys Watt believes (and is herself an exemplar of the trend). She works in community and social development in a research consultancy she and another woman founded. She's worried by the way deregulation has pushed wages down, but still sees flexibility 'in reasonable jobs, reasonably paid' as immensely important. 'I really do feel that the future is happening now, the decisions we make now will create the future and it could go either of two ways – one in which people share work and childcare, or a nightmare alternative with a few people with well-paid jobs and everyone else down below.

'Maybe this is turn-of-the-century stuff but it feels like a time when we've got to start thinking 100, 200 years ahead, think about what we want, think laterally and in a global sense, not in a narrow sense.' What will encourage us to do so? 'For more people to talk and think about the consequences if we don't. It's all interlinked: if we don't look at what we're doing economically it's likely to finish off the environment, or social unrest will become massive.'

Claims that 'generation X' have rejected the Protestant work ethic and want a more sustainable balance between work and the rest of life support her argument. Higher-educated young people in North America and Europe, a new study says, 'want work to be life-friendly' and see their futures less in fixed careers than project-based work. 'A desire to use intellect and have greater control over time ... and that work be varied and worthwhile' are very important. In this young people of both sexes are seen as coming closer to values women have more usually expressed. 'Decades after forecasters first predicted a leisure society, we may at last be seeing a backlash against an out-of-control work culture, demanding more and giving less ...'[24] The need for education and re-training throughout a lifetime also fits well with a different approach to work, skills and personal timetables.

'It is possible to decide what is the level of a good standard of living for everybody,' Glenys Watt believes. 'If we decided so most people could work part time, it's about how we decide to run things. Denmark and also the Netherlands have created a lot of reasonably well-paid part-time work.' She cites the example of Volkswagen workers who chose shorter hours for everyone rather than redundancy for some. But in a recent study of Calvinist attitudes to work, Britain came top. 'When I work in other parts of Europe it's quite noticeable. In Denmark, well you start the morning with coffee and pastries ...

'Time with friends, time for painting, dreaming, gardening – valuing children and elderly people – we could choose all of that. What we value is work, money, getting on. But you work hard and then you're redundant – and that word says it all. The middle part of your life is frenetic, then what?'

Time for Social Policy

Whether change in the workforce can be used for positive ends depends very much on what women do. Political organisation and a greater role for women in decision-making will be critical in ensuring that change benefits both women and those they care for – and men with the vision to want a truly different world. The lack of public confidence in the present economic system and the deep-seated insecurity it is creating calls not for insularity and ever more individualism but for policies debated and shaped by and within communities and for economic decisions placed (again) in a social context.

As things are most men have jobs, and most women have jobs that fit in. We *all* need to have jobs that fit in with *life* – with a sustainable balance. Harriet Harman argues that women are no longer going to be fobbed off 'with claims that the male pattern of a working life is the only possibility. For women now have been behind doors that once were closed to them ... [and know] that they are as good as men ... and that there are new ways of doing almost anything.'[25] The transition to a 'post-industrial economy' must be an opportunity for social transformation. That social transformation could, in turn, hold the key to economic transformation. But it only will if we do not just dream about it, but actively create it. Jean-Yves Boulin believes 'women who are faced with a masculine culture of time are likely to be the driving force behind such change'.[26] Yes and no.

The answer doesn't lie in going back to the 40-hour week for the 40-year lifetime. I doubt if we can. Its disappearance, if exaggerated, is not to be 'mourned', as some argue. The security it offered was at too great a cost in terms of the gendered division of labour, at home and in the public world, and in terms of the power it gave men over women in the family. There is no golden age for us to return to: the dominant organisation of work and systems of labour relations which are now regretted didn't offer equality either. Nor is the answer to accept the price we are currently paying for participation and flexibility. As working patterns become more complex we also urgently need to build new forms of social protection which interact with them, rather than creating, as at present, new and tortuous versions of the poverty trap. Change demands equally flexible social benefits and a stronger safety net, not the weaker one that is being created. Gender must be properly taken into account; and women must no longer be treated as dependants.

The concept of 'stakeholders' in society and in creating common enterprise is a useful one. As Will Hutton argues in *The State We're In* (1995) 'a well-functioning market economy requires skilled workforces, strong social institutions like schools and training centres and a vigorous infrastructure'. A central argument of the Social Justice Commission is that allowing whole swathes of society to be alienated and excluded is against not only social justice but economic sense: 'where social justice is pursued primarily through investment in opportunities (rather than simply supporting the non-employed on benefits), it contributes directly to economic growth'. 'Investing in people,' as the SJC describe it, must explicitly include investing in women, for reasons equally of social justice and economic renewal. The 'social contract' must be rewritten in ways which build in sexual and racial equality. We need both to realise the value of social institutions, as Hutton argues, and to ensure that women play an equal part in them, if women are to have a stake.[27]

There is a growing debate about new ways of working and ways of creating a better balance between work and the rest of life. It is a crucial debate and 'women's work' is central yet women's voices are rarely heard in it. It needs to be given priority. Crisis will create change anyway: Hutton calls this a 'hurricane blowing through the labour market' and Eileen Appelbaum writes that the problems of joblessness and stagnating or declining real wages in the industrial-ised countries are not 'the employment problems ... of an ordinary business cycle' but much more fundamental.[28]

The old model of gendered working time is still dominant. But if our times are truly in transition, if what we are seeing and suffering is a transformation in the organisation of work and production, radical new ways of responding both to work/life tensions and to unem-ployment need to be taken seriously. Women with family responsi-bilities need change in the organisation of work most (though other women and men will benefit), and have been building an understand-ing of how to make it work. Women's experience must become part of how we understand work and time.

A few years ago I wrote about an Italian city whose International Women's Day celebration I'd heard about. I've since wondered if this was a kind of feminist urban myth since I've never been able to confirm it. Instead of bunches of flowers, which are traditional, the city presented women with a new concept of time. Posters pro-claimed 'Time in the city is now woman's time' and announced the launch of an ambitious project to change opening times and tailor them to women's needs. The mayor apparently decided the city's institutions should fit in with women's timetables, not the other way round. Play-centres and crèches would operate in off-peak hours and hairdressers, shops and the labour exchange open for a much longer day. The 'time-engineering project' should fit the lives of women, the mayor said, because 'they are the ones who do most of the running between home and work and who organise the family's time'.

Since the Industrial Revolution, working time has been the central organising principle in our society. We have learnt to deal in monetarised time, time as a traded good. Because of this, unpaid work – housework, childcare, subsistence agriculture and much creative work, and the processes of creating community – has been devalued. We need to recognise and contest working time's hegemony, to dethrone the centrality of paid work and production. We need to do it, yes, but working time must be understood in terms of our whole lifetimes and our multi-dimensional lives. We need to learn to use and value time in different ways. There is a close connection of course – but time is not, after all, money.

Conclusion: Opening Pandora's Box

When I started thinking about this book I had an image in mind of a pair of old-fashioned scales: evidence for 'no change' on one side, 'change' on the other. It seemed as possible then that I would find that the continuities in women's lives outweighed change, and there *are* strong continuities in what we expect of women as mothers and at the centre of family life, in segregated work and low pay and poverty, and in the sexual double standard used against women. But it now seems to me that the evidence weighing down the *change* side of the scales is much heavier. The lid of Pandora's box has been wedged fully open, even if what we found there has brought new complexities.

In an inquiry like this there are no neat ends to tie. (Instead there are still other questions to ask.) But several – interlinked – threads stand out from the pattern.

What has changed least, I think, is the habit of measuring things against a male-defined standard: we still use definitions of work and of progress, what counts as success, the place of caring, and appropriate behaviour along a false axis of reason to emotion, which are a consequence of male pre-eminence in the public sphere. So women's needs are seen as special and additional rather than *ordinary*; women have, as Scottish politician Jeanette Timmins said, always to be saying 'excuse me, I need extra because …' It means that women who lead a 'double life' are seen as doubly burdened, not that men who don't are missing out or irresponsible. It means that women who allow their real lives to show on a public stage are seen as 'trailing evidence of domesticity', as Cynthia Cockburn put it, or 'always bleating about childcare', as another Scottish woman politician said.

This is writ large in the equal pay and sex discrimination legislation. Both were crucial steps and have been beneficial, but, as Valerie Amos cogently argued, we need a fundamental rethink of how we approach equality in law. 'Our legislation is framed so that it applies equally to women and men. And that's fine as a principle but women and men don't start from the same place and all the data demonstrates that there is a differential impact on women of a whole range of social and economic policies. So if you have legislation that starts off from a standpoint of equal treatment it is not going to be able to address structural inequality. You have a built-in contradiction there.' As things stand, measures to address inequality 'look as if you're doing women a favour, you're doing something special. We haven't found a way of trying to deal with the complexity of that.'

Related problems dog progress in political representation. More women in elected positions would change the political power structures which exclude or marginalise women; yet our understanding of equality means that measures to break down that exclusion (particularly quotas) are derided, by women as well as men, as 'positive discrimination' and as unfair to men (and may be found to be legally so). It means that women in all sorts of areas, but most conspicuously in politics, are faced with the problem of 'how do I get there from here'? Women see that the rules of the game suit men more than women, but you have to play by those rules to change it. The involvement of more women would change political practices which exclude women, but until the culture of mainstream politics is changed a lot of women won't want to be involved.

Although the powerful institutions which shape our lives – Parliament, and the criminal justice system especially – remain male defined and male run with their thinking on very familiar tramlines, the world outside them is a different place. This is part of the paradox; contradictory realities running side by side. Women see what's behind doors that were once closed to us and are more confident in our perceptions of what's needed, better able to detect and refuse old boundaries and to say 'No, I want to do it *this* way.'

(Though women who do say that still find themselves on the outside again, often as not.) 'It's not so tangible, just the feeling that you have a language and an articulacy to be able to say "this isn't good enough", or "this is what I want",' Reena Bhavnani said. 'I don't know if you can identify when it happened but in the 1970s you might go into a room of women and it would be far more tentative what you felt you could say. Now there would be lots of women in that room who would say "no, I won't be treated like that" or "I won't put up with that", or "a woman has as much right as a man to ..." It may seem obvious now, but women have a language to be able to express their confidence and their needs which they didn't use to have.' The more so as women define women's needs: what's changed, Fiona Mackay said, is not just that women's concerns have legitimacy but that it is women who are posing the questions. 'It's not Freud but *women* who are asking what do women want.'

The old ways don't work. A way of seeing the world based on an historic masculine pre-eminence is outdated and destructive. This is evident in everything from building motorways, which just mean more traffic and more children with asthma, to a government veto on parental leave – fending off the Eurocrat attack on the distant father traditional to the British way of life – to high finance which allows international speculators to knock away the foundations of industry on which even the monetary system, in the end, depends. Even as I looked at all the evidence of men in charge and women losing out I felt strongly that though it may not be as easy to demonstrate as the high numbers of low-paid women or the small number of women managing directors, none the less the world view which has sustained male dominance is altogether hollow. One more push and it might just topple.

Contradictory beliefs are woven in and out of each other still. But the old explanations and justifications have less and less power. We recognise the old paradigm and it still has influence but we don't believe in it any more. Perhaps this is how it is when the tectonic plates that underlie shared perceptions and structures alike shift and settle in a new configuration. A shift in perception and values is under way, shared by some men.

Another way of expressing this is in terms of 'spaces' which have

been carved out where masculine values were once deeply embedded. If there are deep cracks in a once smoothly constructed surface
some of the debris may be loose and dangerous, but there is far more
room for women to create the lives and (less so) to build the
structures we want. This was something I felt strongly on a sad
occasion, the funeral in Edinburgh of Franki Raffles, the woman
photographer who created the Zero Tolerance campaign and who
died in childbirth in 1994. As the service began the sense of her life as
enclosed in a male-written ritual was strong. But her partner and
daughter and her close friends and colleagues made new room within
an old ceremony to truly express and mourn her life.

That sense of space was exuberantly expressed by Ellen Kelly:
when she was a teenager, she said, not only did she not have any
positive images of lesbians, 'I didn't even know the word. If
somebody in the 1970s had been able to show me role models of me
and my friends the way we are now, you wouldna' have stopped me!
I'd've thought it's all right to be ... whoooeeee!' Zoe Fairbairns
echoed her words, talking about a life with both creative work and an
equal, loving relationship with a man – growing up that had seemed
to her impossible and wrong even to want. Cynthia Cockburn used
the image of new spaces to describe 'the most astonishing, influential
discovery of women!' She remembered an evening in 1974 when she
was involved with a community project and the women went to a
Chinese restaurant together. 'I really had no identification with
women. It was the first time in my life I had ever done anything just
with women. That was a turning point.' There is a kind of alternative
women's world she suggests: 'quite significant spaces – spaces that
are there in every city, every institution ... But for a lot of women
they are hard to find.'

Once our world seemed frozen and fixed. If there are cracks in the
ice which allow new ideas through, new ways to do things and new
ways of thinking and seeing the world then we need to get our
elbows out, or ice axes or whatever fits the metaphor, to widen them.
Or perhaps, like Gerda in *The Snow Queen*, we can melt the ice
through courage and strength of feeling. And make space for a
renewed democracy, for a new economics and a new basis for social
policy. At least, those would be my priorities – write your own list.

The changes over the past twenty-five years have come very quickly to be taken for granted. It's like children growing up – each successive year of growing overlays and partly wipes out your memory of what they were like before. Does that make change vulnerable? Changes in attitude and expectation, and perception and possibility, are easier to assert than measure; can they be safe-guarded? The barriers may be harder to see but aren't women still tripping over them?

These are problems of progress rather than evidence of stasis. In 1928 Vera Brittain commented that Mrs Pankhurst and the women who followed her were luckier in a way than her generation, because they fought 'for a clear-cut issue, which was popular in the sense that it was easily understood ... Today half a dozen things – equal pay, equal opportunities, the right of married women to work, freedom from restrictive legislation, the retention of nationality on marriage – remain to be fought for. They are no less urgent than the franchise merely because less obvious.' Nor have they all been achieved even if they seem obvious now.[1]

Many injustices seemed clearer and easier to argue in the 1960s and 1970s. The issues are more diffuse now. It is like a wall of great stones: you get out of the way the stones that are clearly on the surface and then you start dealing with those that are half-buried in the ground behind it. They were there all the time but you have to get the big stones, the more obvious ones, out of the way to see them. Just keeping on keeping on is harder, Zoe Fairbairns said: 'when you've got a specific target you can go for it ... but once you've hit it then you've got to deal with what happens when you've hit it.'

The very achievements of that time may make change harder to argue for now. When I talked to her, Cynthia Cockburn was doing research on the presence of women and women's interests in the social dialogue (between government, trade unions and employers) in Europe. 'It's not a negative story. There are women present and women's interests are acknowledged and there are women's commit-tees which are considered legitimate. At the same time, there's a huge step still needed to get real parity, or to have a women's vision of the future of Europe in any way central to what happens. It's as if we've made a huge climb and we've reached a plateau and it's now almost inconceivable that we can make the next step. The demands have become less legitimate *because* we already have some representation. The scandal effect of women's exclusion has gone, we really *are* there, we don't have that scandal to strengthen our arm in saying, now give us the moon. They'll say, "You've got the moon," and we'll say, "But we want the sun."'

Partly because of the very success of feminism, alongside other changes in society which threaten current power structures, we face, a time not only of great possibility but also of new dangers. Cynthia Cockburn expressed the sense of danger very clearly: 'When people talk about a male backlash that is really minimising what is happening. To talk of a male backlash is to talk about individual men getting pissed off with uppity women.' She talked about intensifying ethnic nationalisms and religious conflict and about the hegemony of the market economy and loss of the welfare state and the re-emergence of forms of Fascism. 'Those movements are, one could almost say, essentially about repositioning women and re-establishing patriarchal gender relations. Some people would see it as being a by-product of them. I actually think that that is what they are about, about a militarist form of masculinity, and a domestic femininity.

'I think that's been a change. I think we've moved out of relatively safe times for women when women in vulnerable situations could take risks and get away with it; now I think it's only women *not* in vulnerable situations who can take risks.' For women who are poorer, more embedded in the dominant culture, more alone, the world may be more dangerous for women to step out of line in than it was.

Usha Brown talked about the need for women's lives and possibilities in Britain to be understood in an international context. 'Women are doing things they would hardly have thought about twenty-five years ago but global changes are affecting women in this country and throughout the world in different ways, and they affect women in the South in sometimes dangerous ways. This has to be understood as about power, about people who have power retaining it. Nobody gives up power. Nor does anyone see themselves as holding it wrongly. And throughout the world most power still lies with men.'

The Wider View

Thinking about change demands both a global perspective and the perspective of a century. Or perhaps the arguments of the Victorian feminists in the 1850s would be a better starting point, or the determined emphasis on women's role in the home and family which followed Mary Wollstonecraft's *Vindication of the Rights of Woman* in the 1790s. Looking at women's history is to see the same paradox of change and continuity running through the century, and longer.

'Although change had occurred in the political, social and economic status of women, what was more striking was the contested and uncertain nature of gender roles. What is striking is the diversity of women's experience and beliefs. There was no unilinear shift in women's role. By the end of the century some women had experienced changes which led in the direction of greater equality, for others what was significant was the enduring nature of inequalities. For most women some aspects of their lives improved and in other aspects gender divisions were more pronounced.' The historian Eleanor Gordon was talking about women's lives at the end of the nineteenth century. Her words are also true of women's lives at the end of the twentieth.[2]

'The feminist movement of the present day is not very popular,' Vera Brittain wrote in 1927. 'It has a good many openly declared enemies, all of whom appear determined not to understand its true aims and meaning.' Opposition was in part 'gently patronising, lightly chaffing those women who share in feminist activities, and jocosely suggesting their enthusiasm is just a bit behind the times'. Others, most dangerously, she thought, 'maintain that feminism is merely hysterical, since it is now quite unnecessary. Feminists are told, in the words of a weekly paper, that all the strongholds of the enemy have been taken, all the big battles fought and won.' That could also be said of it today.[3]

The recovery of women's history, which has only begun, is immensely important. Taking a longer perspective is to see that there are equal numbers of women in higher education now because women fought for that more than a hundred years ago. It is to see that we only talk today about mothers going out to work as if that was unusual and about women choosing between love and work because

Victorian ideas about 'separate spheres' – which no more fitted the reality of most women's lives then than they do now – hang over us still. That when older women say younger women are not taking the movement further they are repeating complaints to which Vera Brittain replied in 1929 that she was afraid young women had less time to organise for change because at work and at home they were living it.

The comment by Eleanor Gordon was the conclusion of her paper at a conference on Scottish women's history in April 1995 in St Andrews. It was one of several events marking the centenary of women's admission to the university and it felt a bit like a personal anniversary too: I was a student there in the 1970s; the conference was held in the room in which I had sat my finals and hadn't been in since.

I was the first person in my family to go into higher education; I had left university with a sense that I could do things which only a few years before I had never dreamt I could; as a young woman with a lot to contribute. I thought about how many doors had been shut in my face since (though some I've also prised open again), sometimes without explanation, sometimes with apologies, and what that had meant for my sense of myself and my possibilities. I thought about my own generation, at a turning point, energised by a new vision but caught and tangled up in old doubts sometimes, looking forward but sometimes looking back. I thought about my mother whose life has been led between narrow parameters and who holds firmly to a belief in women's place, and my daughters, to whom that makes no sense at all. They are beginning their lives as women in a world which tells them they are equal even as it withholds equality, a world which holds more possibilities for them than women have ever known, but reason to fear as well.

A serious and visionary attempt to address inequality, between women and women, between women and men, would power the renewal of our society which is so badly needed. Workable, everyday equality would revitalise the institutions of this country and end oppression within families. Equality is the missing ingredient in the puzzle of why so much social legislation doesn't work. There has been half a social revolution: we need now to complete it.

At the end of the twentieth century we live in a profoundly unequal world in which power and prosperity is held tightly in the hands of a minority, a world riven by greed and maintained by violence or by complex systems of disinformation and disenfranchisement. Neither capitalism nor communism deliver what they promised. Both have a cost in cruelty, inequality and environmental degradation. An international perspective only underlines how much the male-dominated systems by which this world is run don't work for more than a minority of people, or for the planet.

'We have reached a point of historic crisis', Eric Hobsbawm concludes in *Age of Extremes*. 'If humanity is to have a recognisable future, it cannot be by prolonging the past or present. If we try to build the third millennium on that basis, we shall fail. And the price of failure, that is to say, the alternative to a changed society, is darkness.'[4] I think women will – and must – hold up a light against that darkness: a searchlight if we can, a whole sunrise even – but candles anyway. Women are making change work. We have less to lose and more to gain from it. The questions that women have raised have a greater legitimacy and the ideas we are exploring a greater relevance and urgency than ever before. We must ensure that the variety of women's voices and the values and understanding which come from our experience of life shape further change for ourselves, our children and a new century.

About three quarters of the way through writing this book I realised that what the women I'd talked to had in common was that they are *Making it Work*. It was as true of women living 'ordinary' lives at home with young children or as carers trapped in their homes but not in their ideas, as it was of women on the public stages of media, the arts, politics. They are making it work, with creativity and imagination and commitment, with perseverance and humour and strength. If we go on doing so we will make a better world for everyone.

Notes

Introduction

1   Estimate by the British Medical Association, *Taking Care of the Carers*, February 1995. Equal Opportunities Commission 1995.
2   Equal Opportunities Commission 1994. Union of Shop, Distributive and Allied Workers, 1995.
3   Mary Evans, introduction to Mary Evans (ed), *The Woman Question* (London, Sage 1994).
4   Vicky Randall and Joni Lovenduski, *Contemporary Feminist Politics* (Oxford, OUP 1993). Kate Figes, *Because of her Sex* (London, Macmillan 1994.) Susan Faludi, *Backlash* (London, Vintage 1993). *Everywoman* editorial, November 1994.
5   Naomi Wolf *Fire with Fire* (London, Chatto & Windus 1993). *Social Justice: Strategies for National Renewal* (London, Vintage 1994). Helen Wilkinson, *No Turning Back: Generations and the Genderquake* (London, Demos 1994).
6   *Hansard*, 7 March 1995, 10 March 1994 and 26 March 1975.
7   *Report of the UK to the Fourth World Conference of Women*, Employment Department 1994.
8   *In Search of Equality, Development and Peace*, Women's National Commission, 1994. *Scottish Women's Report to Beijing*, Co-ordinating Group on Representation, 1995. Cynulliad Merched Cymru report to Beijing 1994.
9   Christine Delphy, 'Changing women in a changing Europe', *Women's Studies International Forum*, vol 17 no 2/3, 1994.

Chapter 1

1   See Catherine Itzin ed, *Pornography: Women, Violence and Civil Liberties* (Oxford University Press) 1992, particularly chapter 3.
2   Brigid McConville, *Mixed Messages*, Penguin 1994.
3   *Observer*, 18 August 1994
4   The number of councils who had bought the Zero Tolerance campaign at March 1995. Birmingham City Council Campaign Against Violence Against Women and Children was launched on 25 May 1994, information from the Council Women's Unit, August 1994. Scottish Office press statement and campaign materials, June 1994.
5   Lorna JF Smith, *Domestic Violence*, Home Office 1989. Scottish Women's Aid, 1994. Women's Aid Federation England Annual Report 1993/94.
6   *Daily Mail*, 3 April 1995. Alice Brown, *Englander* Conference, 22 April 1995. *Scotsman*, 13 October 1993.

7   *Further Steps: Towards a Scheme for Scotland's Parliament*, The Scottish Constitutional Commission, October 1994. The electoral contract was formally proposed on 10 March 1995. *Scotsman*/ICM POLL, 11 March 1994.

8   Public Appointments Unit, Office of Public Services and Science, 1994. Employment Department 1994, op. cit.

9   Inter-Parliamentary Union, Series *Reports and Documents* no 18, Geneva 1994.

10   Women's Local Authority Network, February 1995. Scottish Local Government Information Unit 1995.

11   European Parliament, *European Elections 1994: Results and Elected Members*, July 1994. European Commission, March 1995.

12   George Younger, *Scotland on Sunday*, 3 October 1993.

13   *Observer* and *Guardian* reports of the 1993 Conservative Party Conference. Margaret Thatcher, *The Downing Street Years* (London, HarperCollins 1993) and television and radio comments after publication.

14   The Carlton Club (founded by opponents of the 1832 Reform Act) was faced with a dilemma when Margaret Thatcher became leader of the Conservative Party because her position entitled her to honorary membership but women (and non-Conservative voters) had been banned for 140 years. Now the club admits a special category of lady associate members with rights equivalent to guests, but retains a male-only bar and dining room. David Frost interview, 17 October 1993.

15   *The Downing Street Years*, op cit.

16   Wendy Webster, *Not A Man to Match Her* (London, Women's Press 1990).

17   Kenneth Baker, *The Turbulent Years: my life in politics*, (London, Faber 1993).

18   Elizabeth Templeton *A Woman's Place?* (Edinburgh, St Andrew Press 1993).

19   *Scotsman*, 17 June 1994. *Guardian*, 14 March 1994; 11 March 1995.

20   The Church of Scotland decided to permit women ministers in May 1968. *Scotland on Sunday*, 6 September 1992.

21   Haleh Afshar, 'Women and the Politics of Fundamentalism in Iran', *Women Against Fundamentalism* journal vol 1, no 5, 1994. *Sunday Times* 4 September 1994.

22   *Hansard*, 22 March 1995, *Women at Work: The Businesswoman's Perspective*, Institute of Directors, 23 Sept 1994. William Kay, *The Bosses* (London, Piatkus, 1994).

23   *Guardian*, 15 August 1994.

24   *Sunday Mail*, 19 February 1995.

25   *Observer*, 14 August 1994.

26   Women are 13% of police personnel in England and Wales and 12% in Scotland, though they make up a higher proportion of new recruits (29%). Home Office figures for 1992; Chief Inspector of Constabulary Annual Report for Scotland, 1993. Frances Heidensohn, *Women in Control?: the role of women in law enforcement* (Oxford, Clarendon Press 1992). Jennifer Brown, Women's National Commission Seminar, 8 July 1994. *Guardian*, 17 January 1995.

27   Joanna Shapland and Angela Sorsby, Sheffield University Institute for the Study of the Legal Profession, February 1995. *Guardian*, 5 May 1995.

28   *Guardian*, 12 January 1995. Industrial Tribunals Regional Office, March 1995.

29   EOC briefing, 26 October 1994. Gary Bowker, *Taking the Cap Off Discrimination Awards*, Equal Opportunities Review, September 1994. (Excluding the MoD cases, the average award made by industrial tribunals had increased by 45% since 1993).

30   reports in *Guardian* and *Scotsman* in 1994 and 1995. EOC briefing, 21 February 1995.

31   *Guardian*, 2 April 1994.

32   *Independent*, 10 February 1994.

33   *Scotsman*, 14 October 1994. *Guardian*, 14 October 1994.

34   EOC January 1995. *Independent*, 15 December 1994.

35   EOC briefing paper July 1990. *Guardian*, January 1995. *Guardian*, 16 September 1994.

36   Kate Soper, 'Feminism, Humanism and Postmodernism', in Mary Evans (ed) *The Woman Question*, (London, Sage 1994).

37   Simone de Beauvoir, *The Second Sex* (London, David Campbell 1993). Audre Lorde, 'Age, Race, Class and Sex: Women Redefining Difference', in *Sister Outsider* 1984, reprinted in Mary Evans op cit.
38   Mary Evans op cit. Introduction.
39   Liz Stanley, *The Auto/biographical I: the theory and practice of feminist auto/biography* (Manchester University Press 1992), pp 240–242.

Chapter 2

Unless specified otherwise, employment statistics in this chapter are from the Labour Force Survey for 1994 and its Historical Supplement 1994, Social Trends 1994, and the Employment Department, May 1995; and the following articles from the *Employment Gazette*: Richard Bartholomew, Angela Hibbett and Judith Sidaway, 'Lone parents and the labour market', November 1992; Gary Watson and Barbara Fothergill, 'Part-time employment and attitudes to part-time work' May 1993; Frances Sly, 'Mothers in the Labour Market', November 1994.

1   New Earnings Survey 1994. EOC: first annual report, 1976. Calculations by EOC, May 1995 and by Esther Breitenbach for the *Engender Gender Audit* (Edinburgh, Engender 1993). *Women and Men in Britain*, EOC 1993.
2   New Earnings Survey 1994. *Women and Men in Britain*, EOC 1993.
3   Calculation by the Scottish Low Pay Unit, December 1994, using a low pay threshold of two-thirds median adult male earnings. Scottish Low Pay Unit, 1995.
4   *Hansard* written answers, 9 February 1994. 'Part-time work in Britain', TUC Economic and Social Affairs Department, December 1994.
5   Robert Lindley ed, *Labour Market Structures and Prospects for Women*, The Institute of Employment Research at the University of Warwick/EOC 1994. Women's National Commission March 1995. *Scotland on Sunday*, 16 May 1993.
6   *Hansard*, 7 March 1995. *Independent*, 15 June 1995. 1991 Census of Employment by Incomes Data Services, May 1993. IER Warwick/EOC op cit. Susan Harkness, Stephen Machin and Jane Waldfogel, *Women's Pay and Family Income Inequality* (Joseph Rowntree Foundation October 1994).
7   Yvonne Roberts, *Mad About Women* (London, Virago 1992).
8   *Dispatches*, Channel 4, 8 February 1995.
9   Neil Millward, *Targeting Potential Discrimination* PSI/EOC 1995. Louise Corti and Shirley Dex, 'Highly qualified women', *Employment Gazette*, March 1995.
10   Opportunity 2000 Third year report, October 1994, updated March 1995.
11   'The Politics of Equal Opportunity', Janette Webb, University of Edinburgh, unpublished paper.
12   Sue Sharpe, *Just Like A Girl: from the seventies to the nineties* (London, Penguin 1994).
13   Steven McKay and Alan Marsh, *Lone Parents and Work* (Department of Social Security, 1994). Bronwen Cohen and Neil Fraser, *Childcare in a Modern Welfare System*, IPPR 1991. IER Warwick/EOC op cit.
14   Gabrielle Cox, *After the Safety Net*, Low Pay Unit, 1994. *Narrowing the Gender Pay Gap: How Wages Councils work for women*, Pay Equity Project 1993.
15   Esther Breitenbach 'Women's employment in the Lothian economy', *Equal Voice*, STUC September 1994.
16   Louise Corti and Shirley Dex, 1995 op cit.
17   Julia Evetts (ed), *Women and Career: Themes and Issues in Advanced Industrial Societies* (Longman UK 1994).
18   Gillian Pascall 'Women in professional careers: social policy developments' in Julia Evetts op cit.
19   *Progress Report on Women in the Civil Service*: 1984–1994, Cabinet Office Equal Opportunities Division, 1995.
20   Helen Dawson, report to the Local Government Management Board, Birmingham 1994. Esther Breitenbach *Quality Through Equality: Good Practice in Equal Opportunities in Scottish Local Authorities*, EOC 1995.
21   *Independent*, 29 January 1995. Clara Greed, 'Gender and the Built Environment:

grand plans or pragmatic change?', paper given to Edinburgh Planning and Transport conference, 27 May 1995.

22 Julia Evetts op cit. *Hansard*, 26 March 1975. British Medical Association *Equal Opportunities in Medicine*, 1994 (figures for 1992). *Guardian*, 25 April 1995. *Hansard*, 7 March 1995. *Engender Gender Audit*, 1995.

23 Association of University Teachers, for 1993/4. Susan Walsh and Catherine Cassell, *A Case of Covert Discrimination* (London, The Bentinck Group, 1995).

24 Institute of Management, National Management Salary Survey 1994 and 1995. Harriet Harman, *The Century Gap* (London, Vermilion 1993).

25 Janice Morphet, *The Role of Chief Executives in Local Government*, (Longman UK 1993).

26 Rosemary Hutt, *Chief Officer Career Profiles*, Institute of Manpower Studies, 1985. Creative Career Paths in the NHS, reports no 4 (Senior Nurses, 1995) and no 1, (Top Managers, 1992), Institute of Health Service Management Consultants, London. James Buchan, Queen Margaret College, Edinburgh 1995.

27 Alison Tiernay, 'Married Women in Nursing', *Nursing Times 1983. Creative Career Paths* op cit. Reena Bhavnani, *Black Women in the Labour Market: A research review*, EOC 1994. The Royal College of Nursing, 1994.

28 RCN Oct 1993. Unison September 1994.

29 Education Department figures for January 1994. Scottish Office Education Department Bulletin, March 1995 (figures for September 1992). Margaret Macintosh, 'The gender imbalance in Scottish education', *Scottish Affairs, 5* (Edinburgh, autumn 1993).

30 Judith Fewell, 'The protection racket', in Fiona MS Paterson and Judith Fewell (eds), *Girls in their Prime* (Scottish Academic Press, Edinburgh 1990). Research by Oxford Brooks University reported in the *Guardian*, 13 January 1995.

31 Anthony Sampson, *The Essential Anatomy of Britain* (London, Hodder & Stoughton 1992).

32 David Williams, 'How we made local money official', *New Economics*, Spring 1995. Bernadette Vallely, 'Free and Easy', *Everywoman* May 1995.

33 Barbara Castle, *Fighting All The Way* (London, Macmillan 1993).

34 *Equal pay for work of equal value*, EOC 1984. Lorna Russell, *Everywoman*, May 1995. Morley Gunderson, *Comparable Worth and Gender Discrimination: An international perspective* (Geneva, International Labour Office 1994).

35 Jane Jenson, Elisabeth Hagen and Ceallaigh Reddy, *Feminization of the Labour Force: Paradox and Promises* (Cambridge, Polity 1988).

Chapter 3

1 Rebecca Abrams, *Woman in a Man's World: pioneering career women of the 20th century* (London, Methuen, 1993).

2 IER/Warwick op cit. *Report of the All Party Parliamentary Group on Parenting and International Year of the Family UK, Parliamentary Hearings* (London, IYF 1994). *Mothers in Employment*, Employment Committee (HMSO 1995).

3 Ginny Dougary, *The Executive Tart and Other Myths* (London, Virago 1994).

4 British Film Institute TV Projects Unit and the *Independent*, 5 December 1994.

5 Carol Craig, 'Equal Opportunities: A Report and Strategy for BBC Scotland', 1993.

6 Susan McRae, 'Returning to work after childbirth: opportunities and inequalities', *European Sociological Review*, 1993. David Bell and Sheila Rimmer, *Gender and Opportunity in Scotland* (Glasgow, Scottish Enterprise 1992).

7 Rebecca Abrams, 1993 op cit.

8 IYF Factsheet 1 1994. Social Trends 1994.

9 Clare Jones, 'Fertility of the over thirties' *Population Trends 67*, Spring 1992. Jane Bartlett, *Will You Be Mother?* (London, Virago, 1994).

10 Clare Jones, 1992 op cit. Penny Babb 'Birth Statistics 1993' and 'Fertility of the over forties' *Population Trends* no 79 Spring 1995.

11 PT no 67 op cit.

12 Ibid. and no 79 op cit.

13   Sue Innes, *Scotland on Sunday*, 2 January 1994.
14   Kathleen Kiernan, 'The roles of men and women in tomorrow's Europe', *Employment Gazette*, October 1992.
15   Susan McRae, *Maternity Rights in Britain* (London, Policy Studies Institute, 1991). WW Daniel, *Maternity Rights: The experience of women* (London, PSI 1980.) Incomes Data Services Study 550, Maternity Leave, 1994.
16   WW Daniel, op cit. Employment Comittee, op cit.
17   Ibid.
18   EOC January 1995.
19   WW Daniel, op cit.
20   Frances Sly, 1994 op cit. Julia Brannen and Peter Moss, *Managing Mothers: Dual Earner Households after Maternity Leave* (London, Unwin Hyman 1990).
21   Susan McRae, 'mothers employment after childbirth', Policy Studies Insititute, 1995.
22   Frances Sly, 1994 op cit. Parliamentary Question, 17 May 1994. Angela Hibbert and Judith Sidaway, 1992 op cit., David Bell and Sheila Rimmer, op cit.
23   *Employment for the 1990s* Employment Department (HMSO 1989).
24   Institute of Manpower Studies, press release in *Scotland on Sunday*, March 1993.
25   Sue Innes, *Scotland on Sunday*, 30 April 1989.
26   Employment Committee, (1995). Harriet Harman speech *The Childcare Gap*, April 1994. Susan McRae 1991 op cit. Opportunity 2000: Third year report, 1994. Midland Bank 1995.
27   Employment Committee (1995) op cit. Alan Marsh and Stephen McKay, 'Families, Work and the Use of Childcare', Employment Gazette August 1993.
28   Julia Brannen, George Meszaros, Peter Moss and Gill Poland, *Employment and Family Life: a review of research in the UK*, Employment Dept (HMSO 1994).
29   Employment Committee, 1995, op cit.
30   Padraig Flynn at the European Commission Conference 'New Ways of Working' 30 September, 1 October 1993.
31   Maeve Haran, *Having It All* (London, Michael Joseph 1991).
32   Brannen et al 1994 op cit.
33   I o M 1994 Sheena Briley and Marilyn McDougall, Developing Women Managers, (HMSO 1994) op cit. Helen Wilkinson, 1994, op cit.
34   *Independent*, 5 December 1994.
35   Family Policy Bulletin April 1995 (London, Family Policy Studies Centre).
36   BONP, letters to the *Guardian*, March 1992 and April 1995.
37   Lady Howe *Guardian*, 15 April 1995.

Chapter 4

Population statistics in this chapter are from: OPCS up-date, issue 1 Jan 1995; OPCS *Population Trends* numbers 65, 67, 69, 73, 77, 80; Scottish Abstract of Statistics 1993 (HMSO, 1994); *Social Trends* 1994 and 1995; *Regional Trends* 1994 (HMSO 1994) unless specified otherwise.

1   Linda Grant, *Sexing the Millennium* (London, HarperCollins, 1993).
2   OPCS Up-date no 1, 1995.
3   LB Rubin 1983, quoted by Penny Mansfield, 'Expectations and experiences of marriage today', *Journal of Social Work Practice*, Vol 5, no 2 1991.
4   *Cosmopolitan*, March 1995.
5   Susan McRae, *Cohabiting mothers: changing marriage and motherhood?* (London, PSI 1993).
6   Fay Weldon, *Affliction* (London, HarperCollins 1993).
7   Sue Innes, *Scotland on Sunday*, 16 January 1994.
8   *Network First*, 11 January 1994.
9   *Scotland on Sunday*, 16 January 1994.
10   Lorna JF Smith, 1989 op cit. Jane Rooney, *The Hidden Figure: Domestic Violence in North London*, Centre for Criminology, Middlesex University, 1993. Janette

Forman, '*Is there a correlation between child sexual abuse and domestic violence? An exploratory study*', Women's Support Project, Glasgow 1995.

11 Penny Mansfield and Jean Collard, *The Beginning of the Rest of Your Life* (Basingstoke, Macmillan 1988). The next stage of the research will be published by Macmillan in 1996.

12 Michael Murphy and Ann Berrington, 'Household Change in the 1980s: a review' *Population Trends* 73, autumn 1993.

13 Kathleen Kiernan and Valerie Estaugh, *Cohabitation: Extra-marital childbearing and Social Policy* (London, Family Policy Studies Centre, 1993).

14 Kathleen Kiernan and Valerie Estaugh op cit.

15 Kathleen Kiernan, 'The Family: Formation and Fission', in Heather Joshi ed, *The Changing Population of Britain* (Oxford, Basil Blackwell, 1989). 'Annus Mirabilis', *High Windows* (London, Faber and Faber 1974).

16 Kathleen Kiernan and Valerie Estaugh op cit. Susan McRae op cit.

17 Fran Wasoff and Janet Sultanan, University of Edinburgh, forthcoming.

18 Germaine Greer, *Guardian*, 10 December 1994.

19 *Guardian*, 26 April, 1994.

20 Kate Sandham, final year thesis, University of Edinburgh 1994. Paul Gregg and Edward Balls, *Work and Welfare* (London, IPPR 1993).

21 International Year of the Family, Parliamentary Hearings op cit.

22 Patricia Hewitt, *About Time: the revolution in work and family life* (London, IPPR/Rivers Oram 1993).

23 Kathleen Kiernan, 1992 op cit.

24 European Commission press release, December 1993. British Household Panel Survey, 1994 and newspaper reports of it.

25 In 1993 the average age of first marriage was 26 for women and 28 for men in England and Wales and in Scotland slightly lower. In 1970, in marked contrast, the average age of first marriage for women was 21 and the rate of marriage was unusually high: more than nine in ten of women born in 1946 married by 1976, the tail end of the strong pattern of earlier marriages in the 1950s and 1960s. Among Asian women, however, marriage rates are still high at young ages.

26 Michael Anderson, University of Edinburgh, 1994.

27 Sue Morris, Sheila Gibson and Alison Platts, *Untying the Knot: the characteristics of divorce in Scotland* (Scottish Office, 1993) Lord Chancellor's Department, 1995.

28 Ibid.

29 Ibid.

30 IYF Factsheet 1, 1994.

31 Scottish Office and Lord Chancellor's Dept 1995. The steepest increase in the divorce rate was in the first half of the 1970s after divorce was made simpler.

32 Fran Wasoff, University of Edinburgh 1994.

33 *Local Voices, Local Lives*: the story of the Kendoon Community Health Profile, Drumchapel Community Health Project, 1992.

34 *Sunday Times*, 19 May 1994. Demos/*Guardian*, 27 September 1994.

35 the changes introduced in February 1994 decreased payments and phased them in; in January 1995 the ceiling on maintenance was set at 30% of the absent parents' net income (which would benefit higher-earning fathers most) and there were additional allowances.

36 Fran Wasoff, Sue Morris, paper given at *Engender Dialogue*, Edinburgh 5 December 1994.

37 18 July 1990. Alison Garnham and Emma Knights, *Putting the Treasury First: the truth about child support*, London, Child Poverty Action Group, 1994. *Child Support: One Year On* National Association of Citizens' Advice Bureaux, 1994. *The Child Support Agency: Evidence of CAB Clients*, Citizens' Advice Scotland, 1994. *Damned if they Do: Damned if they Don't*, One Plus 1994. *The Child Support Agency's First Year*, One Parent Families, 1994.

38 Karen Clarke, Caroline Glendinning and Gary Craig, *Losing Support: Children and the Child Support Act*, The Children's Society, 1994.

39   Ibid.

40   The CSA formula is based on Income Support levels – which have never before been deemed to be wildly generous.

41   *Observer*, 17 October 1993.

42   Alison Garnham and Emma Knights op cit.

43   *Guardian*, 26 January 1995.

Chapter 5

All statistics quoted in this chapter come from OPCS *Population Trends* numbers 58, 73, 76 and 79, Scottish Abstract of Statistics, 1993, and from *Social Trends 1994* and *1995*, unless specified otherwise.

1   *Observer*, 17 October 1993.

2   *Independent*, January 1994.

3   *Woman's Own* quote from Susan Reinhold, 'Through the Parliamentary Looking Glass' *Feminist Review* no 48, Autumn 1994. The sermon on the mound was so-called because it was delivered in the Church of Scotland Assembly Halls at the top of a hill in Edinburgh called the Mound.

4   *Sunday Times*, 7 March 1993; in the article Professor Halsey made clear he rejected Charles Murray's 'underclass' theories.

5   Vicky Randall and Joni Lovenduski, 1993 op cit. Michelle Barrett and Mary McIntosh, *The Anti-social Family* (London, Verso 1982).

6   IYF Factsheet 1. The IYF UK Committee, chaired by Joanna Foster, was determined not to be drawn into the family values lobby but to generate 'more understanding both of the diversity of families and of their common needs for security and support' (interview with Joanna Foster, 23 September 1994).

7   Julia Brannen and Peter Moss, *Managing Mothers: Dual Earner Households After Maternity Leave* (London, Unwin Hyman 1990).

8   British Household Panel Survey, University of Essex Centre on Micro-social change, 1994.

9   Shere Hite *The Hite Report on the Family* (London, Bloomsbury 1994).

10   Penelope Leach and Patricia Hewitt, *Social Justice, Children and Families* (London, IPPR 1993).

11   *Eurobarometer* special report December 1991. Kathleen Kiernan, 1992 op cit.

12   Michael Murphy and Ann Berrington, 'Household Change in the 1980s: a review' *Population Trends* 73, 1993. The decade saw the most rapid decline in household size in the past half century.

13   Michael Anderson's analysis of OPCS statistics, 1994.

14   *Scottish Daily Express*, 16 September 1994. *Daily Mail*, 20 January 1995.

15   Elizabeth Wilson, 'Revolutionary Mothers', *Diva* issue 5 December 94/January 95. *Independent*, 20 September 1994.

16   *Guardian*, 1 July 1994. *Rights of Women* bulletin autumn/winter 1994.

17   *Rights of Women* bulletin autumn/winter 1994, Angela Mason, 15 June 1995.

18   John Haskey, 'Stepfamilies and Stepchildren in Britain' *Population Trends* 76, 1994.

19   *Eurostat* news release, December 1993. David Coleman, 'Britain in Europe: comparisons of fertility levels and trends', in M Ní Bhrolcháin (ed), *New perspectives on fetility in Britain* (HMSO 1993).

20   Dorothy Rowe, *Time On Our Side* (London, HarperCollins 1994). Germaine Greer, *The Change* (London, Hamish Hamilton 1991).

21   Michael Anderson, 'Today's families in historical context', Report to the Rowntree Foundation, January 1994.

22   Michael Anderson, op cit. 1993 Eurobarometer survey and research quoted in IYF Factsheet 1.

23   IYF Factsheet 4. General Household Survey 1985 (HMSO 1987).

24   GHS 1985 and 1990 (HMSO 1992).

25   IYF UK Parliamentary Hearings, op cit.

26   Kathleen Kiernan, 'The Family: Formation and Fission' in Heather Joshi (ed), *The*

Changing Population of Britain (Oxford, Basil Blackwell, 1989).

27   Penelope Leach and Patricia Hewitt, 1993 op cit.

28   Kathleen Kiernan in Heather Joshi (ed), op cit.

Chapter 6

1   Shirley Henderson and Alison Mackay (eds), *Grit and Diamonds: Women in Scotland Making History 1980–1990* (Edinburgh, Stramullion 1990).

2   Ann Oakley, *Social support and motherhood: the natural history of a research project* (Oxford, Basil Blackwell, 1992).

3   Jane Lazarre, *The Mother Knot* (London, Virago 1987).

4   Sheila Kitzinger, *The Crying Baby* (London, Viking 1989).

5   Julia Brannen and Peter Moss op cit.

6   Ibid.

7   A survey by the Lamplugh Trust in 1994 found that three-quarters of people believed children had become more exposed to personal and physical risk over the past five years. Childline Annual Report, 1993–1994.

8   Vivien Nice, 'In Search of Perfect Mothers', *Social Work Today*, December 1988.

9   Penelope Leach, *Children First* (London, Michael Joseph 1994).

10   Julia Brannen and Peter Moss op cit.

11   Lesley Garner, *How to Survive as a Working Mother* (Harmondsworth, Penguin 1982). Shirley Conran, *Superwoman in Action* (Harmondsworth, Penguin 1979). Mary Kenny, *Woman × Two: How to Cope with a Double Life* (London, Sidgwick and Jackson 1978).

12   *Good Housekeeping*, December 1994.

13   Ginny Dougary, op cit.

14   *Marie Claire* and *Cosmopolitan*, January 1995.

15   Anne Fine, *In Cold Domain* (Viking 1994).

16   See Ann Phoenix, Anne Woollett and Eva Lloyd, (eds), *Motherhood Meanings, Practices and Ideologies*, (London, Sage 1991).

17   The iconic w.l.m activist was young and middle-class. But that is to overlook the role of women in the trade unions, women's groups mainly of mothers, and other working women's groups. Sheila Rowbotham, 'To be or not to be: the dilemma of mothering', Feminist Review no 31, Spring 1989.

18   Micheline Wandor, *Once A Feminist: Stories of a Generation* (London, Virago 1990).

19   Shulamith Firestone, *The Dialectic of Sex* (London, Cape, 1971). Simone de Beauvoir, *The Second Sex*, op cit.

20   Lee Comer, *The Myth of Motherhood* (Nottingham, Bertrand Russell Peace Foundation, 'Spokesman' pamphlet 1972).

21   Sheila Rowbotham, 1989 op cit.

22   Ibid.

23   *First Steps*, February 1995. *She Magazine Guide to Having A Baby*, Spring 1995. Advertisement leaflet for 'Postman Pat's Play School'.

24   *Hausord* 7 March 1995. Jane Bartlett, 1994 op cit. *Guardian* 11, 12, 13 April 1995.

25   Naomi Wolf, 1993 op cit.

26   Christine Delphy, 'Changing women in a changing Europe', *Women's Studies International Forum*, vol 17 no 2/3, 1994.

27   Tuula Gordon, *Feminist Mothers* (Basingstoke, Macmillan 1990).

28   Caroline Quest (ed) *Equal Opportunities: A feminist fallacy* (London IEA Health and Welfare Unit, 1992).

29   Penelope Leach, 1994 op cit.

30   Liz Heron, 'The Mystique of Motherhood', Feminist Anthology Collective, *No Turning Back* (London, The Women's Press 1981).

31   Heather Joshi, 'The Cost of Caring' in Caroline Glendinning and Jane Millar (eds) *Women and Poverty in Britain in the 1990s* (Hemel Hempstead, Harvester Wheatsheaf 1992).

32   Jane Waldfogel, *Women Working for Less*, LSE Welfare State Programme

discussion paper, 1993.

33 IER/Warwick EOC op cit.

34 Anne Harrop and Peter Moss, 'Working Parents: Trends in the 1980s', *Employment Gazette* October 1994 op cit.

35 Anne Harrop and Peter Moss, op cit. IER Warwick/EOC op cit. Susan McRae 1993 op cit.

36 Rosie Jackson, *Mothers Who Leave* (London, Pandora 1994).

Chapter 7

Population statistics in this chapter are from: OPCS *Population Trends* numbers 67, 71, 74, 77 and 79; the *Scottish Abstract of Statistics* 1993 (HMSO, 1994), unless specified otherwise.

1   Margaret Bramall, then Director of the National Council for the Unmarried Mother and her Child, at a conference in Scotland in June 1971. (Conference report, Scottish Council for Single Parents, 1971.)

2   Robert Black was convicted in 1994 of the sexual attacks and murder of three girls; Frederick West committed suicide in January 1995 before trial for the murder of ten girls and women.

3   Peter Lilley, Conservative Party Conference 1992. Lorraine MF Harding, 'Parental Responsibility: the re-assertion of Private Patriarchy', paper given at conference, 'Good Enough Mothering? Feminist Perspectives on Lone Motherhood', University of Leeds, 6 May 1994.

4   Frank Field, *Making Welfare Work* (London, Institute of Community Studies, 1995).

5   *Sunday Times* editorial, 14 November 1993

6   Virginia Bottomley, address on family policy, 27 May 1994. Alan Howarth MP *Guardian*, 5 October 1993. Ian Lang, Scottish Conservative Conference, 1993.

7   Debbie Taylor, *My Children, My Gold* (London, Virago 1994).

8   Susan McRae 1993 op.cit.

9   Jonathan Bradshaw and Jane Millar, *Lone Parent Families in the UK*, Department of Social Security, 1991. Jane Millar, 'State, Family and Personal Reponsibility', *Feminist Review* 48, 1994. One Parent Families 'Key Facts', March 1995.

10 Kathleen Kiernan in Heather Joshi 1989 op cit.

11 Michael Anderson, University of Edinburgh 1994.

12 Penelope Leach and Patricia Hewitt, 1993 op cit.

13 Jonathan Bradshaw and Jane Millar 1991 op cit.

14 Kathleen Kiernan and Valerie Estaugh, 1993 op cit.

15 FPA data for 1993. See Ann Phoenix, *Young Mothers?* (Oxford, Polity 1991).

16 *Teenage Pregnancy in Scotland*, Scottish Forum for Public Health Medicine, February 1995.

17 Scottish Council for Single Parents, 1971 conference report op cit.

18 Scottish Council for Single Parents, 1970 conference papers.

19 S. Weir, A Study of Unmarried Mothers and their Children, Scottish Home and Health department, SCSP 1970. *Single Mothers: the First Year*, Angela Hopkinson (Edinburgh, Scottish Council for Single Parents, 1976).

20 Households below average *income*, HMSO 1994.

21 Hilary Macaskill, *From the workhouse to the workplace: 75 years of one-parent family life* (London, One Parent Families, 1993).

22 Steven McKay and Alan Marsh, *Lone Parents and Work* (DSS 1994). Frances Sly, op cit 1994. Parliamentary Question, 17 May 1994. Angela Hibbett and Judith Sidaway, op cit 1992. EOC submission to the Employment Committee, 15 February 1994.

23 Social Fund figures analysed by Alan Milburn MP, *Guardian*, 23 December 1994. *Little or Nothing* Family Service Units/Save the Children (Glasgow 1995).

24 Jonathan Bradshaw and Jane Millar 1991 op cit. Scottish Council for Single Parents Annual Report 1992–3.

25 *Social Justice: Strategies for National Renewal*, the Report of the Commission on

Social Justice (London, Vintage, 1994).

26   *Report of the Committee on One-Parent Families* HMSO 1974. Hilary Macaskill, op cit.

27   Jane Millar, *Feminist Review* op cit.

28   House of Commons, 10 January 1995.

29   Bronwen Cohen and Neil Fraser, *Childcare in a Modern Welfare System*, IPPR 1991. *Parents, Employment Rights and Childcare*, EOC 1993.

Chapter 8

1   John Major, Conservative conference speech, 8 October 1993.

2   Zoe Fairbairns, *Benefits* (London, Virago 1979).

3   October 1974, the year before Mrs Thatcher became party leader. In an interview in the *Independent* (11 October 1989) he said that the speech and reaction to it ended his chances of leading the Tory Party.

4   Vicky Randall and Joni Lovenduski op cit.

5   Pankhurst Lecture, 18 July 1990.

6   Martin Durham, *Sex and Politics* (Basingstoke, Macmillan Education 1991).

7   Patricia Morgan, *Farewell to the Family? Public policy and family breakdown* IEA 1995, and 'Double Income, No Kids' in Caroline Quest (ed) *Liberating Women . . . from Modern Feminism*, IEA 1994.

8   *Sunday Times*, 22 and 29 May 1994, *Sunday Times*, 28 August 1994. *Independent*, 9 January 1994.

9   *Guardian*, 17 September 1994.

10   See for example the published views of Christie Davies (Reading University and the Social Affairs Unit) and Dr Adrian Rogers, director of the Conservative Family Campaign. Also reports by *Public Eye* 18 March 1994; Michael Howard's reported remarks on adoption, *Guardian* 6 October 1993; *Guardian*, 9 November 1993 (draft cabinet paper).

11   Norman Dennis and George Erdos, *Families without Fatherhood*' (London, IEA 1992).

12   Amitai Etzioni *The Spirit of Community* (Crown, 1993), *The Parenting Deficit* (London, Demos 1993), *Times*/Demos lecture 'Communitarianism', 13 March 1995.

13   Tony Blair's speech accepting leadership of the Labour Party, 21 July 1994; interview on London Weekend Television, 24 July 1994.

14   *Guardian* editorial, 23 March 1995. Speech at Labour Women's Conference, Derby, 1 April 1995.

15   Harriet Harman, Patricia Hewitt and Anna Coote, *The Family Way: A New Approach to Policy-Making*, IPPR Sept 1990. Harriet Harman '*The Century Gap*', (London, Vermilion/Ebury Press 1993).

16   *Looking to the Future: Mediation and the ground for divorce* (HMSO 1993).

17   Statement by the Lord Chancellor, 27 April 1995.

18   Rights of Women bulletin, autumn/winter 1994 op cit.

19   Bradshaw and Millar op cit. *Untying the Knot* op cit. Fran Wasoff, Edinburgh University, 1994.

20   Sara Thornton, Network First 11 January 1994.

21   J Kitzinger and K Hunt, *Evaluation of Edinburgh District Council's Zero Tolerance Campaign*, (University of Glasgow 1993).

22   See 'The Interests of Children at Divorce', Martin Richards, paper given to Family Mediation Scotland, 3 October 1994. Rudolf Shaffer, overview of research on divorce, paper given to Family Mediation Strathclyde 28 October 1994. Monica Cockett and John Tripp, *Children living in re-ordered families*, Joseph Rowntree Foundation, 1994. David Uttings, *Family and parenthood: supporting families, preventing breakdown*, Joseph Rowntree Foundation, 1995.

23   *The Times*, 22 June 1994. *Observer*, 13 June 1993.

24   *Guardian* editorial, 9 November 1993.

25   Norman Fowler, *Guardian*, 9 November 1993. Peter Lilley, Telegraph 21 June 1994. Patricia Morgan 1994 op cit.

26   Melanie Phillips, *Observer*, May 29 1994.

27   *Guardian*, 9 November 1993. *Sunday Times*, 11 July 1993.

28   *The Times* editorial June 1994. Charles Murray, quoted in Bea Campbell, *Goliath* (London, Methuen 1993). AH Halsey, introduction to Dennis and Erdos op cit.

29   Dennis and Erdos op cit. Margaret Thatcher, 18 July 1990. *Sunday Times*, 19 June 1994.

30   Sean French, 'The Fallen Idol', *Father Figures*, Children in Scotland/IYF conference, 23 September 1994.

31   At May 1995 with the Bill going through parliament the government clause (no 4) was close to the provision in the English Children's Act but amendments were proposed which would give automatic parental rights to fathers unless the mother applied to the Court to prevent this (the position recommended by the Scottish Law Commission) and, conversely, to limit the time in which a father could apply to the Courts for parental rights. An amendment to the English legislation to give fathers automatic parental rights has also been discussed.

32   *Family Agenda for Action*, IYF 1994.

33   Tony Blair, *Spectator* Lecture, 22 March 1995.

34   Eric Hobsbawm, *Age of Extremes* (London, Michael Joseph 1994).

35   Ibid.

36   Amitai Etzioni, *Times*/Demos Lecture, 13 March 1995.

37   *The Changing Family*, conference, 5 March 1995, University of Edinburgh Centre for Theology and Public Issues.

38   A number of studies are quoted in Patricia Hewitt, 'About Time', op cit. Research by Jonathan Gershuny quoted in the *Guardian*, 1 April 1995.

39   Bea Campbell, Zero Tolerance debate, 24 March 1994.

40   Tony Blair, 'Crime, family and society', 24 May 1994 Family Breakdown and Criminal Activity' conference, IEA/Family Civic Trust.

41   *Spectator* and *Times*/Demos lectures, op cit.

42   *Herald*, 26 April 1994.

43   For example, Morayo Scanlon, a Scots widow who (at May 1995) is fighting a deportation order on her and her son; Dorothy Nwokedi, who with her four-year-old daughter was deported from Britain in July 1993 in circumstances of considerable brutality; Prakash Chavrimootoo, whose immigration status was threatened because she left a violent husband within a year of marriage.

44   Rights of Women bulletin op cit. Jacqueline Bhaba and Sue Shutter, *Women's Movement: Women under immigration, nationality and refugee law* (Oakhill, Trentham Books 1994).

45   *Breaking up the family*, Churches' Commission for Racial Justice, 1994.

46   *Income and Wealth*, report of the Joseph Rowntree Foundation Inquiry Group, February 1995. Carey Oppenheim, *Poverty: The Facts*, Child Poverty Action Group 1993.

47   Patricia Hewitt, 'Families in Flux', *Political Quarterly* vol 65, no 2, April-June 1994. Household Below Average Income, 1994 op cit.

48   Robin Tennant, *Child and Family Poverty in Scotland: The Facts*, Save the Children, and Glasgow Caledonian University 1995.

49   Quotes from women I have spoken to and from *Poverty Briefing*, Save the Children Child Poverty Resource Unit, 1994.

50   *The Progress of Nations*, UNICEF 1993.

51   *The Progress of Nations*, UNICEF 1994.

52   Report of the Commission on Social Justice, 1994 op cit.

53   Susan Harkness, Stephen Machin and Jane Waldfogel, *Women's Pay and family income inequality*, Joseph Rowntree Foundation October 1994. Helen Penn, *Under Fives: The view from Strathclyde* (Edinburgh, Scottish Academic Press 1992).

Chapter 9

1   Naomi Wolf, 1994 op cit. Helen Wilkinson 1994 op cit.
2   *Women and Men in Britain 1994*, EOC 1994.
3   Helen Wilkinson 1994 op cit.
4   Helen Brown, *Expectations for the Future*, Health Education Authority, 1995.
5   Liz Spencer and Sally Taylor, *Participation and Progress in the Labour Market: key issues for women*, Employment Department 1994.
6   Scottish Forum for Public Health Medicine, 1995 op cit.
7   Spencer and Taylor op cit.
8   Sue Sharpe, 1994 op cit.
9   Introduction to Mothers in Employment report, op cit.
10   Peter Burnill and Andrew McPherson, 'Careers and Gender, The expectations of able Scottish school-leavers in 1971 and 1981', in S Acker and D Warren Piper (eds) *Is Higher Education Fair to Women?* Society for Research in Higher Education, 1984.
11   *Scotland on Sunday*, 23 April 1995.
12   Sue Lees, *Sugar and Spice: sexuality and adolescent girls* (London, Penguin 1993).
13   *Observer*, 7 August 1994.
14   Willings Press Guide 1994 and 1995.
15   *Sugar*, February 1995.
16   *19*, April 1995. *Just Seventeen* 'Feel Like a New You' April 1995.
17   Nick Fisher, *Your Pocket Guide to Sex*, Penguin, 1994.
18   Sue Innes, *Scotland on Sunday*, 27 March 1994.
19   *Perspectives of Women in Television*, Broadcasting Standards Council, May 1994.
20   Amy Raphael, *Never Mind the Bollocks: Women Rewrite Rock* (London, Virago 1995).
21   *Vanity Fair*, August 1993. Victoria Starr, *All You Get is Me* (London, HarperCollins 1994).
22   *Scotsman*, 29 March 1995, 18 May 1995.
23   QED, 'Sex Acts', BBC 1, 28 March 1995.
24   Teenage Growth Study, 1992–1995, Young People's Unit, Royal Edinburgh Hospital. Marion M Hetherington, 'Eating Disorders', in *Food and the Human Condition*, Open University textbook 1994.
25   *Guardian*, 10 June 1992.
26   Jenny Kitzinger, 'I'm sexually attractive but I'm powerful: Young women negotiating sexual reputation', *Women's Studies International Forum*, vol 18 no 2, March/April 1995.
27   Sue Lees, 1993 op cit.
28   Sue Lees, *Guardian* 29 September 1994. Jennifer Temkin, *Guardian* 15 April 1995.
29   Dispatches, 1 March 1995. *Observer*, 26 February 1995.
30   Beverley Brown, Michele Burman and Lynn Jamieson, *Sex Crimes on Trial* (Edinburgh University Press, 1993).
31   Sue Lees, 1994, op cit.
32   Marina Warner, *Managing Monsters: Six Myths of our Time*, the Reith Lectures, (London, Vintage 1994).
33   AIDS/HIV surveillance tables for 1994, Public Health Laboratories Service Aids Centre; Scottish Centre for Infection and Environmental Health.
34   *Sugar*, February 1995.
35   Scottish Forum for Public Health Medicine, 1995 op cit.
36   Carol Becker, *The Invisible Drama; Women and the anxiety of change*, (Golden, Colorado, Fulcrum 1990).

Chapter 10

1   *Sunday Times*, 19 June 1994. Department for Education, 1994.
2   University Statistical Record, 1994: figures for 1993/94 (excluding the universities which were previously polytechnics). Dept. of Education and Science, 1974.

3 Sheila Riddell, Sally Brown and Eileen Turner, *The Impact of Recent Education Reforms on Gender Equality in Scottish Schools*; Gaby Weiner, Madeleine Arriott and Miriam David, *Educational Reforms and Gender Equality in Schools*, EOC forthcoming, Autumn 1995.

4 *Independent*, 6 September 1994.

5 *Science and Mathematics in Schools, A Review,* Office for Standards in Education, (HMSO 1994).

6 *Engender Gender Audit* 1994 and 1995.

7 OFSTED, 1994 op cit.

8 *Gender in Education*, General Teaching Council for Scotland, 1991.

9 Martin Horner, Phd thesis, University of Michigan, 1968

10 *Engender Gender Audit* 1994. Sue Innes (ed) *A Study of Women's Access to Education, Training and Employment Opportunities in Scotland*, Scottish Enterprise/Highlands and Islands Enterprise/Training 2000, 1992. *Report of the UK to the UN Fourth World Conference on Women, 1994*, op cit.

11 Edith Hamilton, *Second Chance* (Greenock 1994). *Guardian Education*, 10 May 1994.

12 'The higher education route to the labour market for mature students', Alice Brown and Janette Webb, *British Journal of Education and Work* 1990; Alice Brown and Janette Webb in 'Career prospects for mature women students: aspirations and achievements', Julia Evetts (ed) *Women and Career: Themes and Issues in Advanced Industrial Societies,* 1994 op cit.

13 Part-time students have no automatic entitlement to a grant and funding available has restrictions which can be harder to meet for students with family commitments. Employers are the main source of support for part-time students but are not a source of help available to 'women returners'.

14 Sue Innes (ed), 1992 op cit.

15 Valerie Walkerdine op cit.

16 *Guardian Education*, 14 March 1995.

17 Sheila Riddell, *Gender and the politics of the curriculum* (London, Routledge 1992).

18 Helen Lucey, Goldsmiths' College London, 1995.

19 *Education Divides: Poverty and Schooling in the 1990s*, Child Poverty Action Group 1995.

20 *School Leaver Destinations – Lothian Region 1993*, Lothian Region Careers Service. Catherine Shaw, *Changing Lives*, PSI 1994.

21 Student association surveys and NUS postal survey of students in London and Manchester, July 1994.

22 *In Search of Equality, Development and Peace*, Women's National Commission 1994. *Scottish Women's Report to Beijing*, 1995 op cit.

23 Jane Lewis and David Piachaud, 'Women and Poverty in the Twentieth Century', in Caroline Glendinning and Jane Millar 1992 op cit.

24 *Income and Wealth: report of the JRF Inquiry Group* op cit.

25 Juliet Cook and Shantu Watt, 'Racism, Women and Poverty' in Caroline Glendinning and Jane Millar 1992 op cit.

26 Reena Bhavnani 1994 op cit.

27 Sheila Lewenhak, *Women and Trade Unions* (London, Ernest Benn 1977).

28 Women and Men in Britain, 1993 op cit. AUT 1994. Louise Corti and Shirley Dex, 1995 op cit.

29 Aileen McColgan *Pay Equity – Just Wages for Women?* (London, The Institute of Employment Rights, 1994). Lorna Russell 1995 op cit.

30 EOC Briefing *Draft Code of Practice on Pay* May 1995.

31 Audrey Wise MP, House of Commons 7 March 1995.

32 *Engender Gender Audit* 1994. Sandra Hutton, Steven Kennedy, Peter Whiteford, *Equalisation of State Pension Ages: The Gender Impact.* EOC 1995.

33 Women's National Commission seminar on poverty, 1995.

34 Sue Innes, *Scotland on Sunday*, May 1993. EOC briefing 1995.

35 Part Time Work in Britain, TUC December 1994.

36   Carol Sexty, *Women Losing Out: Access to housing in Britain today*, Shelter 1990. Hilary Macaskill 1993 op cit.
37   *World in Action*, 5 December 1994.
38   *Putting the Treasury First*, 1994 op cit.
39   Information from Centrepoint 1994. Mandana Hendessi, *Support for young women homeless because of sexual abuse*, CHAR 1992.
40   Sarah Webb, *My Address is Not my Home*, Scottish Council for Single Homeless 1994.

Chapter 11

Employment statistics come from the Labour Force Survey for 1994, unless specified otherwise, with particular reference to the following articles in the *Employment Gazette*: Frances Sly, November 1994 op cit; Gary Watson, 'The flexible workforce and patterns of working hours in the UK' July 1994; Mark Beatson, 'Progress towards a flexible labour market', February 1995.

1   *Guardian*, 9 April 1994, *The Times*, 27 March 1994, *Scotsman*, 4 May 1994, *The Times*, 30 October 1994.
2   Report of the Social Justice Commission, 1994. Census 1991.
3   Frank Field, speech to Low Pay Conference, Accrington, 4 February 1994.
4   Will Hutton, *The State We're In* (London, Jonathan Cape 1995).
5   *Social Trends* 1994. *Population Trends* 79, Spring 1995. Louise Corti and Shirley Dex, March 1995 op cit.
6   Lynne Segal, *Is the Future Female? Troubled thoughts on contemporary feminism* (London, Virago 1987).
7   Incomes Data Services analysis of the 1991 Census of Employment, May 1993.
8   1991 Census.
9   Duncan Gallie, Catherine Marsh and Carolyn Vogler (eds), *Social Change and the Experience of Unemployment* (Oxford University Press, 1994).
10   Frank Field, 1994 op cit.
11   Matilda Quiney, 'Women need the work', *New Economy*, September 1994. *Guardian*, 28 October 1994.
12   Edward Balls and Paul Gregg, *Work and Welfare: Tackling the jobs deficit* (research series for Commission on Social Justice), IPPR 1993.
13   EOC, 7 March 1995.
14   Gillian Shephard, 15 September 1992. *Scotland on Sunday*, 14 August 1994.
15   Matilda Quiney, op cit.
16   Gallie et al, op cit.
17   *The Married Woman: Is She a Person?* (The Open Door Council, London: no author or date on pamphlet but references in text suggest it is between 1933–5).
18   David Bell and Sheila Rimmer, 1992 op cit. TUC, December 1994 op cit.
19   Employment Department evidence to the Employment Committee, 15 February 1994.
20   Gary Watson, Barbara Fothergill, 'Part-time employment and attitudes to part-time work' 1993 op cit. EOC research found many women preferred part-time hours (Catherine Marsh, *Hours of Work of Women and Men in Britain*, 1991); and the 1990 *British Social Attitudes* survey of mothers in employment found that two-thirds of those with school age children would prefer to work school hours even if appropriate childcare was available.
21   Patricia Hewitt, *About Time* op cit.
22   Will Hutton 1995 op cit. Charles Handy, *The Empty Raincoat* (London, Hutchinson 1994).
23   Michael Portillo, speech *Management of Change* conference, London 22 February 1995. Harriet Harman, *The Century Gap* op cit; speech to Labour National Women's Training Day, 2 July 1994.
24   *Independent*, 15 September 1994.
25   Report of the Social Justice Commission, op cit.

26   European network on Families and Work bulletin no 1, Dec 1994. EC Conference New Ways to Work op cit.

27   *Women and Structural Change, New Perspectives* OECD 1994.

28   Will Hutton, *Guardian*, 14 March 1994; Charles Handy 1994 op cit; William Bridges, *How to Prosper in a Workplace Without Jobs* (London, Nicholas Brealey Publishing 1995).

29   LC Hunter and J McInnes, *Employers' Labour Use Strategies*, Employment Dept, 1991.

30   Ibid.

31   Carol Wharton 'Finding Time for the "Second Shift" ', *Gender & Society*, vol 8 no 2, June 1994.

32   Report of the Social Justice Commission op cit. Michael Portillo 1995 op cit.

33   John Curtice and Peter Spencer, 'Flexibility and the Feelgood Factor', University of Strathclyde November 1994; George Callaghan, University of Bristol, Phd thesis 1995.

34   Linda Dickens, *Whose Flexibility? Discrimination and Equality Issues in Atypical Work*, The Institute of Employment Rights, 1992. Employment Committee 1995 op cit.

35   *Guardian*, October 28, 1994. Employment Committee 12 April 1994.

Chapter 12

1   Evidence to the Employment Committee, 8 March 1994. Charles Handy, *The Empty Raincoat*, op cit.

2   Health and Safety Executive and International Labour Office quoted by New Ways to Work, Employment Committee, 8 March 1994.

3   *Open Space*, 29 November 1994.

4   J Rubery, C Fagan, M Smith, 'The Redistribution of Work: Taking into account gender and country-specific differences', research for the European Commission, March 1994.

5   *Scotland on Sunday*, 8 January 1995. J Rubery, C Fagan, M Smith, op cit.

6   *Scotland on Sunday*, 8 January 1995. Catherine Marsh, *Hours of Work of Women and Men in Britain* (HMSO 1991). McInnes and Hunter, op cit.

7   Quoted by New Ways to Work to the Employment Committee, 8 March, 1994.

8   David Hunt, CBI Conference November 1993.

9   Louise Corti and Shirley Dex, 'Informal carers and employment', *Employment Gazette*, March 1995. *Financial Times*, 23 November 1994.

10   *Scotland on Sunday*, 18 September 1994.

11   Jean-Yves Boulin, 'Working Time, Productive Flexibility and Autonomy', EC Seminar, 30 September 1993.

12   Philip Taylor and Alan Walker, *Employment Gazette* August 1994. *Guardian*, 8 November 1994. Evidence to the Employment Committee, 8 March 1994.

13   Reena Bhavnani 1994 op cit.

14   Karen Escott and Dexter Whitfield, *The Gender Impact of CCT in Local Government*, EOC 1995.

15   McInnes and Hunter, op cit. Unison/Local Government Information Unit, *CCT On the Record* 1994. Escott and Whitfield, op cit.

16   *Independent*, 5 December 1994.

17   BIFU 1995.

18   *Scotland on Sunday*, 26 March 1995.

19   *The Best of Both Worlds*, Employment Department 1991.

20   Linda Dickens, op cit.

21   OECD op cit. *Human Resource Management, a trade union response*, TUC 1994.

22   Seminar organised by Unison and the Fabian Society; *Guardian* report 18 April 1994. Eileen Appelbaum and Ronald Schettkat, 'Economic development in the industrialised countries and the prospects for full employment' in Philip Arestis (ed), *The Political Economy of Full Employment* (Edward Elgan, UK. Forthcoming.)

23   Sian Reynolds, 'Women in the Printing and Paper Trades in Edwardian Scotland' in Eleanor Gordon and Esther Breitenbach (eds), *The World is Ill Divided* (Edinburgh, EUP 1990). OECD op cit.
24   *Generation X and the New Work Ethic* (London, Demos 1994).
25   Harriet Harman, *The Century Gap* op cit.
26   Jean-Yves Boulin, 1993, op cit.
27   Will Hutton, 1995 op cit. Report of the Social Justice Commission, op cit.
28   Eileen Appelbaum op cit.

Conclusion

1   Vera Brittain, 'Committees Versus Professions' (1929 unpublished), in Paul Berry and Alan Bishop (eds), *Testament of a Generation: the journalism of Vera Brittain and Winifred Holtby* (London, Virago 1985).
2   Eleanor Gordon, 'The March of the Women', conference, St Andrews University 29 April 1995.
3   Pamphlet published by the Six Point Group, 1927 reprinted in Paul Berry and Alan Bishop, op cit.
4   Eric Hobsbawm, 1994 op cit.

Acronyms used in the text

BBC	–	British Broadcasting Corporation
CBI	–	Confederation of British Industries
CCT	–	compulsory competitive tendering
CFC	–	Conservative Family Campaign
CHAR	–	Housing Campaign for Single People, formerly Campaign for the Homeless and Rootless)
CSA	–	Child Support Agency
ED	–	Employment Department
EOC	–	Equal Opportunities Commission
FPA	–	Family Planning Association
FPSC	–	Family Policy Studies Centre
HEA	–	Health Education Authority
IoD	–	Institute of Directors
IPM	–	Institute of Personnel Management
ITN	–	Independent Television Network
IYF	–	International Year of the Family
LETS	–	Local Economic Trading Systems
MWF	–	Medical Women's Federation
OPCS	–	Office of Population Censuses and Surveys
OPF	–	One Parent Families
PSI	–	Policy Studies Institute
RCN	–	Royal College of Nursing
SCSH	–	Scottish Council for Single Homeless
SJC	–	Social Justice Commission

Index